科思论丛　　本书由中国劳动保障科学研究院资助出版

中国绿色就业研究

RESEARCH ON GREEN EMPLOYMENT IN CHINA

游　钧　张丽宾　等◎著

社会科学文献出版社
SOCIAL SCIENCES ACADEMIC PRESS (CHINA)

Contents

3 International Research on Green Employment

4 Laws and Policies for Green Employment

5 Evaluation of Social Environment for Developing Green Employment in China

6   Case Study: Value Chain Analysis of Solar Water Heater Industry in Dezhou City

前　言

当前我国正处于重化工业的工业化中期阶段，资源短缺、环境恶化、气候变化的矛盾和压力十分突出。2008 年全球金融危机也对我国现有的经济发展模式提出了严峻的挑战，向可持续的经济社会发展模式转变显得更加迫切。危机后的世界各国，特别是发达国家，纷纷采取行动，实施绿色新政，通过投资绿色经济促进经济复苏、创造体面工作，通过促进绿色就业发展减少生存发展的环境压力和气候危机的威胁。我国应对危机出台的一揽子经济刺激措施中，也有相当一部分资金投资于绿色经济。"十二五"时期我国经济发展的核心任务是转变经济发展方式，向绿色、低碳经济转型，这既是世界经济社会发展的趋势，又是我国未来发展的客观要求。

事实上，从 20 世纪 70 年代开始，我国政府就日益重视环境保护工作，制定和实施了一系列政策措施，在 13 个重点行业关停淘汰落后产能；推进传统产业技术改造，提高能源利用效率，实现节能减排；提高资源综合利用水平，大力发展循环经济；加强环境污染治理，大力发展环保产业；加强生态农业建设，实施六大林业工程，增强碳汇能力；等。在这一过程中，一些就业机会被摧毁，一些新的就业机会被创造出来，一些工作岗位的技能要求发生了变化，还有一些就业机会被替代。值得特别强调和高度关注的是，2008 年金融危机后，各国失业率居高不下，创造就业成为各国政策的核心目标。温家宝总理指出："就业是天大的事"；党中央国务院提出"要把就业工作放在更加突出的位置"，"实施就业优先战略"。作为一个占世界 1/4 就业人口、仍然有 40% 多的劳动力从事农业生产、就业的城市化率不到 40%、就业压力巨大的发展中大国，我们必须采取负责任的态度，处理好向绿色、低碳经济转型过程中的就业问题。

在我国制定国民经济和社会发展"十二五"规划前夕，我们于 2009 年开展了"中国绿色就业研究"，目的是在制定"十二五"发展规划的关键时期，促进我国经济发展方式转型，推动制定出台促进绿色就业发展的政策措施，完善我国更加积极的就业政策体系，促进我国经济、环境和就业的协调发展。同时，在当前全球气候变化谈判中，向国际社会介绍我国就业的基本情况，以及我国在推进绿色就业发展方面的实践和努力，从社会维度争取我国作为发展中国家的发展权力和发展空间，进而为尽可能地缓解我国本已严峻的就业形势创造空间。

作为关于中国绿色就业的初始性研究的成果，本书分别对绿色就业的国际研究情况进行了介绍，对中国发展绿色就业的法律和政策环境进行了分析，对太阳能热水器行业进行了价值链技术分析；就发电行业向绿色就业转型的经验、问题和做法进行了问卷调查研究。在上述研究的基础上，本书从绿色就业概念的理论探讨、绿色就业的宏观发展状况、向绿色就业转型的微观实践等方面，进行了初创性的研究探索。研究结果表明：在我国，绿色就业发展空间广阔，潜力无限，应有效地促进体面劳动；同时，向绿色就业的转型需要付出巨大的成本，我们应从我国经济社会发展的实际出发，采取措施，积极有效地促进我国绿色就业的发展。

本书分析了绿色就业的含义和本质属性，指明了绿色就业议题的实质和意义，并从总体上分析了发展绿色低碳经济影响就业的路径，以及我国绿色就业的现状；对我国已采取的促进绿色就业发展的政策措施进行了概括，并提出了较完善和可行的进一步促进绿色就业发展的政策措施建议。

在开展研究的同时，我们深深地感到这方面的研究工作只是开了个头，需要深入研究的方面还很多。首先，需要研究如何在全球气候谈判中发挥就业因素的作用。应对气候变化是为了人的发展，而迄今为止，在谈判中涉及的只是科技因素，包括限制气候升温的程度、减排指标等，而没有考虑人类发展指标。我们可以做些工作，将就业权、发展权纳入气候谈判框架中。其次，需要综述我国采取的发展绿色就业的政策措施。以前我们没有从这个角度考虑过，但实际上我们制定和实施了很多促进绿色就业发展的政策措施，付出了巨大的代价，承担了巨大的成本，也有很多政策创新。我们需要总结和宣传。再次，需要深入开展绿色就业发展的前瞻性研究。环境保护的就业影响是个复杂的过程，间接的就业效应往往大于直接的就业效应，单从某一点的直接影响难以判断整体的就业效应。我们需要在建筑、交通、农业、基础工业等重点行业开展绿色就业研究，摸清绿色低碳发展对就业的影响，一方面为谈判提供论据支撑，另一方面也为我们制定政策、采取措施提供依据。我们已试验了价值链等分析技术，在开展重点绿色就业领域研究时也有技术方法保证。最后，需要开展促进绿色就业发展政策的前瞻性研究，完善我国的就业政策体系。我们已进行的研究仅能就促进绿色就业发展的总的政策提出一些建议，还需要研究不同行业促进绿色就业发展的具体政策。另外，促进绿色就业发展的政策是投资、财政税收等各种政策的综合，也需要研究综合性政策如何促进绿色就业的发展。就中国促进绿色就业发展的政策而言，需要在对现有政策总结、评估的基础上，进行前瞻性、应用性的探讨。

由于可资借鉴的资料有限，我们的研究本身还有很多不足之处，还有更多问题有待进一步深入研究。但是，为了展示中国绿色就业的研究及实践情况，我们仍愿意将我们的研究成果整理成书，以分享给更多的人。希望本书的出版能够有助于相关部门和领域的研究者、决策者、政策执行者进一步深化对绿色就业问题的认识并给予更多的关注，共同推动我国绿色就业的发展。

游钧　张丽宾

2013 年 9 月 23 日

Preface

Currently, China is in the middle stage of industrialization, during which the conflicts due to and pressures from resource shortage, environmental deterioration and climate change are prominent. In 2008, the global financial crisis brought a severe challenge to the existing economic development model of our country, and the transition to a sustainable economic and social development model became more urgent. After the outbreak of the crisis, various countries in the world, especially the developed countries, all took actions to implement Green New Deal, specifically to promote economic recovery and create decent jobs by investing in the green economy, and to reduce the environmental pressure on and the threat of climate crisis to survival and development by promoting the development of green employment. As for China, among a package of economic incentive measures issued to cope with the crisis, there is considerable fund for investment in the green economy. In the period of the "12th Five-Year Plan", the main task of economic development in our country is to transform the model of economic development into a green and low-carbon one, which is not only a trend in global economic and social development, but also an objective requirement for future development of China.

As a matter of fact, since the 1970s, our government has attached more and more importance to environmental protection by formulating and implementing a series of policies and measures. For example, the government has closed 13 key industries for eliminating backward productivity; promoted the technological transformation of traditional industries, improved energy utilization efficiency and achieved energy saving and emission reduction; improved comprehensive utilization level of resources and vigorously developed circular economy; strengthened environmental pollution control and developed environmental industries rapidly; strengthened eco-agricultural construction, implemented Six Key Forestry Programs and strengthened the capacity of carbon sink, etc. During the process, some employment opportunities have been destroyed and some new ones created. Besides, the skills requirements for some jobs have changed and some employment opportunities have been replaced. It requires special emphasis that, since the financial crisis occurred in 2008, the unemployment rate in various countries has stayed high; and creating jobs has become the key policy goal in these countries. Former Premier Wen Jiabao once indicated, "Employment is a most important matter". The CPC Central Committee and the State Council also stated that the government should, "Put employment work in a more prominent position" and "Implement the strategy of the primacy of increasing employment". As a large developing country with working population amounting to 1/4 of the world's total, where as much as 40% of the labor force is still engaged in agricultural production, urbanization rate for jobs is less than 40% and employment pressure is great, we must be responsible and deal with the employment problem properly in the transition to a green and low-carbon economy.

On the eve of the drafting process for the "12th Five-Year Plan" for national economy and social development, we initiated "Research on Green Employment in China" in 2009. The purpose of the study is to provide a reference basis for policy-making in areas such as boosting the transformation of our economic development model, promoting the formulation and issuing of policies and measures for facilitating green employment development, inproving employment policy system to make it more active and accelerating the coordinated development among economy, environment and employment. Meanwhile, in the current negotiations over global climate change, we shall inform the international society about the basic employment situation in China and our country's practices and efforts in promoting green employment development, As a developing country, China must strive for its development right and development space, especially with respect to the social dimension, and alleviate the already severe employment situation in China.

As a preliminary study on green employment in China, this research summarizes international research on green employment, analyzes the legal and political environment for developing green employment in China, conducts technical analysis of the value chain of the solar water heater industry, and uses questionnaire surveys to study the experience, problems and actions in power industry's transition to green employment. On the basis of the above research, this report engages in preliminary exploration of theoretical questions about the concept of green employment, macroscopic development of green employment and the microscopic practices in the transition to green employment. The research results show that: in China, green employment has infinite potential and huge development space, which can effectively promote decent jobs. At the same time, the transition to green employment is costly, and we shall take active and effective measures to accelerate China's green employment development. On the basis of the actual situation of economic and social development in China.

The research analyzing and defining the meaning and essential attributes of green employment, pointing out the essence and significance of the issue of green employment, analyzing how the development of green and low-carbon economy influences employment as well as the overall situation of green employment in our country, summarizing the policies and measures already adopted for promoting green employment development, and raising relatively complete and feasible suggestions on policies and measures for the further promotion of green employment development.

While conducting the research, we deeply realized that research work on this subject has just started and there are still very much hard work to be done. For instance, we need to study how to give play to the role of employment factors in the negotiations over the global climate. As we know, adapting to climate change is necessary for human development. However, so far, only technological factors, including the cap on temperature rise and emission reduction targets, have been covered in the negotiations while human development targets have never been considered. Thus we can work toward integrating employment right and development right into the framework of climate negotiations. In addition, we need to summarize the policies and measures China has adopted for developing green employment. Over recent years, we have never considered things from this perspective. In fact, we have formulated and implemented many policies and measures for facilitating green employment development, with heavy prices paid, huge costs borne but a lot of policy innovations made also. We need to summarize and publicize the results of these practices. Also, we need to develop the prospective study on green employment development. The impact of environmental protection on employment takes a complex process and indirect employment effects is usually greater than direct employment effects, thus it is difficult to judge the overall employment effect based only on the direct influence at a particular point. For this, we need to conduct research on green employment in key industries such as construction, transportation, agricultural and basic industries to find out the impact of green and low-carbon development on employment, which, on the one hand, provides theoretical support for climate negotiations and, on the other hand, offers basis for formulating policies and implementing measures. Since we have experimented with value chain and other analytical techniques, research on green employment in key fields will have guarantee with respect to technical methods. Finally, we need to conduct prospective study on policies for promoting green employment development and for improving the employment policy system in our country. As this report can only provide some suggestions on the general policy for promoting green employment development, we also need to study specific policies for promoting green employment development in the various industries. Additionally, since the policies for promoting green employment development include polices in investment, finance and taxation, we must also study how comprehensive policies affect the development of green employment. As to China's policies for promoting green employment development, we need to make prospective and applicable discussions on the basis of summarizing and assessing the existing policies.

Due to limited information for reference, the research itself has several shortcomings and there are still many problems requiring further study. We hope that the publication of the book can help researchers, decision-makers and policy-executors in relevant departments and fields further deepen their understanding of and concern with the issue of green employment and promote the development of green employment in China.

You Jun and Zhang Libin
September 23, 2013

第一章

绿色就业研究概论

当前我国正处于重化工业的工业化中期阶段，资源短缺、环境恶化、气候变化的矛盾和压力十分突出。金融危机的爆发对我国现有的经济发展模式提出了严峻挑战，向可持续的经济社会发展模式转变显得更加迫切。金融危机后，世界各国特别是发达国家纷纷采取行动，实施绿色新政，通过投资绿色经济促进经济复苏、创造体面工作，通过促进绿色就业发展，减少生存发展的环境压力和气候危机的威胁。我国出台的一揽子经济刺激措施中，也有相当一部分资金投资于绿色经济。向绿色、低碳经济转型，既是世界经济社会发展的趋势，又是我国未来发展的客观要求。

实际上，我国政府一直重视环境保护工作，制定和实施了一系列的政策措施，在 13 个重点行业关停淘汰落后产能；推进传统产业技术改造，提高能源利用效率，实现节能减排；提高资源综合利用水平，大力发展循环经济；加强环境污染治理，大力发展环保产业；加强生态农业建设，实施六大林业工程，增强碳汇能力等。在这一过程中，一些就业机会被摧毁，一些新的就业机会被创造出来，一些工作岗位的技能要求发生了变化，还有一些就业机会被替代，最终导致就业的总量、结构、增量和就业形式发生变化。所以，向绿色、低碳经济的转型会对就业产生重大的影响。作为一个就业人口巨大的发展中国家，我们必须采取负责任的态度，处理好向绿色经济转型的就业问题。

一　绿色就业的概念

绿色就业是一个全新的研究领域，迄今为止，全球还没有被普遍接受的关于绿色就业的准确定义，对这一问题的认识还处于一个日新月异的深化过程中。

（一）绿色就业的范畴

1. 绿色经济

经济绿化即发展绿色经济，是指重新构造企业和基础设施，以提高自然、人文和经济资本投资回报，同时减少温室气体排放、提取和使用较少的自然资源、创造较少的废物和减少社会分化的过程。这样，绿色经济被认为既能创造绿色就业、确保真正可持续的经济增长，又能防止环境污染、全球变暖、资源枯竭和环境退化。

联合国环境规划署领导的绿色经济倡议，旨在帮助各国政府重新制定和瞄准针对清洁技术、可再生能源、供水服务、绿色交通、废物管理、绿色建筑、可持续农业和林业等部门的政策、投资和支出，来绿化其经济。

在实际中，"绿化"主要包括六个方面：一是大力发展对环境影响小的产业，主要是生态农业、生态旅游、有机食品、可再生能源、服务业、高新科技、植树造林等；二是限制那些对环境影响大的产业的过度发展，主要是能源、冶金、建材等重化工业和造纸等轻工业；三是绿化/净化生产过程，通过开发新的生产工艺降低或替代有毒有害物质的使用、高效和循环利用原材料、降低污染物的产生量、对污染物进行净化治理等；四是城市和农村的公共环境设施建设和维护，以及公共环境保护与治理；五是生态环境保护与修复；六是围绕经济绿化发展绿色服务业，包括绿色信贷、绿色技术、绿色设备、绿色保险、绿色认证等。

2. 绿色就业

绿色就业是在经济绿化的过程中产生和发展的，是指从事经过绿化的经济活动的就业和从事绿色经济活动的就业。绿色经济是对产业结构、产品生产的技术和工艺、产品生产的组织方式、生活方式等进行"绿化"，绿色就业就是采用绿色技术、工艺和原材料进行生产的就业，就是从事绿色产品生产和服务的就业，就是直接从事环境和生态保护工作的就业。

国际劳工组织将绿色就业定义为：在经济部门和经济活动中创造的，可以减轻环境影响并最终实现环境、经济和社会可持续发展的体面工作。

与建设资源节约型、环境友好型社会的发展战略相一致，中国的绿色就业可以定义为：国民经济中相对于社会平均水平而言，低投入、高产出，低消耗、少排放，能循环、可持续的产业、行业、部门、企业和岗位上的工作。"低投入、高产出"泛指与提高组织管理水平进而提高生产效率相关的就业。提高生产效率意味着各种生产要素的节约，具有资源节约、环境友好的倾向，是我国从粗放到集约的经济增长模式转变的主要方面，对整个经济都具有基础性的决定性作用，应成为中国绿色就业的要素；"低消耗、少排放"主要指与通过提高技术水平实现通常意义上的能源、资源节约和减少污染物排放相关的就业，是绿色就业的基本要素；"能循环、可持续"既是指总体上生态体系的自我修复和经济、社会发展的可持续的思想，又是指与循环经济、污染治理和生态环境保护相关的就业。

3. 绿色就业与绿色经济的关系

就业本质上是一种经济关系和经济行为，受劳动力市场供求机制调节，受产品市场影响。产品供给的总量和结构、产品生产的技术和工艺、产品生产的组织方式等，决定就业的数量、结构和就业模式。绿色就业是在经济绿化的过程中产生发展的，是绿色经济发展的产物，同时也是推动绿色经济发展的关键力量。

（二）绿色就业的特征

理解绿色就业的概念，需要把握绿色就业的以下特征。

1. 绿色就业具有环境特征

绿色就业具有环境特征，即绿色就业不但要具有体面就业的劳动属性，还强调就业的环境功能。

"绿色就业"特指劳动者从事的经济活动有助于保护或恢复环境质量。从环境功能看，绿色就业具有四个特征：降低能耗与原材料消耗的"非物质化经济"特征，如发展循环经济创造的就业；避免温室气体排放的"去碳化经济"特征，如太阳能热利用及风能就业；将废物与污染降至最低的"环境经济"特征，如安置除尘脱硫设施后电力企业的就业；保护和恢复生态系统和环境服务的"生态经济"特征，如生态农业领域的就业。

绿色就业并非绝对不对环境产生影响，而是指那些对环境的负面影响程度显著低于通常水平、能够改善整体环境质量的就业。绿色就业中不同就业对环境的影响程度不同，因而有"浅绿"就业、"深绿"就业、"浓绿"就业等不同分类，如节能环保汽车属于浅绿就业，而大容量公交系统属于深绿就业，太阳能热利用则属于"浓绿"就业。由于工作环境、劳动条件非"绿色"，现实中，一些绿色就业还不是体面的就业。

2. 绿色就业具有与时俱进的动态特征

绿色就业具有与时俱进的动态特征，既包括对现有就业的改造，又涵盖由于创新而新增的就业。

绿色就业并非都是新的就业。有些绿色就业是以前没有的崭新的工作类型，但是大多数绿色就业是建立在传统专业和职业基础上的，只是工作的内容和能力要求发生了一些变化。即使是完全崭新的产业和新技术创造的完全崭新的绿色就业，其供应链也主要是由钢铁、机器零部件制造等传统产业的工作所构成，只是这些工作的内容发生了一定的变化，有了新的技能要求。

绿色就业既包括直接创造的就业机会，又包括由此带动的间接就业机会，还包括诱导所衍生的就业机会。直接的绿色就业如垃圾处理、污水处理企业的就业；更多是间接的绿色就业，如生产污水处理设备的企业的就业；诱导性就业如电子废弃物回收再利用所带动的就业等。

绿色就业具有与时俱进的特征。评判绿色就业的标准是相对的，与特定背景下的环境标准相关。如发达国家的非绿色就业在发展中国家可能是绿色就业，目前阶段的绿色就业随着经济的发展可能就变为非绿色就业了。

二　我国绿色就业的发展现状

绿色就业在我国已有较长的发展过程。我国环保事业从20世纪80年代就开始了，已形成环保产业；植树造林从新中国成立以来就开始了，年年植树造林；太阳能产业从20世纪90年代开始发展，已具有相当规模；风力发电发展迅猛，生物质能发电也得到发展；工业企业三废治理力度不断加大，淘汰落后产能陆续关停了一些污染和能耗大户；发展循环经济、废品回收利用正在规范发展。在这一过程中，已形成一定规模的绿色就业。

（一）传统就业中与绿色就业发展关联度高的行业和就业群体

涉及绿色就业的行业遍布各行各业。根据温室气体排放量的多少、以自然资源作为原材料的程度、对经济的贡献率，以及对就业和收入的贡献率等指标来衡量，绿色就业主要集中在六类经济部门，即可再生能源、建筑、交通、基础工业、农业和林业。从与绿色就业发展关联度高的重点行业的就业情况来看①，不包括农业共涉及8423万人，包括农业则涉及39867万人。其中，能

---

① 这里仅指法人单位的就业情况。

源、资源①行业 1253.3 万人，冶金业② 464.3 万人，非金属矿制品业 872.5 万人，轻工业③ 597.6 万人，化工业④ 1136 万人，建筑业 3253 万人，交通业 653.3 万人，水力、环境和公共设施方面 193 万人，占二三产业单位就业的比重分别为 6%、2%、4%、3%、5%、15%、3%、1%，合计占 39%。考虑到个体经营户就业以及漏统的灵活就业人员，人数应该更多，比重应该更大。虽然与绿色就业发展关联度高的重点行业就业人数众多，但迄今为止，这些行业中只有很小的一部分真正属于绿色就业，大部分则是需要转化才能变为绿色就业的岗位。

（二）重点行业绿色就业发展现状和发展前景分析

总体上，向绿色低碳经济转型的直接就业效应并不乐观，必须注重扩展间接就业效应。向绿色低碳经济转型，能源行业主要是调整能源结构，发展可再生能源和新能源，提高能效。传统能源行业就业将减少，除了太阳能以外，新能源带动的直接就业有限；原材料行业和加工制造业主要是通过技术改造、节约资源和加强资源综合利用，技术改造、技术进步通常都会导致直接就业减少；建筑业主要是开发节能建筑和对建筑物进行能效改造，节能建筑发展受制于市场需求，直接就业前景并不乐观；交通行业主要是发展公共交通系统，发展公共交通系统的直接就业效应也较小；农业主要是发展生态农业，林业主要是营林造林、发展生态林业等。由于土地资源有限，林业和农业新创造绿色就业的潜力也受到限制，主要是就业替代。间接就业效应主要是环保产业发展带动的就业贡献。向绿色就业转型，最终导致就业的总量、结构、增量和就业形式发生变化。

1. 环保相关产业的就业⑤

近年来，国家加大了环境保护基础设施的建设投资，有力地拉动了环境保

---

① 包括采矿业和电力、燃气及水的生产和供应业。

② 包括黑色金属冶炼及压延加工业和有色金属冶炼及压延加工业。

③ 主要包括皮革、毛皮、羽毛（绒）及其制品业，木材加工及木、竹、藤、棕、草制品业，家具制造业，造纸及纸制品业。

④ 包括石油加工、炼焦及核燃料加工业，化学原料及化学制品制造业，医药制造业，化学纤维制造业，橡胶制品业，塑料制品业。

⑤ 国家环境保护总局、国家发展和改革委员会、国家统计局联合于 2006 年 4 月发布了 2004 年由环保产业协会具体执行的《全国环境保护相关产业状况公报》。此次调查为一次性全面调查，调查基准时间为 2004 年，实施时间为 2005 年 2 月至 8 月。调查范围覆盖了全国除台湾地区、香港和澳门特别行政区以外的 31 个省、自治区和直辖市专业或兼业从事环境保护产品生产、资源综合利用、环境保护服务、洁净产品生产的全部国有及环保相关产业年销售（经营）收入 200 万元以上的非国有企业或事业单位。

护相关产业的市场需求，环境保护相关产业已成为国民经济结构的重要组成部分。根据《全国环境保护相关产业状况公报》，2004 年，全国环保环境保护相关产业国有单位和年销售（经营）收入 200 万元以上的非国有单位从业人员 159.5 万人，其中，以水污染治理设备和空气污染治理设备为主的环保产品行业从业人数 16.8 万人；以再生资源回收利用和固体废物综合利用为主的资源综合利用行业从业人数为 96 万人；以环境工程设计与施工服务和污染治理设施运营服务为主的环境保护服务业从业人数 17 万人；以节能产品、低毒低害产品、低排放产品和有机食品为主的洁净产品从业人数 23.3 万人。

环保产业发展迅速。据环保产业协会的统计，2008 年，我国环保产业单位 3.5 万家，从业人员 300 多万人，占当年非农就业人数的 0.66%。可以预见，随着国家《节能环保产业发展规划》的制订出台和实施，环保产业从业人员还将有更大的增加，预计达到上千万人。

2. 新能源行业的就业[①]

大力发展可再生能源是我国的基本战略。可再生能源是全新的行业，其发展必然会带动就业增加。根据有关研究，到 2007 年年底，全国新能源行业总的就业人数约为 110 万人，主要分布在太阳能、风能和生物质能行业，其他行业较少，占当年非农就业的 0.24%。如表 1-1 所示。

表 1-1　新能源行业就业人数

单位：人

行业	太阳能热水器	太阳能光伏	太阳能热发电	风能	生物质能	其他行业	合计
人数	800000	100000	150	20000	200000	1000	1121150

据有关研究[②]，每创造一个直接工作岗位，风能需要投资 115 万元，太阳能光伏电池需要 91 万元，太阳能热利用需要 70 万元，生物质能需要 14 万元。总体看来，可再生能源单位就业所需投资都远远高于传统产业所需投入。对于中国这样一个发展中国家，这样的工作岗位实在是太过昂贵。中国的一次能源结构以煤为主。2005 年中国一次能源消费中，煤炭所占的比重为 68.9%，石

---

① 国家发改委能源所有关研究。

② Peter Poschen：《绿色工作：定义、方法及其对低碳发展的贡献》，中国绿色就业经验分享研讨会，2009 年 3 月 30 日。

油为 21.0%，天然气、水电、核电、风能、太阳能等所占比重为 10.1%，而在同年全球一次能源消费构成中，煤炭只占 27.8%，石油占 36.4%，天然气、水电、核电等占 35.8%。中国以煤为主的能源结构在未来相当长的时期内难以根本改变。尽管到 2020 年将实现可再生能源在能源供应中的比重达到 20%，可以创造出更多就业机会，预计将达到 220 万人，但可再生能源行业与传统原有能源业的就业机会并不会像美国那样出现逆转。在较长时期内，传统能源行业就业仍然占主体。当然，新能源行业的发展将带动如风电设备制造、工业原材料等行业的发展，从而带动大量的间接就业。

3. 建筑节能改造的就业①

在我国经济持续高速增长和城市化进程的快速推进中，建筑业发展迅猛。建筑业的能源强度最高，推进建筑节能是我国节能减排的重要领域。相关法律法规和政策要求，新建建筑的设计和建造都要采用节能型的建筑结构、材料、器具和产品，提高保温隔热性能，减少采暖、制冷、照明的能耗；要对既有民用和公共机构建筑进行节能改造。

新建节能建筑和现有建筑节能改造将创造大量就业机会。自 2005 年起国家开展建筑节能试点城市工程开始，试点城市相关就业岗位大大增加。仅就现有建筑节能改造而言，我国既有建筑面积高达 420 多亿平方米。2006 年以前建设的绝大部分建筑不节能，不节能的锁定效应将长达至少 30 年。420 亿平方米既有建筑中，如果仅改造 1/3，以 200 元/平方米计算，市场价值就达 28000 亿元。有关报告指出，建筑节能改造可以新增大约 1260 万就业岗位。②

通过建筑节能改造发展绿色就业面临一些瓶颈。建筑节能改造一般需要较高的初期投资，不能吸引开发商的兴趣；既有建筑改造技术含量高，仅以住宅建筑节能改造为例，就包括建筑外围护结构节能改造、采暖制冷设备更新、供热计量改造等，需要大量各类专业技术工种，而建筑业中技术工人短缺，建筑工人中只有 1/5 接受过培训；此外，相关法律法规并没有得到有效贯穿执行，验收与监管环节依然是空白。这些都制约着建筑行业绿色就业的发展。

---

① 莫争春：《现有建筑的能源效率和绿色就业》，中国绿色就业经验分享研讨会，2009 年 3 月 30 日。
② 王伟光、郑国光主编《应对气候变化报告（2009）》，社会科学文献出版社，2009。

4. 发电行业的就业

在发展可再生能源的同时，我国还通过淘汰落后产能等措施，提高能效、节能减排。其中，电力行业是节能减排的大户。这些环保措施在保护环境的同时，对就业产生影响。根据相关研究[1]，2020 年前，"上大压小"关停小火电机组将使 60 万人的就业受到影响。据本课题组对火电企业的调查，因机组关停而失去岗位的职工，其中只有 1/10 能够在新建的大机组的辅助岗位重新就业，其余的 50 万人重新就业存在困难，需要就业帮助。

同时，由于火电行业安装脱硫设施，同期火电脱硫行业预计可以创造 108 万个直接、间接和引致的就业岗位，包括设备运行和维护增加的约 3.18 万个就业岗位和脱硫设备制造业创造的 30 万个就业岗位。

5. 林业绿色就业

森林是最大的"储碳库"和最经济的"吸碳器"，在这方面的就业潜力巨大，主要有三个方面：一是通过造林再造林、退化生态系统恢复、建立农林复合系统、加强森林可持续管理创造的就业；二是木材生产和加工；三是林产化工、林机制造、森林旅游、森林食品、森林药材、经济林、花卉和竹产业等。

根据相关研究，每增加 1 公顷森林面积，可以增加一个就业岗位。我国从 2002 年开始实施六大林业重点工程，10 年的造林任务达 0.76 亿公顷，预计可安置 2280 万人的就业，平均每年 200 多万人。根据《中国林业年鉴(2008)》，我国已建立各类森林公园 1200 多处，2001 年全国森林公园接待游客达 8300 万人，创造综合收入 500 多亿元，直接或间接创造各种就业岗位 350 万个。中国竹林面积、蓄积量和竹材年产量均居世界首位，被誉为竹子王国，竹产业的发展尚有很大潜力；此外，花卉业也是世界最具活力的产业之一，中国有悠久的花卉栽培史，品种丰富，开发和就业潜力巨大。按照林业就业 3000 万人推算，占农业就业的 9.5%。

另一方面，保护林业资源，也使以开发利用天然林资源为主的 135 个大型森工企业（国有林业局）出现严重的就业问题。大约有 41.28 万集体所有制职工没有得到安置，48.4 万名富余职工的安置资金不足。由于林区产业结构单一，岗位有限，造成很大部分职工失业或季节性失业。林业向绿色低碳经济转型承担了巨大的就业成本。

---

[1] 中国社会科学院：《中国低碳发展与就业的实证研究课题总报告》，2009 年 12 月。

对于我国绿色就业发展现状及未来发展前景的研究还尚待深入。目前，我国太阳能热水器行业从业人数占世界的96％；估计有1000万人从事各种形式的回收业，仅电气回收就有70万人；目前全球新增建筑的50％以上在以中国为主的亚洲，提高建筑能效也将提供大量就业机会。我国绿色就业发展潜力巨大。同时，发展绿色就业也要付出相应的代价。淘汰落后产能不但使一部分职工面临失业的威胁，还增加了巨大的职工安置的经济和社会成本；绿色发展对劳动者的就业能力提出严峻挑战，技能转换和提升成本巨大；一些新的绿色岗位被创造出来，但所需投入巨大，技术成本高昂，并且以替代原有岗位为主。发展绿色就业任重而道远。

三 促进我国绿色就业发展的思路

（一）准确把握发展绿色就业的含义

发展绿色就业有利于促进就业。提出绿色就业有利于促进政府尽早制定绿色人力资源开发战略，顺应绿色低碳经济的发展。从长远看，绿色就业是发展方向，空间广阔，具有可持续发展的潜力，能够促进体面劳动。绿色就业直接导致劳动生产率和企业效益的提高，有利于劳动报酬的更快提高和收入分配中劳动份额的增长；通过推进各种环保措施整合发展成不断延伸的绿色产业链条，蕴藏着的大量就业机会，长期来看必将抵消传统产业中工作岗位的减少，而且新创造的就业机会更具安全性、经济性和稳定性；节能环保措施在生产过程中的使用，能大大改善工人的作业环境，从而增进工人的安全和健康保障；实施节能环保推动技术进步和产业升级，促进劳动技术含量的提高，有利于改善劳动者的技能素质。我们关于发电行业绿色就业的具体案例研究确实表明，绿色就业岗位比非绿色就业岗位更具职业安全性，绿色就业比非绿色就业更体面，企业采取环保措施有利于促进体面就业。按照建设生态文明的基本国策，我国应坚定不移地实施绿色就业战略，将促进绿色就业发展纳入现行的扩大就业战略中，制定相关政策措施，在持续扩大就业的过程中推动绿色就业的发展。

国际社会提出"绿色就业"的概念、发起"绿色就业"倡议，其根本目的，一是想表达"向绿色低碳经济转型所创造的绿色就业机会大于被摧毁的非绿色就业机会"的观点，以便从就业角度来呼应国际社会提倡的"向绿色低碳经济转型"的思想；二是将绿色就业纳入体面劳动中，提高国际劳工标准。在肯定其促进就业的积极意义的同时，必须指出的是，国际社会提出的"绿色就业"倡议对发展中国家发展绿色就业所面临的约束条件没有给予足够重视。正如向绿色低碳经济转型要考虑转型成本和条件一样，向绿色就业转型也是有成本的。事实上，我国政府、企业、劳动者和社会都默默无闻地承担了巨大的绿色就业转型成本。如政府的脱硫电价补贴、对风电上网电价的补贴、对森工企业职工的一次性安置费用、建立下岗职工再就业中心的政策等；如很多企业因为职工无法安置而无法退出，进行技术改造增加成本，发电企业承担了安置关停小火电机组职工的责任，对他们进行培训和岗位安置等；如被关停小企业的职工失去工作岗位，难以实现再就业等。向绿色就业转型的社会成本也非常巨大，一些关停企业的职工为各种权益而上访，一些职工虽然被重新安置，但由于心理和现实落差，积累了不满情绪。

从近20年国际政治经济局势来分析，全球气候变化的话题越炒越热，已经成为国际社会政治经济博弈的一个重要方面，成为西方发达国家重新划分世界政治经济格局的主要工具。绿色就业的提出并被纳入劳工标准中，自然也就成为发达国家在全球气候变化谈判博弈中的一个重要维度。我们必须清醒地认识到提出发展绿色就业可能带来的两面性影响；必须清醒地认识到，对于我们这样一个占世界1/4就业人口、仍然有40%的劳动力从事农业生产、就业的城市化率不到40%、每年有800万农村剩余劳动力向城市转移就业、城镇就业人口中1/3为灵活就业、每年的非农就业需求在3000万人而经济增长所创造的就业岗位仅有1000多万人的发展中国家，在较低的成本下促进就业，仍然是我们保障公民基本就业权利的唯一可行路径。我们应趋利避害，在制定和实施绿色就业转型战略时，考虑我们正处于工业化的中期，市场经济体制还不够完善，就业压力持续加大，就业结构还比较落后，考虑我们的财力和社会可承受的能力，必须充分考虑向绿色就业转型的经济和社会成本。

(二) 促进绿色就业发展的思路

绿色就业发展战略的总体目标，是以绿色就业作为方向来积极扩大就业。大力开发新的绿色就业机会，稳定现有绿色就业机会，将绿色经济发展对就业的积极影响最大化；在调整产业结构、向绿色经济转型的过程中，注重保障劳动者的合法权益，将环境对就业的消极影响最小化；通过人力资源开发促进绿色经济发展。在最大限度保护环境的同时，采取措施，将失业率控制在社会可承受的范围内，不能因为发展绿色就业而导致失业率上升、劳动者收入水平下降，使失业问题加重，甚至超过经济社会可承受的程度。通过积极推动绿色就业的发展，最终实现环境和社会可持续的经济增长。

发展绿色就业要把握以下几个原则。

1. 促进绿色经济发展要充分重视其对就业的影响

我国正处于能源消耗量大的工业化发展中期，适度的能源消耗是经济发展所必需的，低碳发展实际上是限制能源利用的水平和规模，最终会限制发展、限制就业。因此，在全球气候变化谈判（IPCC）中，要明确态度，现在大气中发展中国家排放的二氧化碳累积不到 10%，我们有为发展继续排放的充分权利。要充分考虑就业因素，需要找到一个合适的点，避免承担不适当的义务，导致巨大的就业压力，进而对我国经济社会发展产生负面影响。同时，积极争取国际资金和技术，在促进经济发展的同时减缓温室气体排放。

2. 采取分类促进原则

绿色就业的发展有两种情况：一类是市场自发创造的，如废品回收行业的就业；一类是政府推动创造的，如火电行业的就业。对于不同性质的绿色就业，必须在促进就业的大前提下，采取不同的措施和策略，不能一概而论，不能"一刀切"。对于市场自发创造的绿色就业，政府就业促进的原则是坚持市场化原则，政府的作用是消除不利于市场机制发挥作用的干扰因素，更多、更好地提供就业服务；对于政府推动创造的绿色就业，必须坚持政策干预的就业促进原则，制定专门的就业促进政策。

3. 产业政策、环保政策与就业政策并重同步

发展经济、保护环境、促进就业都是为了民生，三者要并重，不能偏废。既不能因为发展经济而忽略环境保护和就业促进，又不能为保护环境而制约经济发展和增加就业，更不能采取没有就业增长的发展模式，必须坚定不移地朝着经济绿化的方向，量力而行，循序渐进，采取综合配套的政策杠杆，协调推进产业结构优化升级、环境不断改善和就业数量扩大、就业质量提高。这意味着，要在充分考虑充分就业目标的前提下，鼓励绿色产业的发展，有序推动传统产业绿化，逐步完善环保标准。

实现三者的协调推进，关键是要做到政策同步，在制定产业政策和规划时，必须有同步的就业政策和规划；制定环保政策和规划时，必须有同步的就业政策和规划；制定就业政策和规划时，必须考虑对经济发展和环境保护的作用。

4. 绿色就业促进政策需要对绿色就业本身进行调整

绿色就业是个发展的事物，一些绿色就业本身并不是体面就业；一些绿色就业有利于保护环境但并非低碳就业；一些低碳就业又不利于环境保护，如生物质能源种植要用化肥，会造成污染；一些就业是绿色就业，但不符合产业发展要求，如产能过剩的光伏发电和发电设备制造就业；一些就业是绿色就业，但不适合资源禀赋特点，如我国土地资源有限，不适合发展生物质能源。因此，对于绿色就业并非要一味地鼓励发展，还要进行政策调控。在制定绿色就业促进政策时，要从中国实际出发，确定对绿色就业进行干预的领域和程度。

（三）促进绿色就业发展的政策建议

制定促进绿色就业发展的政策，就是要绿化更加积极的就业政策体系。一方面将"绿色"的观念植入现行的政策体系中，另一方面，将以往相关的政策纳入这一政策体系，如资源枯竭城市的就业政策、水库移民的政策、政策性关闭破产企业的政策等。在此基础上，对我国现行的积极就业政策体系进行充实完善，最终形成中国的绿色就业政策体系。

一是要用法律手段保证绿色就业的发展。对产业政策和环保政策进行就业评估，制定以就业为核心的环境保护的社会评价指标体系，在各种产业规划和环保规划中，列入就业评价指标，把产业政策和环保政策对就业的影响评估作为项目审批的前置程序；修改完善相关法律，将对产业政策和环境保护的就业评估法制化。

二是加大政策扶持力度，促进绿色就业发展。绿化人力资源市场机制，建立绿色就业企业认证制度、绿色职业资格认证体系，绿化公共就业服务体系；绿化现行的积极就业政策，将现有的政策扩展到向绿色经济转型中就业受到影响的群体；通过政策扶持，开发一批绿色有潜力的就业岗位；在新农村建设和西部大开发中，大力扶持发展生态农业、特色农业、特色农产品加工业和特色生态乡村旅游业等，开发农村绿色就业岗位，并带动农村公共服务需求，创造绿色公共服务就业岗位；扶持绿色就业型小企业发展带动就业。

三是制订绿色技能开发计划，促进绿色职业的发展。加快绿色职业标准开发建设，开发绿色培训专业标准和绿色技术训练标准，逐步完善我国绿色职业谱表及绿色职业培训标准体系；制定和实施我国绿色产业技术技能提升规划，全面提升劳动者绿色技能水平，为绿色发展提供所需的人力资源；绿化现行的创业培训；强化向绿色就业转型中的转岗转业培训；逐步开展绿色职业从业资格认证和绿色技能鉴定考核工作；建立覆盖各类劳动者的绿色职业技能开发体系。

四是加强对绿色就业领域劳动者的权益保障。在绿色就业发展中，促进提高从业人员薪酬待遇和参加社会保险，改善安全卫生条件，健全工会组织和功能，促进绿色就业劳动者获得符合体面劳动原则的工作条件和工作待遇，提高就业安全性和保障性。

五是社会伙伴共同促进绿色就业。发展绿色就业必须在政府、雇主和职工之间达成共识。工会组织可以积极参与到促进绿色就业发展的工作中。雇主在考虑经济效益的同时，必须承担绿色发展的社会责任，要尽可能将绿色就业与经济效益统一起来。在劳动关系三方协商机制中突出绿色就业的发展战略，促进绿色就业发展。

六是完善促进企业绿色发展的环境。加快完善环保标准；逐步完善政策的激励和诱导机制，使绿色技术和实践的采用者在市场竞争中处于有利地位；不断完善绿色发展的融资机制，争取国际的技术和资金支持，为发展绿色经济、创造绿色工作融资。

七是在国际气候谈判中，建立就业补偿机制。迄今为止，国际气候谈判的焦点只集中在各国的减排指标上，而没有考虑减排的社会成本。为此，应在谈判中建立就业补偿机制，对发展中国家由于减排导致负面就业影响予以资金、技术或减排指标的补偿。

中国绿色就业研究

一 中国研究绿色就业的背景

(一) 国际背景

联合国系统长期关注全球环境和生态的可持续，近年来气候变化也成为最受关注的热点，并且在 2008 年开始的金融危机中，将绿色新政作为经济复苏的重要推动力。在这个过程中，技术、制度和经济是讨论的重点，而社会和劳动维度较少得到关注。2007 年，国际劳工组织（ILO）联合联合国环境规划署（UNEP）、国际雇主组织和国际工联，共同发起绿色就业项目，首次将就业、劳动力市场、社会公正等可持续发展的社会维度纳入环境和生态可持续发展的讨论中，旨在帮助各国保护并创造环境可持续的生产性的体面工作，确保各行各业都严格遵守环境标准和劳工标准，并确保向绿色经济的公平转型。可以说，绿色就业是一个全新的研究领域，对这一问题的认识在全球都处于日新月异的深化过程中。中国作为一个人力资源大国，在发展绿色就业方面也得到国际社会的关注。

(二) 国内背景

中国政府在长期高度重视环境和生态问题的同时，逐步重视在环境保护的同时促进就业。1984 年中国政府发布了《国务院关于环境保护工作的决定》，确立"保护和改善生活环境和生态环境，防止污染和自然环境破坏，是我国社会主义现代化建设中的一项基本国策"。2006 年国务院出台了《国务院关于落实科学发展观加强环境保护的决定》，提出"经济社会发展必须与环境保护相协调"，提出加强环境保护，大力发展循环经济，积极发展环保产业和相关产业，培育新的经济增长点和增加就业。保护环境和生态逐步带动绿色经济发展，进而带动绿色就业增加。

发展绿色就业与中国政府的发展战略思路是一致的。中国政府在 2003 年就提出树立"全面、协调、可持续"的科学发展观，"统筹人与自然和谐发展""构建社会主义和谐社会"的概念，将"人与自然和谐相处"作为和谐社会的六大特征之一，实现生产发展、生活富裕、人民群众安居乐业。2006 年提出把"资源利用效率显著提高，生态环境明显好转"作为构建和谐社会的九大目标之一，要求转变增长方式，提高发展质量，推进节约发展、清洁发展、安全发展，实现经济社会全面可持续发展。由此可见，中国在建设生态文明思想的指导下，生产方式、消费方式的转变会自发带动绿色就业的发展，同时政府已经直接关注到了绿色就业，并已采取了很多措施促进绿色就业发展，在促进绿色就业发展中保障劳动者权益。这与国际倡议是完全一致的。

事实上，中国的绿色就业无论从总量和增速看，都对全球绿色就业做出重大贡献。例如，中国太阳能热水器从业人员达到 60 万人，占世界太阳能热水器行业从业人员的 96%。中国估计有 1000 万人从事各种形式的回收业，仅电器回收就有 70 万人。六大林业工程预计将创造 2000 万就业机会。目前全球新增建筑的 50% 以上在以中国为主的亚洲，提高建筑能效也将提供大量就业机会。同时，很多非绿色就业机会将消失，如仅关停小火电一项就将使 50 万职工失去工作岗位，采用非木材纸浆和造纸也将使上千万人的工作受到影响。

中国在促进绿色就业发展方面也有很多有效的政策干预实践。如早在 20 世纪 90 年代，就针对"煤炭、森工"等五类企业职工就业问题出台过专门的政策，针对资源枯竭城市也出台过专门的政策，针对三峡库区迁建企业也出台过专门的政策。还专门出台政策规范政策性关闭破产企业的职工问题。此外，还有很多扶持创业和产业发展的政策。最全面的政策还是在解决国有企业下岗分流基础上逐步归纳总结形成的、行之有效的、更加积极的就业政策体系，包括人力资源开发政策、促进下岗失业人员再就业的就业政策、调整劳动关系的政策、完善就业保障的政策等。

总之，中国在发展绿色就业方面，战略思路与国际一致，绿色就业发展速度很快，也有很多政策实践。在中国制订"十二五"发展规划的关键时期，需要在明晰中国绿色就业概念的基础上，进一步向全社会推行绿色就业的理念；需要对我国绿色就业的实践进行总结，以推动各方面共同促进绿色就业的发展；对现有相关政策进行评估，不断丰富和完善我国的就业促进政策。同时，在当前积极应对全球气候变化的形势下，作为一个发展中大国，也需要采取负责任的态度，处理好向绿色经济转型的就业问题。

（三）研究现状

中国的绿色就业是一项全新的研究，没有现成的可资借鉴的成果。已有的相关研究主要有以下几类。

1. 关于绿色经济的相关研究①

虽然绿色就业是一个全新的题目，但国内有很多关于绿色经济的探讨。绿色经济是指能同时产生环境效益和经济效益的人类活动，由两部分组成：一是对原有经济系统进行绿化或生态化改造的活动，包括开发新的生产工艺、降低或替代有毒有害物质的使用、高效和循环利用原材料、降低污染物的产生量、对污染物进行净化治理等。二是发展对环境影响小或有利于改善环境的产业，包括生态农业、生态旅游、有机食品、可再生能源、服务业、高新科技、植树造林等绿色产业。绿色经济包括循环经济、低碳经济和生态经济。循环经济主要解决环境污染问题，低碳经济主要针对能源结构和温室气体减排，生态经济主要指向生态系统（草原、森林、海洋、湿地、沙漠等）的恢复、利用和发展。

促进绿色经济发展的环境政策主要包括：提高环境准入门槛、促进产业结构优化；加强环境保护管理和执法；把环保要求纳入生产、流通、分配、消费全过程；制定和实施环境经济政策，创设有利于环境保护的激励机制。

2. 国外的相关研究

国际劳工组织（ILO）联合联合国环境规划署（UNEP）、国际雇主组织和国际工联于 2008 年发布的报告——《绿色工作：在低碳可持续发展的世界实现体面劳动》，是关于绿色就业的首份权威研究成果，对绿色就业进行了如下总结。

（1）资源短缺、环境恶化和气候变化已经对人类社会的可持续发展构成严重威胁。实现环境、经济和社会的协调可持续发展是人类社会共同的唯一选择，即向绿色低碳经济转型。这会产生巨大的绿色工作机会。

---

① 夏光：《积极促进绿色经济发展的环境政策》，中国绿色经济国际论坛，2009 年 11 月。

（2）绿色工作是指在各行各业中对保护和恢复环境质量做出贡献的工作。绿色工作的概念不是绝对的，它随着时间而演变。同时，"绿色"的程度不同，不同的绿色工作对保护和恢复环境质量的作用程度是不同的。

（3）向绿色低碳经济转型会使一些工作被替代甚至消失，一些新的就业机会被创造出来。

（4）绿色工作遍布各个行业和部门。根据温室气体排放量的多少、以自然资源为原材料的程度、对经济的贡献率，以及对就业和收入的贡献率等指标来衡量，绿色工作主要集中在可再生能源、建筑、交通、基础工业、农业和林业六类经济部门。

（5）绿色工作遍布生活的各个方面、各个角落。各种职业、各种技能、各种教育水平都有绿色工作。

（6）绿色工作主要来源于部门或行业内部的工作转化。大多数绿色工作是建立在传统专业和职业基础上的，只是工作的内容和能力要求发生了一些变化。即使是完全崭新的产业和技术创造的完全崭新的绿色工作，其供应链也主要是由钢铁、机器零部件制造等传统产业的工作构成，只是这些工作的内容发生了一定变化，有了新的技能和绩效要求。

（7）技能差距和技能短缺共同制约了绿色经济的发展。缩小现存的技能差距和预测未来的需求是向绿色低碳经济转型的根本。

3. 国内的相关研究

目前国内还没有关于绿色就业的研究。相关的研究主要有"向低碳经济转型对就业的影响"，主要对火电行业"上大压小"、营林造林等对就业的影响进行了定量研究和预测。

关于绿色经济的研究对绿色就业进行了理论模型的推算，关于低碳就业的研究也进行了理论模型的估算，关于绿色工作的研究对绿色工作做了全新的全面探索。这些都为本项研究提供了有效的启发和借鉴。

（四）研究目的和研究框架

开展中国绿色就业研究的目的是出台促进绿色就业发展的政策措施，最终将其纳入中国更加积极的就业政策体系中，促进我国环境和就业的协调发展。在保护环境的同时，大力开发新的绿色就业机会，稳定现有绿色就业机会；在调整产业结构、向绿色经济转型的过程中，注重保障劳动者的合法权益。将环境对就业的积极影响最大化，将环境对就业的消极影响最小化，在最大限度保护环境的同时，采取措施，将失业率控制在社会可承受的范围内，最终实现环境和社会可持续的经济增长。根据中国的国情和目前的研究现状，绿色就业研究需要回答以下问题。

1. 什么是绿色就业

绿色就业是个全新概念，阐述清楚这一概念，是推广理念、开展研究的基础。

2. 就业绿化的全景

就业绿化是全方位的，涉及国民经济的各个部门和领域。这是研究绿色就业的前提。比如在中国，许多行业与环境和气候变化联系紧密，从业人员需要"靠天吃饭"，如农业、渔业和旅游业等，他们的生计非常容易受到环境的影响。

3. 就业绿化对劳动者的影响

如在气候变化适应方面，一些领域的投资可以为易失业人群提供更多、更好的就业机会；如某些企业转换到可持续生产模式，在短期内需要在就业模式方面做出重大调整，一些劳动者会面临失去工作岗位或进行技能提升的问题；如新的能源和产业政策可能给绿色就业创造了机遇。

4. 如何有效促进绿色就业的发展，保障劳动者的就业权利

制定合理的就业转化措施，使工人参加教育与再培训计划，然后使其获得从事其他环境友好型工作的渠道或者获得经济赔偿；如一些城市围绕水资源保护、城市绿化、"一退双还"、防风固沙、发展农业产业化和龙型经济，帮助年龄偏大的下岗职工实现再就业；如工会和企业的合作等。

二　中国绿色就业的概念

（一）现有的绿色就业的概念

绿色就业是一个全新的研究领域，对这一问题的认识在全球都处于日新月异的深化过程中。迄今为止，国际上关于绿色就业有以下一些界定。

一种定义[1]，"绿色就业是指经济上可行的，同时能够减少环境影响、实现可持续发展的就业"。还有一种定义[2]，"绿色就业是指对环境的影响低于平

---

[1] 转引自 ILO 亚太地区局专家 Ivanka Mamic 会议发言材料，中国绿色就业研讨会，2009 年 1 月 21 日，北京。

[2] 转引自 ILO 亚太地区局专家 Ivanka Mamic 会议发言材料，中国绿色就业研讨会，2009 年 1 月 21 日，北京。

均水平、能够改善整体环境质量的任何的新兴工作"。

国际劳工组织对绿色就业的定义，"绿色就业是在经济部门和经济活动中创造的体面劳动，它能够减少环境影响，最终在环境、经济和社会层面实现可持续发展"。

在报告《绿色工作：在低碳、可持续发展的世界实现体面劳动》（UNEP、ILO、ITUC）中，绿色就业被定义为："在农业、工业、服务业和管理领域有助于保护或恢复环境质量的工作。"绿色就业有四个基本特点：一是能够减少能源和原材料消耗（"非物质化经济"）；二是避免温室气体排放（"无碳化经济"）；三是保护和恢复生态系统；四是减少废物和污染。

美国明尼苏达州 Task Force 机构将"绿色就业"定义为"绿色经济的就业机会，包括绿色产品、可再生能源、绿色服务和环境保护四个产业部门的就业"。其中，绿色产品是指为了减少环境影响、改善资源使用效率而生产的产品，它主要应用于建筑、交通、消费产品和工业产品四个领域。可再生能源是指太阳能、风能、水能、地热能、生物燃料等能源。绿色服务是指为帮助企业和消费者个人使用绿色产品或技术提供各类服务的产业或职业，还包括能源基础设施建设以及与能源效率、农业、再循环和废物管理相关的职业。环境保护是指与能源、空气、水以及土地资源的保护相关的产业。

第一种定义是一种强调绿色就业的经济和环保属性的模糊定义，第二种定义是强调环境影响的新兴就业，ILO 的定义强调的是体面劳动特性，UNEP 等报告的定义强调的是绿色就业的行业和技术特性，TF 机构的定义则是指绿色产业的就业。以上各种定义都从不同侧面对绿色就业进行了定义，但都没有完整概括绿色就业的范畴和特性。

（二）中国绿色就业的定义

1. 理论定义

绿色是指生态环境良好。为了可持续发展，需要对人类的经济活动和生存环境进行绿化，也就是对产业结构、产品生产的技术和工艺、产品生产的组织方式、生活方式等进行绿化。从实践出发，绿化具体包括六个方面：一是多发展对环境影响小的产业，主要是生态农业、生态旅游、有机食品、可再生能源、服务业、高新科技、植树造林等；二是限制发展对环境影响大的产业，主要是能源、冶金、建材等重化工业，造纸等轻工业；三是绿化/净化生产过程，通过开发新的生产工艺降低或替代有毒有害物质的使用、高效和循环利用原材

料、降低污染物的产生量、对污染物进行净化治理等；四是城市和农村的公共
环境设施建设和维护，以及公共环境保护与治理；五是生态环境保护与修复；
六是围绕经济绿化发展绿色服务业，包括绿色信贷、绿色技术、绿色设备、绿
色保险、绿色认证等。

绿色就业指所有使经济活动和生存环境绿化（变得更绿、更环保）的就
业，它有如下特性或规定性。

• "绿色就业"强调的是就业的环境功能，特指这种就业有助于保护或
恢复环境质量，而不是强调就业本身的劳动属性。虽然国际劳工组织强调体面
就业必须是绿色就业，但现实中，一些绿色就业本身并不一定是体面的就业，
一些体面的就业也不一定是绿色的就业。

• 从其环境功能来看，绿色就业具有四个特征，即降低能耗与原材料消
耗的"非物质化经济"特征，避免温室气体排放的"去碳化经济"特征，将
废物与污染降至最低的"环境经济"特征，保护和恢复生态系统和环境服务
的"生态经济"特征。

• 体现上述四种特征、实现绿色就业的方式包括：宏观层面上调整生产
结构，使用新的替代能源和原材料，发展低碳经济，发展循环经济，发展环境
保护产业等；微观层面主要是改进生产技术，提供相关服务等。

• 绿色就业并非是绝对不对环境产生影响的就业，是指那些对环境的负
面影响程度显著低于通常水平、能够改善整体环境质量的就业。也就是说，绿
色就业本身可以有"深绿""浅绿"等不同分类，非绿色就业也可以有"黑
色""棕色"等不同分类。

• 就业绿化的程度，或者说绿色就业在整个就业中所占的比重，与发展
水平和发展方式相关。经济越发达，就业绿化的程度越高。以工业、建筑业为
主的第二产业比重越高，经济增长方式越粗放，就业绿化的程度越低。也就是
说，绿色就业的发展具有不可超越的客观性和历史阶段性，我们可以促进但不
可能跨越发展阶段。

• 评判绿色就业的标准是相对的，与特定背景下的环境标准相关。如发
达国家的非绿色就业在发展中国家可能就是绿色的，目前阶段绿色的就业可能
随着经济的发展就成为非绿色的就业了。也就是说，绿色就业具有动态发展
性。

• 绿色就业遍布各行业，分布在资源开采、转化、流通、生产消耗、废

物产生、消费等各个环节，在建设、生产、技术、设备、工艺、服务等各个方面，具有巨大潜力和发展前景。根据温室气体排放量的多少、以自然资源为原材料的程度、对经济的贡献率，以及对就业和收入的贡献率等指标来衡量，低碳报告认为绿色就业主要集中在六类经济部门，即风能、太阳能、生物能等可再生能源部门和建筑、交通、基础工业、农业和林业等部门。

• 绿色就业同时具有产业、行业和部门的非均衡性。通常，相对第二产业，第三产业的就业更加绿色；在 19 个国民经济部门中，农业、水利、电力、制造业、建筑业、交通运输业的就业平均绿色程度相对较低；制造业中，电力、钢铁、建材、电解铝、铁合金、电石、焦炭、煤炭、平板玻璃、轻工（造纸、化工、印染）等行业的就业绿色程度相对较低。

• 绿色就业涉及各种职业、各种技能、各种教育水平的劳动者，从简单体力劳动到技术工人，从手工业者和创业者到高素质技师、工程师和经理，都可以是绿色就业。绿色就业为管理人员、科学家、技师及各类普通劳动者都提供了机会，同样也能为那些最需要工作的就业困难群体提供机会，如青年人、妇女、农民、农村人口及贫民窟的居民。

• 绿色就业并非都是新的就业。一些绿色就业是以前没有的崭新的工作类型，但是大多数绿色就业是建立在传统专业和职业基础上的，只是工作的内容和能力要求发生了一些变化。即使是完全崭新的产业和技术创造的完全崭新的绿色就业，其供应链也主要是由钢铁、机器零部件制造等传统产业的工作构成，只是这些工作的内容发生了一定的变化，有了新的技能和绩效要求。也就是说，绿色就业是对现有就业的逐步改造，以及在现有就业基础上的新创造。

• 绿色就业既包括直接创造的就业机会，又包括由此间接带动的就业机会，还包括诱导衍生的就业机会。直接的绿色就业如环保设备企业、直接保护环境的企业的就业，如垃圾处理、污水处理。更多是间接的、在不同产业和不同企业中的就业。环保要求提高后，各个领域都会受到影响，包括生产和消费等环节。政策、科研、金融（信贷、保险、证券）、监管、贸易等都是间接就业。因此，研究绿色就业需要统筹考虑直接就业、间接就业以及衍生就业。

• 绿色就业需要技能提升。技能差距和技能短缺共同制约了绿色经济的发展。生产链中最弱的环节决定可能获得的绩效水平。没有合格的创业者和技术工人，可获得的技术和投资就不能被利用或不能实现预期的环境收益和经济收益。缩小现存的技能差距和预测未来的需求是向绿色低碳经济转型的根本。

一味强调高端技能和教育将导致劳动力市场供求不匹配，因而培训"绿领"工人很重要。评估绿色工作的潜力并对这些工作进行监控，将有利于中长期职业教育培训体系的应对，使技能开发与政策和投资之间相联系。

- 与解决就业问题主要依靠中小企业一样，小企业和基层社区可以创造大量的绿色就业。

- 绿色就业的发展过程包括四种情况：产生一些新的就业机会，一些现有的就业机会消失，一些就业机会被替代，一些就业的技能要求发生变化，最终对就业的总量、结构、增量和就业形式产生影响。

- 绿色就业实际上只是个容易叫得响的口号，名词本身没有重要意义。倡议绿色就业的根本目的，或者说绿色就业的根本意义在于两个方面：一是引起人们对"'经济绿化'对扩大就业、创造体面就业的挑战和影响"的重视；二是希望通过"就业绿化"推动经济绿化。

- 根据我国正处于工业化中期、城乡二元劳动力转移也处于中期的国情，以及建设生态文明的基本国策，我国应坚定不移地实施绿色就业战略，将绿色就业纳入现行的扩大就业战略中，制定相关政策措施，在持续扩大就业的过程中，推动绿色就业的发展。

- 从人力资源部门的角度，绿色就业发展战略的目标有三个方面：一是以绿色就业为主扩大就业，不能因为发展绿色就业而使失业问题加重，甚至超过经济社会可承受的程度；二是在绿色就业发展中，促进劳动者权益保护；三是通过人力资源开发，促进绿色经济发展。

2. 政策定义

根据中国国民经济和社会发展规划，以及相应的每年的政府工作安排及行业和部门的发展规划和政策措施，与建设资源节约型、环境友好型社会的发展战略相一致，中国的绿色就业可以定义为，国民经济中相对于社会平均水平而言，低投入、高产出，低消耗、少排放，能循环、可持续的产业、行业、部门、企业和岗位上的工作。

"低投入、高产出"泛指与提高组织管理水平进而提高生产效率相关的就业。提高生产效率意味着各种生产要素的节约，具有资源节约、环境友好的倾向，是我国从粗放到集约的经济增长模式转变的主要方面，对整个经济都具有基础性的决定性作用，应成为中国绿色就业的要素；"低消耗、少排放"主要指与通过提高技术水平实现通常意义上的能源、资源节约和减少污染物排放相关的就业，是绿色就业的基本要素；"能循环、可持续"既是指总体上生态体系的自我修复和经济、社会发展的可持续的思想，又是指与循环经济、污染治理和生态环境保护相关的就业。

这一定义是从中国经济社会的发展阶段、面临的主要问题、应对各种挑战的战略、政策措施出发，与世界趋势一致下界定的。中国是一个中低收入的、处于工业化、城市化阶段的发展中国家，面临的主要问题是满足人口生存基本需要的资源、环境压力巨大，过于粗放的经济增长模式和低的要素生产率。中国《国民经济和社会发展第十一个五年规划纲要》提出，要实现人口、资源、环境相协调的可持续发展，为此要建立"低投入、高产出，低消耗、少排放，能循环、可持续"的国民经济体系，建设资源节约型、环境友好型社会。转变经济增长方式、提高投入产出效率，与节约资源、保护环境、治理污染、减少排放是一致的；是适应与减缓的统一。这"18字方针"既概括了国民经济发展的战略部署，又决定了中国绿色就业的范畴。与 UNEP 绿色就业的定义相比，这一定义更全面和综合：除节约资源、低排放、低污染、保护和修复生态环境四点外，还明确强调了低投入和"能循环、可持续"的特征，体现了中国经济发展的阶段特征，以及从宏观意义上保护环境可持续发展的整体思想。

3. 绿色就业的范畴

绿色就业包括低碳就业和环保就业。环保就业是指低污染（传统排放）的就业模式。低碳就业主要是指低能耗、低污染（传统排放）、低排放（二氧化碳）的就业模式。低碳发展的思想在时间和空间上都比环保发展的思想晚了20年，低碳发展的套路和做法与环保发展的思路和做法完全不一样，低碳就业与环保就业也不同。

传统污染物排放是区域性的、局部的。降低传统污染物排放有利于低碳发展，但不是100%是低碳的。反过来，气候变化对环境污染影响不大，因而低碳发展对环境保护也影响不大。总之，环保的就业不一定都是低碳的，低碳的就业也不一定是环保的就业。低碳就业与环保就业有交叉，但不完全相同。

污染是内政，发达国家早在30年前就解决了污染问题，国外的环保产业需求相对稳定，新增环保就业机会有限，因而他们不太关心低污染的就业，而主要关注全球性的碳排放问题，因此绿色就业主要指低碳就业。发展中国家则不同。我们仍然处于工业化发展阶段，保护环境、清洁发展仍然是一个重要问题，因此，发展中国家的绿色就业不仅包括低碳就业，而且包括环保就业，二者不可偏废。

三 中国绿色就业发展的法律、制度、政策环境

从污染控制、恢复生态到建设生态文明，修正工业文明弊端，中国政府从思想上正在实现三个转变：一是从重经济增长、轻环境保护转变为保护环境与经济增长并重，二是从环境保护滞后于经济发展转变为环境保护与经济发展同步，三是从主要用行政办法保护环境转变为综合运用法律、经济、技术和必要的行政办法解决环境问题。[①] 这种战略思路的转变决定了绿色就业发展的大背景。

（一）环境保护相关立法

1979 年 9 月 13 日第五届全国人大第十一次会议通过了《环境保护法（试行）》，这是中国第一部关于环境保护的法律。此后，环境与资源保护法律体系逐步形成。主要立法包括以下几类。

一是生态与自然资源保护方面的法律，包括《土地管理法》《水法》《森林法》《草原法》《水土保持法》《野生动物保护法》等。二是环境污染防治和公害控制的法律法规，主要是针对大气、水、固体废物、噪声、放射性污染防治方面的法律，以及与之配套的环境质量标准和污染物排放标准，包括《固体废物污染环境防治法》《水污染防治法》《大气污染防治法》，以及《水污染防治法实施细则》等。三是资源节约和综合利用方面的法律法规，如《节约能源法》。四是促进循环经济和清洁生产的法律法规，如《清洁生产促进法》《可再生能源法》，以及《循环经济促进法》。五是关于特定环境行政制度的法律，以及国务院和主管行政部门颁布的配套规章，如《环境影响评价法》《建设项目环境保护管理条例》《建设项目环境影响评价文件分级审批规定》。

（二）相关产业政策

绿色发展最终落实到产业政策上。相关的产业政策主要有以下内容。

1. 发展可再生能源，优化能源结构

《节约能源法》《国民经济和社会发展第十一个五年规划纲要》《节能减排综合性工作方案》《国家环境保护"十一五"规划》《中国应对气候变化国家

---

① 周生贤：《生态文明建设：环境保护工作的基础和灵魂》，第五届环境和发展中国（国际）论坛资料。

方案》，以及《中国应对气候变化的政策与行动》《新能源产业振兴和发展规划》，提出要优化发展能源工业，优化能源的生产和消费结构。

加快火力发电的技术进步，优化火电结构，加快淘汰落后的小火电机组，大力发展高效、洁净发电技术；加快发展水电、太阳能热利用（太阳能热水器、太阳灶）、沼气等技术成熟、市场竞争力强的可再生能源，积极推进技术基本成熟、开发潜力大的风电、生物质发电、太阳能发电、生物液体燃料（非粮原料燃料乙醇、生物柴油、户用沼气池、规模化养殖场沼气工程、农林生物质固体成型燃料）等可再生能源技术的产业化发展；积极发展核电；进一步推进煤炭清洁利用，不断加强对煤层气和矿井瓦斯的利用，研究二氧化碳捕获与封存技术。

未来中国能源结构战略是，2010 年前后，可再生能源占到能源消费的 10% 左右，战略定位是补充能源；2020 年前后，可再生能源占到能源消费的 15% 左右，战略定位是替代能源；2030 年前后，可再生能源占到能源消费的 25% 左右，战略定位是主流能源；2050 年前后，可再生能源占到能源消费的 40% 左右，战略定位是主导能源。

可再生能源是高新技术和新兴产业，是新的经济增长领域，可以有效拉动装备制造等相关产业的发展，有利于调整产业结构、促进经济增长方式转变、扩大就业，还有利于节能减排。

2. 淘汰落后生产能力

2006 年，国务院发布了《国务院关于加快推进产能过剩行业结构调整的通知》，规定一是要制定更加严格的环境、安全、能耗、水耗、资源综合利用和质量、技术、规模等标准，提高准入门槛。二是淘汰落后生产能力，依法关闭一批小企业（小火电、小钢铁、小水泥、小煤矿），分期分批淘汰一批落后生产能力。三是推进技术改造，围绕提升技术水平、改善品种、保护环境、保障安全、降低消耗、综合利用等，对传统产业实施改造提高。

电力、钢铁、建材、电解铝、铁合金、电石、焦炭、煤炭、平板玻璃等13 个行业是节能降耗和污染减排的重点领域。2007 年 1 月，国务院批转了国家发展改革委、能源办《关于加快关停小火电机组的若干意见》，提出了"上大压小"政策，就是将新建电源项目与关停小火电机组挂钩，在建设大容量、高参数、低消耗、少排放机组的同时，相对应关停一部分小火电机组；2007年，国家发展和改革委员会（简称国家发改委）先后与 28 个省（区、市）签订了《关停和淘汰落后钢铁生产能力责任书》；水泥行业立窑水泥企业停止原来的生产；有色金属行业淘汰落后铜、铅、锌冶炼产能和小预焙槽电解铝产能；轻工行业淘汰造纸、酒精、味精、柠檬酸、低能效冰箱（含冰柜）、皮革、含汞扣式碱锰电池、白炽灯的落后产能；纺织行业加快关闭污染严重的印染企业，重点淘汰印染、化纤落后产能，加速淘汰棉纺、毛纺落后生产能力；石化行业淘汰 100 万吨及以下低效低质落后炼油装置，农药行业淘汰一批高毒高风险农药品种，加快淘汰电石、甲醇等产品的落后产能。

2007 年 11 月制订的《国家环境保护"十一五"规划》提出，在确定钢铁、有色、建材、电力、轻工（造纸、化工、印染）等重点行业准入条件时充分考虑环境保护要求，新建项目必须符合国家规定的准入条件和排放标准；对于已无环境容量的区域，禁止新建增加污染物排放量的项目；对消耗高、污染重、技术落后的工艺和产品实行强制淘汰。

"十一五"期间，全国关停小燃煤火电机组 5000 万千瓦以上；关停和淘汰炼铁能力 8917 万吨、炼钢能力 7776 万吨，涉及企业 917 家；淘汰落后水泥产能 2.5 亿吨；淘汰落后铜冶炼产能 30 万吨、铅冶炼产能 60 万吨、锌冶炼产能 40 万吨、小预焙槽电解铝产能 80 万吨；淘汰落后制浆造纸 200 万吨以上、低能效冰箱（含冰柜）3000 万台、皮革 3000 万标准张、含汞扣式碱锰电池 90 亿只、白炽灯 6 亿只、酒精 100 万吨、味精 12 万吨、柠檬酸 5 万吨的生产能力；淘汰 230 万吨化纤落后产能；淘汰 100 万吨及以下低效低质落后炼油装置。仅山西省钢铁、焦化、火电、小煤矿等淘汰落后产能行业，就涉及职工 13 万人。[①]

"十一五"时期淘汰落后生产能力情况如表 2 - 1 所示。

表 2 - 1　"十一五"时期淘汰落后生产能力一览

行业	内容	单位	"十一五"时期	2007 年
电力	实施"上大压小"，关停小火电机组	万千瓦	5000	1000
炼铁	300 立方米以下高炉	万吨	10000	3000
炼钢	年产 20 万吨及以下的小转炉、小电炉	万吨	5500	3500
电解铝	小型预焙槽	万吨	6.5	10

① 劳动和社会保障部：《淘汰落后产能和节能减排职工安置有关情况调研报告》，2007。

续表

行业	内容	单位	"十一五"时期	2007 年
铁合金	6300 千伏安以下矿热炉	万吨	400	120
电石	6300 千伏安以下炉型电石产能	万吨	200	50
焦炭	炭化室高度 4.3 米以下的小机焦	万吨	8000	1000
水泥	等量替代机立窑水泥熟料	万吨	25000	1000
玻璃	落后平板玻璃	万重量箱	3000	600
造纸	年产 3.4 万吨以下草浆生产装置、年产 1.7 万吨以下化学制浆生产线、排放不达标的年产 1 万吨以下以废纸为原料的纸厂	万吨	650	230
酒精	落后酒精生产工艺及年产 3 万吨以下企业（废糖蜜制酒精除外）	万吨	160	40
味精	年产 3 万吨以下味精生产企业	万吨	20	5
柠檬酸	环保不达标柠檬酸生产企业	万吨	8	2

3. 推进传统产业的技术改造提高，减少污染物排放

2007 年 6 月，国务院印发《节能减排综合性工作方案》，提出促进节能减排的 45 条政策措施，其中对传统产业进行技术改造的政策主要包括：加快现役火电机组脱硫设施的建设，使现役火电机组投入运行的脱硫装机容量达到 2.13 亿千瓦。新（扩）建燃煤电厂必须同步建设脱硫设施并预留脱硝场地。大力推进煤炭洗选工程建设，推广煤炭清洁燃烧技术。加大造纸、酿造、化工、纺织、印染行业工业废水污染治理和技术改造力度。

4. 节约能源，提高能源利用效率，减少污染物排放

2006 年发布的《国务院关于加强节能工作的决定》和 2007 年 6 月国务院印发的《节能减排综合性工作方案》，提出工业、交通和建筑节能的具体措施：工业节能要突出抓好钢铁、有色金属、煤炭、电力、石油石化、化工、建材等重点耗能行业和年耗能 1 万吨标准煤以上企业的节能工作；推进建筑节能，大力发展节能省地型建筑，推动新建住宅和公共建筑严格实施节能 50% 的设计标准，直辖市及有条件的地区要率先实施节能 65% 的标准；积极推进节能型综合交通运输体系建设，加快发展铁路和内河运输，优先发展公共交通和轨道交通，加快淘汰老旧铁路机车、汽车、船舶，鼓励发展节能环保型交通工具，开发和推广车用代用燃料和清洁燃料汽车；引导商业和民用节能，并确立了十大重点节能工程。

5. 推动循环经济试点，实现清洁生产，减少污染物排放

国家通过制定并实行《清洁生产促进法》《固体废物污染环境防治法》《循环经济促进法》《城市生活垃圾管理办法》《废弃电器电子产品回收处理管理条例》等法律法规，发布《促进产业结构调整暂行规定》《关于加快发展循环经济的若干意见》《"十一五"资源综合利用指导意见》，以及《国家环境保护"十一五"规划》《中国应对气候变化的政策与行动》白皮书等政策文件，提出发展循环经济的总体思路、近期目标、基本途径和政策措施，并发布循环经济评价指标体系。

2006 年发布的《国民经济和社会发展第十一个五年规划纲要》第六篇制订了关于发展循环经济的规划，提出发展循环经济，坚持开发节约并重、节约优先，按照减量化、再利用、资源化的原则，在资源开采、生产消耗、废物产生、消费等环节，逐步建立全社会的资源循环利用体系。《节能减排综合性工作方案》提出要在钢铁、电力、化工、煤炭等重点行业加强废水循环利用。

建立循环经济示范区，就 36 种主要产品扩展了循环经济试点。

6. 提高资源综合利用水平

资源综合利用方面的目标是，到 2010 年资源综合利用产业得到快速发展；资源利用效率有较大幅度提高，工业固体废物综合利用率达到 60%；综合利用产品在同类产品中的比重逐步提高，形成一批具有一定规模、较高技术装备水平、资源利用率较高、废物排放量较低的综合利用企业。

资源综合利用的重点领域包括：矿产资源综合利用、"三废"综合利用、再生资源回收利用、农林废弃物综合利用。"十一五"期间资源综合利用的重点工程包括：共、伴生矿产资源综合开发利用工程；大宗固体废物资源化利用工程；再生金属加工产业化工程；废旧家用电器、废旧轮胎等再生资源产业化工程；再生资源回收体系建设示范工程；农业废弃物（秸秆、畜禽粪便）和木材综合利用工程；推进建筑垃圾的综合利用。

7. 加强环境污染治理

实施危险废物和医疗废物处置工程和生活垃圾无害化处置工程，推进固体废物综合利用。到"十一五"末期，将建立 31 个省级危险废物集中处置中心，300 个设区市的医疗废物集中处理中心，以及配套的国家和省级技术支持和监管能力建设项目，总计投资需要 150 亿元。

在废水处理方面，一是要加快城市污水处理与再生利用工程建设。到

2010 年，城市污水处理率不低于 70%；到 2015 年，全国新建城镇污水管网约达到 16 万公里，新建污水日处理能力 4200 万吨，城市污水处理率达到 85%。二是加强工业废水治理。重点抓好占工业化学需氧量排放量 65% 的"国控重点企业"的废水达标排放和总量削减。

8. 大力发展环保产业

《国民经济和社会发展第十一个五年规划纲要》将发展大型高效清洁发电装备、环保及资源综合利用装备作为振兴装备制造业的重点领域。提出以环境保护重点工程为需求，大力发展环保装备制造业；以环境影响评价、环境工程服务、环境技术研发与咨询、环境风险投资为重点，积极发展环保服务业。例如，在资源综合利用方面，重点发展废品回收利用，再生水、微咸水、海水淡化等非常规水资源化，高效冷却节水，报废汽车、废旧轮胎、废旧家电、电子废物和尾矿再利用等。在污染治理设施建设运营和咨询服务方面，重点推进城市污水、垃圾、危险废物等环境设施建设运行市场化；规模化工业废水处理、电厂脱硫、除尘设施专业化运营；大力发展环境保护的技术咨询和管理服务。2012 年 6 月 16 日，国务院印发了《"十二五"节能环保产业发展规划》。

9. 减少农业、农村温室气体排放

通过继续推广低排放的高产水稻品种和半旱式栽培技术，采用科学灌溉技术；强化高集约化程度地区的生态农业建设，加强对动物粪便、废水和固体废弃物的管理，加大沼气利用力度等措施，努力控制甲烷排放增长速度。

10. 推动植树造林，增强碳汇能力

改革和完善现有产业政策，抓好林业重点生态建设工程。继续实施植树造林、推进天然林资源保护、退耕还林还草、京津风沙源治理、防护林体系、野生动植物保护及自然保护区建设等林业重点生态建设工程，抓好生物质能林基地建设。

中国《国民经济和社会发展第十二个五年规划纲要》提出，到 2015 年，单位国内生产总值二氧化碳排放量降低 17%，单位工业增加值用水量降低 30%，农业灌溉用水有效利用系数提高到 0.53；非化石能源占一次能源消费的比重达到 11.4%，单位国内生产总值能源消耗降低 16%，主要污染物排放总量显著减少，化学需氧量、二氧化硫排放量分别减少 8%，氨氮、氮氧化物排放量分别减少 10%；森林覆盖率提高到 21.66%，森林蓄积量增加 6 亿立方米。

(三) 相关经济政策

经济政策是促进环境保护的重要杠杆。中国政府正在积极完善促进环境保护的相关政策措施，主要有以下几个方面。

1. 财政政策

财政支出包括政府对环境保护的直接投资、财政补贴、政府"绿色"采购制度、环境性因素的财政转移支付等。

政府对环境保护的直接投资主要是环境污染治理投入。设立环境整治与保护补助的专项资金，不断增加中央环保专项资金投入，充分发挥中央财政资金的引导和示范作用；通过国债资金支持一批重点生态建设和污染治理项目，主要用于京津风沙源治理，西部中心城市环保设施建设，"三河三湖"污染防治，污水、垃圾产业化及中水回用，北京环境污染治理，森林生态效益补偿等项目。自 1998 年起，中央政府不断加大对欠发达的中西部地区的财政援助，把生态建设与农村基础设施建设、产业开发结合起来，实施退耕还林、还草政策，调整农业结构，增加农牧民收入。

目前广泛应用的补贴主要有对治污项目的补贴（如脱硫电价补贴）、对生态建设项目的补贴、对清洁生产项目的补贴、对环境科研的补贴、对生产环境友好型产品的补贴等。

2003 年 1 月 1 日起实施《政府采购法》，2004 年年底财政部与国家发改委的《节能产品政府采购实施意见》于 2005 年 1 月 1 日起正式实施，成为我国第一个政府采购促进节能与环保的具体政策规定。

2. 税收政策

在增值税方面，一是鼓励资源综合利用的税收政策。对企业利用废渣等生产的资源综合利用产品免征增值税、减半征收增值税或实行增值税"即征即退"办法；对废旧物资回收经营单位销售收购的废旧物资免征增值税，对生产企业购买废旧物资允许抵扣进项税额。二是鼓励清洁能源和环保产品的税收政策。对利用风力生产的电力和列入《享受税收优惠政策新型墙体材料目录》的新型墙体材料产品，包括非黏土砖、建筑砌块、建筑板材 14 类共 23 种产品，实行增值税减半征收。三是鼓励污水处理的优惠措施。自 2001 年 7 月 1 日起，对各级政府及主管部门委托自来水厂随水费收取的污水处理费，免征增值税。

在消费税方面，2009 年 1 月 1 日实施成品油税费改革，有利于节能环保的小排量车发展，从长远来看有利于新能源汽车的产业化发展。

在所得税方面，一是规定企业利用"三废"等废弃物为主要原料进行生产的，可在 5 年内减征或者免征所得税。二是对专门生产当前国家鼓励发展的环保产业设备（产品）的免税政策。三是对国家鼓励发展的环保产业设备实行投资抵免、加速折旧政策。

在资源税方面，1988 年 4 月开征了资源税，1994 年进一步扩大了征收范围。目前正在研究碳税政策。在出口退税政策方面，取消包括各种矿产品精矿、原油等资源性产品在内的出口退税政策，将铜、镍、铁合金、炼焦煤、焦炭等部分产品的出口退税率降为 5%，对"两高一资"产品的出口退税率大幅下降甚至全额取消。在房产税、城镇土地使用税、车船使用税、契税等地方税种中，也有一些有利于生态环境保护的措施。

3. 金融政策

2007 年 7 月 30 日，国家环保总局联合中国人民银行、银监会出台《关于落实环境保护政策法规防范信贷风险的意见》，要求人民银行和银监会配合环保部门，引导各级金融机构按照环境经济政策要求，对国家禁止、淘汰、限制、鼓励等不同类型企业的授信区别对待。尤其要对没有经过环保评估审批的项目不可提供新增信贷，避免出现新的呆坏账。

2007 年 12 月，环境保护部与中国保监会联合出台《关于环境污染责任保险工作的指导意见》，正式启动了绿色保险制度建设。提出在"十一五"期间初步建立符合我国国情的环境污染责任保险制度，在重点行业和区域开展环境污染责任保险的试点示范工作，以生产、经营、储存、运输、使用危险化学品企业，易发生污染事故的石油化工企业，危险废物处置企业等为对象开展试点。2012 年以后，环境污染责任保险将在全国推广。

2009 年 2 月，国家环保部提出将加强新建项目的环境准入，将逐步废除不利于环保的相关补贴和税收优惠，对达不到环保要求、严重污染环境的企业，取消其享受有关税收优惠。此外，将进一步拓展绿色贸易政策，定期公布企业污染物排放达标公告，凡未被列入达标公告的企业所生产的产品禁止出口，并在目前柠檬酸、电解铝等行业公告的基础上，逐步向其他重污染行业扩展。

四　中国绿色就业的现状

绿色就业在中国已有较长的发展过程。中国环保事业从 20 世纪 80 年代就开始了，已形成环保产业；植树造林从新中国成立以来就开始了，年年植树造林；太阳能产业从 20 世纪 90 年代开始发展，已具有相当规模；风力发电这些年发展迅猛，生物质能发电也得到发展；工业企业"三废"治理力度不断加大，淘汰落后产能陆续关停了一些污染和能耗大户；发展循环经济、废品回收利用正在规范发展。在这一过程中，已形成一定规模的绿色就业，同时，也有一些经验做法。

（一）环保相关产业就业①

近年来，国家加大了环境保护基础设施的建设投资，有力地拉动了环境保护相关产业的市场需求，环境保护相关产业已成为国民经济结构的重要组成部分。根据 2004 年《全国环境保护相关产业状况公报》，环境保护相关产业不仅包括污染控制与减排、污染清理及废物处理等方面提供产品与技术服务的狭义内涵，而且包括涉及产品生命周期过程中对环境友好的技术与产品、节能技术、生态设计及与环境相关的服务等。根据公报，2004 年全国环境保护相关产业从业人员 159.5 万人，其相关产业领域构成情况如表 2－2 所示。

表 2－2　2004 年全国环境保护相关产业领域构成

项目	合计	环境保护产品	资源综合利用	环境保护服务	洁净产品
从业单位总数(个)	11623	1867	6105	3387	947
从业人数(万人)	159.5	16.8	95.9	17.0	23.3
年收入总额(亿元)	4572.1	341.9	2787.4	264.1	1178.7
单位平均从业人数(人)	137	90	157	50	246
单位人均收入(万元)	29	20	29	16	51

列入调查范围的环境保护产品②共计 594 个类别，5501 项产品，以水污染治理设备和空气污染治理设备为主。环保产品行业单位平均从业人数为 90 人，单位人均收入 20 万元。

---

① 国家环境保护总局、国家发展和改革委员会、国家统计局联合于 2006 年 4 月发布了 2004 年由环保产业协会具体执行的《全国环境保护相关产业状况公报》。此次调查为一次性全面调查，调查基准时间为 2004 年，实施时间为 2005 年 2 月至 8 月。调查范围覆盖了全国除台湾地区、香港和澳门特别行政区以外的 31 个省、自治区和直辖市专业或兼业从事环境保护产品生产、资源综合利用、环境保护服务、洁净产品生产的全部国有及环保相关产业年销售（经营）收入 200 万元以上的非国有企业或事业单位。

② 环境保护产品指用于防治环境污染、保护生态环境的设备、材料和药剂、环境监测专用仪器仪表。包括水污染治理设备、空气污染治理设备、固体废物处理处置与回收利用设备、噪声与振动控制设备、放射性与电磁波污染防护设备、污染治理专用药剂和材料、环境监测仪器等。

资源综合利用①以再生资源回收利用和固体废物综合利用为主。资源综合利用行业单位平均从业人数为 157 人，单位人均收入 29 万元。

在全国环境保护服务业②从业人员中，有从事环境技术与产品研发的 1.6 万人，从事环境工程设计与施工的 5.3 万人，从事污染治理设施运营（生活污水治理设施运营、工业废水处理设施运营、除尘脱硫处理设施运营、工业废气处理设施运营、生活垃圾处理设施运营、危险废物处理设施运营、自动连续监测设施运营、其他设施运营）的 5.2 万人，环境监测从业人数 2.7 万人，环境咨询服务从业人数 1.5 万人。我国环境保护服务以环境工程设计与施工服务和污染治理设施运营服务为主。环境保护服务行业单位平均从业人数为 50 人，单位人均收入 16 万元。

本次调查统计包括 9 类洁净产品③，即有机食品及其他有机产品、低毒低害产品、低排放产品、低噪声产品、可生物降解产品、节能产品、节水产品及其他产品。纳入调查统计的洁净产品 52 类，产品 1492 项，以节能产品、低毒低害产品、低排放产品和有机食品为主。洁净产品行业单位平均从业人数为 246 人，单位人均收入 51 万元。

● 武汉首开电子废物回收超市，防止电子垃圾污染，实现资源循环利用

早在 2006 年，湖北省发改委的相关报告就表明，湖北省已进入电器报废高峰期。全省每年约报废 30 万台电视机、20 万台冰箱、30 万台洗衣机。电子垃圾含有大量铅、锡、汞等有毒、有害物质，如处理不当，会污染土地和水源，是继化工、冶金、造纸、印染之后的又一环境杀手。目前，近九成的城市废弃家电被流动商贩低价收走，并由小作坊拆解或被焚烧、填埋，污染严重。

电子垃圾的金属含量比矿山高出好多倍。在专业化的处理工厂，采取无害

---

① 资源综合利用指对废弃资源和废旧材料的加工处理，利用废弃物生产各种产品。主要包括在矿产资源开采过程中对共生、伴生矿进行综合开发与合理利用；对生产过程中产生的废渣、废水（液）、废气、余热、余压等进行回收和合理利用；对社会生产和消费过程中产生的各种废旧物资进行回收和再生利用。

② 环境保护服务指与环境相关的服务贸易活动。本次调查主要包括环境技术与产品的研发、环境工程设计与施工、环境监测、环境咨询、污染治理设施运营、环境贸易与金融服务等。

③ 洁净产品指在产品的整个生命周期内（包括新产品的生产、消费及使用后的回收与再利用）对环境友好的产品。这类产品既具有一般商品的特性，又在生产、使用和处理处置过程中符合特定的环境保护要求，与同类产品相比，具有低毒少害、节约资源的环境功能。

化、机械化的专业手段，能从 1 吨干电池中提炼出 350 公斤氧化锌、300 公斤锰铁合金、5 公斤镍合金，总价值约 2000 元，无废水、废渣排放；分离出的金属粉末用作工业原料出售；分离出的塑料则被加工成型材；而且电子垃圾可以无限循环使用。废旧电器是另一座亟待开采的"精矿"，其金属含量超过 30%。

资料来源：《人民日报》（海外版）2009 年 3 月 19 日第 2 版。

环保产业拥有巨大的市场机会。随着国家环保事业的发展，环保产业必将创造更多就业岗位。据环保产业协会最新统计，目前我国环保产业从业人员已超过 300 万人。UNEP 预测，废物处理与循环利用对降低重工业影响非常有效，已创造就业机会超过 1200 万个，其中，1000 万个在中国。中国有世界上最大的水泥、钢铁企业，有巨大的就业前景。

（二）新能源行业就业[①]

大力发展可再生能源是中国的基本战略。可再生能源是全新的行业，其发展必然会带动就业增加。根据国家发展和改革委员会能源研究所的有关研究，截至 2007 年年底，全国新能源行业总的就业人数约为 110 万人，主要分布在太阳能、风能和生物质能行业，其他行业较少。如表 2－3 所示。

表 2－3　新能源行业就业人数

单位：人

太阳能热水器	太阳能光伏	太阳能热发电	风能	生物质能	其他行业	合计
800000	100000	150	20000	200000	1000	1121150

据有关研究[②]，每创造一个直接工作岗位，风能需要投资 115 万元，太阳能光伏电池需要投资 91 万元，太阳能热利用需要投资 70 万元，生物能需要投资 14 万元。总体看来，可再生能源单位就业所需投资都远远高于传统产业所需投入。对于中国这样一个发展中国家，这样的工作岗位实在是太过昂贵。中国的一次能源结构以煤为主。2005 年中国的一次能源消费构成中，

---

① 国家发改委能源所有关研究。
② Peter Poschen：《绿色工作：定义、方法及其对低碳发展的贡献》，中国绿色就业经验分享研讨会，2009 年 3 月 30 日。

煤炭所占的比重为68.9%，石油为21.0%，天然气、水电、核电、风能、太阳能等所占比重为10.1%；而在同年全球的一次能源消费构成中，煤炭只占27.8%，石油占36.4%，天然气、水电、核电等占35.8%。中国作为发展中国家，工业化、城市化、现代化进程远未完成，为进一步实现发展目标，未来能源需求将合理增长，这也是所有发展中国家实现发展的基本条件。同时中国以煤为主的能源结构在未来相当长的时期内难以根本改变。尽管到2020年将实现可再生能源在能源供应中的比重达到20%，可以创造出更多就业机会，预计将达到220万人，但可再生能源行业与传统原有能源业的就业机会并不会像美国那样出现逆转。在较长时期内，传统能源行业就业仍然占主体。

（三）建筑节能改造的就业①

在我国经济持续高速增长和城市化进程的快速推进中，建筑业发展迅猛。建筑业的能源强度最高，推进建筑节能是我国节能减排的重要领域。相关法律法规和政策要求，新建建筑的设计和建造都要采用节能型的建筑结构、材料、器具和产品，提高保温隔热性能，减少采暖、制冷、照明的能耗；要对既有民用和公共机构建筑进行节能改造。

新建节能建筑和现有建筑节能改造将创造大量就业机会。自2005年国家开展建筑节能试点城市工程开始，试点城市相关就业岗位大大增加。仅就现有建筑节能改造而言，我国既有建筑面积高达420多亿平方米。2006年以前建设的绝大部分建筑不节能，不节能的锁定效应将长达至少30年。420亿平方米既有建筑中，如果仅改造1/3，以200元/平方米计算，市场价值就达28000亿元。有关报告指出，建筑节能改造可以新增大约1260万就业岗位。②

通过建筑节能改造发展绿色就业面临一些瓶颈。建筑节能改造一般需要较高的初期投资，不能吸引开发商的兴趣；既有建筑改造技术含量高，仅以住宅建筑节能改造为例，就包括建筑外围护结构节能改造、采暖制冷设备更新、供热计量改造等，需要大量各类专业技术工种，而建筑业中技术工人短

---

① 莫争春：《现有建筑的能源效率和绿色就业》，中国绿色就业经验分享研讨会，2009年3月30日。
② 王伟光、郑国光主编《应对气候变化报告（2009）》，社会科学文献出版社，2009。

缺，建筑工人中只有 1/5 接受过培训；此外，相关法律法规并没有得到有效贯穿执行，验收与监管环节依然是空白。这些都制约着建筑行业绿色就业的发展。

（四）火电行业"上大压小"对就业的影响

在发展可再生能源的同时，中国还通过淘汰落后产能等措施，提高能效、节能减排。其中，电力行业是节能减排的大户。这些环保措施在保护环境的同时，对就业产生负面影响。中国社会科学院"中国低碳发展与绿色就业研究"课题组，根据对发改委、某电力集团及江西、山西等 12 个电厂的调研与统计数据，测算了关停小火电机涉及的就业人数：2007 年全国关停小火电机组 553 台，共计 1438 万千瓦，涉及人员 12.25 万人，其中在职人员 9.1 万人，退休人员 3.15 万人。全国平均每关停 1 万千瓦小火电机组涉及需要重新安置人员 62 人。全国关停小火电机组影响就业人数情况为：①2003～2008 年已经受到就业影响的人数：3809 万千瓦×62 人/万千瓦＝236158 人；②2009～2020 年潜在就业影响人数：5980 万千瓦×62 人/万千瓦＝370760 人。

据本课题组对火电企业的调查，因机组关停而失去岗位的职工，其中只有 1/10 能够在新建的大机组的辅助岗位重新就业，其他绝大多数职工重新就业存在困难。按照上述测算，2020 年前，因关停小火电机组就业受到影响的 60 万人中，50 多万人需要就业帮助。

（五）林业绿色就业

森林是最大的"储碳库"和最经济的"吸碳器"，在这方面的就业潜力巨大，主要有三个方面：一是通过造林再造林、退化生态系统恢复、建立农林复合系统、加强森林可持续管理创造的就业；二是木材生产和加工；三是林产化工、林机制造、森林旅游、森林食品、森林药材、经济林、花卉和竹产业等。

自 1980 年至今，中国投入大量资金用于全面加强林业生态建设、实施林业重点工程、扩大森林资源总量、增加森林碳汇功能。根据森林覆盖率指标测算，到 2010 年森林覆盖率达到 20% 时，将新增就业 1779.5 万人。

根据《中国林业年鉴（2008）》，中国从 2002 年开始实施六大林业重点工程，10 年的造林任务达 0.76 亿公顷，预计可安置 2280 万人就业。2007 年共完成造林面积 268 万公顷，其中，"三北"及长江流域等重点防护林体系建设工程 57.4 万公顷，群众投工投劳折资 36857 万元，按 2007

年集体单位平均工资 6007 元推算，总共为 61356 人提供了一年的工作，为 245427 人提供了 3 个月的全时工作；天然林资源保护工程全部在册职工 98 万人。①

表 2 - 4 为中国碳汇林业就业潜力测算（2003～2050 年）。

表 2 - 4　中国碳汇林业就业潜力测算*（2003～2050 年）

年份	森林覆盖率（%）	森林面积（万公顷）	森林碳储量（10 亿吨碳）	森林碳汇价值（10 亿美元）	新增造林（万公顷）	新增就业数（万人）
2003	18.21	17490.92	14.43	158.73	—	—
2010	20	19210.20	15.85	174.35	1719.28	474
2020	23	22091.73	18.23	200.53	4600.81	1268
2050	26	24973.26	20.60	226.6	7482.34	2026

注：就业数按每公顷平均 103.5 工日，每人工作 100 工日核算；碳汇价格设定为 11 美元/吨碳。
* 中国社会科学院"中国低碳发展与绿色就业研究"课题组。

根据《中国林业年鉴（2008）》，中国已建立各类森林公园 1200 多处，2001 年全国森林公园接待游客达 8300 万人，创造综合收入 500 多亿元，直接或间接创造各种就业岗位 350 万个。

林副产业方面中国竹林面积、蓄积量和竹材年产量均居世界首位，被誉为竹子王国，竹产业的发展尚有很大潜力；此外，花卉业也是世界最具活力的产业之一，中国有悠久的花卉栽培史，品种丰富，开发和就业潜力巨大。

2007 年年末，全国林业系统在册职工共计 184.92 万人，其中在岗职工人数 139.58 万人。在国有林业经济单位中，从事农林牧渔业的 111.6 万人，约占 84%；公共管理和社会组织中 8.8 万人，约占 6.6%；水力环境和公共设施管理业中 3.75 万人，约占 2.8%；科学研究技术服务和地质勘查业中 2.73 万人，占 2%；制造业中 2.6 万人，约占 2%。如表 2 - 5 所示。

联合国粮食农业组织估测，森林恢复可创造 1000 万个绿色工作机会。农业仍然是提供就业机会最多的行业，全球有 13 亿农民，绿色就业主要集中在有机农业和生物燃料。

---

① 国家林业局编《中国林业年鉴（2008）》，中国林业出版社，2008。

表 2 – 5　2007 年林业系统在岗职工人数情况

单位：万人，%

		合计		133.3	100.0
		企业		55.9	41.9
		事业		69.3	52.0
		机关		8.2	6.2
国有经济单位	农林牧渔业	小计		111.6	83.7
		木材及竹业采运企业		46.5	34.9
		国有林场		34.7	26.0
		国有苗圃		3.4	2.6
		林业工作站		12.4	9.3
		木材检查站		2.1	1.6
		种苗站		0.7	0.5
		病虫害防治站		1.1	0.8
		治沙站		0.1	0.1
		其他		10.5	7.9
	采矿业			0.1	0.1
	制造业	小计		2.6	2.0
		非木质林产品加工业		0.2	0.2
		木材加工及竹藤棕草制品业	小计	1.96	1.5
			锯材木片加工	0.17	0.1
			人造板制造	1.4	1.1
			木制品制造	0.37	0.3
			竹藤棕草制品制造	0.01	0.0
		林产化学产品制造业		0.1	0.1
		专用设备、仪器仪表制造业		0.04	0.0
		工艺品制造业		0.027	0.0
		其他		0.3	0.2
	电力燃气及水的生产和供应业			0.4	0.3
	建筑业			0.3	0.2
	批发和零售业			0.66	0.5
	科学研究技术服务和地质勘查业	小计		2.73	2.0
		其中	科技交流和推广服务	0.4	0.3
			规划设计管理	0.69	0.5

续表

国有经济单位	水力环境和公共设施管理业	小计		3.75	2.80
		其中	自然保护区管理	1.28	1.00
			野生动植物保护	0.1	0.10
	教育			0.86	0.60
	卫生社会保障和福利事业			0.6	0.50
	公共管理和社会组织			8.8	6.60
	其他			0.87	0.70
集体经济单位				2.58	—
其他各种经济单位				3.7	—
总计				139.58	—

中国还把植树造林与扩大就业和国内消费相联系，可谓一举多得。河北省承德市从2004年起探索"绿色就业"模式，目前已安置下岗失业人员2400多人，每年财政投入120多万元，已植树262万株，使城市绿化率由24.3%提高到34.6%。近日，网络上关于雇用农民工种树等话题引起热议，也反映了人们对"植树造林＋就业"模式的关注。在金融危机的影响下，在我国部分地区，越来越多的农民工返乡务林，实现了"一人承包、全家就业""城里下岗、山上创业"。

资料来源：《承德市"绿色就业"模式开启再就业新空间》，新华网2007年11月24日。

关于中国绿色就业的现状还尚待研究。仅就上述分析可以看出，尽管中国对全球的绿色就业做出了巨大贡献，但中国的绿色就业只是刚刚起步，相对于7.6亿的就业人口而言，绿色就业的比重还很低。特别是，由于中国的就业结构还比较落后，劳动者的整体素质不高，淘汰落后产能将使一些岗位消失，一部分职工面临失业的威胁；采取环保措施会使一些岗位要求发生转变，劳动者会面临技能转换的挑战；虽然一些新的绿色岗位会被创造出来，可能会为一些劳动者创造就业机会，但相对于需要就业的庞大群体而言数量还极其有限。同时，经济发展也会面临就业的挑战。一些产业可能由于人才短缺而得不到充分发展；一些产业可能由于冗员太多而难以尽快退出，结构性失业可能会进一步加重，需要深入研究向绿色就业转变的过程。

五 发电企业向绿色就业的转型

为了了解向绿色就业转型中面临的问题，以便提出促进向绿色就业顺利转型的政策建议，本课题组选择发电行业开展了问卷调查和深度访谈。在中国，发电行业是国民经济的命脉部门，有上百万人的职工队伍；也是温室气体排放大户，是国家环保政策调控的大户，受国家政策影响最深；同时，随着能源结构的调整，也是绿色就业潜力巨大的部门。为此，本课题组选择发电行业开展向绿色就业转型的研究。

（一）发电行业特点

1. 发电行业受国家政策影响最深

发电行业是国家调控改革的重要领域。首先，1984 年实行电、网分家改革，发电企业开始面临市场竞争，主要原材料煤的价格已经市场化，而上网电量及电价受制于国家和电网公司。其次，从 1997 年开始，国家在电力行业实行"上大压小"、淘汰落后产能政策，陆续关停一部分小火电，安排大火电项目。最后，从 20 世纪 90 年代开始，国家鼓励发展新能源，电力企业纷纷在新能源领域大量投资，抢占市场，特别是风电、水电项目迅猛增长。

2. 发电企业以国企为主

发电行业由五大国有电力企业垄断。国有企业都是"红色公司"，长期都积极承担企业社会责任，对职工高度负责，在企业结构调整过程中，始终对职工采取内部安置的办法，不向社会排放人员。

3. 发电行业安全第一

电力关系国计民生，发电行业安全生产要求高，企业生产实行半军事化管理，确保安全生产、万无一失。因此，企业的安全生产措施都比较健全和严格，对员工要求也较高，职工的待遇也比较好，职工队伍也很稳定。

4. 发电行业是知识密集型行业、非劳动密集型行业

这一行业特点决定了发电企业职工的整体文化素质和技能水平在各行业中处于较高水平，企业招收的全部是大中专毕业生。

这一行业特点也决定了发电企业职工需要长期培训。大机组集控运行需要复合型技能人才，技术跨度大，培训周期长，短期只是认知培训，岗

位过程中的培训最重要。大学毕业生首先要从最基层的班组做起，经过
1～2年的岗位培训才能作为普通工人上岗；成为班组长或技师则要更长的
时间。

这种行业特点和培训特点还决定了发电行业职工只能在本行业内部转岗。
由于常年在岗培训形成的技术过专，很难再适应别的行业要求；并且转岗也受
到当地经济环境的影响。即使在本行业转岗，虽然每台发电机组的控制系统差
不多，但每台机组的设备安装都不同，职工转到不同企业都得重头学。在整个
火电行业技术升级、电力供给充足的背景下，职工再就业难度很大，形势非常
严峻。

（二）研究方法

首先，课题组在天津市、内蒙古自治区呼和浩特市和乌兰察布市选择了8
家电厂，在8家企业分别召开了由厂长及综合部门、财务部门、生产技术部
门、人力资源部门、工会、环保部门人员参加的企业管理人员座谈会和职工座
谈会，着重了解不同类型企业在开展绿色就业、向绿色经济转型过程中的实际
情况、困难与问题。其次，发放职工问卷600份，回收有效问卷587份。调查
对象严格定义为一线操作职工，并兼顾不同类型工作机组、不同年龄、不同性
别、不同学历层次职工。样本既有绿色岗位，又有非绿色岗位。另外，每个企
业被调查员工的数量占所属企业员工的比重控制在一定比例之内。总体上看，
样本具有代表性。

从研究目的出发，按职工所在岗位的能源类型与机组大小进行分类，分为
风电和火电机组，其中，火电机组以"上大压小"的一般标准20万千瓦为标
准，分成大火电（20万千瓦以上）和小火电（20万千瓦及以下）两组。各组
数据情况如表2-6所示。

表2-6 问卷基本情况

问卷类型	能源类型	频 数	百分比	有效百分比	累计百分比
有 效	风 能	52	8.9	9.1	9.1
	大火电	361	61.5	63.1	72.2
	小火电	159	27.1	27.8	100.0
	合 计	572	97.4	100.0	
缺 失		15	2.5	—	—
合 计		587	100.0	—	—

（三）被调查企业信息及其向绿色经济的转型

1. 被调查企业的基本信息

首先，课题组在天津市、内蒙古自治区呼和浩特市和乌兰察布市选择了8家电厂，其中，3家电厂是新型现代化发电厂的代表；1家是清洁能源电厂的代表；2家是老火力发电企业的代表；还有1家既有老的小机组，又有新的大机组，是综合性企业的代表。1家是地方发电企业的代表，其他则属于五家国有发电集团。8家电厂基本情况如表2-7所示。

被调查企业职工的劳动工具以自动控制工具为主。从目前所使用的主要劳动工具的情况看，主要使用自动控制工具的调查对象占各组总体的比例，风电最高，为74.5%；大火电机组最低，为52.5%（见表2-8）。这与各机组工种的分布有关。风电企业是完全现代化的管理系统，机械化、自动化程度高，即使是一般岗位的职工，也以自动化操作为主，因此，以自动控制工具为主的职工比重最高。大火电机组技能岗位所占比重低于小火电机组，相应的以自动控制工具为主的职工比重就低一些。

表 2-7 8家电厂基本情况

	呼市电厂1	呼市电厂2	呼市电厂3	呼市电厂4
职工人数	362	1061	238	330
样本数	100	70	45	35
成立时间	2005	1954	1999	1956
所有制类型	国有企业	国有企业	合资企业	国有企业
机组类型	Phase III	Phase I, II, III	Phase III	Phase I, II

	乌兰察布市电厂	天津大港区发电厂	天津东丽发电有限公司	天津河西区发电有限公司
职工人数	193	1923	2302	801
样本数	50	100	100	100
成立时间	1989	1974	1960	1992
所有制类型	合资企业	国有企业	国有企业	国有企业
机组类型	—	Phase I, II, III	Phase I, III	Phase I, II

值得注意的是，不同机组自动控制工具的自动化程度是不同的。如小火电机组和大火电机组生产工艺和流程基本相同，但主控室的设备是不同的。另外，还有一些半自动化的操作工具，在归类时也可能有差异。

表2－8　发电企业分机组职工劳动工具情况

单位：%

种　类	手工工具	自动控制工具
风　电	25.5	74.5
大火电	47.5	52.5
小火电	37.7	62.3

2. 发电企业的绿色转型对就业的影响

所有被调查者所在的企业都采取了环保措施。大火电企业采取的环保措施包括：安装进口发电机组；加大投入，引进或进行节能技术改造，如引进先进的中水处理、布袋除尘、石灰石－石膏湿法脱硫工艺、等离子点火等节能环保技术，采取安装高效除尘器、安装固定式隔音罩、在输煤系统端部安装旋风水浴式除尘器等环境保护措施，开展发电废弃物粉煤灰和石膏的综合利用、开展海水淡化等；加强机组节能降耗工作的管理和研究；开展造林绿化等。大火电企业在向绿色经济转型中面临的问题主要是经营方面的问题：国家环保政策标准的不断提高，对企业的生产经营带来的压力；为提高生产效率需要不断更新机器设备，要求大量的资金投入。对职工的影响主要表现在需要常规性的不断的技能提升。

小火电企业的环保措施主要是脱硫改造。一家电厂脱硫系统改造后，公司的厂用电率增加近1.3%，供电煤耗增加4.3克/千瓦时。由于增加了大量的设备，使公司的运营维护成本大大增加，每年新增维护、材料及水的费用将近1500万元。脱硫改造对员工素质提出要求。公司将当年新入厂大学生中的优秀学员分配到除尘车间，进行脱硫的前期准备，并外派到其他电厂调研脱硫设备的安装和运行情况，跟班进行现场见习和实习。同时，外派检修人员到脱硫设备制造企业进行脱硫设备的实习。脱硫设备安装投产后，进行全程培训工作的跟踪和考试。

另一项重要的环保措施是"上大压小"，关停机组的生产人员需要裁减转岗，如何安置富余人员是公司面临的非常棘手的问题。公司通过劳资双方协商机制，职工代表和工会领导参与企业裁员及员工安置，尽量避免职工待遇发生明显变化。一些企业虽然至今尚未"上大压小"，但预计今后3～5年将实施。

发电企业在"上大压小"、节能减排的过程中，从本行业、本企业特点出发，充分考虑企业人力资源的特点，因地制宜地想方设法安置富余职工，不将他们排向社会。对于一部分关停机组的职工，根据新机组的需要，经过培训后，安置到新机组的辅助岗位上；对于不能重新上生产岗的富余职工，企业的安置渠道多种多样，具体如下。

一是安置到检修队伍，发挥他们常年在机组工作的经验和专长，鼓励他们到本企业外主动承揽检修业务。

二是利用企业下属的"三产"，安置各类富余人员。如天津一家近 2000 人的老火电企业，下辖 12 家"三产"企业，涉及餐饮、住宿、食品、物流、建材、施工等行业。"三产"企业已经面向社会发展，成为天津市的纳税大户。仅开发海水淡化一项业务，就解决了 60 人的就业问题。但是搞多种经营与企业所在的地理区位有关系，如内蒙古自治区的经济环境就不如天津，企业发展三产就不一定有竞争力。

三是在一些岗位实行岗位分享，降低劳动强度，相应的职工的收入会受到影响。

风电企业则不断扩建新的风电场，并不断提升单机设备的装机容量。这一方面引发了该行业对劳动力的大量需求，导致人员流动率高，为此，企业需要支付较高的人工成本。另一方面随着企业的迅速扩张，职工技能总处于不断提升的过程中。

3. 金融危机对企业的影响

2008 年全球金融危机以来，由于用电需求减少，火电机组运行负荷降低，职工就业受到一定的影响，有一定比例的职工有减薪的情况。金融危机对风电企业的影响不明显，风电组 98% 的调查对象所在企业没有发生缩短工时、暂时放假、减薪、待岗培训等情况。如表 2-9 所示。

表 2-9 金融危机对发电企业用工的影响

单位：%

企业类型	2008 年金融危机以来,公司是否有下列情况发生？					
	缩短工时	暂时放假	减薪	待岗培训	其他	没有以上情况发生
风电	0	0	2.0	0	0	98.0
大火电	1.5	0.3	18.1	0.5	1.5	78.1
小火电	0	0	38.6	1.2	0	60.2

（四）发电行业不同机组职工队伍基本情况

不同发电企业之间劳动力的构成是相似的。如表2－10所示。

表2－10 8家企业劳动力的基本信息

指标	呼市电厂1		呼市电厂2		呼市电厂3		呼市电厂4	
性别	男：54.09% 女：45.91%		男：63.9% 女：36.1%		男：65.1% 女：34.9%		男：72.1% 女：27.9%	
年龄（岁）	37.98	男：39.43	33.88	男：34.33	36.84	男：36.02	35.43	男：35.20
		女：36.14		女：33.09		女：38.36		女：36.00
平均工龄（年）	9.06	男：9.71	5.45	男：5.78	14.44	男：12.62	10.85	男：10.41
		女：8.19		女：4.89		女：17.73		女：11.92
教育水平（年）	5.31	男：5.00	5.52	男：5.45	4.75	男：4.61	5.55	男：5.53
		女：5.68		女：5.63		女：5.00		女：5.58
户口性质	90.4%	—	86.0%	—	96.8%	—	90.7%	—

指标	乌兰察布市电厂		天津大港区发电厂		天津东丽发电有限公司		天津河西区发电有限公司	
性别	男：48.4% 女：51.6%		男：77.7% 女：22.3%		男：66.7% 女：33.3%		男：79.6% 女：20.4%	
年龄（岁）	41.03	男：42.93	37.77	男：37.42	39.55	男：40.38	34.79	男：34.32
		女：39.13		女：38.95		女：37.88		女：36.74
平均工龄（年）	21.67	男：18.31	16.76	男：16.31	19.43	男：20.02	12.52	男：11.70
		女：19.94		女：18.40		女：18.27		女：15.16
教育水平（年）	4.42	男：4.13	4.78	男：4.77	3.65	男：3.91	4.46	男：4.47
		女：4.69		女：4.81		女：3.12		女：4.40
户口性质	96.8%	—	98.9%	—	100%	—	94.8%	—

说明：年龄为均值比较；平均工龄为均值比较；教育水平以学历得分计，对文化程度进行赋值（初中及以下"1分"，普通高中和职高"2分"，技校和中专"3分"，高职"4分"，大专"5分"，大学"6分"，硕士及以上"7分"）；户口性质为本市非农户口所占比重。

1. 年龄及相关情况

（1）小火电组职工的平均年龄最大

总体看，小火电机组职工的平均年龄为39.1岁，大于风电的38岁和大火电的36.3岁。小火电人员年龄结构偏大，30岁以下的只有10%，31～40岁所占的比例最大，占到该组总体的60%。如图2－1所示。

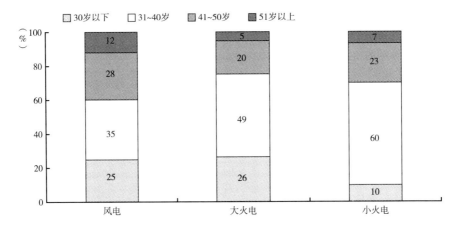

图 2-1 发电企业分机组职工年龄结构

（2）小火电职工平均入职年限最长

各组职工的入职年限最短的为 1～2 年，最长的为 37～38 年，基本相同。但从平均入职年限看，小火电机组最长，为 17.84 年，比大火电机组（12.97 年）约长 5 年，接近风电组平均入职年限（9.10 年）的 2 倍。

划分入职年限期间后，可以发现：风电组中 46% 的人入职年限在 1～5 年，新员工所占的比例最大，另外其他三个年限区间的人数分布相对均衡；大火电组职工的入职年限分布比较均衡，入职年限在 1～5 年和 11～20 年的员工所占的比例都在 37% 左右；小火电组中超过一半的员工入职年限在 11～20 年，此外入职超过 20 年的员工还占到 30%，新员工所占比例很小，只有不到 10% 入职在 1～5 年。如图 2-2 所示。

2. 职工的文化及技能水平

（1）小火电组职工平均文化程度最低

对文化程度进行赋值（初中及以下"1 分"，普通高中和职高"2 分"，技校和中专"3 分"，高职"4 分"，大专"5 分"，大学"6 分"，硕士及以上"7 分"），则风电组职工的平均学历得分最高，为 5.30 分，小火电组职工的平均学历得分最低，为 4.25 分，比风电组低了 1.05 分。

风电是一个新兴的行业，企业职工队伍的文化程度最高，不存在初中及以下学历，大专及以上学历的比例达到 90%。大火电机组也多是新建机组，职工文化程度也较高，大专及以上学历的职工比例也较高，达到 71%。此外，还有超过 20% 的技校和中专学历的职工。小火电机组中拥有大专及以上学历

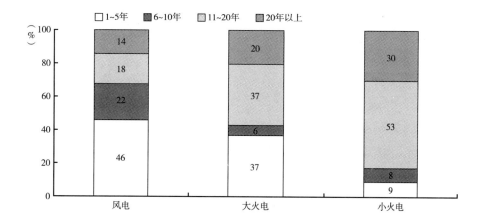

图 2 - 2 发电企业分机组职工入职年限

的调查对象所占的比例明显低于其他两组，只有 56.6% 。技校和中专学历的
职工比例较高，达到 25.3% 。如表 2 - 11 所示。

表 2 - 11 发电企业分机组职工文化程度

单位：%

企业类型	初中及以下	普通高中	职高	技校	中专	大专	大学	硕士及以上
风 电	0	4.0	0	2.0	4.0	38.0	50.0	2.0
大火电	2.4	3.3	3.0	10.5	9.8	26.1	43.1	1.8
小火电	4.9	3.6	9.6	10.8	14.5	25.3	27.7	3.6

（2）大龄职工的平均受教育程度低

30 岁以下、31～40 岁、41～50 岁、51 岁以上职工的平均学历得分分别为
5.56 岁、4.66 岁、4.42 岁和 2.88 岁。从受教育程度看，绝大多数的 30 岁以
下职工都接受了高等教育，这一比例远高于其他年龄组。相反，51 岁以上年
龄组中近 80% 的职工都没有接受过高等教育。如图 2 - 3 所示。

（3）小火电组技术工人的比重最高

从被调查员工的职业技能情况看，发电行业员工素质整体较高，绝大多数
具有职业资格证书。小火电组中具有职业资格证书的员工所占的比例最高，为
90.2% ；风电组和大火电组情况差不多，分别为 84.8% 和 83.8% 。如表 2 - 12
所示。

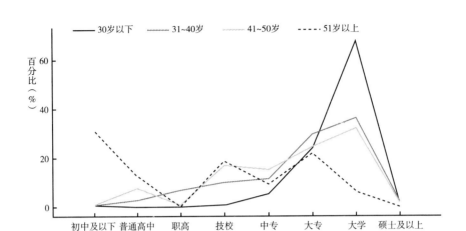

图 2-3 分年龄段职工教育程度结构

表 2-12 发电企业分机组职工职业资格证书情况

单位：%

企业类型	您是否拥有职业资格证书？	
	有	无
风 电	84.8	15.2
大火电	83.8	16.2
小火电	90.2	9.8

从技能/技术等级结构看，风电组主要集中在中级技术职称、高级技术职称和技师；大火电组主要集中在高级技工、中级技工和中级技术职称；小火电组的情况与大火电组差别不大，也主要集中于中级技工、高级技工和中级技术职称。也就是说，风电企业员工以专业技术人员和技师为主体，而火电企业员工以中高级技工和专业技术人员为主体。如表 2-13 所示。

表 2-13 发电企业分机组职工技能等级情况

单位：%

企业类型	无	初级技工	中级技工	高级技工	技师	高级技师	初级专业技术职称	中级专业技术职称	高级专业技术职称
风 电	6.5	13.0	6.5	2.2	15.2	2.2	10.9	28.3	15.2
大火电	4.2	7.7	24.7	25.3	6.8	1.2	6.5	18.2	5.4
小火电	2.7	4.1	27.0	24.3	8.1	1.4	8.1	17.6	6.7

（4）技能等级和专业技术职务基本与年龄正相关

从技能等级情况看，30 岁以下年轻人中一半为中级和初级技工；31～40
岁职工中高级工的比重最高，接近 30%；51 岁以上职工中技师所占比重高于
其他年龄组，并且超过 60% 的职工有中级及以上技能等级。从职称情况看，
31～40 岁年龄段职工中有近 40% 的人有中级及以上专业技术职称，这一比重
较高的年龄组其次是 41～50 岁年龄组，再次是 51 岁以上年龄组，表明技能等
级和专业技术职务基本与年龄正相关。如图 2－4 所示。

分性别情况看，男性职工的技能等级普遍高于女性，但女性的专业技术职
务级别普遍高于男性。说明两性职工的岗位性质有明显差异。如图 2－5 所示。

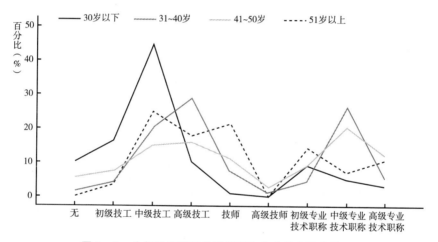

图 2－4　分年龄段职工技能等级和专业技术职务情况

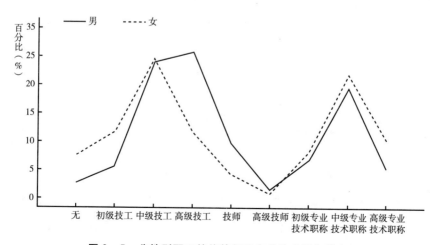

图 2－5　分性别职工技能等级和专业技术职务情况

3. 职工身份

(1) 小火电组中100%为本市非农户籍

职工的户口性质反映出很多问题。风电企业由于特殊的工作条件，实行长班倒，通常十天半月连续在岗不能回家，因此，招收了相对较多的外地非农户籍的职工。大火电机组由于生产效率提高，定员相对较少，因此会雇用一些本市农业户籍、外省区市的非农或农业户籍的职工。而小火电机组基本上是很多年前建厂时招收的职工，都是本市非农户籍的职工。如表2－14所示。

表2－14　发电企业分机组职工户籍情况

单位：%

企业类型	本市非农	本市农业	外省区市非农	外省区市农业	其他
风　电	90.4	1.9	7.7	0	0
大火电	93.7	3.3	0.8	0.8	1.4
小火电	100.0	0	0	0	0

(2) 小火电组100%都是正式职工

发电企业基本上都是正式职工。其中，风电企业使用了少量劳务派遣工，大火电机组使用了少量临时工，小火电企业由于存在冗员，全部都是正式工，如表2－15所示。这些都符合企业的生产实践需要。

表2－15　发电企业分机组职工就业身份情况

单位：%

企业类型	正式职工*	劳务派遣工	小时工	农民合同工**
风　电	96.2	3.8	0	0
大火电	98.5	1.0	0.2	0.2
小火电	100.0	0	0	0

* 正式职工包括固定期限劳动合同职工和无固定期限劳动合同职工。

** 农民合同工指签订短期合同的农民工。

(3) 小火电组技术岗位职工比重最高

被调查职工的工种情况显示，风电机组、大火电机组、小火电机组职工中，技能岗位职工所占比重依次提高，普通工种和熟练工种所占比重依次降低。这可能表明，电力企业技能工人的培养需要较长的周期，小火电机组由于存续时间长，技能岗位职工所占比重较高，风电和大火电机组运行时间短，因而技能岗位职工所占比重相对较低。也可能是由于风电和大火电机组的专业化程度更高，分工更细、更明确，技能岗位的劳动生产率较高，需要较多的非技能岗位配套。风电企业其他岗位比重较高，是因为风电企业一般人员规模都较小，有一些管理岗位也被调查了。如图2-6所示。

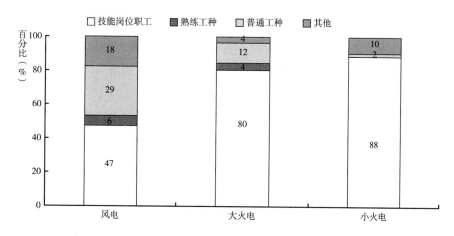

图2-6　发电企业分机组职工工种分布

（3）职工普遍签订劳动合同

不论什么性质的用工，基本都与公司签订了劳动合同。其中，风电组职工以无固定期限合同为主，比例高达80.4%。风电组的固定期限劳动合同的具体期限较短，均值为4.62年。

大火电和小火电机组职工签订无固定期限劳动合同的比例也较高，接近60%。虽然有40%左右的被调查职工签订了固定期限合同，但合同的期限相对较长，均值分别为6.27年和5.80年，固定合同的最高年限达到了20年和10年，比风电组的最高值5年高出许多。如表2-16所示。

表2-16　发电企业分机组职工劳动合同签订情况

单位：%

企业类型	无固定期限	有固定期限	以完成一定任务为期限的劳动合同	不清楚
风　电	80.4	15.7	0	3.9
大火电	55.0	40.6	0.3	4.1
小火电	59.3	38.3	0	2.4

对于签订固定期限合同的调查对象来说，基本上所有的人都愿意与企业续签劳动合同，而且绝大部分也认为这种意愿是能够实现的。火电机组签订固定期限合同的职工中，也有少量的职工认为续签合同存在不确定性。如表 2-17 所示。

表 2-17　发电企业分机组职工对能否续签劳动合同的看法

单位：%

企业类型	能够	不能够	现在很难说
风　电	100.0	0	0
大火电	90.3	0.6	9.1
小火电	94.3	0	5.7

4. 求职及职业变动情况

（1）小火电组职工主要通过国家分配实现就业，风电企业主要通过工作调动实现就业

历史上，电力系统是国有企业，人员都由国家分配，年龄在 40 岁以上的职工基本都是通过国家分配实行就业的。从 1993 年实行市场化就业机制以后，企业用工主要通过企业和毕业生双向选择的市场化招聘方式满足用工需要，而不再实行国家分配，企业招用的也都是大学毕业生。由于有成熟的招聘渠道和较高的待遇，企业不会通过职业介绍机构介绍、亲戚朋友推荐等市场化方式招人。

风电是新兴行业，国内大学还没有专业毕业生，因此，主要通过本企业内部人员岗位调整、培训上岗，以及不同企业之间的流动来满足人员需求。调查显示，41.2% 的风电职工是通过调动工作的方式进入企业的。如表 2-18 所示。

表 2-18　发电企业分机组职工求职方式

企业类型	国家分配	调动工作	自己应聘/应招	企业兼并或重组	职业介绍机构介绍	亲戚朋友推荐	劳务派遣机构派遣	其他
风　电	43.1	41.2	7.8	0	0	2.0	3.9	2.0
大火电	60.1	19.0	16.5	0.5	0.2	1.5	0.2	2.0
小火电	80.5	4.9	11.0	0	0	0	0	3.6

（2）发电行业职工岗位变动以内部流动为主

职工岗位变动频率与机组运行年限有关。小火电由于运行时间长，岗位发生过变动的职工比例就高一些。在经历过岗位变动的职工中，各机组中都有近1/4的职工变动过一次工作岗位；对于小火电机组，职工中经历过二次工作岗位变动的比例最大，约为1/4；而对于风电和大火电机组，职工中经历过三次及以上工作岗位变动的比例高于经历过二次工作岗位变动的比例。如图2-7所示。

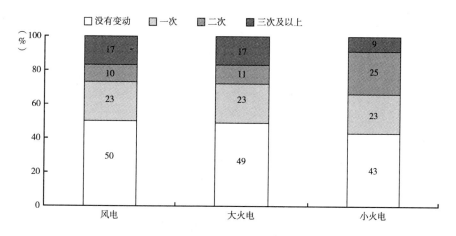

图2-7 发电企业分机组职工岗位变动情况

（五）发电行业不同机组职工劳动状况

1. 工作时间

（1）小火电机组职工中有更多的人是轮班制

轮班制在小火电组中较为普遍，该组约一半的调查对象所从事的工作为轮班制；而风电和大火电机组的这一比例约为1/3。如表2-19所示。风电企业由于远离城市，职工实行长班倒，一般连续工作10~15天，然后休息10~15天。每班2~3人，值班期间相互轮班。可以说，采取环保措施后，更多的劳动者可以享受正常的工时制。

（2）发电行业加班加点现象普遍，但权益基本能得到保障

加班加点在各组中都是普遍的现象，被调查对象中表示过去一年加过班的比重都在85%以上，从小火电、大火电到风电，这一比重逐步提高。如表2-20所示。

表 2 - 19   发电企业分机组职工轮班情况

单位: %

企业类型	轮班制	非轮班制
风 电	33.3	66.7
大火电	31.6	68.4
小火电	49.4	50.6

表 2 - 20   发电企业分机组职工加班情况

单位: %

	过去一年,您是否加班加点过?	
企业类型	是	否
风 电	93.5	6.5
大火电	89.3	10.7
小火电	87.7	12.3

绝大部分职工加班加点都按国家规定获得了加班工资或补休。由于长倒班的情况,风电企业职工加班加点以补休为主,占到近60%,剩余的40%则得到加班工资。

火电机组职工加班加点则以加班工资为主,60% ~70% 的加班加点职工能得到基本工资,还有不到10%的职工可以被安排补休。小火电机组的职工中,反映加班加点后既没有补休、又没有得到加班工资的比例高于大火电机组。如表 2 - 21 所示。

表 2 - 21   发电企业分机组职工加班后补休、补贴情况

单位: %

企业类型	全部得到加班工资	部分得到加班工资	没得到加班工资	单位安排补休	说不清楚
风 电	20.0	20.0	0	57.5	2.5
大火电	18.4	50.6	15.8	9.0	6.2
小火电	44.4	19.4	26.4 *	9.7	0

* 一些岗位工种实行综合计算工时和不定时工作制,职工加班可以不支付加班费。

加班加点取决于行业性质,由于职工民主决策和参与管理,职工对加班加点都能理解。

2. 工资和福利

（1）风电组职工平均年收入最高，小火电组职工收入分配差距最大

风电组职工的平均年收入最高，为 51687.50 元，比平均值最低的小火电组高出近 1 万元。从职工年平均收入的标准差看，从风电到大火电、再到小火电，职工收入差距越来越大。如表 2 - 22 所示。

表 2 - 22　发电企业分机组职工年收入情况

企业类型	极小值	极大值	均　值	标准差
	过去一年年收入			
风　电	27000	100000	51687.50	14715.446
大火电	7500	120000	46792.74	17750.316
小火电	15000	95000	42219.34	20373.406

对年收入进行分组，风电组的收入呈正态分布格局，40001 ~ 50000 元中等收入水平的比重占 41%，高收入和低收入的都越来越少，收入分配具有科学合理性；火电机组的平均年收入基本呈递减分布，即低收入组所占比重最大，越高收入组所占比重越小。大火电机组有近一半的被调查者年收入低于 4 万元，小火电机组更甚，超过 70% 的被调查者年收入低于 4 万元。如图 2 - 8 所示。

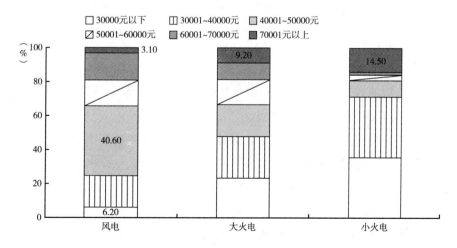

图 2 - 8　发电企业分机组职工年收入结构

从相关分析看，年龄、入职年限与年收入呈明显正相关关系，年龄越大，收入越高。而学历得分与年收入负相关。

发电企业收入分配的总体原则是向一线职工倾斜，拉开收入差距。低收入职工的比重越高，说明机组中非一线职工的比重越高。

（2）发电企业职工的福利待遇较好

几乎所有的被调查职工都享受住房补贴或（和）公积金（风电组94.2%，另两组均达到97%）。

各组在伙食/误餐补贴、交通补助方面差距明显。风电组中只有不到1/3的调查对象能得到伙食/误餐补贴，而大火电组中却有超过3/4的人能享受该待遇。风电组只有26.9%的人能得到交通补助，而小火电组中该比例是风电组的2倍，大火电组情况最好，达到73%。如图2－9所示。

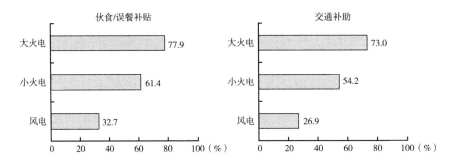

图 2－9 发电企业分机组职工误餐补贴和交通补贴情况

此外，发电企业还定期为职工进行健康体检和对困难人员给予生活补助，在这两个方面，各组之间也存在差异。就健康体检而言，火电机组好于风电企业，几乎所有的大火电企业被调查职工都享受到了健康体检，而火电机组有不到20%的职工没有享受到这一待遇。

对困难人员的生活补助，风电企业有约40%的被调查职工表示企业有这项福利，而大火电和小火电机组职工中分别有不到60%和50%表示企业有这项福利。如图2－10所示。

3. 社会保障

（1）职工参加社会保险的情况好于社会总体情况

从法定的五项社会保险的参保情况看，几乎全部被调查的职工都参加了城镇职工基本养老保险和基本医疗。风电企业职工基本都参加了失业保险和工伤

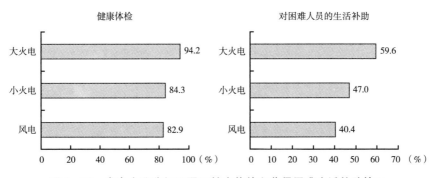

图 2 - 10 发电企业分机组职工健康体检和获得困难生活补助情况

保险，而火电机组职工中有少部分被调查职工没有参加上述两项保险，小火电机组中没有参加上述两项保险的职工比例以及不清楚是否参加的职工比例都高于大火电机组。各组参加生育保险的比例都稍低，小火电组的情况最差，有32%的被调查职工明确表示没有参加生育保险，还有16%的职工表示不清楚。风电组和大火电组的情况稍好些。如图 2 - 11 所示。

除基本社会保险外，发电企业都有企业年金。各组差距不大，风电组相对较好。

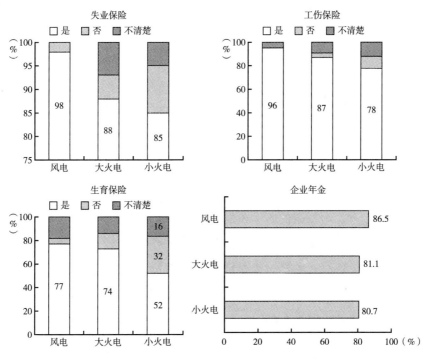

图 2 - 11 发电企业分机组职工社会保险情况

分年龄段看，总体上年龄越大，参保情况越好。分性别看，男性各项保险参保情况普遍好于女性。如表2-23和图2-12所示。

表2-23 分年龄段职工参保情况

单位：%

社会保险险种	参保率			
	30岁以下	31~40岁	41~50岁	51岁以上
养老保险	98.5	99.7	99.2	100.0
医疗保险	100.0	100.0	100.0	99.2
失业保险	81.6	90.9	86.0	93.9
工伤保险	84.1	84.0	85.3	93.8
生育保险	60.9	70.0	77.0	84.6
商业保险	25.0	25.1	26.5	7.7

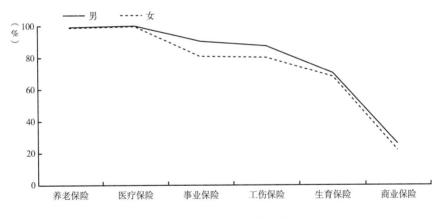

图2-12 分性别职工参保情况

4. 工作环境

（1）火电和风电机组的职业危害存在显著差异

本次调查设置了高温、噪声、粉尘、辐射四项职业危害内容。可以明显看出风电企业的绿色就业特征：没有被调查对象认为存在高温危害，只有不到2%的人认为有粉尘危害，不到1/5的人认为有噪声危害，不到1/3调查对象认为在工作中面临辐射危害。

相反，火电机组呈现出明显的非绿色就业特征：大火电组中有近2/3的调查对象认为工作中存在噪声危害，小火电组中该比例更是超过了75%；两个火电组中均有 2/3 左右的调查对象认为在工作中存在粉尘危害；均有超过一半的调查对象认为工作中存在高温危害；分别有 42.4% 和 44.6% 的被调查对象认为有辐射危害。如图 2-13 所示。

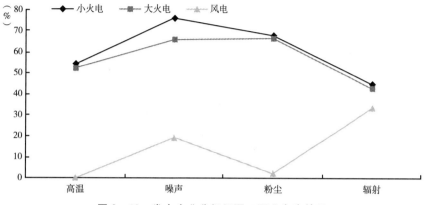

图 2-13　发电企业分机组职工职业危害情况

　　分性别看，除辐射危害外，男性职工中反映有高温、噪声和粉尘危害的比重都大于女性职工。这也反映了发电企业一线职工以男性为主的特征。分年龄段看，对职业危害反映大的群体是 30 岁以下的职工以及 51 岁以上的职工，这可能是因为这两个群体对职业危害敏感。分工种情况看，技能岗位职工中认为有职业危害的比重最高，高于普通工种和熟练工种。这反映了发电企业知识技能密集型的特点。如图 2-14、图 2-15、图 2-16 所示。

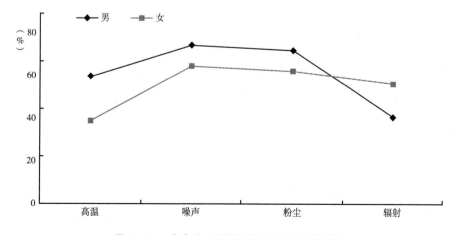

图 2-14　发电企业分性别职工职业危害情况

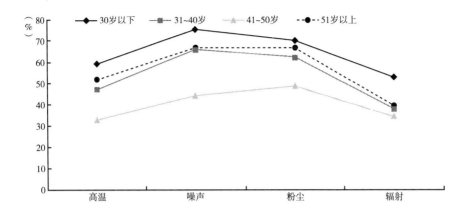

图 2-15　发电企业分年龄职工职业危害情况

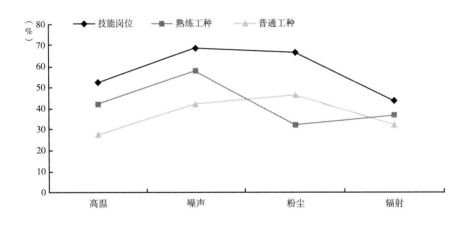

图 2-16　发电企业分岗位职工职业危害情况

（2）职工对工作场所的环境状况评价总体满意，但风电和火电差别显著

风电组中大部分人认为"环境很好"，有76.9%的调查对象选择该选项。两个火电组中分别有18.2%和13.3%的人认为"环境很好"，大部分认为"环境一般"。如图2-17所示。

从分性别、年龄和工种的职工对工作环境的评价看，有一个有趣的发现，女性职工比男性职工对工作环境的总体评价稍好；年龄越大，职工对工作环境的总体评价越高；普通工种和其他工种的职工对工作环境的总体评价最高，其次是熟练工种，技能岗位职工对工种环境的总体评价最差。如图2-18、图2-19、图2-20所示。

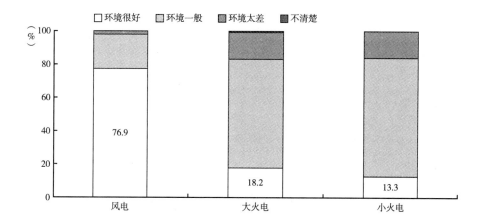

图 2 - 17　发电企业分机组职工对工作场所环境的评价情况

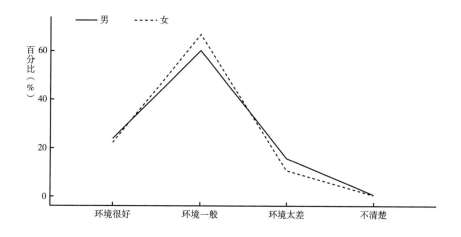

图 2 - 18　发电企业分性别职工对工作场所环境的评价情况

（3）劳动保护措施

在各组采取的劳动保护措施中，职业危害最小的风电企业劳动保护措施最完善，而职业危害最大的小火电机组的劳动保护措施最不完善。

近 90% 的风电企业被调查职工表示企业进行了安全教育，而小火电机组的这一比例不到 75%；近 85% 的风电企业被调查职工表示工作场所配备有安全措施，而小火电机组的这一比例不到 65%；三组都有 92% 左右的职工表示企业发放劳保用品。如图 2 - 21 所示。

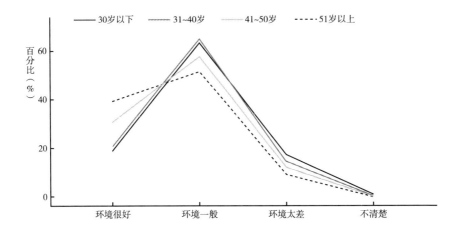

图 2-19　发电企业分年龄对工作场所环境的评价情况

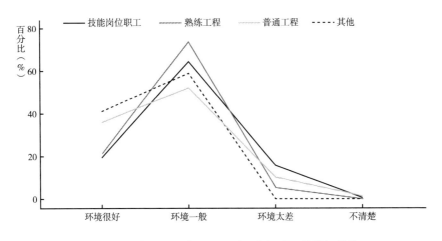

图 2-20　发电企业分岗位职工对工作场所环境的评价情况

（4）风电组职工的健康状况最好

风电企业调查对象的 98% 身体状况都是"健康"，而火电企业中身体"健康"的调查对象不到 80%，还有不到 20% 的职工身体健康状况一般。小火电机组职工的健康状况总体比大火电机组差，有近 5% 的职工体弱多病。大火电机组还吸纳了 0.3% 的残疾人就业。这些残疾人主要是企业发展过程中致残的，将他们安置在适合的工作岗位上，体现了企业的社会责任意识。如图 2-22 所示。

与职工对工作环境的评价相似，从职工总体健康状况来看，女性职工好于

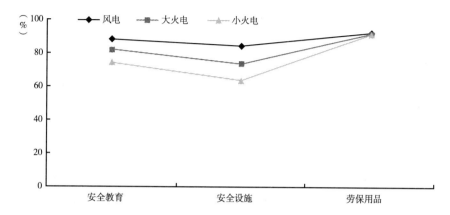

图 2 - 21　发电企业分机组职工企业安全措施情况

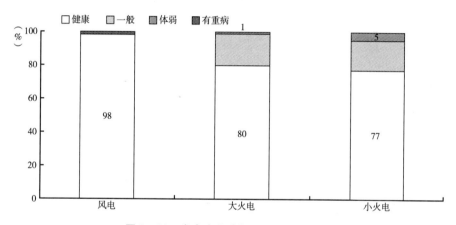

图 2 - 22　发电企业分机组职工健康情况

男性职工；年轻职工好于年长职工；普通工种好于熟练工种，熟练工种好于技能岗位。

（5）职业病情况

从职业病发生情况看，风电组情况最好，除了 11% 的人不清楚公司是否发生过职业病，其他 89% 的调查对象所在公司均没有职业病发生；两个火电组中均有超过 1/4 的人不清楚本公司的职业病发生情况，但大火电组中有 47% 的调查对象所在公司发生过职业病，而小火电组中这一比例更高，为 55%。如图 2 - 23 所示。

需要特别注意的是，职工职业病的发生情况随着年龄的增大而增大，并且技能岗位职工职业病的发生比例高于其他岗位职工。如图 2 - 24、图 2 - 25 所示。

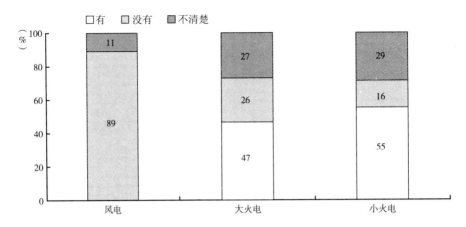

图 2 - 23　发电企业职业病发生情况

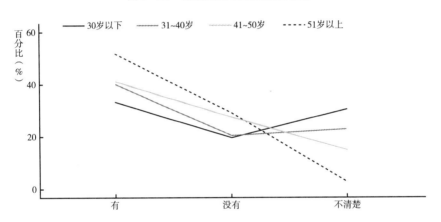

图 2 - 24　发电企业职工分年龄职业病发生情况

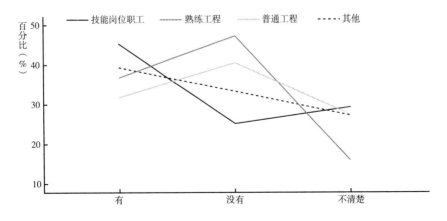

图 2 - 25　发电企业职工分工种职业病发生情况

对本题的文本答案内容进行简要分析，可以发现矽肺是调查对象所在企业里已发生的最常见的职业病，此外还有神经衰弱、耳鸣等。首先，火力发电企业的主要职业病种是矽肺病，主要是因为作业环境中排放大量烟尘不能彻底清洁。其次，噪声污染也是发电企业的重要污染源，再加上为满足 24 小时生产的轮班工作制，使得一部分职工有耳鸣、神经衰弱等职业病。如图 2－26 所示。

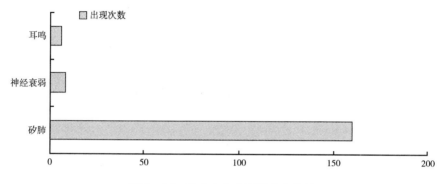

图 2－26　发电企业主要职业病情况

被调查对象对发生职业病的风险评估在各组间差别明显。风电组中没有人认为"风险很大"，大部分人认为"不会发生"和"风险一般"。两个火电组中均有近 1/3 的调查对象认为"风险很大"，而且也均有近一半的人认为"风险一般"；其中小火电组只有 1.2% 的调查对象认为不会发生职业病。如图 2－27 所示。

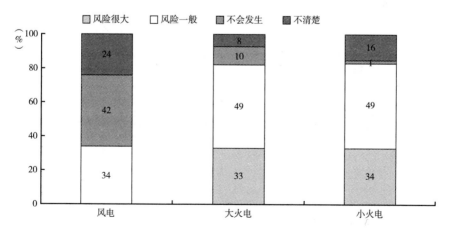

图 2－27　发电企业分机组职工对发生职业病风险的认识

（六）发电企业分机组职工劳动关系状况

所有被调查员工所在公司都有工会。超过90%的调查对象是工会成员，各组差别不大；并且工会或工人代表基本都能参与民主管理，参与到公司改革和结构调整的协商中。其中，风电组的民主管理参与情况稍好于其他组，近90%的调查对象所在企业工会或工人代表可以参与到公司改革和结构调整的协商之中；而两个火电组的这一比例分别只有81.6%和80.5%。如表2-24所示。

表2-24　发电企业分机组职工参与企业民主管理情况

单位：%

公司让工会或工人代表参与到公司改革/结构调整的协商中吗？		
企业类型	是	否
风　电	89.8	10.2
大火电	81.6	18.4
小火电	80.5	19.5

（七）发电行业不同机组职工的培训情况

1. 发电企业不断变化的技能要求

风电组中超过70%的调查对象认为工作所需技能和使用设备/工具的变化很多。大火电机组中，有近不到一半的职工感受到工作所需技能和使用设备/工具的变化很多，各还有近1/4的调查对象认为"变了一点"或"没有太多变化"。小火电机组中，只有1/4强的职工感觉工作所需技能和使用设备/工具的变化很多，超过70%的职工感觉只有很小的变化或没什么变化。如图2-28所示。

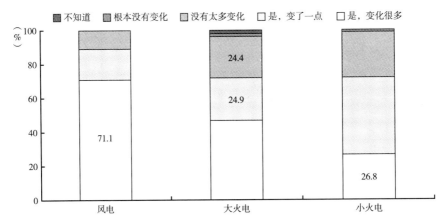

图2-28　发电企业采取环保措施对职工劳动工具和技能要求的影响

2. 被调查企业开展的培训

员工培训是发电企业一项最重要的常规性工作，越是老企业，员工培训越规范。成为一名发电企业的合格员工，通常要经过以下培训。

一是上岗培训。新员工入厂后，一般先接受半个月岗前入厂教育培训，主要包括厂规和厂纪、安规、消防、触电急救与心肺复苏、生产过程、劳动合同与社会保险等内容的讲解；入厂教育结束后，进入现场实习；见习结束后，进行岗位实习，即生产过程实习，要经过现场跟班实习、监护下值班、独立值班等步骤的培养过程。经过以上学习培训后，新员工经转正考试合格后，成为正式员工，历时一年。新员工从入厂到顶岗成为主值班员一般至少需要 5 年的时间。新员工入厂后，一般和有经验的技术人员签订师徒协议，进行一对一的培训。

二是设备专门培训。企业引进新设备，一般合同约定由设备厂家进行培训。一般赴厂家培训一次，在设备安装调试期间再现场培训一次；有些聘请行业专家进行系列讲座；有的是赴同类电厂调研、选择委托培训单位现场跟班学习、仿真机培训等；还与高校合作办学组织专业基础理论学习。如天津一家企业在加装脱硫设备时，将当年新入厂大学生中的优秀学员分配到除尘车间，进行脱硫的前期准备，并于当年外出到电厂调研脱硫设备的安装和运行情况，并跟班进行现场见习和实习。同时，外派检修人员进行脱硫设备的实习。脱硫设备安装投产后，进行全程培训工作的跟踪和考试。利用公司级除尘和脱硫专业考试进行综合考核。

三是日常培训。日常培训采取定时和不定时相结合的方式进行。如有的公司规定，运行班组每轮值有一个学习班，专门用于培训。检修班组每周有一个下午利用两个小时进行培训学习。现场培训采用不定时培训，有问题随时进行讲解，常常进行抽考。

培训形式一般要求班组每月每人必须进行技术讲解、现场考问、技术问答、技术考试、反事故演练的培训。每月公司培训中心不定时抽查。对培训效果主要通过公司级、车间级考试进行综合评价。每年公司级考试覆盖全部生产岗位及主要管理岗位。考试成绩与公司人才工程测评挂钩，重奖优秀人员。

四是对特殊工种人员采用统一管理、统一培训、统一考试、统一发证、统一复试的原则。送出参加行业培训取证，全面实行国家职业资格准入制度，强化特种设备作业人员培训取证管理，以制度的形式给以规范。

五是鼓励职工利用业余时间参加岗位需要的专业对口的学历教育，毕业后按公司学历教育奖励管理规定奖励报销部分学费，以进一步改善职工队伍的能级结构，提高职工专业素质和学习能力。

加强培训是发电企业应对环保产生的就业影响的重要措施。在企业采取环保措施之后，超过2/3的风电组员工所在公司组织过相关的培训，大火电组这一比例达到了59%，小火电组中有42.5%的职工所在的公司组织过相关培训。对所接受过的职业培训，职工的评价都很高，对培训的需求也很高。职工参与企业民主管理，最关心的是技能培训问题。如表2-25所示。

表2-25　发电企业在采取环保措施后的培训情况

单位：%

企业采取环保措施后,公司组织过相关的培训吗?		
企业类型	有	没有
风　电	67.7	32.3
大火电	59.0	41.0
小火电	42.5	57.5

公司高度重视节能环保，采用科普宣传、问卷调查、知识竞赛等提高职工的环保意识。职工在生产、生活中的环保意识普遍提高，对企业采取环保措施理解、支持、积极推动。

3. 被调查企业职工对培训的满意度

从员工接受培训的情况看，整体而言，火电企业员工的培训情况较好，超过97.5%的火电员工接受过培训；风电组相对较差，只有88.5%的风电员工接受过培训。如表2-26所示。

表2-26　发电企业分机组职工培训情况

单位：%

企业类型	有培训	没有培训
风　电	88.5	11.5
大火电	97.5	2.5
小火电	97.6	2.4

（1）分类培训情况

按培训类型看，风电企业员工的培训情况总体好于火电企业，在资格培训、继续教育、适应性培训方面，风电企业参加过培训的职工比重都高于火电企业，只有参加过技术等级培训的员工比例低于火电企业。如表 2 - 27 所示。

表 2 - 27　发电企业分机组职工参加各类培训情况

单位：%

	资格培训		适应性培训		技术等级培训		继续教育	
	没有	有	没有	有	没有	有	没有	有
风　电	48.1	51.9	69.2	30.8	57.7	42.3	57.7	42.3
大火电	64.8	35.2	84.6	15.4	38.2	61.8	66.0	34.0
小火电	72.3	27.7	83.1	16.9	34.9	65.1	75.9	24.1

（2）职工对培训效果的评价高，培训需求也很高

对所接受过的职业培训，各组被调查者评价都很高。在风电组中，所有调查对象的评价都集中在"很有用处"或"有些用处"，不存在对培训的负面或一般评价。而火电组中还有少数被调查者对培训的评价不高。

员工对培训的需求都很高。75%以上的被调查者认为为了适应公司或部门的技术发展，自身需要更多的培训；相比而言，小火电组员工对培训的需求低于其他组。如表 2 - 28 所示。

表 2 - 28　发电企业分机组职工的培训需求和评价

单位：%

企业类型	为了适应公司或部门的技术发展,您认为您需要更多的培训吗?		您对所接受过的职业培训评价如何?				
	需要	不需要	很有用	有些用	一般	用处不大	没用
风　电	88.4	11.6	61.9	38.1	0	0	0
大火电	86.5	13.5	51.0	35.0	12.2	1.3	0.5
小火电	76.8	23.2	54.9	29.3	8.5	7.3	0

（八）发电企业不同机组职工的职业安全感、工作满意度及关注的问题

1. 对职业安全性的自我感受

总体上，被调查职工感觉自身就业是相对安全的。风电组中，76.9%的调

查对象认为"就业很可靠",还有19.2%认为"比较可靠"。而大部分的火电组调查对象认为就业"比较可靠",两组中认为"很可靠"的还有20%左右。火电组中有较小比例的调查对象认为就业岗位具有不确定性。如图2-29所示。

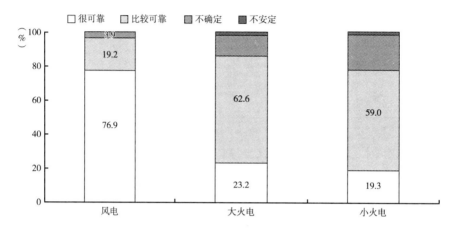

图 2-29　发电企业分机组职工的职业安全感

从年龄分组情况看,职工年龄越大,对职业安全性的自我评价越高。从工种和性别分组情况看,各组之间的差异不大。如图2-30所示。职工对职业安全性的自我评价与受教育程度不是明显相关,各类受教育程度的职工职业安全感都较高,唯有硕士及以上学历的职工中有较大比例的人认为"不确定",这主要与个人的职业取向有关。

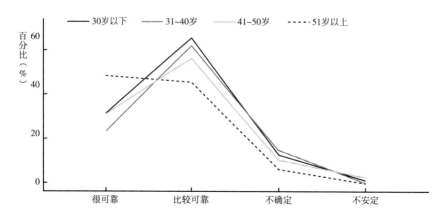

图 2-30　发电企业分年龄段职工的职业安全感

2. 职业安全的影响因素

分析就业不确定/不安定的原因，在仅有的 3.9% 就业不确定的风电组成员中，现有技能限制是他们共同的原因。而大火电组成员中认为就业不确定的原因依重要程度排序分别是：政府支持不够、行业竞争激烈、现有技能限制、行业发展需求。小火电组成员中认为就业不确定的原因依重要程度排序分别是：政府支持不够、现有技能限制、行业发展需求与合同期限短。如表 2 – 29 所示。

表 2 – 29　发电企业分机组职工对就业不确定的原因评价

企业类型	劳动合同期限短	我现在的技能所能从事的工作越来越有限	这一行业竞争越来越激烈	政府政策对就业支持力度不够	行业发展需要的人员越来越少	其他
风　电	0	100.0	0	0	0	0
大火电	13.2	15.1	18.9	34.0	15.1	3.7
小火电	18.8	18.8	6.2	31.2	18.8	6.2

3. 对就业状况的满意度

虽然火电企业职工对就业前景有所担忧，但被调查职工对就业现状的整体评价还是满意的。风电组员工对就业状况的满意程度非常高，超过一半的人"非常满意"，还有 42.6% 的人"较满意"；不存在对就业状况不满意的情况。两个火电组中，虽然"非常满意"所占的比重不高，但大部分调查对象都持"较满意"的态度；不满意就业状况的员工所占的比重较小。如图 2 – 31 所示。

4. 职工参与企业民主管理最关心的是技能培训问题

几乎所有调查对象都认为企业应该多听取工人的意见。职工最关心的是技能培训问题。各组都有过半的被调查员工有强烈的技能培训需求，风电组中强调这一需求的比例高达 3/4，两火电组也有一半以上的员工强调这一需求。

火电机组职工还最关注工资问题。小火电机组有 57% 的被调查职工表示了对工资的关注。风电组员工对工资的关注度最低，这可能是由于该组员工对自身当前的工资水平已经比较满意——平均收入水平最高，本组员工间收入差距相对最小，而且不存在因企业采取环保措施而造成收入减少的现象。

工作安全也是各组职工最关心的问题之一，其中小火电机组员工最关注这

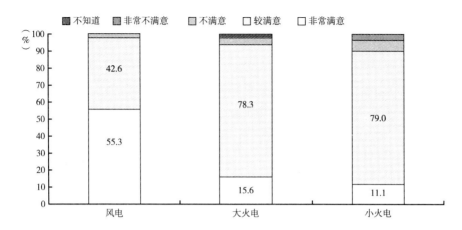

图 2-31　发电企业分机组职工的就业满意度

一问题，这可能是因为该组实际工作安全条件最差。

大火电组员工还比较关注"介绍新技术"和"工人向新岗位的转换"问题，这可能与部分员工从小火电组转岗到大火电组需要学习新技术有关。也有少部分职工关注"解雇与赔偿"的问题。再一次说明发电行业职工的就业是比较稳定的。如图 2-32 所示。

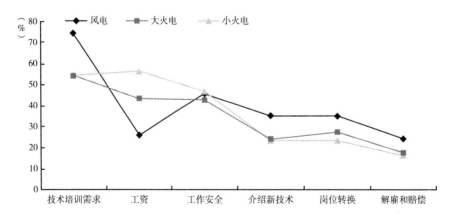

图 2-32　发电企业分机组职工参与企业民主管理最关心的问题

（九）小结

1. 发电行业结构调整对就业的总体影响

（1）发电行业结构调整对直接就业的负面影响大

首先，新能源行业吸收就业的潜力有限。仅就三类机组而言，30 万千瓦的风电、大火电、小火电的就业潜力分别为 30~50 人、300~500 人以及 1000 多人。技术进步、能源供给结构调整将导致能源行业就业需求大量减少。

其次，上大机组能吸收的人数也有限。一方面，大机组本身需要的就业人数就少；另一方面，因小机组淘汰而失去工作岗位的人员，只有约 1/4 的人经过培训能重新上辅助岗位，其余 3/4 的人员只能靠企业想其他办法安置。

最后，企业上脱硫设施等环保措施创造的直接就业数量有限。一台机组实施脱硫改造能增加 1~2 个就业岗位，一般企业约有 5 台机组，最多可以创造 10 个就业岗位。

总之，就电力行业而言，"上大压小"、发展可再生能源，都是一个技术进步的过程。在电力供应一定的情况下，对劳动力的需求会大大减少。在创造新的更高质量就业岗位的同时，被摧毁的就业岗位的数量远远大于被创造出来的新的就业岗位。

（2）发电行业结构调整会使就业问题不断加重

对于现存的还未被列入淘汰范围的小火电而言，生存空间也越来越窄。机组生产效率低于大机组，在同样的市场环境下，小机组的运行成本远高于大机组。为适应环保要求，小机组必须做很多技术改造，导致厂用电等所有指标都增加，进一步加大企业运行成本。石灰石等原材料涨价，对小机组的影响也远大于对大机组的影响。

在这种形势下，小火电新增就业非常有限。由于机组建立时间早，员工年龄结构相对老化，入职年限相对较长，文化程度偏低，技能水平也越来越落后。而发电行业关停小机组是必然趋势，一旦面临关停，未来职工安置问题需要密切关注。

（3）能源产业政策导致不同行业和地区的就业形势发生变化

发电行业结构调整导致直接就业减少，另一方面则带动间接就业和诱致性就业增加。如脱硫设备环保产业链的延伸为社会做出了巨大贡献：企业脱硫使用石灰石作为生产原料，带动了石灰石生产厂家的就业增加；脱硫后产生的石膏可以用于房屋装修，也带动了汽车运输业的就业；带动脱硫设备生产和运行维护企业的就业。发展风力发电则可以带动风电设备生产、安装的就业等。也就是说，发电行业关停小火电损失了就业，上下游产业及相关产业所在的行业和地区增加了就业。能源产业政策导致不同行业和地区的就业形势发生变化。

2. 发电行业环保措施对就业的影响

（1）小企业采取环保措施面临较大生产经营困难

以脱硫改造为例，火电企业普遍进行了老机组的脱硫除尘改造，新机组安装高效脱硫除尘设施。上脱硫设施企业普遍要投入巨资；脱硫系统改造完成后，系统运行维护增加了厂用电率，增加了供电煤耗；增加了大量的设备，每年新增大量维护、材料及水的费用。企业的运营维护成本因此增加了10%。政府对安装脱硫设施机组的上网电价补贴为每度电1.5分，而企业的实际成本核算下来是每度电2分，电价补贴远远无法弥补成本的增加。大企业有能力进行环保投入，而这对小企业来说则是不小的经济负担。小企业面临两难：不按照环保要求进行污染治理，企业根本就不可能生存下去，就失去了竞争的资本；上环保设施又增加成本负担，使企业面临就业困难。

（2）老职工再就业难

火电企业管理经历了一个不断科学合理化的过程。最早的一期机组（主要是已关停或行将关停的小火电）实行岗位分专业管理，运行岗分为汽机、锅炉和电气运行三种岗位。这种模式的特点是，专业技能使用时间比较长，专业性强而技能的复合性低，员工再接受跨专业知识技能的难度比较大。二期机组主要是20世纪90年代前后建的以20万千瓦为主的机组，岗位管理基本属于承上启下的阶段，大家都在努力学习跨专业知识，有一部分职工有能力向复合型技能转变。三期机组主要是不断新建的以30万千瓦为主的机组，企业基本打算实行全能型值班员岗位，以往机组的一些老员工很难适应新的岗位需要。由于年龄、技能老化，学习新技术难度大，岗位转换的心理落差也大，他们再就业比较困难。

（3）关停小火电时企业内部职工的阻力大

发电企业的收入分配原则是向一线职工倾斜，一线员工的收入是辅助岗位或三产岗位职工收入的10倍。小火电机组关停后，原来一线的员工只能转到辅助岗位，收入大大下降。虽然企业可以想方设法安置职工就业，但是下岗职工仍然会有不满情绪。

再加上行业发展对劳动者素质的要求越来越高，这些无法被新机组吸纳到一线岗位的小机组职工对自己的职业前景也不可能有好的预期，就业的不安全感增强。

另外，企业生存空间收窄、运行成本不断加大的压力，也折射到了职工身上，增强了他们就业的不安全感和不满情绪。火电企业职工关于影响就业安全性的原因中，政府支持不够被排在首位。

3. 风电和火电行业就业比较

（1）风电行业比火电行业提供更高的职业安全性

行业发展前景从根本上决定了职工就业的安全性和保障性。风电是正处于大发展时期的朝阳产业，用工需求旺盛，职工不需要为有没有岗位发愁。他们所担心的是自己是否有足够的技能承担起工作。风电企业签订固定期限合同的职工，基本上所有的人都愿意与企业续签劳动合同，而且绝大部分也认为这种意愿是能够实现的。总体上表明风电行业职工就业的安全性很高。

而小火电企业职工则担心现有的岗位能否保得住。由于火电行业受市场因素影响的程度越来越大，竞争越来越激烈，技术进步导致生产所需的人员越来越少，对越来越多职工的就业安全性带来根本性的影响，其次才是个人技能的问题。火电机组签订固定期限合同的职工中，有少量的职工认为续签合同存在不确定性。表明火电机组中存在相对大的人员调整的空间。

（2）风电行业就业比火电行业就业更具灵活性，更少归属感

从用工形式看，风电企业使用了少量劳务派遣工，大火电机组使用了少量临时工，而小火电企业全部都是正式工；从员工身份看，风电企业招收了相对较多的外地户籍职工，大火电机组雇用了一些本市农业户籍和外省市户籍的职工，而小火电机组基本上是很多年前建厂时招收的职工，都是本市非农户籍的职工；从合同期限看，风电机组固定期限劳动合同的合同期限比火电机组的短；从各类机组职工的求职方式看，风电企业用工机制最灵活；从员工流动情况看，风电和大火电机组职工变动工作岗位的频率较高。这些都说明，绿色就业的灵活性总体上高于非绿色就业。

就业灵活性提高的另一面，是职工对企业的归属感降低。对于骨干员工，一旦发现更好的就业机会，就会跳槽，企业想留的人留不住；对于一些具有就业替代性的经常性岗位，为了避免不想要的人难解聘，企业主要聘用文化程度较低的临时工来满足需要，这部分职工大概占企业职工的10%。临时工虽然工资水平与正式职工差不多，但不享受企业年金、住房公积金等福利待遇，他们的归属感也不强。

实施《劳动合同法》后，企业把临时工全部转为劳务派遣用工，实行同工同酬，企业的解雇成本和用工成本将增加，用工灵活性将降低，这也是企业

面临的新问题。

（3）风电行业的就业比火电行业的就业更体面

首先，从工作场所环境看，风电对职工健康状况的影响最小。火电特定的生产操作方式下，检修都是在现场，高温、噪声都难以避免，因此对职工健康的影响较大。新老机组的工作环境差别比较大。老机组当初的设计理念是生产为先，对人的关注度不够，新机组的工作环境越来越多地考虑人的因素，工作环境不断改善。

风电也有新的问题。由于风电厂远离城市，职工一般都是在工厂连续工作10～15天，然后在家休息10～15天的大班轮班制，一个风电厂一般只有几个人，长此以往，人的沟通能力受到影响；另外，露天作业受自然条件影响大，设备检修和运行管理对体质要求比较高，因此，对从业人员的年龄、性别都有要求，一般20多岁的年轻男性比较适合。

第二，从收入情况看，受国家大力发展新能源产业的政策影响，风电上马速度快，就业机会多。但由于人员储备少，导致这一行业的收入水平高于火电行业。企业为了避免人才流失太快，往往给予职工较高的收入和较好的福利待遇。传统火电行业整体经营状况还可以，整体上保持了职工收入的稳定。但在采取环保措施的过程中，一些非绿色的岗位虽然依然存在，但收入水平有所下降。

第三，从加班情况看，风电行业加班情况比较普遍，加班加点的员工一般都能得到加班费或安排补休，但不同机组之间情况有所差别，风电组中全部能得到加班费，而小火电机组中较多的人没得到加班费。

第四，从受金融危机冲击情况看，金融危机对风电企业的影响不明显，而火电企业受到一定的冲击。

另外，从劳动工具、工时制度、职工参加社会保险、企业的福利待遇、职工的健康状况、职业病、企业采取的劳动保护措施、职工对工作环境的满意度、职工参与企业民主决策等方面的情况看，绿色就业的情况都好于非绿色就业，体现了体面就业的特征。

（4）企业采取环保措施有利于促进体面就业

企业采取环保措施后，就生产所需技能和设备/工具而言，风电组变化很多，小火电机组也有一定的变化；职工的工作时间总体上保持稳定，但风电企业职工的工作时间有较大增加，小火电组职工中也有超过1/4的职工工作时间有所增加；各机组的工作强度都有所增加；风电机组近60%的职工收入水平增加，小火电机组也有近 1/4 的职工收入增加了。总体上看，企业采取环保措施后，在生产所需技能和设备/工具、收入、工作时间以及劳动强度方面，各机组都有积极的变化和改善。企业采取环保措施有利于促进体面就业。

六　促进绿色就业发展的原则和政策建议

作为关于中国绿色就业的初始性研究，本研究报告从绿色就业概念的理论探讨、绿色就业的宏观发展状况、向绿色就业转型的微观实践等方面，进行了初创性的研究探索，初步结论是，绿色就业发展空间广阔，潜力无限，能够促进体面劳动。

向绿色发展转型、大力发展绿色经济，是中国未来经济社会发展的方向和必然趋势，已经并将继续创造更多新的朝阳产业，成为新的经济增长点，带动新的经济增长和就业增加。遍布各行各业、惠及各类劳动者的大量的绿色就业岗位亟待开发。

保护环境是个持续发展的过程，绿色就业具有无限可持续发展潜力。以脱硫设施为例，以前上的脱硫炉型技术还不成熟，磨损严重，维护工作量大，成本高。脱硫运行岗的工作环境比较好，脱硫检修岗的工作环境就差一些，因为员工要进入炉内检修，气味很重。目前设备还在健康期，不需要频繁检修；将来过了五六年，维护的工作量可能增加。所以环保投入是个持续的、不断技术进步的过程，绿色就业因而是个持续发展的过程。

绿色就业直接导致劳动生产率和企业效益的提高，有利于劳动报酬的更快提高和收入分配中劳动份额的增长；通过推进各种环保措施整合发展成不断延伸的绿色产业链条，蕴藏着的大量就业机会，足以抵消传统产业中工作岗位的减少，而且新创造的就业机会更具安全性、经济性和稳定性；节能环保措施在生产过程中的引用，能大大改善工人的作业环境，从而增进工人的安全和健康；实施节能环保推动技术进步和产业升级，促进劳动技术含量的提高，有利于改善劳动者的技能素质。总之，绿色就业有利于促进体面劳动。

人力资源政策的唯一的选择，就是顺应绿色发展的大趋势，有效促进绿色就业发展。

（一）促进绿色就业发展的指导思想和基本原则

1. 分类促进原则

绿色就业的发展有两种情况：一类是市场自发创造的，如废品回收行业的就业，一类是政府推动创造的，如火电行业的就业。对于不同性质的绿色就业，必须坚持不同的就业促进思路和原则，不能一概而论，不能一刀切。对于市场自发创造的绿色就业，政府就业促进的原则是坚持市场化原则，政府的作用是消除不利于市场机制发挥作用的干扰因素，更多、更好地提供就业服务。对于政府推动创造的绿色就业，必须坚持政策干预的就业促进原则，制定专门的就业促进政策。

2. 产业政策、环保政策与就业政策并重、同步

发展经济、保护环境、促进就业都是为了民生，三者要并重，不能偏废。既不能因为发展经济而忽略环境保护和就业促进，又不能为保护环境而制约经济发展进而对就业产生不利影响，更不能采取没有就业增长的发展模式，必须坚定不移地朝着经济绿化的方向量力而行、循序渐进，采取综合配套的政策杠杆，协调推进产业结构优化升级，环境不断改善和就业数量扩大、就业质量提高。这意味着，要在充分考虑充分就业目标的前提下，鼓励绿色产业的发展，有序推动传统产业绿化，逐步完善环保标准。

实现三者的协调推进，关键是要做到政策同步，即制定产业政策和规划时，必须有同步的就业政策和规划；制定环保政策和规划时，必须有同步的就业政策和规划；制定就业政策和规划时，必须考虑对经济发展和环境保护的作用。

3. 促进低碳发展要重视就业影响

中国正处于能源消耗量大的工业化发展中期，适度的能源消耗是经济发展所必需的，低碳发展实际上是限制能源利用的水平和规模，最终会限制发展，限制就业。因此，中国要充分考虑就业因素，需要找到一个合适的点，利用国际资金和技术，在促进经济发展的同时减缓温室气体排放。

4. 绿色就业促进政策需要对绿色就业本身进行调整

一些绿色的就业本身不是体面就业；一些绿色就业有利于保护环境但并非低碳就业，如脱硫要释放碳；一些低碳就业又不利于环境保护，如生物质能源种植要用化肥，会造成污染；一些就业是绿色就业，但不符合产业发展要求，如产能过剩的光伏发电和发电设备制造就业；一些就业是绿色就业，但不适合资源禀赋特点，中国土地资源有限，不适合发展生物质能源。因此，对于绿色就业并非要一味地鼓励发展，还要进行政策调控。在制定绿色就业促进政策时，要从中国实际出发，确定对绿色就业进行干预的领域和程度。

5. 分行业制定促进绿色就业发展的专门政策

绿色就业遍布各行各业、各个层次的劳动者，各行业千差万别。因此，在总的指导思想和原则下，必须进行分行业的调查研究，制定分行业的促进绿色就业发展的专门政策。

（二）促进绿色就业发展的政策建议

中国 1992 年开始正式建立市场经济体制，20 世纪 90 年代中期开始大规模的国有企业改制，1998 年开始在全国实行减员增效、下岗分流的再就业工程，使近 3000 万国有企业职工通过再就业中心由国家职工转变为社会人。这一政策在 2002 年结束。在总结再就业政策经验的基础上，于 2002 年创立了有中国特色的积极就业政策体系。经过 3 年的探索实践，在 2005 年对积极就业政策体系进行了进一步的扩展、充实、延伸和提高，在经历了 2008 年的金融危机后，进一步完善充实为更加积极的就业政策体系。

国际劳工组织充分肯定中国积极就业政策，认为这一政策体系包含了现有各国就业政策的所有元素：重积极促进就业的作用，并包含提前预防失业的措施；岗位开发与技能开发并重；重创业。不但体现了体面工作的本质特征，而且还有执行力。

制定促进绿色就业发展的政策，就是要绿化更加积极的就业政策体系。一方面将"绿色"的观念植入现行的政策体系中，另一方面，将以往相关的政策纳入这一政策体系，如资源枯竭城市的就业政策、水库移民的政策、政策性关闭破产企业的政策等。在此基础上，对更加积极的就业政策体系进行充实完善，最终形成中国的绿色就业政策体系。

目前，中国每年的非农岗位就业需求在 3000 万人左右，而目前经济增长所创造的就业岗位仅在 1000 万人左右。加速经济发展、扩大就业仍然是政府最迫切、最首要的任务。在这种就业形势下，制定促进绿色就业发展的政策必须处理好以下几个问题：一是不能由于发展绿色就业引起较大的就业波动，必须做好相应的就业预案；二是在农业劳动力难以在短缺内完全转移的情况下，政策应支持农业领域劳动密集型的就业绿化的措施；三是像其他政策一样，发展绿色就业也应在非公有制部门着力，包括个体、私营企业、乡镇企业等。一方面因为这些单位的就业占到多数，另一方面是因为其就业绿化的潜力也比较大；四是灵活就业目前依然是新增就业的重要渠道，发展绿色就业应避免对这一就业渠道的扼杀。

根据本项研究，提出以下促进绿色就业发展的政策建议。

1. 用法律手段保证绿色就业的发展

（1）对产业政策和环保政策进行就业评估

首先，制定以就业为核心的环境保护的社会评价指标体系。在各种产业规划和环保规划中，用科学的方法列入就业评价指标，包括项目可能带动的新增就业数、项目可能造成的就业减少数、项目对地方人力资源供求形势的影响、项目对居民收入水平的影响、地方发展此项目的人力资源匹配情况等。

其次，制定就业预案。建立就业评价指标后，需要建立就业预案，即应对项目对就业影响的政策措施。如可能造成失业，则要制定应对失业的预案；如对人力资源供给提出需要，则需要制订人力资源供给方案等。这些预案主要涉及资金保证等问题。

再次，编制好就业预算。建立就业评价指标和就业预案后，就需要建立就业预算，即项目就业的成本效益核算，包括就业核算和资金核算。

最后，进行项目评估。把产业政策和环保政策对就业的影响评估作为项目审批的前置程序。

（2）修改完善相关法律，将对产业政策和环境保护的就业评估法制化

首先，要在环境保护、主要产业以及人力资源和社会保障事业的"十二五"规划中，分别提出促进绿色就业发展的目标，最终在《国民经济和社会发展第十二个五年规划纲要》中，明确提出产业发展和环境保护的就业指标，推动"十二五"时期我国绿色就业的发展。

其次，在"十二五"时期实践的基础上，逐步修订相关法律法规，包括《环境保护法》《循环经济促进法》《能源节约法》《就业促进法》《劳动合同法》等，在"职业能力开发条例"、《社会保险法》等新的法律法规制定中，纳入绿色就业的要素，使促进绿色就业发展逐步法制化。

2. 促进绿色就业发展的政策措施

（1）绿化人力资源市场机制，促进绿色就业发展

一是建立绿色就业认证制度，促进企业发展绿色就业。建立绿色就业认证制度，对于绿色行业的企业、非绿色行业的绿色企业，授予绿色就业企业称号，作为享受相关政策扶持的一个参考。如列入政府绿色采购清单。

二是建立绿色职业资格认证体系，促进劳动者向"绿领"转变。逐步完善我国的职业资格认证体系，开发绿色职业标准，鼓励劳动者参加绿色职业资

格认证，促进越来越多的劳动者从事绿色就业。

三是绿化公共就业服务体系。在公共就业服务机构建立绿色就业服务专区，收集和发布绿色就业岗位信息，促进绿色就业岗位的供求匹配。并通过劳动保障社区平台，将绿色就业岗位的信息传递给每一位劳动者。

（2）绿化现行的积极就业政策，促进绿色就业发展

目前，中国的积极就业政策主要是针对下岗失业人员的。绿化积极的就业政策，就是将现有的政策扩展到向绿色经济转型中就业受到影响的群体，包括国有林场改制职工，电力、钢铁、建材、电解铝、铁合金、电石、焦炭、煤炭、平板玻璃、造纸等13个行业淘汰落后产能而关停的企业职工等，国家的产业政策、制度因素使他们的就业受到影响，应给予他们政策性的就业扶持，包括促进企业稳定岗位的政策，以及促进劳动者就业的政策。

一是鼓励企业雇用人员。运用税收优惠、社会保险补贴、担保贷款和贴息等政策杠杆，鼓励企业雇用向绿色经济转型中就业受到影响的群体。对企业利用现有设施、场地和技术发展多种经营，多渠道分流本企业职工的，给予劳动就业服务企业的税收优惠等政策扶持。

二是帮扶企业克服困难，尽可能创造就业。对处于向绿色生产转型期间、有吸纳员工就业潜力的企业，通过缓缴社会保险费，降低社会保险费费率，给予社会保险补贴、岗位补贴、职业培训补贴等措施，鼓励企业稳定职工队伍，不裁员或少裁员。

三是鼓励自主创业。通过免费创业培训、定额减免税费和提供小额担保贷款等政策，鼓励这些人员自主创业。对于从事个体经营、家庭手工业以及私营企业的，免收行政事业性收费，并予以税金减免；对缺乏经营资金的，给予一定数额的小额担保贷款及相应的财政贴息。通过实行税费减免、场地安排、小额担保贷款及贴息等政策和提供创业咨询及开业服务，为劳动者自谋职业和自主创业创造良好环境。

四是通过公共就业服务和再就业培训，促进再就业。政府的公共就业服务机构为这些人员提供免费就业服务。重新培训夕阳产业从业人员，重视资源替代产业和技术的培训，促进他们顺利实现转岗。对于参加培训的人员提供培训费补贴，以及职业技能鉴定补贴。

五是对困难群体实行就业援助。政府开发公益性岗位，优先安排就业困难人员，并给予社会保险费补贴和岗位补贴。对于从事灵活就业的人员，给予社

会保险补贴。针对就业困难人员等重点人群，统筹安排就业。

六是对一部分老职工实行提前退休。有一些老职工再培训、重新就业比较困难，可以考虑实行提前退休的政策，让他们体面地退出劳动力市场。

七是做好对困难地区的就业援助。对向绿色经济转型中就业受损的地区，特别是中西部经济欠发达地区，要有中央财政的专项转移支付，用于帮助这些地区解决就业问题。

（3）通过政策扶持，开发一批绿色就业岗位

一些绿色就业有很强的市场竞争力，无须政策扶持就已经发展得蓬蓬勃勃，如环保设备、洁净产品、有机食品创造的就业等。但总体上，绿色就业还是新兴事务，很多绿色就业还需要政策扶持才能较快地发展起来，并不一定需要很多资金投入，但会有巨大的就业潜力。

如一些城市开展了废旧物资统一回收利用的试点，但竞争不过小商贩的回收队伍。可以开发社区废旧物资回收加工岗位，形成网络，在起步阶段给予岗位补贴或社保补贴，促进绿色就业发展起来，等行业正规以后，再让其在市场中发展。

又如，中国每年高校培养大量环保专业的毕业生就业困难，而企业又招不到需要的人，感到人才短缺。如果规定每个企业都必须雇用一名环境评估师，则可以创造可观的就业机会。从《中国环境统计年鉴（2008）》中可以看出，中国工业企业专职环保人员中，有 18.8 万人分布在实行工业固体废物汇总的70612 个工业企业中，6463 人在 2681 户企业中从事环境保护档案工作。按照第一次全国经济普查，如果将全国 516.9 万个法人单位、682.4 万个产业活动单位都配备一名环保工作人员，就可以创造 1200 万个就业岗位。

（4）在新农村建设和西部大开发中开发绿色就业岗位

农村绿色就业的天地广阔。农业是国民经济的基础，生态环境建设是基本国策，农村经济就是小国民经济。发展农业型的知识密集产业，即以阳光为直接能源、靠光合作用进行生产、充分利用生物资源和现代生产技术、进行流水式生产的农/林/草/沙/海产业，是农村的未来，也是绿色就业的源泉。西部日照时间长、土地及各种资源丰富，是发展农业型的知识密集产业潜力最大的地区。农村地区绿色就业主要包括以下六个方面。

一是发展生态农业就业。生态农业是科技和劳动密集型的结合，通过生产高效、节约资源能源的绿色食品，可以增加 20% 农村劳动力的就地转化，收入比普通农民增加 50% 以上。

二是发展特色农业就业。根据市场和区域优势，发展特色农业，是现代化农业生产的方向，可以带动一批专业户、专业村，促进农民增收致富。

三是发展特色农产品加工业就业。特色农产品加工是农工商的联合体。以公司或者农民合作社为龙头，将农户和加工业连接起来，形成经营链，是促进农村工业化的重要途径。

四是发展特色生态乡村旅游业，可以实现产业、产值、就业年增长15%。

五是发展新能源产业。农村能源消费增长快，发展包括生物质能、粪便秸秆沼气等，既有助于满足农村地区的能源需求，又是绿色就业的重要领域。

六是在农村经济发展的基础上，带动农村公共服务需求，创造绿色公共服务就业岗位。

促进农村绿色就业发展，首先要建立资源和生态补偿机制，征收生态资源税，实现末端产业对源头产业、成品对资源、二三产业对第一产业的补偿。将征收来的生态资源税，用于发展农村绿色公共服务，如改善村容村貌、改善农村供水系统和卫生设施等。

其次，要完善现行的促进大学毕业生到基层就业的相关政策，引导技术人员到农村办绿色产业。农村缺的是专业人才和企业家，而不是村官。将促进大学毕业生到基层就业的政策开展到农村从事绿色公共服务的大学生，要把创业带动就业的政策延伸到农村绿色创业中。

再次，要加大宣传力度，让更多的人认识到农村绿色就业的广阔空间。相对于能源、工业等对 GDP 影响大的行业，农业的经济效益不显著，农村绿色经济往往不受重视。但事实上它是既有科技含量、又密集使用劳动力，有巨大发展前景的新兴行业。在统筹城乡就业发展中，应将促进农村绿色就业发展作为重要内容，加以开发。

最后，加强农村劳动者的教育。当前，农村劳动力素质与农村经济发展需要的矛盾巨大。农村的"3860部队"，难以承担起农村绿色经济发展的重任。通过发展农村绿色经济，吸收一批有知识、有技能的劳动者到农村，同时，加大对农村劳动力的针对性培训，将有利于改善农村人力资源状况，促进农村地区的可持续发展。

（5）扶持绿色就业型小企业发展带动就业

小企业永远都是创造和吸收就业的主体，绿色就业也不例外。界定绿色就业型小企业，发给《绿色就业劳动组织证书》，作为享受相关扶持政策的依据。对绿色就业型小企业要提供信贷支持，可在 3 年内减征或者免征所得税，免税期满后，可减半征收所得税 2 年等，给予适当补助。对创办绿色就业型小企业的，3 年内免征营业税、个人所得税、城市维护建设税和教育费附加等；提供小额信贷；简化工商登记手续，或者发给"绿色就业劳动组织证书"，不再办理工商营业执照。制定科技促进政策，推动绿色科研成果和技术成果的应用和推广，促进"绿领"人才创业。

3. 制订绿色技能开发计划，促进绿色职业的发展

向绿色就业转型，技能开发是关键。一方面，要将现有的各种培训绿化，如农村实用技能培训、阳光培训、雨露计划、农村劳动力转移就业技能培训、创业培训等，要将绿色技能开发融入这些培训项目中；另一方面还需要开发制订新的技能开发计划。

（1）调查绿色职业现状，制定绿色职业职谱

我国已经有很多绿色职业，一些绿色职业已纳入职业资格认证体系，如环境影响评价工程师、再生资源回收、污水处理工，以及太阳能利用工、沼气生产工等。一方面要分行业继续挖掘绿色职业，另一方面要加快绿色职业标准开发建设，并依据职业标准开发绿色培训专业标准和绿色技术训练标准，逐步完善我国绿色职业谱表及绿色职业培训标准体系。

（2）制订绿色产业技术技能提升规划

制订和实施中国绿色产业技术技能提升规划，全面提升劳动者绿色技能水平，为绿色发展提供所需的人力资源。

为此，要制订分行业的绿色技术技能纲要和人力资源需求规划。对于新技术技能，可以联合行业、高校，建立新技术技能开发机构，逐步探索人才培养模式。如皇明集团的职业技术学院正不断开发太阳能热利用的各项技术及专业人才的培养。现行的教育制度、培训制度对这种新的技术技能要从制度上接纳和推动。对于相对成熟的技术技能，则应出台激励政策，如用失业保险金鼓励企业开展面向全体职工的绿色技能培训，用培训补贴的政策鼓励各类教育培训机构开展培训，用培训券的形式鼓励劳动者积极参加培训。

（3）绿化现行的创业培训

包括绿色创业的理念、绿色产业的技能、绿色创业的项目等。

（4）强化向绿色就业转型中的转岗转业培训

非绿色就业退出的途径，一是转岗，二是转业，三是彻底退出劳动力市

场，即岗位替代、岗位转换和岗位消失。实现向绿色就业的公正转型，必须对这些岗位上的职工进行技能提升转换再培训。

岗位替代的转岗培训，主要是技能转换培训，可以由本企业开展，社会提供帮助。岗位转换的培训，即转业培训，难度比较大，因为职工所需技能并非原企业的专长，就需要政府和社会来提供。如在丧失工作机会的行业与地区，政府应制订专门的转业培训计划，设立专项资金，开展真正意义上的技能培训。

（5）逐步开展绿色职业从业资格认证和绿色技能鉴定考核工作

根据绿色职业标准，制定"绿领"人才评估考核标准，逐步开展绿色职业从业资格认证和绿色技能鉴定考核工作。

（6）建立覆盖各类劳动者的绿色职业技能开发体系

绿色职业遍布各行各业、涉及各类劳动者，绿色职业技能开发也需要覆盖各类劳动者。要通过各类职业技术学校、社区培训中心、公共就业服务机构、企业等各种渠道传播绿色就业的概念和技能，使新成长的劳动力具备绿色职业意识；为失业人员提供绿色的再就业培训；为困难企业职工提供技能提升培训和转岗转业培训；为农民工提供绿色职业技能培训；为退役士兵提供免费的绿色职业培训；为大学生和想创业的人员提供绿色创业培训；为在职人员提供绿色技能提升培训。运用培训补贴政策，扩大培训规模，延长培训时间，提高培训的针对性和有效性。

4. 加强对绿色就业领域劳动者的权益保障

绿色就业有助于环境保护，但有些绿色就业劳动者的权益并没有得到很好的保护。第一种情况是，工作环境不好，如风电企业职工工作受自然环境影响大，还要实行长班轮班制。需要有特殊的补偿机制来解决长班倒的问题，除了给予津贴、改善企业福利设施外，最主要的是解决好职工子女教育的问题。

第二种情况是，工作报酬低，缺乏社会保障，特别是一些灵活就业群体。如目前遍布大街小巷的废品回收人员。尽可能使他们的就业正规化，有助于提高他们的就业稳定性和安全性，提高收入水平。

第三种情况是，一些绿色就业的就业保障性降低，劳动合同期限短，企业随意解雇员工，劳动者权益时常受到侵犯，主要是中小企业和私营企业。健全执法监督，健全企业集体谈判机制，有助于提高劳动者的就业保障性。

第四种情况是，劳动关系不和谐。如皇明集团新入职大学生与公司有很多矛盾，公司认为大学生从工作态度、能力等方面都不适应工作需要，职工认为企业要求太过分，不时发生冲突。薪酬水平低，职工流失率高。帮助企业提高管理水平，健全管理机制，建立和谐劳动关系，才最终有利于促进绿色就业发展。

5. 社会伙伴共同促进绿色就业

发展绿色就业必须在政府、雇主和职工之间达成共识。雇主在考虑经济效益的同时，必须承担绿色发展的社会责任，要尽可能将绿色就业与经济效益统一起来。在劳动关系三方协商机制中突出绿色就业的发展战略，促进绿色就业发展。

工会组织可以积极参与到促进绿色就业发展的工作中。一是开展技术提升活动，努力提高职工绿色就业能力。如通过积极开展以绿色发展为主要内容的专题培训、咨询等工作，编写相关读物，举办相关讲座，帮助职工掌握绿色生产的新技能、新方法；如不断征集挖掘、总结推广职工创造的绿色操作技术和小窍门，帮助职工提高节约资源的能力；又如大力开展有关的岗位练兵、技术比赛等活动，激发职工提高自身技能的积极性。

二是参与企业管理、加强对企业绿色发展的群众监督。如把职工参与管理贯穿于企业生产经营的全过程，发动职工从岗位做起，从点滴着手，认真查找薄弱环节，采取措施堵塞漏洞，减少资源浪费，提高资源利用率，促进环境保护；如了解企业环保情况，检查企业节约环保工作，积极协助企业制订规划、落实责任，使环保的各项措施落到实处；又如建立职工监督员队伍，加强群众监督。

6. 加强宣传，创造全社会促进绿色就业发展的氛围

多开展形式多样的活动，通过对绿色就业典型事例、重点项目、重大活动的宣传，逐步促进全社会形成了解绿色就业、崇尚绿色就业、发展绿色就业的氛围。如开展街头宣传；开展征集表彰职工合理化建议的活动；组织发布职工节能减排技术创新成果；开展节能环保知识竞赛，评选表彰一批"绿色就业"的先进集体和个人，广泛宣传他们的先进事迹，推广他们的创新成果。

7. 完善促进企业绿色发展的环境

（1）完善环保标准

目前，中国环境保护的标准体系正在建设之中，很多行业还缺乏环境标准，或者标准体系不完善。因此，环保标准体系的建设应进一步加快。同时，

环保标准应该是让大部分企业都能做到，而不是只有少数企业能做到。国家在制定环保标准时，应充分考虑国情，一要允许企业分步到位；二要考虑企业实际情况，通过资金投入、政策投入等，使企业落实环保标准成为可能，而不能不考虑对社会的实际影响，特别是对就业的影响，强行实施环保标准。

（2）采取激励与惩罚措施，促进企业可持续发展

不履行环保责任，实际上就是将应承担的环境和社会成本外部化。促使企业向绿色发展转变，一是要逐步完善政策的激励和诱导机制，使绿色技术和实践的采用者在市场竞争中处于有利地位。如加大对没有经济回报或暂时没有经济回报的环保产品和服务的财政补贴。二是要加强执法。现在国有企业一般都会执行国家的环保政策，但是一些小型的私营企业却不能严格执行国家标准。应加大对小企业的整治力度和环保执法力度。

（3）不断完善绿色发展的融资机制

环保技术的开发、应用、传播在向绿色经济转型中起关键作用，而环保技术应用的关键是资金。需要不断创新融资机制，包括征收资源税、环境税、碳税等，为发展绿色经济、创造绿色工作融资。同时，争取国际技术和资金支持。

8. 在国际气候谈判中，建立就业补偿机制

迄今为止，国际气候谈判的焦点只集中在各国的减排指标上，而没有考虑减排的社会成本。为此，应在谈判中建立就业补偿机制，对发展中国家由于减排导致的负面就业影响予以资金、技术或减排指标的补偿。

绿色就业的国际研究

发展绿色节能环保产业，推行低碳经济发展模式，利用可再生能源，是未来经济社会可持续发展的必由之路。通过发展环保产业、低碳经济和可再生能源的途径，创造就业岗位，更是应对金融危机冲击下国内就业压力剧增的一剂良方。本研究旨在总结世界各国在环保产业、低碳经济和可再生能源领域的相关立法、政策和措施，为中国绿色就业事业的发展提供借鉴。

一　绿色就业的含义

目前，绿色就业（绿色工作）并没有严格统一的定义。

一种定义①，"绿色就业是指经济上可行的，同时能够减少环境影响，实现可持续发展的就业"。

还有一种定义②，"绿色就业是指对环境的影响低于平均水平、能够改善整体环境质量的任何的新兴工作"。

国际劳工组织对绿色就业的定义是，"绿色工作是在经济部门和经济活动中创造的体面劳动，它能够减少环境影响，最终在环境、经济和社会层面实现可持续发展的企业和经济"。

在报告《绿色工作：在低碳、可持续发展的世界实现体面劳动》（UNEP、

---

① 转引自 ILO 亚太地区局专家的 Ivanka Mamic 的会议发言材料，中国绿色就业研讨会，2009 年 1 月 21 日，北京。
② 转引自 ILO 亚太地区局专家的 Ivanka Mamic 的会议发言材料，中国绿色就业研讨会，2009 年 1 月 21 日，北京。

ILO、ITUC）中，绿色就业被定义为："在农业、工业、服务业和管理领域有助于保护或恢复环境质量的工作。"绿色就业有四个基本特点：一是能够减少能源和原材料消耗（"非物质化经济"）；二是避免温室气体排放（"无碳化经济"）；三是保护和恢复生态系统；四是减少废物和污染。

美国明尼苏达州 Task Force 机构将"绿色就业"定义为："绿色经济的就业机会，包括绿色产品、可再生能源、绿色服务和环境保护四个产业部门的就业。"其中，绿色产品是指为了减少环境影响、改善资源使用效率而生产的产品，它主要应用于建筑、交通、消费产品和工业产品四个领域。可再生能源是指太阳能、风能、水能、地热能、生物燃料等能源。绿色服务是指为帮助企业和消费者个人使用绿色产品或技术提供各类服务的产业或职业，还包括能源基础设施建设以及与能源效率、农业、再循环和废物管理相关的职业。环境保护是指与能源、空气、水以及土地资源的保护相关的产业。

二 国际环保产业政策

（一）美国的环保产业政策

美国的环保产业（包括国有企业和私人企业）两种形式①：一是历史上存在的公共基础设施，如提供饮用水、废水处理和废弃物管理；二是随着国内环保法规的制定和实施而迅速崛起的企业，绝大多数是私人公司，主要从事污染控制、污染补救等业务。环保产业包括与下列活动有关的创造产值的所有企业：①遵守环保法规；②环境评价、分析和保护；③污染控制、废弃物管理以及污染的补救；④水、回收物和清洁能源的供应和运输；⑤能够提高能源和资源效率、提高生产力和促进经济可持续发展的技术活动。

美国的环境保护产业政策归纳起来有以下几个方面。

1. 实施严格的环境标准和法规是环保产业发展的基础

美国于 1963 年制定出第一部《清洁空气法》，对燃烧矿物燃料排放的污染物进行了限制。随着美国加强对污染的控制，1970～1990 年，美国先后 3 次修改了《清洁空气法》，且一次比一次严格。在此期间，由于实施了日益严格的环境法规，作为污染控制手段的美国大气污染控制设备市场也有了突飞猛进的发展，新技术、新工艺不断得到开发，市场也不断呈上升趋势。此外，美

---

① 陈吕军、温东辉、陈维敏：《美国环保产业发展的现状》，《环境保护》2002 年第 9 期。

国的《清洁水法》也在控制水污染方面直接促进了环保产业的迅速发展。

2. 采用经济刺激手段是美国环保产业发展的推动力①

环保产业与其他行业相比尚属新兴产业，美国在发展环保产业过程中，采用了许多经济手段作为法律、法规手段的补充，刺激企业达到环境标准或遵守环保法律、法规。其采用的经济刺激手段主要包括：

（1）财政补贴

政府通过立法等措施对与环境产业及相关项目给予一定的资金补助。例如，美国《联邦水污染控制法》中规定：在污水处理管理计划得到良好实施的前提下，城市污水处理厂只要采用联邦环保局认定的"最佳实用处理技术"，均可向联邦环保局申请补助，经批准可以获得很大比例的建设补助费。自20世纪70年代初开始，美国联邦政府就鼓励各州建立"水污染控制周转基金"，并可以从联邦政府取得一定比例的补助金列入其中，以减轻联邦政府的财政压力。

（2）税收刺激

政府一般对商业企业征收固定资产税，但为了鼓励企业安装环保设施，在地方税收方面采取了减免税的特别措施。

（3）征收排污清理费

美国联邦环保局在2000年5月，对污染美国加州的圣费南度谷饮用水源的51家企业处以3725万美元的赔偿金，用于支付清洁圣费南度谷饮用水源水库所需要的费用。

（4）排污权交易

1979年，美国政府率先提出了排污权交易的整体政策，规定了一定区域范围内污染物排放的总量以及环境质量的最低标准，对一些难以控制、治理费用大的污染源增加排污，对其他的污染源则削减排放。到1986年，美国已初步建立了一整套较为完整的排污权交易体系。1990年，美国在控制二氧化碳、二氧化硫排放上首次实施了排污权交易，并取得了成功，所花费用只有采取"逐厂控制"措施所需费用的一半。

排污权交易是在某一区域范围内根据环境纳污能力，在实行总量控制的前提下，政府通过市场将排污权分配给企业，体现出较强的公平性和效率性，有

---

① 谷文艳：《美国环保产业发展及其推动因素》，《国际资料信息》2000年第5期。

助于区域经济发展和环境保护协调一致，因此，这一政策有很大的发展前景。

3. 增加环保资金投入，使环保产业发展具有原动力①

环保资金的投入是环保产业发展的保障。美国在减少污染、保护环境过程中所投入的资金量是相当可观的，而且呈增长势头。如1991年美国治理环境费用的总额达1290亿美元，1995年美国用于减少和控制污染的费用达1700亿美元。

美国环保资金的投入并非只由政府来承担，企业的参与也成为环保资金的重要来源。正是政府和企业在环保资金方面的大量投入，使用于污染防治的各种新技术、新产品不断开发和利用，促使环保产业更为兴旺和活跃。

4. 加速环保产业的技术创新，提高环保产业的国际竞争力

美国在经济、技术各个领域是一个全方位的超级大国，尤其在高新技术产业和新兴产业领域，为了保持其大国地位，除了在投入方面加以倾斜之外，更重要的是发挥美国在科技方面领域领先的优势，以科技优势推进环保产业的发展，保证环保产业与其他产业（尤其是高新技术产业）相匹配，在国际环保产业市场上占据领先的位置。

（二）英国的环保产业政策

英国环保产业发展面临许多困难，如法规、资金和市场及技术等。资金短缺非常突出，尤其在开业和拓展新业务时，资金更显不足。而投资者也往往不愿在环保产业投资，认为环保项目风险高、政策不稳定。

英国于1994年出台了《减少环保产业控制法案》，近年来英国为解决阻碍环保产业发展面临的瓶颈问题的主要措施包括：环保法规的改革和技术创新；研究与开发政策；高新技术在工业中的应用；促进和协助开发出口业务；国际贸易和国际环保政策；建立环保产业数据库。

当前，英国环保产业政策有以下特点和趋势②：

（1）环保产业基本政策中，增加对技术含量高的环保措施的支持。

（2）支持环保研究和开发。

（3）促进英国环保产业发展的国家战略。

（4）环保法规改革。

环保法规改革包括：①逐步规范英国各主要环保企业，促进英国环保产业

① 亦冬：《浅析美国成为环保产业大国中的政府行为》，《环境保护》2003年第10期。
② 章坚庭：《英国环保产业现状及发展趋向》，《全球科技经济瞭望》1999年第4期。

标准进入世界最高水平；②加强环保法规的实施管理，保证完全按英国和欧盟的标准执行；③研究制定遵守环保法规的优惠政策，以鼓励厂家积极选用创新环保技术，积极创造研究与开发支持条件，向环保投资者提供税收优惠政策；④利用政府采购计划来激发国内环保技术和服务市场的发展，加大英国环保基础设施建设的投入。

（5）环保技术与服务国际化。

（6）开发环保技术与服务创新技术研究的新途径，以期在鼓励创新活动管理方面取得新突破，以减少创新活动的障碍。

（三）比利时的环保政策

比利时国家虽小，但它是欧盟的创始国之一，与西欧其他国家一样，在过去几十年的经济和社会发展中，比利时走过了一段漫长的弯路，吃够了"先污染、后治理"的苦果，并从中吸取了惨痛的教训。比利时联邦政府为重视本国的环境治理工作，早在 1991 年就制订了"环境技术研究与开发计划"。1995 年，政府再次综合研究和分析了全国的环境现状，并重点围绕大气、水、垃圾和土壤四个环境领域，开展各种研究与技术开发活动。其政策要点可归纳为[1]：

（1）围绕大气、水、垃圾和土壤四大环境领域，联邦政府和各大行政区政府加强组织和协调，并给予有力的财政支持。

（2）积极支持和扶持工业企业（包括中小企业）参与环保新技术、新工艺和新产品的开发。

（3）每项技术的开发确保其高技术的特点及长期的安全性，并能适应多种环保领域，而不应只限于某一个领域。

（4）组织精兵强将（重点是科研机构和企业）共同攻克大型环保设备的技术难题，研制并开发本国新一代高水平设备和装置。

（5）制定各类环保新产品的统一国际标准。

（6）加强环境领域的各种专职人员和技术干部培训，为未来的环境保护培养和储备优秀专业人才。

（7）加强国际合作，特别是加强与欧盟和各成员国之间的合作，积极参与欧盟研究与技术开发总体规划。

---

① 周宏春：《环保产业政策的国际比较》，《节能与环保》2002 年第 10 期。

三　世界有关国家的低碳经济政策与措施

（一）欧盟：向高能效低排放方向转型①

欧盟委员会提出的一揽子能源计划，旨在带动欧盟经济向高能效、低排放的方向转型，并以此引领全球进入"后工业革命"时代。

欧盟一直是应对气候变化的倡导者，积极推动国际温室气体的减排行动。自英国提出"低碳经济"之后，欧盟各国不同程度地给予积极评价并采取了相似的战略。

欧盟大力倡导低碳经济的原因同样来源于对保障整个欧盟体系能源和气候安全的考虑。作为世界第一大经济体系和第二大能源消费体系，欧盟本身的能源匮乏问题始终是其经济社会发展的最大障碍之一。

2009 年，整个欧盟是全球最大的石油和天然气进口者，其 82% 的石油和 57% 的天然气都来源于其他国家和地区，到 2025 年其油气进口率更将突破 93% 和 84%。这其中，能源最为匮乏的西欧发达国家（如法国和德国）将尤为依赖进口能源。20 世纪多次发生的"石油危机"，促使了欧盟各国对石油替代能源以及更加清洁安全的可再生能源的开发利用，而 2006 年开始的新一轮世界能源价格飙升以及之后两年俄罗斯分别与乌克兰和白俄罗斯之间的石油天然气纠纷对于欧盟国家所带来的影响，极大地凸显了欧盟潜在的能源危机和能源政策的脆弱性。

为了进一步推动能源供应的多元化以及实现《京都议定书》所规定的温室气体减排目标，欧盟各国领导人于 2007 年 3 月通过了欧盟委员会提出的一揽子能源计划，从而带动欧盟经济向高能效、低排放的方向转型，并以此引领全球进入"后工业革命"时代。

根据该计划，欧盟承诺到 2020 年将可再生能源占能源消耗总量的比例提高到 20%，将煤炭、石油、天然气等一次能源的消耗量减少 20%，将生物燃料在交通能耗中所占的比例提高到 10%。此外，欧盟单方面承诺到 2020 年将温室气体排放量在 1990 年的基础上减少 20%，如果其他的主要国家采取相似行动则将目标提高至 30%，到 2050 年希望减排 60% ~ 80%。而 2007 年年底，欧盟委员会通过了欧盟能源技术战略计划，明确提出鼓励推广"低碳能源"

---

① 《经济日报》2009 年 3 月 25 日第 11 版。

技术，促进欧盟未来能源可持续利用机制的建立和发展。

以法国和德国为首的欧盟主要国家的政府长期以来在节能和环保领域投入巨大，促进了环境、能源及相关产业的技术升级。与此同时，欧盟国家利用其在可再生能源和温室气体减排技术等方面的优势，积极推动应对气候变化和温室气体减排的国际合作，力图通过技术转让为欧盟企业进入发展中国家能源环保市场创造条件。

（二）英国推行低碳经济的实践

英国是最早提出"低碳"概念并积极倡导低碳经济的国家。2003 年，英国政府《能源白皮书》提出了四个目标：一是在 2050 年之前将英国二氧化碳排放量减少 60% 左右，并在 2020 年取得切实进展；二是保证可靠的能源供应；三是在英国和更广泛的范围内促进有竞争力的市场；四是保证每个英国家庭在经济能力可承受范围内，获得最充分的供热。

为实现以上目标，英国采取的主要措施[1]有以下几个方面。

1. 建立自由化和有竞争优势的市场

自由、有竞争优势的市场是能源政策的基础。精心设计的市场体制具有良性竞争能力，能产生合理的价格，提供更为安全的能源，选择更多，并且在市场机制下真正体现货币的价值。

2. 推行相关标准和条例

英国推行《能源效率标准》和修订新的《建筑物监管条例》来提高能源使用效率，减少二氧化碳排放量。在推行《能源效率标准》时，英国环境食品与农村事务部（Department for Environment, Food and Rural Affairs, DEFRA）确立整体目标以及相关法规；能源市场管理局（Office of Gas and Electricity Markets, OFGEM）负责管理监督工作；而供应商则既期望能进一步有效利用能源，同时又想要优先节约家庭能源消耗。

3. 利用可再生能源

可再生能源在降低碳排放量方面也起到重要作用，同时通过开发更清洁的技术、产品及工艺来提高能源的可靠性，改善行业竞争能力。到 2003 年，英国有 3% 的电力供应来自可再生能源。目前英国政府已经制定了如下目标：只要成本能被消费者接受，到 2010 年英国可再生能源的发电量占总发电量的

---

① 靳志勇：《英国实行低碳经济能源政策》，《全球科技经济瞭望》2003 年第 10 期。

10%。也就是说，英国每年需要新增 1250 兆瓦的可再生能源发电。与此同时，为了达到 2050 年减少 60% 的二氧化碳排放量的目标，英国需要增加 30% ~ 40% 的可再生能源发电。

英国的实践证明，经济增长和低碳排放是可以同时实现的。向低碳前进，既是应对气候变化的方法，又是经济繁荣的机会。在过去 10 年间，英国实现了 200 年来最长的经济增长期，经济增长了 28%，温室气体排放减少了 8%。英国的成功经验主要可以概括为两个方面①：

一方面，通过立法应对气候变化。近年来，英国一直把应对气候变化、发展低碳技术与经济作为英国经济社会发展的重要战略。2007 年 6 月，英国公布了《气候变化法案》草案，明确承诺到 2020 年，削减 26% ~ 32% 的温室气体排放，到 2050 年，实现温室气体的排量降低 60% 的长远目标。法案提出要成立气候变化委员会，专门负责就英国在碳减排方面的投入、政策机制等具体问题向政府提出建议。法案还制订了未来 15 年的计划，为促成碳减排这一重要目标的实现、确保企业和个人向低碳科技领域投资提供了一个明确的框架。

另一方面，积极应用政策工具是英国发展低碳经济的另一举措。

在家庭领域，英国政府提出到 2016 年所有新建住宅全面实现零碳排放。政府的环境、食品与乡村事务部设立了碳信托基金，提供节能服务和贷款等；家用电器采用欧盟标准；运用降低增值税等财政工具，制定燃料贫困补助措施；为居民提供信息和建议；设立节能信托基金，负责提供绿色住房服务、建立能源标识、建筑节能绩效证书制度等。

在企业领域，英国政府规定 20 兆瓦以上机组都要加入碳排放交易系统；设立"碳信托"基金，负责提供碳管理、能源审计和贷款（对中小型企业提供低息或无息贷款）等服务，安装智能计量表，建立建筑能效证书制度；引入财政激励，推出了"气候变化税"，政府与重工业能源用户签订自愿协议，如果他们能够通过新的投资实现较低的排放，就不需要支付全税，最高可免税 80%。

英国还积极倡导碳捕获与埋存（CCS）技术。在与低碳经济相关的众多技术创新方面，英国政府尤其关注碳捕获与埋存（CCS）技术对于在世界范围内实现温室气体控制目标所能够起到的关键作用。

---

① 《经济日报》2009 年 3 月 25 日第 11 版。

（三）意大利的低碳经济发展政策

当前，意大利正在大力发展低碳经济，甚至是零碳经济，主要是通过节能减排的政策和措施以及技术开发来影响意大利的经济政策和经济发展。由于意大利的能源80%以上都依靠进口，因此意大利更加注重可再生能源和新能源的开发和利用，更加重视伴随着《京都议定书》的实施、欧洲总体能源政策以及世界能源市场变化带来低碳经济的发展。

由于意大利政府重视落实《京都议定书》的义务，其采取的政策措施主要是通过提高能源效率、发展可再生能源并鼓励低碳技术的开发，以降低主要能源生产和消耗领域的二氧化碳排放水平，包括鼓励可再生能源发展的"绿色证书"制度、新近出台的2015法案中的能源一揽子计划以及向欧盟提出的能源效率行动计划等。

1. "绿色证书"制度

为支持可再生能源的发展，意大利政府从1992年开始实施所谓的CIP6机制，以保证购买价格的方式支持可再生能源发电厂的建设。根据可再生能源项目的建设费用、运行和维护费用、燃料费用、促进发展的费用以及可再生能源设备的种类、全部或部分用于可再生能源和能源产品是全部出售或是仅出售剩余产品等不同情况，规定了不同的购买价格，从政策导向上推动可再生能源的发展。1999年以后，意大利通过立法的形式开始实行"绿色证书"制度。

2. 能源效率行动计划

根据欧盟的节能目标：2016年能源消耗节约9%，意大利向欧盟提出了能源效率行动计划以及已经实施和即将实施的措施。其行动包括三个方面。

（1）已经实施的措施继续实施几年，如对建筑物进行能源认证，给予石油液化气减少税赋，建立生态汽车园以及减少污染的激励措施；对农业能源系统的优惠措施，对高效率工业电机的税收减免；对高效率家用电器的税收减免；推动高产出的联合发电装置等。

（2）即将实施和正在讨论的一些措施。如欧盟关于生态设计的法令：规定所有产品或服务，都必须有符合欧盟规定的能耗标签。

（3）从2009年开始，将汽车二氧化碳平均排放限制在140克/公里，并相应节能23260亿千瓦时/年，占总节能目标的18%。

（四）德国发展低碳经济的政策措施

德国作为发达的工业国家，能源开发和环境保护技术处于世界前列。德国政府实施气候保护高技术战略，将气候保护、减少温室气体排放等列入其可持续发展战略中，并通过立法和约束性较强的执行机制制定气候保护与节能减排的具体目标和时间表。

1. 实施气候保护高技术战略

为实现气候保护目标，从 1977 年开始，德国联邦政府先后出台了 5 期能源研究计划，最新一期计划从 2005 年开始实施，以能源效率和可再生能源为重点，通过德国"高技术战略"提供资金支持。2007 年，德国联邦教育与研究部又在"高技术战略"框架下制定了气候保护高技术战略。

2. 提高能源使用效率，促进节约

（1）征收生态税。生态税是以能源消耗为对象的从量税，是德国改善生态环境和实施可持续发展计划的重要政策。

（2）鼓励企业实行现代化能源管理。发挥工业经济巨大的节能潜力是德国气候保护的重要目标。德国工业还蕴藏着巨大的提高能效的潜力，如动力装置、照明系统、热量使用和锅炉设备等都有进行节能改造的空间。德国政府计划在 2013 年之前与工业界签订协议，规定企业享受的税收优惠与企业是否实行现代化能源管理挂钩。对于中小企业，德国联邦经济部与德国复兴信贷银行已建立节能专项基金，用于促进德国中小企业提高能源效率，基金主要为企业接受专业节能指导和采取节能措施提供资金支持。

（3）推广"热电联产"技术。德联邦政府为支持热电联产技术的发展和应用，制定了《热电联产法》（2002 年 4 月生效）。该法主要规定了以热电联产技术生产出来的电能获得的补贴额度，如 2005 年年底前更新的热电联产设备生产的电能，每千瓦可获补贴 1.65 欧分。德国政府计划，到 2020 年将热电联产技术供电比例较目前水平翻一番。

（4）实行建筑节能改造。德国政府计划每年拨款 7 亿欧元用于现有民用建筑的节能改造，另外还有 2 亿欧元用于地方设施改造，目的是充分挖掘建筑以及公共设施的节能潜力。

3. 大力发展可再生能源

政府通过《可再生能源法》保证可再生能源的地位，对可再生能源发电进行补贴，平衡了可再生能源生产成本高的劣势，使可再生能源得到了快速发展。在广泛发展各种可再生能源的同时，德国也确定了以下几个重点领域。

（1）促进现有风力设备更新换代、发展海上风力园。

（2）促进可再生能源的使用。德国 1991 年出台了《可再生能源发电并网法》，规定了可再生能源发电的并网办法和足以为发电企业带来利润的收购价格。

（3）德国还制定了《可再生能源供暖法》，促进可再生能源用于供暖，计划到 2020 年，将可再生能源供暖的比例提高到 14%（2006 年为 6%）。

4. 减少二氧化碳排放

（1）发展低碳发电站技术。德国政府认为，尽管可再生能源发展迅速，但褐煤和石煤发电站在中期和长期内还将继续发挥作用，因此必须发展效率更高、应用清洁煤技术的发电站。

（2）降低各种交通工具的二氧化碳排放。针对机动车，德国目前新售出汽车的平均二氧化碳排量约为 164 克/公里，而根据欧盟规定，到 2012 年新车二氧化碳排量应达到 130 克/公里。

对于载重汽车，德国自 2005 年开始在联邦高速公路和几条重要的联邦公路上对 12 吨以上的卡车征收载重汽车费，此举对提高货运效率、增加低排量汽车比例起到了积极的作用。

针对空运，德国政府积极主张将其列入欧洲二氧化碳排量交易系统中，以促进竞争。同时，德国政府也支持"欧洲航空一体化"建议，希望通过一体化将航空领域产生的二氧化碳减少 10%。

（3）排放权交易。德国于 2002 年开始着手排放权交易的准备工作，当时联邦环保局设立了专门的排放交易处，并起草相关法律，目前已形成了比较完善的法律体系和管理制度。

（五）日本：低碳行动计划草案使减排目标具体化[①]

2007 年，日本提出了新的防止全球变暖对策——"福田蓝图"，其减排长期目标是到 2050 年温室气体排放量比目前减少 60% ~ 80%。2007 年 7 月 26 日，日本政府公布了为实现低碳社会而制订的行动计划草案，其中包括大幅度降低太阳能发电设备价格等内容。与此同时，日本一直重视能源多样化，并在提高能源使用效率方面做出了很多努力。

日本是《京都议定书》的发起和倡导国，由于国内的能源资源匮乏，日

---

① 《经济日报》2009 年 3 月 25 日第 11 版。

本一直重视能源的多样化，并在提高能源使用效率方面做出了很多努力。日本投入巨资开发利用太阳能、风能、光能、氢能、燃料电池等替代能源和可再生能源，并积极开展潮汐能、水能、地热能等方面的研究。

日本还通过各项法规和激励措施，鼓励和推动节能降耗。除了注重产业结构的调整，停止或限制高能耗产业发展，鼓励高能耗产业向国外转移外，日本还制订了节能规划，对节能指标做出了具体的规定，对一些高耗能产品制定了特别严格的能耗标准。

日本将光伏发电作为重点领域来推动，并提出在 2030 年前将太阳能发电量提高 20 倍。仅夏普公司的光伏发电设备就占到世界的 1/3，在日本排名第 2～4 位的企业的光伏发电设备也占到 24%。如今，日本已经成为全球最大的光伏发电设备出口国，占据了市场主导地位。2007 年 5 月，日本经济产业省提出一项新计划，决定在未来 5 年投入 2090 亿日元发展清洁汽车技术，目的不仅是要大大降低燃料消耗，而且要降低温室气体的排放量。

四 国外的可再生能源政策

国外鼓励可再生能源发展的政策主要体现在目标引导、价格激励、财政补贴、税收优惠、信贷扶持、出口鼓励、科研和产业化促进等方面。①

（一）目标引导

制定发展战略或发展路线图是世界上大多数国家的成功经验。许多发达国家发展可再生能源的思路是：国家制定一定阶段的可再生能源的具体发展目标和计划，在发展目标框架之下，制定一系列的优惠政策，并通过市场经济的手段鼓励各界投资和利用可再生能源。

1997 年欧盟颁布了《可再生能源发展白皮书》，规定 2010 年可再生能源要占欧盟总能源消耗的 12%，2050 年可再生能源在整个欧盟国家的能源构成中要达到 50% 的雄伟目标。2001 年欧盟部长理事会提出了关于使用可再生能源发电的共同指令，要求欧盟国家到 2010 年，可再生能源在其全部能源消耗中占 12%，在其电量消耗中可再生能源的比例达到 22.1% 的总量控制目标。欧盟成员国根据该指令，制定了本国的发展目标，如英国和德国都承诺，2010

---

① 李俊峰、时璟丽：《国内外可再生能源政策综述与进一步促进我国可再生能源发展的建议》，《可再生能源》2006 年第 1 期。

年和 2020 年可再生能源的比例将分别达到 10% 和 20%；西班牙表示，2010 年其可再生能源发电的比例就可以达到 29% 以上；丹麦制订了名为"21 世纪的能源"的能源行动计划，在 2030 年前，可再生能源在整个国家能源构成中的比例将每年增加 1%。北欧部分国家提出了利用风力发电和生物质能发电逐步替代核电的战略目标。

1999 年，澳大利亚宣布了支持可再生能源发展的国家目标，到 2010 年，可再生能源发电量应增加到 255 亿千瓦时，相当于全国总发电量的 12%；可再生能源的供应量将增加 2%。

日本自 1993 年开始实施"新阳光计划"，以加速光伏电池、燃料电池、氢能及地热能等的开发利用，1997 年又宣布了 7 万太阳能光伏屋顶计划，目标是到 2010 年安装 760 万千瓦的太阳能电池。

美国能源部提出了逐步提高绿色电力的发展计划，制定了风力发电、太阳能发电和生物质能发电的技术发展路线图，希望通过风力发电、太阳能发电、生物质能发电等来提高绿色能源的比例。

（二）价格激励

目前国际上可再生能源价格政策主要是针对电力产品。从表现形式上说，价格政策主要有以下几方面。

1. 固定价格

固定价格即政府直接明确规定各类可再生能源产品的市场价格。德国是这类价格政策的代表国家，德国通过法律的形式，根据可再生能源技术类型和项目资源条件，制定不同的可再生能源电价。世界上大约有 10 多个国家采用这种价格机制，主要在欧洲。这种机制的特点是可以根据政府的意愿，促进各种可再生能源技术的均衡发展，也可以推动某些可再生能源技术的优先发展。

2. 浮动价格

一些国家采用浮动价格，以常规电力的销售价格为参照系，制定一个合适的比例，然后随常规电力的市场变化而浮动。例如，西班牙政府规定可再生能源电价在常规电力销售电价 80% ~ 90% 的范围浮动，但每年具体的价格水平由发电企业和输电企业在浮动范围内协商确定。

3. 市场价格

通过强制配额（即要求能源企业在生产或销售常规电力的同时，必须生产或销售规定比例的可再生能源电量）和交易制度（政府对企业的可再生能源发电核发绿色交易证书，绿色交易证书可以在能源企业间买卖，价格由市场决定），发挥市场自身的调节作用，达到提升可再生能源产品价格的目的。此时的可再生能源发电价格为平均上网电价与绿色交易证书的价格之和。英国、澳大利亚和美国的部分州实施了这类政策。在这种情况下，政府制定了对未完成强制配额的企业予以惩罚的额度。这一额度往往成为可再生能源发电交易成本的上限。在此价格机制下，不同的可再生能源电力得到的是相同的价格，但价格水平随时都在随可再生能源市场供需情况而变，总价格又随电力市场的变化而浮动。

（三）财政补贴

财政补贴政策是最为常见的经济激励措施，形式多样。

1. 投资补贴

投资补贴即对可再生能源项目开发投资者进行直接补贴。在没有明确制定价格政策的国家，投资补贴非常普遍，并且覆盖多种可再生能源技术，如希腊对所有可再生能源项目提供投资额 30% ~50% 的补贴，瑞典提供 10% ~25%，印度为风电提供 10% ~15% 的投资补贴。在制定了价格政策的国家，投资补贴常常与价格政策互补，如比利时对可再生能源电力实施了优惠电价政策，对除了发电外的其他可再生能源项目提供 10% ~20% 的投资补贴。荷兰在绿色电价的基础上，对个人投资风电提供 20% 的补贴。除了固定电价外，西班牙还为投资成本高的光伏发电项目提供 40% 的补贴。英国也在统一的市场电价基础上，为投资成本高的海上风电项目提供 40% 的补贴。欧洲大多数国家还对个人投资或参股的可再生能源项目进行补贴。不论采取什么补贴形式，各国政府都有详细的规定可以参照。补贴机制的优点是可以调动投资者的积极性、增加生产能力、扩大产业规模，缺点是这种补贴与企业生产经营状况无关，不能起到刺激企业更新技术、降低成本的作用。

2. 产品补贴

产品补贴即根据可再生能源设备的产品产量进行补贴。这种补贴的优点显而易见，即有利于增加产量，降低成本，提高企业的经济效益，这也是美国、丹麦、印度目前正在实施的一种激励措施，如美国在其能源政策法规中制定的三项鼓励风电的措施之一是风电可以得到产品补贴。

3. 用户补贴

用户补贴即对消费者进行补贴。例如，欧洲大部分国家均对太阳能热水器的用户提供 20% ~60% 的补贴，澳大利亚为安装太阳能热水器系统的用户直接提供每套 500 澳元的补贴。对消费者的补贴也不是一成不变的，而是随市场的发展和技术的进步而调整，例如，日本对家庭用户安装光伏发电产品的补贴额度，起初是 40%，现在逐步降低到 10% 以下，并准备在适当的时候取消补贴。

（四）税收优惠

1. 可再生能源税收优惠

各国支持的方式不一样，技术领域也不同，如印度风力发电机整机进口关税税率为 25%，但对散件进口关税实行零税率；希腊对所有可再生能源项目和产品免税；丹麦对个人投资风电，葡萄牙、比利时、爱尔兰等国家对个人投资可再生能源项目均免征所得税；此外爱尔兰还对一般企业投资风能、生物质能、光伏和水电项目的资金免征企业所得税等。

2. 对非可再生能源实施强制性税收政策

如瑞典和英国对非可再生能源电力均征收电力税。强制性税收政策，尤其是高标准、高强度的收费政策，不仅能起到鼓励开发利用清洁能源的作用，而且能促使企业采用先进技术、提高技术水平。

（五）信贷扶持

低息或贴息贷款等金融政策可以减轻企业还本付息的负担，有利于降低生产成本，但政府需要筹集一定的资金以支持贴息或减息，贷款数量越大，贴息量越大，需要筹集的资金也越多。因此，资金供应状况是影响这一政策持续进行的关键性因素。目前德国对风电项目和光伏项目正在实施低利率贷款；意大利从 2001 年开始对在屋顶及建筑的其他部分安装小型光伏系统提供相当于项目投资 85% 的免息贷款。

（六）出口鼓励

发达国家主要利用对外援助渠道，包括为发展中国家提供各类赠款、政府贷款和混合贷款等，增加其本国设备制造企业的出口，帮助设备制造企业拓展海外市场。例如，丹麦、荷兰通过赠款和政府贷款，推动风机产品出口；西班牙、日本则利用援助渠道推动其太阳能产品出口。

（七）科研和产业化共同促进

除了利用上述政策在总体上推动可再生能源产业化发展之外，大多数国家还对本国的制造业予以强有力的扶持。

首先是科研先行。发达国家在科技和研发方面投入很大，如建立国家实验室和研究中心，为机构和企业提供技术指导、研发资金和补贴等技术支持。美国、丹麦、德国、西班牙、英国、印度等国家都有专门的国家可再生能源机构，统一组织和协调国家的可再生能源技术的研发和产业化推进。

其次是市场开拓。例如，丹麦和西班牙在其风力发电设备制造业发展的初期，均要求电力公司每年必须安装一定数量的风力发电机，支持设备制造企业迅速形成规模化生产能力。大多数欧洲国家在进出口信贷中均要求以购买其设备为前提，帮助企业开拓国际市场。

五 能源利用和应对气候变化的绿色技术对中国就业的影响

（一）影响的五大领域

经济的发展和人口居住结构的变迁，带来了一个严峻的挑战，即二氧化碳的排放。经济的增长和人口向城镇集聚，都可能带来更大规模的二氧化碳排放，将对环境产生深刻影响。但通过绿色技术的发展和应用，有可能在今后的发展过程中，找到实现可持续发展的重要机遇，也将给我国的就业带来新的气象，主要表现在五大领域，即以电力为主体的能源行业、以汽车使用为主体的交通运输行业、高排放的工业领域、建筑和家电领域、生态领域（包括农业和林业）。

第一，在能源领域，随着绿色能源技术的发展，必将采用更加清洁的能源来取代传统的石油和煤炭。即使在传统的石油和煤炭领域中，也将会因为绿色技术的发展使其内部结构产生变化，比如绿色煤炭、绿色发电等。二氧化碳捕获和储存，可能成为未来能源中极其重要的部分。中国有比较丰富的风力资源和太阳能资源，绿色能源中，最有发展潜力的是风能和太阳能的利用。伴随着绿色新技术的应用，必然会影响这些领域从业人员的技能结构，同时也会大量伴生新的职业形态。

第二，在高排放工业领域，实现绿色工业的价值观，最重要的技术是有效管理高排放工业的废弃物和城市生活的废弃物，并将这些废弃物通过新的技术转化为新的能源和材料。中国绿色工业的持续发展，需要将已投入到生活中的生活垃圾和工业垃圾转化为新的动力。在未来的发展中，随着废弃物利用技术的不断推广，从业人员技能结构必将随之发生变化，新职业也会不断产生。

第三，在绿色建筑和家电领域，设计和建造更加节能的公用和民用建筑已成为当今一个明显的趋势，即在建筑中使用更加节能的照明设备和其他家用电器，达到减少二氧化碳排放的目的。面对城镇化迅速发展的状态，这是未来社会可持续发展中一个不可忽视的重要领域。某些技术的利用将极大地减少和有效地控制因为人类活动所产生的二氧化碳排放。如一些企业的自有办公大楼中，开始启用一个新职业，他们被称为能源管理师，来解决建筑的能源使用和管理系统。很多企业的节能措施显然已经收到了明显的效果。当然更重要的是要设计和建造更加节能的建筑，使得我们的能源利用更加有效。再如有一个非常重要的、新的设计思想和设计技术，叫"被动设计"，并产生了一个新的职业，叫作被动设计师，就是如何有效利用既有条件，包括利用地形、气候等各种特征来使建筑的能源利用更加有效。

第四，在交通运输领域，绿化的路径可能是使用清洁能源、使用混合动力汽车，最终将大范围地使用电动汽车，以减少和控制排放。这种变化将使汽车的制造、销售、维修等环节，包括配套行业职业活动发生深刻变革。

第五，在绿色生态领域，绿色路径主要在能够大量造林，农业领域更好的水土保持及化肥的充分利用和有效管理，使我们的生态能够得到恢复和保存中国的碳汇。在这个领域，已经出现了一些新的职业，比如施肥指导师或化肥管理师，防止化肥滥用，充分利用肥效，最终减少化肥使用。

（二）总体趋势

总体而言，这些领域中的绿色革命可能产生的就业和职业变化的趋势如下。

首先，新职业的产生，如绿色煤电中整体煤气化联合循环技术的应用，正在产生对专业技术人员的需求；风能和太阳能的利用人员，将在未来的就业市场中成为极受欢迎的人才；城市废弃物管理技术人员，可以把垃圾变成动力的技术人员、碳捕获和储存的技术人员；等等。目前，能效技术工程师、能源管理师、节能工程师已开始在社会中发挥作用。

其次，技术变革引起的更多的是职业内部的调整，如在上述五大领域中，这些技术的利用必将使几乎所有的从业人员面临知识和技能的调整、更新和升级。同时，关联行业的从业人员也将发生技能调整。例如，城市规划工程师将需要理解和应用诸多绿色技术，他们的知识和能力结构势必发生重大调整。

最后，传统领域和传统岗位可能面临萎缩，甚至消失。比如，在电力领域，随着绿色电力技术的利用和机会的把握，传统能源的利用将呈下降趋势。整个能源工业体系中所留存的传统岗位及从业人员必将伴随总量的减少和结构的调整，产生岗位的萎缩和就业容量的减少。

有关数据表明，在很多绿色领域，由于新职业的产生，就业机会正在不断增长。据联合国统计，到 2030 年，仅风能领域的就业容量就将比 2005 年增长 7 倍。在中国，仅可再生能源领域所创造的就业量也是一个巨大的数字。据有关部门统计，2007 年，全国新能源行业的就业总量约为 110 万人。可见，这对于解决中国就业问题、促进绿色就业，无疑具有重大意义。

六　中国劳动力状况对能源利用和应对气候变化工作的影响

劳动力状况也会影响环境保护、能源利用和应对气候变化等领域的工作目标是否可以实现。劳动力素质和技能状况是影响绿色技术应用和推广的主要障碍之一。毫无疑问，环境保护、能源利用和应对气候变化等领域的绿色技术需要从业人员具备相应的技术知识或专业技能。但总体而言，我国劳动力素质相对不高，技能结构比较单一，这将是未来我国人力资源开发战略的重大挑战。绿色人才正在成为绿色技术应用的瓶颈。此外，绿色思维和绿色技能在现有的教育领域和其他社会经济政策中未能得到足够的重视，将成为制约我国绿色政策目标实现的重要因素。

七　社会伙伴对能源利用和应对气候变化的影响

一些社会伙伴，如工会组织和企业等，在实现环境保护、能源利用和应对气候变化等领域的工作目标中，也发挥着至关重要的作用。如节能减排政策的顺利开展、能源利用和应对气候变化措施的有效执行，都离不开工会的大力支持，更离不开企业的切实落实与积极配合。

第四章

中国绿色就业的相关法律政策

改革开放以来，中国经济高速增长，人民收入水平大幅度提高，大量人口摆脱了贫困。但是，中国的发展也是不平衡的，在经济增长获得巨大成就的同时，环境形势十分严峻，主要表现在：污染物排放量超过环境承载能力，许多城市空气污染严重，土壤污染面积扩大，生态破坏严重，水土流失量大面广，生物多样性减少，生态系统功能退化。发达国家上百年工业化过程中分阶段出现的环境问题，在我国近20多年来集中出现，呈现结构型、复合型、压缩型的特点。未来15年我国人口将继续增加，经济总量继续扩大，资源、能源消耗持续增长，环境保护面临的压力越来越大。但是，由于我国正处在工业化、城镇化快速发展阶段，面临着发展经济、消除贫困和减少污染的多重压力，为了促进就业、消除贫困和提高人民的生活水平，我国必须保持较高的经济增长速度；但在生态环境已受到严重破坏的情况下，中国必须改变粗放型增长和"先污染、后治理"的模式，大力发展绿色经济，促进绿色增长。

为了促进向绿色发展模式的转型，中国出台了一系列法律、法规和政策，建立了包括环境保护法律、产业政策，以及环境经济政策在内的法律政策框架体系。这些政策将环境保护作为新的经济增长点，使环保工作成为经济增长的商机和动力，而不是经济发展的额外成本和负担。这些政策的出台，将有助于协调环境保护和经济发展的关系，促进绿色产业的发展。2008年爆发了席卷全球的金融危机，尽管金融危机对我国的经济发展造成了一定的影响，但是这次金融危机也给经济结构调整带来了机遇。我国将节能减排和生态工程作为"扩内需、保增长"的重点之一，据估计4万亿元投资计划中将有约

2000 亿～3000亿元投向这一领域，这将极大地刺激传统就业岗位的转化和绿色就业岗位的创造。

一　绿色发展的立法和政策体系框架

对绿色发展和绿色就业的立法和政策体系框架如图 4 - 1 所示。

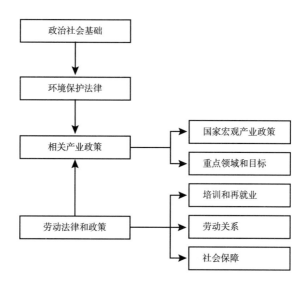

图 4 - 1　绿色发展和绿色就业的立法和政策体系框架

二　我国绿色发展的社会政治基础

1984 年 5 月国务院发布了《国务院关于环境保护工作的决定》，确立"保护和改善生活环境和生态环境，防治污染和自然环境破坏，是我国社会主义现代化建设中的一项基本国策"，并决定成立国务院环境保护委员会，负责研究审定有关环境保护的方针、政策和规划要求，并组织协调全国的环境保护工作。

《中共中央关于制定国民经济和社会发展第十一个五年规划的建议》提出，要大力发展循环经济，并将发展循环经济作为建设资源节约型、环境友好型社会和实现可持续发展的主要途径。2006 年 3 月国务院发布的《国民经济和社会发展第十一个五年规划纲要》（2006～2010 年）将节约资源作为我国的基本国策。

在对待环境保护与经济建设的关系问题上，中国政府的工作重心从 2006

年开始发生了根本性的调整。[①] 1989 年出台的《环境保护法》第四条规定"环境保护工作同经济建设和社会发展相协调",其实质是经济建设优先于环境保护。但是,2006 年的第六次全国环境保护大会上,温家宝总理强调要从重经济增长轻环境保护转变为保护环境与经济增长并重,在保护环境中求发展。该次大会之后,2006 年 2 月国务院出台了《国务院关于落实科学发展观加强环境保护的决定》,把环境保护摆上更加重要的战略位置,提出"经济社会发展必须与环境保护相协调",从根本上提高了环境保护工作的地位,将环境保护与经济发展并重。此外,该决定还提出加强环境保护,大力发展循环经济,积极发展环保产业和相关产业发展,培育新的经济增长点和增加就业,这为绿色就业发展提供了政治基础。

2006 年 10 月,在中共中央《关于构建社会主义和谐社会的若干重大问题的决定》中,把"资源利用效率显著提高,生态环境明显好转"作为构建社会主义和谐社会的九大目标之一,要求转变增长方式,提高发展质量,推进节约发展、清洁发展、安全发展,实现经济社会全面可持续发展。

2007 年 5 月,国务院颁布了《中国应对气候变化国家方案》,提出了中国应对气候变化的指导思想、原则与目标,中国应对气候变化的相关政策和措施。2009 年 8 月,全国人大常务委员会通过了《关于积极应对气候变化的决议》,是我国最高立法机构首次就应对气候变化问题做出决议。决议着重从五个方面阐述了积极应对气候变化的切实措施:一是强化节能减排,努力控制温室气体排放;二是增强适应气候变化能力;三是充分发挥科学技术的支撑和引领作用;四是立足国情发展绿色经济、低碳经济;五是把积极应对气候变化作为实现可持续发展战略的长期任务纳入国民经济和社会发展规划,明确目标、任务和要求。

三 环境保护相关立法

1979 年 9 月 13 日由第五届全国人大第十一次会议通过的《环境保护法(试行)》,是我国第一部关于环境保护的法律;此后我国环境立法工作不断推进,具有中国特色的环境与资源保护法律体系已经基本形成。中国环境立法演

---

① 孙佑海:《改革开放以来我国环境立法的经验和存在问题》,《中国地质大学学报》(社会科学版)2008 年第 8 (4)期。

变的总体趋势是从末端治理到清洁生产，发展循环经济；从污染控制到生态保护；从以行政命令为主导的环境管理到利用技术、经济、法律、教育等多种手段的环境管理；从强调国家在环境管理中的作用到强调政府、企业、公民在环境保护过程中的综合作用。①

（一）我国的环境和自然资源保护法律概况

在全国层面，我国的环境和自然资源保护立法大致包括以下几类。

第一类为综合性的环境保护法律，主要是《环境保护法》。《环境保护法》是国家对环境保护的方针、政策、原则、制度和措施的基本规定，其特点是原则性和综合性的法律规范。这部法律确定的基本原则包括：将环境保护纳入经济和社会发展计划，实行经济发展与环境保护相协调的原则；以防为主、防治结合、综合治理的原则；环境影响评价制度、排污收费制度、限期治理制度、许可制度等。

第二类是以环境污染防治和公害控制为目的的法律法规。主要是针对大气、水、固体废物、噪声、放射性污染防治方面的法律，以及与之配套的环境质量标准和污染物排放标准。包括《固体废物污染环境防治法》《水污染防治法》《大气污染防治法》，以及《水污染防治法实施细则》等。

第三类为自然生态与资源保护方面的法律，包括《土地管理法》《水法》《森林法》《草原法》《水土保持法》《野生动物保护法》等。

第四类为资源节约和综合利用方面的法律法规，如《节约能源法》。

第五类为促进循环经济和清洁生产的法律法规，如《清洁生产促进法》《可再生能源法》，以及《循环经济促进法》。

第六类为关于特定环境行政制度的法律，以及国务院和主管行政部门颁布的配套规章，如《环境影响评价法》《建设项目环境保护管理条例》《建设项目环境影响评价文件分级审批规定》。

（二）主要立法简介

1.《可再生能源法》（2006年1月1日生效）

《可再生能源法》将可再生能源的开发利用列为能源发展的优先领域，鼓励和支持可再生能源并网发电，鼓励清洁、高效地开发利用生物质燃料，鼓励

---

① 李勇进等：《中国环境政策演变和循环经济发展对实现生态现代化的启示》，《中国人口·资源与环境》2008年第5期。

发展能源作物，鼓励单位和个人安装和使用太阳能热水系统、太阳能供热采暖和制冷系统、太阳能光伏发电系统等太阳能利用系统。《可再生能源法》还提出鼓励和支持农村地区的可再生能源开发利用。为此，将提供再生能源发展专项资金、财政贴息的优惠贷款，以及税收优惠。

2.《节约能源法》（修改后的《节约能源法》于2008年4月1日起生效）

《节约能源法》规定"节约资源是我国的基本国策，国家实施节约与开发并举、把节约放在首位的能源发展战略"。《节约能源法》进一步加强了对工业节能的规范，力图从法律层面保证节能减排工作的深入。修改后的《节约能源法》强调对"重点用能单位"加强监管，规定"重点用能单位"应当每年向管理节能工作的部门报送上年度的能源利用状况报告。

修改后的《节约能源法》明确了我国将在节能方面采取的激励政策，包括对生产、使用法律规定推广目录的需要支持的节能技术、节能产品，实行税收优惠等扶持政策；通过财政补贴支持节能照明器具等节能产品的推广和使用，在政府采购中优先列入取得节能产品认证证书的产品、设备；在金融支持方面，法律规定国家引导金融机构增加对节能项目的信贷支持，实行有利于节能的价格政策，来引导用能单位和个人节能。

此外，《节约能源法》还规定，实行节能目标责任制和节能考核评价制度，将节能目标完成情况作为对地方人民政府及其负责人考核评价的内容。

3.《循环经济促进法》（2009年1月1日生效）

《循环经济促进法》规定在生产、流通和消费等过程中实行减量化、再利用、资源化；在技术可行、经济合理和有利于节约资源、保护环境的前提下，按照减量化优先的原则实施。此外，《循环经济促进法》为促进循环经济发展做出了一系列重大的制度安排。

● 建立循环经济规划制度。要求县级以上人民政府及有关部门编制国民经济和社会发展规划及年度计划，编制环境保护、科学技术等规划，应当包括发展循环经济的内容。

● 建立总量调控制度。县级以上地方人民政府应当依据上级人民政府下达的本行政区域主要污染物排放、建设用地和用水总量控制指标，规划和调整本行政区域的产业结构，促进循环经济发展。

● 建立生产者责任延伸制度。《循环经济促进法》区分不同情况，对生产者等主体在产品废弃后应当承担的回收、利用、处置等责任做了明确规定。

● 对重点企业实行重点管理。对钢铁、有色金属、煤炭、电力、石油加工、化工、建材、建筑、造纸、印染等行业年综合能源消费量、用水量超过国家规定总量的重点企业，实行能耗、水耗的重点监督管理制度。

● 强化产业政策的规范和引导。《循环经济促进法》强调产业政策的制定应当符合发展循环经济的要求。

● 建立合理的激励机制，主要包括：设立循环经济发展专项资金；对循环经济重大科技攻关项目实行财政支持；对促进循环经济发展的活动给予税收优惠；对有关循环经济项目实行投资倾斜；实行有利于资源节约和合理利用的价格政策等。

4.《废弃电器电子产品回收处理管理条例》（2011 年 1 月 1 日生效）

● 国家对废弃电器电子产品实行多渠道回收和集中处理制度。

● 国家对废弃电器电子产品处理实行资格许可制度。

● 国家建立废弃电器电子产品处理基金，用于废弃电器电子产品回收处理费用的补贴。电器电子产品生产者、进口电器电子产品的收货人或者其代理人应当按照规定履行废弃电器电子产品处理基金的缴纳义务。

● 明确了生产者、销售者、回收经营者、处理企业应当承担的责任。例如，生产者、进口电器电子产品的收货人或者其代理人生产、进口的电器电子产品应当符合国家有关电器电子产品污染控制的规定，采用有利于资源综合利用和无害化处理的设计方案，使用无毒无害或者低毒低害以及便于回收利用的材料；电器电子产品销售者、维修机构、售后服务机构的责任是在其营业场所显著位置标注废弃电器电子产品回收处理提示性信息。

四 国家关于绿色发展的产业政策

我国在促进绿色发展方面的产业政策有以下特点。

（一）通过采取不同政策取向，促进产业结构调整，形成低投入、低消耗、低排放和高效率的节约型增长方式

国家控制高耗能、高污染行业过快增长，鼓励发展低能耗、低污染的先进生产能力。2005 年 11 月，国务院通过了《促进产业结构调整暂行规定》；12 月，经国务院批准，国家发展和改革委员会发布了《产业结构调整指导目录》。这些文件划分了重点鼓励、限制和淘汰的三类产业，并采取了不同的政策取向。

1. 鼓励类产业

主要生产对经济社会发展有重要促进作用，有利于节约资源、保护环境、产业结构优化升级，需要采取政策措施予以鼓励和支持的关键技术、装备及产品。对鼓励类投资项目给予信贷支持、税收优惠，以及其他优惠政策支持。

2. 限制类产业

主要生产工艺技术落后，对产业结构没有改善；不利于安全生产；不利于资源和能源节约；不利于环境保护和生态系统的恢复；低水平重复建设比较严重、生产能力明显过剩的产业。对属于限制类的新建项目，投资管理部门不予审批、核准或备案，各金融机构不得发放贷款，土地管理、城市规划和建设、环境保护、质检、消防、海关、工商等部门不得办理有关手续。

3. 淘汰类产业

主要生产不符合有关法律法规规定，严重浪费资源、污染环境、不具备安全生产条件、需要淘汰的落后工艺技术、装备及产品。对淘汰类项目，禁止投资，各金融机构应停止各种形式的授信支持，并采取措施收回已发放的贷款，各地区、各部门和有关企业要采取有力措施，按规定限期淘汰。

《产业结构调整指导目录》包括农业、水利、煤炭、电力、交通、信息、钢铁、有色金属、石油化工、建材、机械、轻纺、服务业、环境和生态保护、资源节约及综合利用等 20 多个行业，其中鼓励类 539 条，限制类 190 条，淘汰类 399 条。

（二）建立重点行业环境准入制度

2006 年，国务院发布了《国务院关于加快推进产能过剩行业结构调整的通知》，提出运用经济、法律和必要的行政手段，推进产能过剩行业结构调整。一是要制定更加严格的环境、安全、能耗、水耗、资源综合利用和质量、技术、规模等标准，提高准入门槛。二是淘汰落后生产能力，依法关闭一批破坏资源、污染环境和不具备安全生产条件的小企业，分期分批淘汰一批落后生产能力，如淘汰达不到产业政策规定规模和安全标准的小煤矿。第三是推进技术改造，围绕提升技术水平、改善品种、保护环境、保障安全、降低消耗、综合利用等，对传统产业实施改造提高。

2007 年 11 月制订的《国家环境保护"十一五"规划》提出，在确定钢铁、有色、建材、电力、轻工等重点行业准入条件时充分考虑环境保护要求，新建项目必须符合国家规定的准入条件和排放标准，对于已无环境容量的区域，禁止新建增加污染物排放量的项目。2009 年 2 月，国家环境保护部提出将加强新建项目的环境准入，将逐步废除不利于环保的相关补贴和税收优惠政策，对达不到环保要求、严重污染环境的企业，取消其享受有关税收优惠政策。此外，将进一步拓展绿色贸易政策，定期公布企业污染物排放达标公告，凡未被列入达标公告的企业所生产的产品禁止出口，并在目前柠檬酸、电解铝等行业公告的基础上，逐步向其他重污染行业扩展。①

（三）发展循环经济，建设资源节约型、环境友好型社会

国家通过制定并实行《清洁生产促进法》《固体废物污染环境防治法》《循环经济促进法》《城市生活垃圾管理办法》《废弃电器电子产品回收处理管理条例》等法律法规，发布《促进产业结构调整暂行规定》《关于加快发展循环经济的若干意见》《"十一五"资源综合利用指导意见》以及《国家环境保护"十一五"规划》《中国应对气候变化的政策与行动》白皮书等政策文件，提出发展循环经济的总体思路、近期目标、基本途径和政策措施，并发布循环经济评价指标体系。

2006 年发布的《国民经济和社会发展第十一个五年规划纲要》（简称《纲要》）第六篇做出了关于发展循环经济的规划。《纲要》提出要落实节约资源和保护环境的基本国策，建设低投入、高产出，低消耗、少排放，能循环、可持续的国民经济体系和资源节约型、环境友好型社会。《纲要》提出发展循环经济，坚持开发节约并重、节约优先，按照减量化、再利用、资源化的原则，在资源开采、生产消耗、废物产生、消费等环节，逐步建立全社会的资源循环利用体系。

（四）优化能源结构

《节约能源法》《国民经济和社会发展第十一个五年规划纲要》《节能减排综合性工作方案》《国家环境保护"十一五"规划》《中国应对气候变化国家方案》以及《中国应对气候变化的政策与行动》提出要优化发展能源工业，有序发展煤炭，尽快提高可再生能源在能源结构中的比重，优化生产和消费结构。

《中国应对气候变化的政策与行动》强调，要把发展水电作为促进中国能

---

① http://www.chinaenvironment.com/view/ViewNews.aspx? k = 20090227103959087，环境保护网，2009 年 3 月 20 日。

源结构向清洁低碳化方向发展的重要措施；同时加快火力发电的技术进步，优化火电结构，加快淘汰落后的小火电机组，大力发展高效、洁净发电技术。要推进生物质能源的发展，以生物质发电、沼气、生物质固体成型燃料和液体燃料为重点，大力推进生物质能源的开发和利用。

开发利用可再生能源是开拓新的经济增长领域、促进经济转型、扩大就业的重要选择，可再生能源也是高新技术和新兴产业，快速发展的可再生能源已成为一个新的经济增长点，可以有效拉动装备制造等相关产业的发展，实现调整产业结构，促进经济增长方式转变，扩大就业。

五　绿色发展的主要目标和重点领域

（一）主要目标

《国民经济和社会发展第十一个五年规划纲要》提出了"十一五"期间万元国内生产总值能耗由 2005 年的 1.22 吨标准煤下降到 1 吨标准煤以下；单位工业增加值用水量降低 30%。"十一五"期间，主要污染物排放总量减少 10%，到 2010 年，二氧化硫排放量由 2005 年的 2549 万吨减少到 2295 万吨，化学需氧量（COD）由 1414 万吨减少到 1273 万吨；全国设市城市污水处理率不低于 70%，工业固体废物综合利用率达到 60% 以上。

（二）重点领域

1. 淘汰落后产能

加大淘汰电力、钢铁、建材、电解铝、铁合金、电石、焦炭、煤炭、平板玻璃等行业落后产能的力度。我国政府出台了水泥、电解铝、电力、钢铁等 13 个行业的结构调整指导意见，依法关闭了一批小火电、小钢铁、小水泥、小煤矿。这些关停措施对于节约能源、水资源和减少污染方面具有重要作用。例如，先进的钢铁厂和小钢铁厂在耗电、耗水、排污方面有着天壤之别：在耗电方面，某些经济大省小电炉钢厂吨钢约耗电 700 千瓦时，而这些地区比较先进的炼钢企业吨钢耗电仅 300 千瓦时；在耗水方面，许多小电炉钢厂生产用水基本不循环利用，废水直排入河，一些现代化钢铁企业生产用水循环率可以达到 98%；在排污方面，小电炉钢厂每立方米烟气含尘量达 500 毫克，而现代化钢铁企业仅 25 毫克。

电力行业是节能降耗和污染减排的重点领域。2007 年 1 月，国务院批转了国家发展改革委、能源办《关于加快关停小火电机组的若干意见》，提出了

"上大压小"政策，就是将新建电源项目与关停小火电机组挂钩，在建设大容量、高参数、低消耗、少排放机组的同时，相对应关停一部分小火电机组。"十一五"期间"上大压小"工作的具体目标是：一要确保全国关停小燃煤火电机组 5000 万千瓦以上；二要通过关停小火电机组，形成节约能源 5000 万吨标准煤以上、减少二氧化硫 160 万吨以上的能力；三要建成一批大型高效环保机组和其他清洁能源、可再生能源发电机组。2007 年我国共关停小火电机组553 台，共计 1438 万千瓦。

钢铁行业是节能减排的另外一个重点行业。2007 年，国家发展和改革委员会先后与 28 个省（区、市）签订了《关停和淘汰落后钢铁生产能力责任书》。根据责任书，"十一五"期间，我国将累计关停和淘汰炼铁能力 8917 万吨、炼钢能力 7776 万吨，涉及企业 917 家。2007 年，我国已经淘汰落后炼铁产能 4659 万吨、落后炼钢产能 3747 万吨。

水泥行业：到 2008 年年底全国将有 1066 家立窑水泥企业停止原来的生产，停产的立窑企业带来大约 32 万工人失业；[1]"十一五"期间淘汰落后水泥产能 2.5 亿吨。

有色金属行业：到 2009 年，淘汰落后铜冶炼产能 30 万吨、铅冶炼产能60 万吨、锌冶炼产能 40 万吨；到 2010 年年底，淘汰落后小预焙槽电解铝产能 80 万吨。

轻工行业：截至 2008 年年底，我国已经淘汰造纸落后产能 547 万吨、酒精落后产能 94.5 万吨、味精落后产能 16.5 万吨、柠檬酸落后产能 7.2 万吨。到 2011 年，我国将淘汰落后制浆造纸 200 万吨以上、低能效冰箱（含冰柜）3000 万台、皮革 3000 万标张、含汞扣式碱锰电池 90 亿只、白炽灯 6 亿只、酒精 100 万吨、味精 12 万吨、柠檬酸 5 万吨的生产能力。

纺织行业：加快关闭污染严重的印染企业；到 2011 年，重点淘汰 75 亿米高耗能、高耗水、技术水平低的印染能力；淘汰 230 万吨化纤落后产能；加速淘汰棉纺、毛纺落后生产能力。

石化行业：对炼油行业采取区域等量替代方式，到 2011 年，淘汰 100 万吨及以下低效低质落后炼油装置。对农药行业依据行政法规，淘汰一批高毒高风险农药品种。加快淘汰电石、甲醇等产品的落后产能。

---

[1] http://www.gghf.org.cn/xm/hd4-1.htm，国家落后产能转产基金，2009 年 6 月 9 日。

2. 工程减排，减少污染

在削减二氧化硫排放量方面，以火电厂建设脱硫设施为重点，加快现役火电机组脱硫设施的建设，使现役火电机组投入运行的脱硫装机容量达到 2.13 亿千瓦。新（扩）建燃煤电厂除国家规定的特低硫煤坑口电厂外，必须同步建设脱硫设施并预留脱硫场地。此外，以占工业二氧化硫排放量 65% 以上的国控重点污染源为重点，严格执行大气污染物排放标准和总量控制制度，加快推行排污许可制度。继续抓好煤炭、钢铁、有色、石油化工和建材等行业的废气污染源控制。大力推进煤炭洗选工程建设，推广煤炭清洁燃烧技术。

控制固体废物污染，推进其资源化和无害化。实施危险废物和医疗废物处置工程和生活垃圾无害化处置工程，推进固体废物综合利用。到"十一五"末期，将建立 31 个升级危险废物集中处置中心，300 个设区市的医疗废物集中处理中心，以及技术支持和监管能力建设项目，总计投资需要 150 亿元。① 重点推进煤矸石、粉煤灰、冶金和化工废渣、尾矿等大宗工业固体废物的综合利用。到 2010 年，工业固体废物综合利用率达到 60%。推进建筑垃圾及秸秆、畜禽粪便等综合利用。建立生产者责任延伸制度，完善再生资源回收利用体系，实现废旧电子电器的规模化、无害化综合利用。

在废水处理方面，一是要加快城市污水处理与再生利用工程建设。到 2010 年，城市污水处理率不低于 70%，所有城市都要建设污水处理设施。为达到这一目标，将新增城市污水处理规模 5000 万吨/天，改造和完善现有污水处理厂及配套管网，投资 2100 亿元。② 二是加强工业废水治理。重点抓好占工业化学需氧量排放量 65% 的"国控重点企业"的废水达标排放和总量削减。

3. 节约能源，提高能源利用效率

工业、交通和建筑是节能的主要领域。2006 年发布的《国务院关于加强节能工作的决定》提出的措施包括如下内容。

一是工业节能，突出抓好钢铁、有色金属、煤炭、电力、石油石化、化工、建材等重点耗能行业和年耗能 1 万吨标准煤以上企业的节能工作。

二是推进建筑节能，大力发展节能省地型建筑，推动新建住宅和公共建筑

---

① http://www.gghf.org.cn/xm/hd4-1.htm，国家落后产能转产基金，2009 年 6 月 9 日。

② 国家环境保护总局科技标准司、中国环境保护产业协会编《中国环境保护产业市场供求指南（2006）》，中国环境科学出版社，2007。

严格实施节能 50% 的设计标准，直辖市及有条件的地区要率先实施节能 65% 的标准。

三是加强交通运输节能。积极推进节能型综合交通运输体系建设，加快发展铁路和内河运输，优先发展公共交通和轨道交通，加快淘汰老旧铁路机车、汽车、船舶，鼓励发展节能环保型交通工具，开发和推广车用代用燃料和清洁燃料汽车。

四是引导商业和民用节能。

4. 发展可再生能源，优化能源结构

对于未来可再生能源在我国能源结构中的战略定位是，2010 年前后，可再生能源占到能源消费的 10% 左右，战略定位是补充能源；2020 年前后，可再生能源占到能源消费的 15% 左右，战略定位是替代能源；2030 年前后，可再生能源占到能源消费的 25% 左右，战略定位是主流能源；2050 年前后，可再生能源占到能源消费的 40% 左右，战略定位是主导能源。

为实现这个战略目标，2008 年 3 月国家发展和改革委员会制定的《可再生能源发展"十一五"规划》提出，要加快发展水电、太阳能热利用、沼气等技术成熟、市场竞争力强的可再生能源，尽快提高可再生能源在能源结构中的比重。积极推进技术基本成熟、开发潜力大的风电、生物质能发电、太阳能发电、生物液体燃料等可再生能源技术的产业化发展，为更大规模开发利用可再生能源奠定基础。具体目标如下。

• 在水电方面，"十一五"时期，全国新增水电装机容量 7300 万千瓦。

• 在生物质能方面，到 2010 年，全国生物质能发电装机容量达到 550 万千瓦；增加非粮原料燃料乙醇年利用量 200 万吨，生物柴油年利用量达到 20 万吨；农村户用沼气池达到 4000 万户，建成大型沼气工程 6300 处，沼气年利用量达到 190 亿立方米；农林生物质固体成型燃料年利用量达到 100 万吨。初步实现生物质能商业化和规模化利用。

• 在风电方面，到 2010 年，风电总装机容量达到 1000 万千瓦。

• 太阳能方面，到 2010 年，太阳能热水器累计安装量达到 1.5 亿平方米，太阳能发电装机容量达到 30 万千瓦。

• 农村可再生能源方面，到 2010 年，全国户用沼气池达到 4000 万户，规模化养殖场沼气工程达到 4700 处，农村户用沼气年产气量达到 150 亿立方米；农村地区太阳能热水器的总集热面积达到 5000 万平方米，太阳灶保有量达到

100 万台。

5. 促进资源综合利用

资源综合利用方面的目标是，到 2010 年资源综合利用产业得到快速发展，资源利用效率有较大幅度提高，综合利用产品在同类产品中的比重逐步提高，形成一批具有一定规模、较高技术装备水平、资源利用率较高、废物排放量较低的综合利用企业。

资源综合利用的重点领域包括：矿产资源综合利用、"三废"综合利用、再生资源回收利用、农林废弃物综合利用。

"十一五"期间的资源综合利用的重点工程包括：①共、伴生矿产资源综合开发利用工程；②大宗固体废物资源化利用工程；③再生金属加工产业化工程；④废旧家用电器、废旧轮胎等再生资源产业化工程；⑤再生资源回收体系建设示范工程；⑥农业废弃物和木材综合利用工程。

6. 大力发展环保产业

《国民经济和社会发展第十一个五年规划纲要》将发展大型高效清洁发电装备，环保及资源综合利用装备作为振兴装备制造业的重点领域。

《国家环境保护"十一五"规划》提出，以环境保护重点工程为需求，大力发展环保装备制造业；以环境影响评价、环境工程服务、环境技术研发与咨询、环境风险投资为重点，积极发展环保服务业。例如，在资源综合利用方面，重点发展废品回收利用，再生水、微咸水、海水淡化等非常规水资源化，高效冷却节水，报废汽车、废旧轮胎、废旧家电、电子废物和尾矿再利用等。在污染治理设施建设运营和咨询服务方面，重点推进城市污水、垃圾、危险废物等环境设施建设运行市场化；规模化工业废水处理、电厂脱硫、除尘设施专业化运营；大力发展环境保护的技术咨询和管理服务。

7. 农业减排

减少农业、农村温室气体排放。通过继续推广低排放的高产水稻品种和半旱式栽培技术，采用科学灌溉技术；强化高集约化程度地区的生态农业建设，加强对动物粪便、废水和固体废弃物的管理，加大沼气利用力度等措施，努力控制甲烷排放增长速度。

8. 林业

国家林业局发布了《应对气候变化林业行动计划》（简称《行动计划》），贯彻落实《中国应对气候变化国家方案》中关于林业在应对全球变暖中的作用。《行动计划》提出了 22 项主要行动，包括林业减缓气候变化的 15 项行动和林业适应气候变化的 7 项行动。发展林业，应对气候变化的主要领域包括：实施林业重点生态工程，实施能源林培育和加工利用一体化项目，合理开发和利用生物质材料，加强木材高效循环利用等。全国森林覆盖率三个阶段性目标确定：2010 年达 20%，2020 年达 23%，2050 年达 26% 以上，森林碳汇能力不断提高并最终保持相对稳定。在造林方面，中国正在实施的六大林业重点工程，今后 10 年的造林任务达 0.76 亿公顷，预计可安置 2280 万人就业。生物质能林基地建设是我国政府应对气候变化的另外一个积极举措。根据国家林业局编制的《全国能源林建设规划》，"十一五"期间中国要建设能源林示范基地 1000 多万亩（66.7 万公顷）；到 2020 年，能源林达到 2 亿亩（1334 万公顷），可以提供 600 多万吨生物柴油，满足 1100 多万千瓦装机容量发电厂的燃料需求。

六　与绿色发展相关的劳动保障政策

向绿色发展模式转型对就业的影响体现在：第一，绿色职业和绿色岗位的增加。例如，可再生能源的发展会为新能源部门、相关制造部门、咨询服务部门创造大量的就业机会，如城市废弃物回收管理、火力发电厂的二氧化碳捕集、碳排放交易员、环境影响评估等岗位。第二，有些灰色岗位可能面临萎缩，甚至是消失。例如，传统能源利用行业，如水泥、钢铁、化工、有色金属等重点行业落后产能的淘汰，意味着不符合行业标准的企业被关闭、兼并重组或者企业的某些生产线被拆除，导致相关工作岗位消失。第三，现有岗位的工作内容和技能要求发生变化。例如，依赖化肥和农药的种植转向有机种植转变，农民需要掌握绿肥、通过生物控制有害昆虫等技术，城市规划工程师将需要理解和应用更多的绿色技术，火力发电设备升级改造后由原来的分体运行改为集控运行后，相关操作和技术人员工作内容和技能要求都会发生相应的变化。要保障传统岗位向绿色岗位的顺利转型和绿色岗位的开发，必须有相应的劳动保障政策提供支持。目前，我国在这方面的政策包括职业培训政策，就业促进政策，被关闭、兼并、转产企业的职工裁减、补偿、重新安置、转岗培训等政策。

（一）职业培训方面

1. 职业资格和职业培训体系

我国的职业培训体系包括就业前培训、在职培训、再就业培训。此外，我国还建立了职业标准和资格鉴定制度，由国家制定职业技能标准或任职资格条件，政府认定的考核鉴定机构对劳动者进行技能水平或职业资格的评价和鉴定，合格者获得相应的国家职业资格证书。国家职业资格证书分为五个等级，即初级（国家职业资格五级）、中级（国家职业资格四级）、高级（国家职业资格三级）、技师（国家职业资格二级）、高级技师（国家职业资格一级）。已经制定国家标准、与绿色就业相关的职业包括环境影响评价工程师、再生资源回收工、污水处理工，以及太阳能利用工等。

对从事技术复杂、通用性广，涉及国家财产、人民生命安全和消费者利益的职业（工种）的劳动者，必须经过培训，并取得职业资格证书后，方可就业上岗，如沼气生产工。

2. 鼓励实训基地建设，提高职业院校毕业生的技能和实操能力

从2004年开始，中央财政职业教育专项资金将对符合条件的各级各类职业院校实训基地进行扶持，以提高职业院校学生的技能水平和实操能力。中央财政专项资金支持的职业教育实训基地的模式包括两种：区域综合性实训基地和专业性实训基地。该项目启动初期，中央财政将重点扶持建设数控技术、汽车维修技术、计算机应用与软件技术、电工电子技术、建筑技术等5个专业领域的实训基地，后来重点扶持的专业领域逐步扩大，2009年，教育部规定专业性实训基地项目将以八个领域为重点，同时兼顾能源环保等专业。中央财政专项资金重点支持以下几类院校和培训机构：一是以就业为导向，培养大量社会紧缺的技能型人才，毕业生就业率高的；二是在深化职业教育教学改革、加强校企合作等方面都有所突破和创新的；三是在社会培训、下岗职工再就业培训、农村劳动力转移培训等方面做出突出贡献的。中央财政资金主要用于实训基地设备更新和购置。对于中央财政支持的中等职业学校实训基地建设，地方财政要提供配套资金。

3. 鼓励学生参加中等职业教育

中等职业学校1~2年级农村户籍的学生、县和镇的非农户口学生，以及城市家庭经济困难学生每生每年可获得1500元补助。

4. 大力推行针对农民工的职业技能培训

中国共产党十七大明确提出加强农村劳动力转移就业培训。此后，有关部门制订了由财政支持的农民工培训计划，其重点是职业技能培训。技能培训是结合农村劳动力转移的地区、产业、职业目标，以及农村劳动力在适应转移就

业方面存在的技能欠缺，有针对性地开展相关技能培训。例如，2003 年农业部、劳动保障部等六部委共同制订的 2003 ~ 2010 年全国农民工培训规划。2005 年劳动保障部制订了农村劳动力技能就业计划，提出 5 年内对 4000 万进城务工的农村劳动者开展职业培训。

5. 鼓励企业开展职工培训，提高其职业技能水平

《高技能人才培养体系建设"十一五"规划纲要》（2006 ~ 2010 年）鼓励企业加大对生产、服务一线技能劳动者，特别是高技能人才[①]培训工作的经费投入。企业要按相关规定足额提取职工工资总额的 1.5% ~ 2.5% 作为职工教育经费，重点保证高技能人才培养。

企业进行技术改造和项目引进，应按规定比例提取职工技术培训经费，并列入项目成本。对自身没有能力开展职工培训，以及未开展高技能人才培训的企业，县级以上地方政府可依法对其职工教育经费实行统筹，由劳动保障部门统一组织培训服务。

职工经单位同意参加脱产半脱产培训，应享受在岗人员同等工资福利待遇。对参加当地紧缺职业（工种）高技能人才培训、达到相应职业资格且被企业聘用的人员，企业可给予一定的培训和鉴定费补贴。

6. 应对金融危机的特别职业培训计划

为应对国际金融危机对我国的影响，保持就业局势稳定，人力资源和社会保障部、国家发展和改革委员会、财政部决定实施特别职业培训计划，从2009 ~ 2010 年，重点对四类群体开展有针对性的职业培训。

一是对困难企业在职职工开展在岗的技能提升培训和转岗转业培训，是该计划的核心内容。工作的重点是在受金融危机影响大、职工人数多、生产经营困难的大中型企业积极开展职工在岗培训。开展这方面培训所需资金按规定从企业职工教育培训经费中列支，不足部分可由企业所在地政府就业专项资金予以适当支持。困难企业可凭相关证明，向当地人力资源和社会保障、财政部门提出申请，经人力资源和社会保障部门审核、财政部门复核后，由当地财政部门按最高不超过培训费用 50% 的标准，将补贴资金直接拨入企业在银行开立

---

① "高技能人才"是指在生产、运输和服务等领域岗位一线的从业者中，具备精湛专业技能，在关键环节发挥作用，能够解决生产操作难题的人员。主要包括技能劳动者中取得高级技工、技师和高级技师职业资格及相应职级的人员。

的基本账户。

二是对失去工作返乡的农民工开展职业技能培训或创业培训。可根据农民工转移就业要求和劳务输出意愿开展技能培训，为其今后继续外出打工创造条件；也可根据当地产业结构调整、企业技术改造和新开工建设项目的需求，积极组织开展订单培训。同时，要对具备一定的创业意识和创业条件的返乡农民工，组织其参加创业培训，帮助他们提高自谋职业和自主创业的能力。农民工参加各类职业培训，可按规定由就业专项资金和相关专项资金给予补贴。

三是对失业人员开展 3～6 个月的中短期技能培训，帮助其实现再就业。失业人员大体分为两类，一类是就业转失业人员（包括在城镇继续找工作的失业农民工），这类人有工作经验和一定的技能，要紧密结合当地重点拓展的就业领域、符合产业调整政策的行业和需要发展的职业（工种），重点开发面向城市社区就业的服务类技能培训项目，采取灵活多样的培训形式和手段，突出培训的实用性。另一类是已进行失业登记的大学生，这类人具备一定的理论知识却缺少实际工作技能，要结合其专业背景，组织其参加相关领域的技能培训，突出操作技能训练，提高其就业能力。对失业人员中有创业意愿和需求的，也可组织其参加创业培训。对各类失业人员开展培训所需的资金，可按规定由就业专项资金和失业保险基金给予补贴。

四是对新成长劳动力开展 6～12 个月的储备性技能培训，提高其就业能力。在特殊时期，对新成长劳动力开展培训，要适当延长培训期限。要采取有力措施，扩大技工院校招生，根据国家产业结构调整情况，指导学校根据劳动力市场需求预测情况，有计划地加快培养一批高素质的后备技能人才。有条件的地区还可以组织退役士兵等群体参加职业培训。对新成长劳动力开展培训所需资金，按规定由当地就业专项资金和相关专项资金给予补贴。

（二）促进下岗失业人员再就业的就业政策

1. 通过公共就业服务和再就业培训，促进下岗失业人员再就业

政府的公共就业服务机构为下岗失业人员提供免费就业服务；对帮助下岗失业人员再就业的民营职业介绍机构提供职业介绍补贴。对于参加培训的下岗失业人员提供培训费补贴，以及职业技能鉴定补贴。

2. 鼓励下岗失业人员自主创业

通过创业培训、定额减免税费和提供小额担保贷款等政策，鼓励下岗失业人员自主创业。下岗失业人员可以免费参加创业培训；对于符合条件的下岗失

业人员从事个体经营的，三年内免收行政事业性收费，并以每户每年8000元纳税额为限，对超过限额的税金予以减免；对缺乏经营资金的，给予5万元以下小额担保贷款及相应的财政贴息。

3. 鼓励企业雇用下岗失业人员

运用税收优惠、社会保险补贴、担保贷款和贴息等政策杠杆，鼓励企业雇用下岗失业人员。对于商贸、服务企业，按照新招下岗失业者人数，以每人每年4000元为限，三年内相应核减企业的纳税额，并给予社会保险补贴。对于符合条件的劳动密集型小企业，提供担保贷款和财政贴息。

4. 对困难群体实行就业援助

政府开发公益性岗位，优先安排就业困难人员，并给予社会保险费补贴和岗位补贴。对于从事灵活就业的人员，给予社会保险补贴。

（三）与绿色就业相关的促进大学生就业的优惠政策

1. 大学生见习制度

人力资源和社会保障部建立了离校未就业高校毕业生见习制度，以丰富高校毕业生的工作经验，增强其市场就业竞争。在选择见习基地的时候应优先考虑当地重点发展的优势产业，见习岗位应具备一定的技术含量和业务内容。毕业生实习期间由企业支付一定的基本生活费，高校毕业生在同一单位见习时间一般为3～12个月。

2. 创业支持

对有创业愿望的，则提供项目开发、方案设计、风险评估、开业指导、融资服务、跟踪扶持等"一条龙"创业服务。

（四）规范企业破产、关闭或裁员情况下劳动关系的解除程序

《劳动合同法》第四十一条规定了裁员的程序：在企业依照《企业破产法》规定进行重整、企业转产、重大技术革新或者经营方式调整，经变更劳动合同后，仍需裁减人员的，并且裁减人员二十人以上或者裁减不足二十人但占企业职工总数百分之十以上的，用人单位提前三十日向工会或者全体职工说明情况，听取工会或者职工的意见后，裁减人员方案经向劳动行政部门报告，可以裁减人员。

企业裁减人员时，应当优先留用下列人员：①与本单位订立较长期限的固定期限劳动合同的；②与本单位订立无固定期限劳动合同的；③家庭无其他就业人员，有需要抚养的老人或者未成年人的。

用人单位依照本条第一款规定裁减人员，在六个月内重新招用人员的，应当通知被裁减的人员，并在同等条件下优先招用被裁减的人员。

企业不得解除劳动合同的情形包括：①从事接触职业病危害作业的劳动者未进行离岗前职业健康检查，或者疑似职业病病人在诊断或者医学观察期间的；②在本单位患职业病或者因工负伤并被确认丧失或者部分丧失劳动能力的；③患病或者非因工负伤，在规定的医疗期内的；④女职工在孕期、产期、哺乳期的；⑤在本单位连续工作满十五年，且距法定退休年龄不足五年的；⑥法律、行政法规规定的其他情形。

《劳动合同法》第四十四条规定，用人单位被依法宣告破产的、用人单位被吊销营业执照、责令关闭、撤销或者用人单位决定提前解散的，劳动合同终止。对于国有企业关闭和破产程序，国务院《关于进一步加强就业再就业工作的通知》第十七条规定，国有企业实施重组改制和关闭破产，职工安置方案须经企业职工代表大会或职工大会讨论通过，凡职工安置方案和社会保障办法不明确、资金不落实的企业，不得进入重组改制和破产程序。

（五）在企业破产、关闭或者裁员情况下员工的保障问题

1. 企业破产、关闭或者裁员情况下对员工的补偿

我国的国有企业破产制度是伴随着经济体制改革进程逐步建立和完善的，因此在国有破产企业的资产处置和职工安置等方面，存在着大量的行政因素，法律与政策并行。

政策方面，国务院从 1994 年开始陆续发布了一些行政规范，包括《关于在若干城市试行国有企业破产有关问题的通知》《国务院关于在若干城市试行国有企业兼并破产和职工再就业有关问题的补充通知》，1996 年国家经贸委、中国人民银行也发布了《关于试行国有企业兼并破产中若干问题的通知》，对依照这些规范进入破产的企业的职工安置给出了超越法律规范的特殊优惠，在用于清偿的破产财产上明确土地使用权必须首先用于解决职工安置问题，甚至已抵押的土地所有权变现也可以用于偿付职工安置费，并将职工住房及其他社会性资产如幼儿园等排除在破产财产之外；而实际清偿的范围和标准也有所突破。此外，在国务院确定的 111 家试点城市，如果破产企业的职工选择自谋职业，那么可一次性付给安置费，标准不高于试点城市的企业职工上年平均工资收入的 3 倍，具体标准由清算组根据职工工作年限、职务职级等具体情况确定。也就是说，一次性安置费的适用范围为全国兼并破产协调小组批准的计划

内破产项目企业的职工；对于计划内破产项目企业的职工，安置费与经济补偿金不得同时领取。对于试点国有破产企业进入破产程序后，职工的生活费从破产清算费中支付。

法律方面，我国 1986 年颁布了适用于国有企业破产的一般性法律规范《企业破产法（试行）》，明确"破产企业所欠职工工资和劳动保险费用"按第一顺序清偿；2002 年《最高人民法院关于审理企业破产案件若干问题的规定》中，把"职工解除劳动合同补偿金"和"职工集资款"也列为第一顺序清偿。自 2007 年 6 月 1 日起开始施行的新《企业破产法》依然为政策性破产留出了空间，规定在该法施行前国务院规定的期限和范围内的国有企业实施破产的特殊事宜，按照国务院有关规定办理。《企业破产法》明确规定，破产财产在优先清偿破产费用和共益债务后，列入第一顺序清偿的包括"所欠职工的工资和医疗、伤残补助、抚恤费用，所欠的应当划入职工个人账户的基本养老保险、基本医疗保险费用，以及法律、行政法规规定应当支付给职工的补偿金"。破产企业欠缴的社会保险费用为第二顺序，对抵押债权虽然也规定在职工债权分配不足时可以占用，但对时间和范围有严格的限定。

根据《劳动合同法》的规定，在破产和裁员的时候，企业必须向劳动者支付经济补偿金。经济补偿按劳动者在本单位工作的年限，每满一年支付一个月工资的标准向劳动者支付。六个月以上不满一年的，按一年计算；不满六个月的，向劳动者支付半个月工资的经济补偿。劳动者月工资高于用人单位所在直辖市、设区的市级人民政府公布的本地区上年度职工月平均工资三倍的，向其支付经济补偿的标准按职工月平均工资三倍的数额支付，向其支付经济补偿的年限最高不超过十二年。

2. 企业破产、关闭情况下的提前退休政策

现行政策规定了企业破产时符合条件的职工可以提前退休的制度。例如，《北京市国有破产企业职工分流安置暂行办法》规定，破产企业的在职职工，在法院宣告破产当月，男年满 55 周岁、女年满 45 周岁经本人申请，可以办理退休手续，但在提前退休期间内的养老金酌减。

第五章

中国发展绿色就业的社会环境评估

中国发展绿色就业的时期，正处于工业化、城市化、市场化、国际化交织并进、经济社会全面发展的关键时期，同时还面临着经济快速增长与资源消耗、生态保护之间的矛盾和挑战。国内外的实践证明，高投入、高消耗、高污染的经济增长方式是不可持续的，要立足于走新型工业化和可持续发展的道路，建立资源节约型和环境友好型社会。

中国的就业问题十分突出。中国每年新增就业人口 1000 万人，下岗失业人员数百万，农村剩余劳动力数千万，如果经济增长不达到 8% ~9% 甚至更高，社会稳定就难以保障。中国城市化进程以每年 1% ~1.5% 的速度递增，城市基础设施建设的需求将拉动化工、建材、冶金等污染负荷重的行业规模持续扩大；区域经济发展水平由东向西呈递减趋势，越是深入内地，生态环境越是脆弱，经济发展与生态环境保护的矛盾相当突出。

作为一个负责任的发展中大国，中国政府高度重视促进绿色发展问题，并创造了良好的促进绿色发展的社会环境。本报告从中国促进绿色发展的经济政策（包括财政政策、税收政策和金融政策）、中国促进绿色发展的公众意识、中国促进绿色发展的科学技术环境、中国促进绿色发展的社会支持体系四个方面对中国发展绿色就业的社会环境进行评估。

一 中国促进绿色发展的经济政策

（一）中国促进绿色发展的财政政策

财政投入是十分重要的宏观经济调控政策手段，具体包括：政府对环境保护的直接投资、财政补贴、政府"绿色"采购制度、环境性因素的财政转移支付等。

1. 中国政府绿色预算支出政策

政府对环境保护的直接投资主要用于环境污染治理。2001～2005年,中央财政对环境保护累计投入1100多亿元。

(1) 逐年增加环保事业费,保障环保部门履行职能

"十五"期间,中央财政通过部门预算累计安排环保事业费10.6亿元,年均增长25.3%,重点支持开展环境监测、环保执法、环境标准制(修)订等专项工作。

(2) 增加环保资金投入,发挥中央财政资金的引导作用

中央环保专项资金总额从2001年的0.3亿元增加到2005年的9.3亿元,累计安排专项支出14.5亿元,保障了专项工作的顺利实施,带动了地方政府和社会资金参与环境保护。

(3) 通过国债资金支持重点生态建设和污染治理项目

"十五"期间,中央财政通过国债资金,直接安排生态建设和污染治理方面的支出累计达1083亿元,主要用于京津风沙源治理,西部中心城市环保设施建设,"三河三湖"污染防治,污水、垃圾产业化及中水回用,北京环境污染治理,森林生态效益补偿等项目。

2. 中国政府绿色采购政策

2004年财政部与国家发改委发布《节能产品政府采购实施意见》,成为我国第一个政府采购促进节能与环保的具体政策规定。这一政策从2005年1月1日起正式实施。一些地方政府出台了一些环保采购标准,如青岛市财政局和市环保局2005年12月27日发布了《绿色采购环保产品政府采购清单》(第一批),选定了该市第一批政府绿色采购环保产品清单。

3. 中国政府绿色财政转移支付政策

自1998年起,中央政府不断加大对欠发达的中西部地区的财政援助,把生态建设与农村基础设施建设、产业开发结合起来,实施退耕还林、还草政策,增强了地方环保事业投入的能力。

4. 中国政府设立促进绿色环境发展的专项资金

近年来,中国政府增加了环境整治与保护的专项资金,省级财政也设立了相应的"绿色"环境发展与保护的专项资金。如浙江省2000～2003年安排17

亿元专项资金，用在与生态建设有关的"生态农业与新农村建设""生态公益林建设""万里清水河道建设""生态环境治理""生态城镇建设""碧海建设""绿色文化建设"等工程上，改善了生态环境。

5. 中国政府绿色财政补贴（贴息）政策

目前广泛应用的补贴主要有对治污项目的补贴、对生态建设项目的补贴、对清洁生产项目的补贴、对环境科研的补贴、对生产环境友好型产品的补贴等。

（二）中国促进绿色发展的税收政策

与绿色发展有关的税种体现在两方面：一是对开采和使用自然资源（包括土地）的单位和个人征收的资源税、城镇土地使用税、耕地占用税，对保护资源和促进绿色发展有直接作用；二是如消费税、城市维护建设税等税种，对促进绿色发展有间接作用。

有利于绿色发展的各种税收主要反映在增值税、企业所得税中。此外，消费税和一些地方性税种中都有所体现。

1. 中国政府绿色增值税政策

中国政府实行绿色增值税政策，大体可以分为以下几类。

（1）鼓励资源综合利用产品的优惠措施

主要有：①对企业利用废液（渣）生产的黄金、白银，免征增值税（财税字〔1995〕44 号、财税〔1996〕120 号）。②对企业生产的原料中掺有不少于 30% 的煤矸石、石煤、粉煤灰、烧煤锅炉的炉底渣（不包括高炉水渣）的建材产品（包括商品混凝土），免征增值税，其掺兑比例既可以按重量计算，又可以按体积计算（国税函〔2003〕1151 号、财税字〔1995〕44 号、财税字〔1996〕20 号）。③对利用煤矸石、煤泥、石煤、油母页岩生产的电力，且煤矸石、煤泥、石煤、油母页岩用量（重量）占发电燃料的比重达到 60%（含 60%）以上的，减半征收增值税（财税〔2004〕25 号、财税〔2001〕198 号）。④对企业以林区"三剩物"和"次小薪材"为原料生产加工的综合利用产品，在 2005 年 12 月 31 日之前由税务部门实行增值税"即征即退"办法。⑤对燃煤电厂烟气脱硫副产品（包括二水硫酸钙含量不低于 85% 的石膏、浓度不低于 15% 的硫酸、总氮含量不低于 18% 的硫酸铵），实行增值税"即征即退"的政策（财税〔2004〕25 号）。

（2）促进废旧物资回收的优惠措施

对废旧物资回收经营单位原来实行增值税先征后返 70% 的优惠政策，从

2001 年 5 月 1 日起，改为销售收购的废旧物资免征增值税，而对属于增值税一般纳税人的生产企业，购买废旧物资允许按普通发票注明金额的 10% 计算增值税抵扣进项税额（财税〔2001〕78 号）。

（3）鼓励清洁能源和环保产品的优惠措施

对利用风力生产的电力和列入《享受税收优惠政策新型墙体材料目录》的新型墙体材料产品，包括非黏土砖、建筑砌块、建筑板材 14 类共 23 种产品，实行增值税减半征收。

（4）污水处理的优惠措施

自 2001 年 7 月 1 日起，对各级政府及主管部门委托自来水厂随水费收取的污水处理费，免征增值税（财税〔2001〕97 号）。

2. 中国政府绿色消费税政策

2009 年 1 月 1 日，酝酿了 14 年的成品油税费改革正式实施，取消了原在成品油价外征收的公路养路费、航道养护费、公路运输管理费、公路客货运附加费、水路运输管理费、水运客货运附加费等六项收费；将价内征收的汽油消费税单位税额每升提高 0.8 元，即由每升 0.2 元提高到 1 元，柴油消费税单位税额每升提高 0.7 元，即由每升 0.1 元提高到 0.8 元，其他成品油消费税单位税额相应提高；明确国内成品油价格实行与国际市场原油价格有控制的间接接轨，以国际市场原油价格为基础，加国内平均加工成本、税收、流动环节费用和适当利润确定。同时规定对成品油进口环节消费税进行调整。

从保护环境和节约资源的角度看，此次成品油税费改革的适时推出，极大推进了我国税收体系的绿色化程度，主要表现在以下两个方面。

（1）成品油税费改革，促使消费者改变汽车消费观念

成品油税费改革实施后，汽油、柴油等成品油消费税将实行从量定额计征，而不是从价计征。这意味着征税多少与油品价格变动没有关系，只与用油量多少相关联。这一改革无疑会促使消费者改变汽车消费观念，鼓励购买节油汽车和发展公共交通。同时将推动汽车行业的产业结构升级，促进新能源和新技术的应用。

（2）成品油税费改革，促进新能源汽车产业化发展

成品油税费改革后，不仅有利于节能环保的小排量车发展，而且从长远来看有利于新能源汽车的产业化发展。

3. 中国政府绿色所得税政策

近年来，为进一步促进绿色发展，中国出台了一些资源节约、环境保护的

所得税专项政策。主要内容如下。

（1）企业利用"三废"免税政策

规定企业利用废水、废气、废渣等废弃物为主要原料进行生产的，可在 5 年内减征或者免征所得税（财税〔1994〕1 号），具体包括：①企业在原设计规定的产品以外，综合利用本企业生产过程中产生的、在《资源综合利用目录》内的资源作主要原料生产的产品的所得，自生产经营之日起，免征所得税 5 年；②企业利用本企业外的大宗煤矸石、炉渣、粉煤灰作主要原料生产建材产品的所得，自生产经营之日起免征所得税 5 年；③为处理利用其他企业废弃的在《资源综合利用目录》内的资源而新办的企业，经主管税务机关批准后，可减征或者免征所得税 1 年。

（2）对专门生产当前国家鼓励发展的环保产业设备（产品）的免税政策

规定对专门生产《当前国家鼓励发展的环保产业设备（产品）目录》内设备（产品）的企业（分厂、车间），在符合独立核算、能独立计算盈亏的条件下，其年度净收入在 30 万元（含 30 万元）以下的，暂免征收企业所得税；超过 30 万元的部分，依法缴纳企业所得税（国经贸资源〔2000〕159 号、国经贸资源〔2002〕23 号）。

（3）对国家鼓励发展的环保产业设备实行投资抵免、加速折旧政策

中国政府规定企业技术改造项目凡使用《当前国家鼓励发展的环保产业设备（产品）目录》（第一批）中的国产设备，按照财政部、国家税务总局《关于印发〈技术改造国产设备投资抵免企业所得税暂行办法〉的通知》（财税字〔1999〕290 号）的规定，享受投资抵免企业所得税的优惠政策，并可实行加速折旧办法。

（4）公益性捐赠扣除政策

自 2004 年 1 月 1 日起，对企事业单位、社会团体和个人等社会力量，通过中华环境保护基金会用于公益救济性的捐赠，准予在缴纳企业所得税和个人所得税前金额扣除（财税〔2004〕172 号）。

（5）对生产性外商投资企业的优惠政策

对从事污水、垃圾处理业务的外商投资企业，可以认定为生产性外商投资企业的，享受"两免三减半"优惠（国税函〔2003〕388 号）。

4. 中国政府促进资源节约利用的税收政策

为促进资源的合理利用，限制对资源的滥采滥用，1988 年 4 月开征了资

源税，1994 年的税制改革中，进一步扩大了征收范围。虽然中国开征了资源税，但是，总体上中国的资源税制度还很不完善，突出表现在资源税征收项目不全，如中国目前没有对水资源、生物资源（如森林、草原、海洋渔业资源）征收资源税。

5. 中国政府促进绿色发展的出口退税政策

在出口退税方面，为限制高污染、高能耗及资源性产品出口，中央财政陆续采取了一系列措施，如取消包括各种矿产品精矿、原油等资源性产品在内的出口退税政策。另外，将铜、镍、铁合金、炼焦煤、焦炭等部分产品的出口退税率降为 5%。对"两高一资"产品（高污染、高能耗、资源型产品）的出口退税率大幅下降甚至全额取消，体现优化产业结构调控目标。

6. 中国政府促进绿色发展的其他税收鼓励措施

在房产税、城镇土地使用税、车船使用税、契税等地方税种中，也有一些有利于生态环境保护的措施，主要包括：由国家财政部门拨付事业经费的环保单位自用的房产、土地、车船，免征房产税、城镇土地使用税和车船使用税；对改造的废弃土地（1988 年国务院令第 17 号）、水利设施及其保护用地（〔1989〕国税地字第 14 号）、林业系统的林区及有关保护用地（国税函发〔1991〕1404 号），免征城镇土地使用税；环保部门使用的各种洒水车、垃圾车船（国发〔1986〕90 号），环卫环保部门的路面清扫车、环境监测车（财税地〔1987〕3 号），市内公共汽车、电车（财税地字〔1986〕8 号）等免征车船使用税。此外，2004 年 1 月 1 日至 2010 年 12 月 31 日期间，国有林区天然林资源保护工程实施企业和单位用于天然林保护工程的房产、土地和车船分别免征房产税、城镇土地使用税和车船使用税；对由于国家实行天然林资源保护工程造成森工企业的房产、土地闲置一年以上不用的，暂免征收房产税和城镇土地使用税（财税〔2004〕37 号）。

（三）中国促进绿色发展的金融政策

1. 中国政府绿色信贷政策

2007 年 7 月 30 日，原国家环保总局联合中国人民银行、银监会出台《关于落实环境保护政策法规防范信贷风险的意见》，全国有 20 多个省市出台了具体实施方案，工行、建行、兴业银行等一批银行实施了"环保一票否决"。该意见成为绿色信贷的基础文件。要求人民银行和银监会配合环保部门，引导各级金融机构按照环境经济政策要求，对国家禁止、淘汰、限制、鼓励等不同类型企业的授信区别对待。尤其要对没有经过环评审批的项目不可提供新增信贷，避免出现新的呆坏账。

2008 年 11 月 6 日，环境保护部和世界银行联合出版了《促进绿色信贷的国际经验：赤道原则及 IFC 绩效标准与指南》一书。该书全面介绍了"赤道原则"的内涵，社会和环境可持续性的绩效标准，62 个行业的环境、健康与安全指南。该书的出版，是我国绿色信贷政策走向深入的一个重要标志，同时也是完善绿色信贷技术体系的一个新起点。

2. 中国政府环保产业融资政策

目前，中国企业绿色经济项目的融资规模日趋扩大，仅从其中环保项目融资来看，"九五"和"十五"期间，中央财政统计的拨款分别为 3516 亿元和 8395.1 亿元，根据国家环保总局的规划，"十一五"期间，全社会环保融资达到 13750 亿元，约占同期 GDP 的 1.6%。但同时也应看到融资问题已经成为我国环保产业化发展的主要瓶颈。目前，中国环保企业除政府投资以外，主要通过间接融资方式等筹集资金。一方面，大型环保项目由国家通过政策性银行作为专项贷款方式融入资金，由于存在外部性等问题，缺口部分较难从其他商业银行获得；另一方面，那些具有成长性、效益可观的中小环保企业贷款难、担保难。

3. 中国政府环境污染责任保险政策

2007 年 12 月，环境保护部与中国保监会联合出台《关于环境污染责任保险工作的指导意见》，正式启动了绿色保险制度建设。该意见提出要初步建立符合我国国情的环境污染责任保险制度，在重点行业和区域开展环境污染责任保险的试点示范工作，以生产、经营、储存、运输、使用危险化学品企业，易发生污染事故的石油化工企业、危险废物处置企业等为对象开展试点。2012 年以后，环境污染责任保险将在全国推广。

如湖南省在 2008 年推出了保险产品，确定了化工、有色、钢铁等 18 家重点企业，已有 7 家投保。江苏省 2008 年推出了船舶污染责任保险，由中国人民保险集团股份有限公司、中国平安保险公司、太平洋保险公司和永安保险公司 4 家保险公司组成共保体，承保 2008～2009 年度江苏省船舶污染责任保险项目。湖北省于 2008 年启动了环境污染责任保险试点工作，在武汉城市圈范围进行试点，武汉市专门安排 200 万元资金作为政府引导资金，为购买保险企业按保费 50% 进行补贴。沈阳市率先在地方立法方面实现突破，在于 2009

年 1 月 1 日起实施的《沈阳市危险废物污染环境防治条例》中明确规定，"支持和鼓励保险企业设立危险废物污染损害责任险种；支持和鼓励产生、收集、贮存、运输、利用和处置危险废物的单位投保危险废物污染损害责任险种"。

二　中国促进绿色发展的经济政策对就业的影响

（一）中国促进绿色发展的财政政策对就业的影响

1. 中国政府绿色预算支出政策不仅直接拉动绿色就业，而且通过乘数效应带动社会投资增加了绿色就业

财政政策通过其乘数效应从两个方面扩大就业总量。一是直接效应。财政支出直接形成产业资本，创造了就业岗位。中国政府通过逐年增加环保事业费、环保资金及国债资金等投入，支持了一大批重点生态建设和污染治理项目，直接扩大了绿色就业总量。二是间接效应。中国政府逐年增加的财政支出会因乘数效应使国民收入成倍增加，而中国经济的持续增长必将促使绿色就业人数增长。

在金融危机背景下，中国实行积极的财政政策既有效地推动了经济企稳回升，又增加了就业岗位。据人力资源和社会保障部劳动科学研究所测算，中国政府的 4 万亿元投资将能够带动 2416 万个就业岗位。

2. 中国政府绿色预算支出政策对小企业支持有限，就业岗位的增加潜力有待挖掘

中国政府绿色预算支出政策在促进绿色就业方面作用很大，但也存在一些缺陷，主要是对小企业的支持力度不足，帮扶不够。小企业是推动中国国民经济发展、促进就业的重要力量。而政府财政支出政策对小企业的支持力度有限，如在政府绿色采购政策中没有制定购买中小企业产品的配额，对中小企业的各种创业指导、信息服务、市场开拓等扶持较弱等。

（二）中国促进绿色发展的税收政策对就业的影响

1. 中国税收政策已经形成促进绿色发展的良好政策导向

中国现行税收政策已经形成了鼓励资源节约、保护环境、限制污染的政策导向，与政府的收费制度和排污许可制度、财政补贴等其他有关措施相配合，在减轻或消除污染、节约和合理利用资源、加强环境保护、促进中国可持续发展方面发挥了积极的作用。

2. 中国政府绿色税收政策促进就业效果显著

1994 年税制改革以来，中国出台了一系列促进就业的税收优惠政策。包括：2002 年以前针对待业人员、四残人员、部队转业干部和退役士兵就业再就业的税收优惠政策；2003～2005 年陆续出台的针对服务型企业、新办企业、下岗失业人员的税收优惠政策；2006 年又出台了侧重于鼓励企业吸纳就业，鼓励自谋职业和自主创业，鼓励国有大中型企业主辅分离、辅业改制的税收政策；为应对金融危机，2008 年 9 月至 2009 年 2 月，中国政府出台了七个促进就业的文件，实施了六大举措。通过改善创业环境，在税费减免、小额担保贷款等方面对自主创业人员给予了大力支持，发挥就业倍增效应，带动了其他劳动者就业。

与政府采取的财政支出政策、投资政策、采购政策、转移支付政策相比，税收优惠激励政策与市场化运作相结合的形式效果明显，作用也更加持久。截至 2004 年 6 月 30 日，全国已有 229 万名下岗职工享受了各项再就业税收优惠政策，税务部门已落实再就业减负税额 107.29 亿元，减免税务登记工本费 3635 万元。

3. 中国政府绿色税收政策使中小企业在吸纳就业方面的贡献进一步加大

2008 年度一项上规模民营企业调研结果显示，在国际金融危机影响下的中国民营企业表现出很强的抗逆性，在规模性指标和社会贡献方面依然保持较高的增长水平。这些企业利润空间虽然受到挤压，但在税收、就业方面的贡献进一步加大。2008 年民营企业 500 家缴税总额共计 1484.46 亿元，户均 2.97 亿元，同比增长 12.76%，其中，缴税超过 1 亿元的企业有 341 家。在吸纳就业方面表现尤为突出，总就业人数为 413.27 万人，比 2007 增加了 68.5 万人，同比增长 19.87%。

中小企业被誉为"创造就业岗位的机器"，据统计，我国中小企业就业人数占就业总人数的 70%，在新增就业机会中占 80%。目前发展绿色就业的重要增长点也在中小企业，可以看出，中小企业已经成了中国劳动力的"蓄水池"，中小企业的发展速度直接关系到中国的绿色就业水平。国家应制定差别税率结合财政政策扶持和鼓励中小企业。因而，促进绿色发展的税收政策需要继续向中小企业倾斜。

（三）中国促进绿色发展的金融政策对就业的影响

1. "适度宽松"的货币政策为绿色就业提供了良好的发展空间

自适度宽松的货币政策实施以来，金融支持经济发展的力度得到增强。2009 年上半年人民币各项贷款增加 7.4 万亿元，同比增多 4.9 万亿元。贷款的快速增长有利于从总量上促进经济较快发展，为促进绿色就业提供良好的发展空间。

2. 金融政策缺少对中小企业的支持，中小企业融资难的问题仍然十分突出

按照世界性的就业规律，农村剩余劳动力转移、城镇新增劳动力、结构调整和体制改革挤出的劳动力会随着产业的变动更多地向中小型企业集中。与大企业相比，中小企业在资金、信息、人才、技术、管理等方面都处于劣势，因而扶持中小企业应成为中国促进绿色发展的金融政策建设中重点关注的内容。

当前我国实行的促进绿色发展的金融政策对中国绿色经济的发展是积极有利的，但对作为我国吸纳就业主力军的中小企业的支持力度明显不够，小企业资金短缺、融资困难、发展乏力等问题尤为突出，这在很大程度上限制了就业容量的扩大。融资成本高和小企业扶持政策不到位是小企业面临的主要问题，要突破这一瓶颈，需要融资政策的倾斜、支持和帮助。

三 中国促进绿色发展的公众意识

（一）中国促进绿色发展的宣传和公众参与

绿色发展不仅仅需要政府和企业的参与，更需要公众的参与，才能从根本上形成绿色发展的长期推动力。中国一直重视促进绿色发展领域的教育、宣传和公众参与。

人力资源和社会保障部劳动科学研究所"企业职工绿色就业状况调查"数据显示，80.1%的职工工作场所有环境保护行动或相关规章制度；89.4%的企业有有关循环、回收再利用和减少排放的行动。

"2007年中国公众环境意识调查"显示，有超过七成的中国公众对环境保护的重要性、必要性和紧迫感有较高认识。随着年龄下降，人们对环保重要性评价逐步提高；受教育程度越高，其环境意识和环境行为越高。城市常住人口对环保重要性评价高于农村常住人口。八成中国公众认为环保并非仅是政府的责任，而与个人密切相关。

（二）中国促进绿色发展的社会认知程度

近年来，国家通过提出贯彻落实科学发展观、建设和谐社会和坚持走可持

---

① "2007年中国公众环境意识调查"由"中国环境意识项目"主办，中国社科院社会学所承担全面工作，于2007年12月实施。该调查采取入户方式，调查对象为15~69岁的中国城乡居民，调查样本量为3001人，涵盖全国20个省/自治区/直辖市。

续发展道路等先进理念，不断引导全社会提高绿色发展意识，树立人与自然和谐发展思想。国家把建设资源节约型和环境友好型社会作为教育和新闻宣传的重要内容，利用各种手段普及绿色发展方面的相关知识，提高全社会的认知程度。

"2007 年中国公众环境意识调查"显示，中国公众环境保护认知呈高知晓率与低正确率并存的特征：有超过八成的被调查者听说过至少 1 项有关环境保护的概念；但仅有 10% 的人能够正确指出他们所了解的环境保护概念的确切含义。

中国已出版大量与气候变化相关的出版物、影视和音像作品，创办了中国气象电视频道，建立了资料信息库，利用大众传媒进行气候变化方面的知识普及。人力资源和社会保障部劳动科学研究所"企业职工绿色就业状况调查"数据显示，收看/收听电视、广播成为公众接受环境保护知识及信息的最主要渠道。如图 5 - 1 所示。

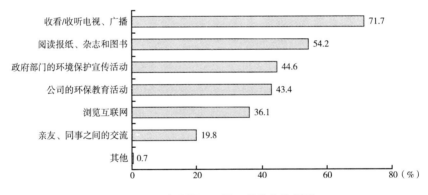

图 5 - 1　企业职工了解环保信息的渠道

（三）中国公众参与绿色发展的实际行动

从 1992 年开始，中国连续举办 18 届全国节能宣传周活动。2007 年国家发布了《节能减排全民行动实施方案》，在全国范围内组织开展"节能减排全民行动"，包括家庭社区行动、青少年行动、企业行动、学校行动、军营行动、政府机构行动、科技行动、科普行动、媒体行动九个专项行动，形成政府推动、企业实施、全社会共同参与的节能减排的工作机制。通过创建"节约型政府机构"等行动，发挥了政府机构和政府工作人员的节能导向作用。

"2007 年中国公众环境意识调查"显示，国家公务员等职业群体环境意识相对较高。凡职业的组织化程度较高、所需受教育程度较高的职业人群，其对环保问题的认知及环境意识就较高。这主要是由于较高的组织化程度保障了这些职业人群有更多的机会接受其职业组织所提供的环保信息、环保活动，能够从更大的范围内了解环境问题。

中国实施企业节能减排宣传教育活动，发动职工参与企业节能减排管理。通过重塑家庭生活消费新模式，搭建节能减排社区平台，积极鼓励公民及社会团体自愿参与植树造林，采取全民限制和有偿使用塑料袋等活动，增强公民的节能减排意识。积极开展以节能减排为内容的学校主题教育和社会实践活动，培养学生树立节能环保意识。近年来，一些社会团体和非政府组织也以多种形式加入全民节能减排行动，发挥了积极作用。

人力资源和社会保障部劳动科学研究所"企业职工绿色就业状况调查"数据显示，96.9%的企业职工听说过垃圾分类；98.1%的企业职工能够正确地回答出垃圾分类的相关知识。资源节约已成为中国公众主要的环境保护行为。从企业职工的环境保护行为看，采取的环境保护行为主要以能降低生活支出或有益自身健康的行为为主，较高比例的企业职工能够做到以下环保行为：购物时不使用塑料袋、外出就餐时不使用一次性餐具、对生活垃圾分类处理、将废旧电池投入专门的回收桶、使用节能产品、随时关紧水龙头、看完电视或用完电脑后拔掉插头等。

（四）中国企业职工对环保的满意度评价

人力资源和社会保障部劳动科学研究所"企业职工绿色就业状况调查"数据显示，55.8%的企业职工对中央政府的环保工作满意；48.2%的企业职工对本地政府的环保工作满意；64%的企业职工对本企业的环保工作满意；60.9%的企业职工对本企业遵守环保法规的自觉性满意；62.3%的企业职工对媒体的环保宣传工作比较满意；93.9%的企业职工认为企业应参与和支持环境保护事业，这是企业社会责任的重要部分，不仅资金支持，而且要实行环保措施，减少污染。

四　中国促进绿色发展的科学技术环境

科学技术进步是促进绿色发展的核心手段。无论是提高能源转换和利用效率、减少能源消耗，还是开发利用可再生能源、优化能源结构，都依赖于先进技术的研究、开发与推广。从长远来看，是否掌握相关核心技术也将体现一个国家的综合竞争力。

（一）中国促进绿色发展科技工作取得的成就

中国是当今世界上最大的发展中国家，国家高度重视绿色发展问题，并采取了一系列措施积极应对。《中国应对气候变化国家方案》明确提出要依靠科技进步和科技创新应对气候变化，"要发挥科技进步在减缓和适应气候变化中的先导性和基础性作用，促进各种技术的发展以及加快科技创新和技术引进步伐等"，并将"先进适用技术开发和推广"作为温室气体减排的重点领域，包括煤的清洁高效开发和利用技术、油气资源勘探开发利用技术、核电技术、可再生能源技术、输配电和电网安全技术等。中国政府还颁布了《中国应对气候变化科技专项行动》作为《中国应对气候变化国家方案》的科技支撑。中国还将低碳技术作为优先领域，纳入《国家中长期科学和技术发展规划纲要》（国务院，2007）。从技术方向上看，该纲要跟踪了发达国家提出的先进能源技术的研发方向；在具体措施上，提出要加大研发投入，提高自主创新能力，将技术引进与国内消化、吸收、创新相结合，加快先进技术产业化的步伐；同时提出要加强法律、法规等减缓气候变化的制度和机制建设，逐步形成促进先进能源技术大规模产业化发展的法律、法规体系和政策激励机制。

中国通过国家科技攻关计划、国家高技术研究与发展计划、国家基础研究发展计划等先后组织开展了一系列促进绿色发展的科技项目，重点研究了全球气候变化预测与影响、中国未来生存环境变化趋势、全球环境变化对策与支撑技术、中国重大气候和天气灾害形成机理与预测理论、能源清洁高效利用技术、节能和提高能源效率、可再生能源和新能源开发利用技术等。

同时，中国还积极参与全球环境变化的国际科技合作，如地球科学系统联盟（ESSP）框架下的世界气候研究计划（WCRP）、国际地圈－生物圈计划（IGBP）、国际全球变化人文因素计划（IHDP）和生物多样性计划（DIVERSITAS）等四大国际科研计划，以及全球对地观测政府间协调组织（GEO）和全球气候系统观测计划（GCOS）等，开展了具有中国特色又兼具全球意义的全球变化基础研究。

通过国家科技计划的支持和国际科技合作，中国在气候变化的基础科学研究、气候变化的影响与对策研究、控制温室气体排放和减缓气候变化的技术开发和应用、气候变化的社会经济影响分析及减缓对策研究等方面取得了许多成果和重要进展，编制完成了《气候变化国家评估报告》。同时科研基础设施建设和人才培养与科研机构建设也得到显著加强。上述成果为中国应对气候变化提供了有力的支撑，同时也为中国气候变化科技工作的进一步发展奠定了坚实的基础。

（二）中国促进绿色发展的科学技术目标

2020 年中国促进绿色发展的科学技术目标是：气候变化领域的自主创新能力大幅度提高；一批具有自主知识产权的控制温室气体排放和减缓气候变化关键技术取得突破，并在经济社会发展中得到广泛应用；重点行业和典型脆弱区适应气候变化的能力明显增强；参与气候变化合作和制定重大战略与政策的科技支撑能力显著提高；气候变化的学科建设取得重大进展，科研基础条件明显改善，科技人才队伍的水平显著提高；公众的气候变化科学意识显著增强。

（三）中国促进绿色发展的重点任务

1. 气候变化的科学问题

包括具有自主知识产权的新一代气候系统模式、气候变化的检测与归因、气候变化监测预测预警技术、亚洲季风系统与气候变化、中国极端天气/气候事件与灾害的形成机理、冰冻圈变化过程与趋势、生态系统能量转化、物质循环对气候变化的响应。

2. 控制温室气体排放和减缓气候变化的技术开发

包括节能和提高能效技术、可再生能源和新能源技术、煤的清洁高效开发利用技术、油气资源和煤层气勘探和清洁高效开发利用技术、先进核能技术、二氧化碳捕集与封存技术、生物固碳技术和其他固碳工程技术、农业和土地利用方式控制温室气体排放技术。

3. 适应气候变化的技术和措施

包括具有自主知识产权的气候变化影响评估模型、气候变化对中国主要脆弱领域的影响及适应技术和措施、极端天气/气候事件与灾害的影响及适应技术和措施、气候变化影响的敏感脆弱区及风险管理体系的建立、气候变化对重大工程的影响及应对措施、气候变化与其他全球环境问题的交互作用及应对措施、气候变化影响的危险水平及适应能力、适应气候变化案例研究。

4. 应对气候变化的重大战略与政策

包括应对气候变化与中国能源安全战略、未来气候变化国际制度、中国未来能源发展与温室气体排放情景、清洁发展机制与碳交易制度、应对气候变化与低碳经济发展、国际产品贸易与温室气体排放、应对气候变化的科学技术战略。

（四）面临的问题

中国能否利用后发优势在工业化进程中实现绿色经济发展，在很大程度上取决于资金和技术能力。对中国来说，主要是技术的获取和消化吸收，并且能提高技术创新能力。一方面技术上受到各种以军事技术管制等为由的限制，另一方面由于自身缺乏消化吸纳能力，技术引进后，消化吸纳不够，缺乏维护保养和使用方面的技能，先进的技术也产生不了效用。中国技术创新能力尚弱，是技术的净进口国。虽然《联合国气候变化框架公约》规定，发达国家有义务向发展中国家提供技术转让，然而实际进展与预期相去甚远，清洁发展机制（CDM）项目对发展中国家的技术转让也十分有限。因此，非常有必要通过制度化的手段，解决好知识产权保护和技术转让的关系问题。中国应该积极利用国际公约框架内外的各种途径促进发达国家向中国的技术转让。

五　中国促进绿色发展的社会支持体系

（一）中国已建立健全的应对气候变化的管理体系

中国政府于1990年成立了应对气候变化相关机构，1998年建立了国家气候变化对策协调小组。为进一步加强对应对气候变化工作的领导，2007年成立国家应对气候变化领导小组，由国务院总理担任组长，负责制定国家应对气候变化的重大战略、方针和对策，协调解决应对气候变化工作中的重大问题。2008年进一步加强了对应对气候变化工作的领导，国家应对气候变化领导小组的成员单位由原来的18个扩大到20个，具体工作由国家发展和改革委员会承担，领导小组办公室设在国家发展和改革委员会，并在国家发展和改革委员会成立专门机构，专门负责全国应对气候变化工作的组织协调。为提高应对气候变化决策的科学性，成立了气候变化专家委员会，在支持政府决策、促进国际合作和开展民间活动方面做了大量工作。

目前，各地区、各部门已建立应对气候变化的管理体系、协调机制和专门机构，建立了地方气候变化专家队伍，根据各地区在地理环境、气候条件、经济发展水平等方面的具体情况，制定了应对气候变化的相关政策措施，建立了与气候变化相关的统计和监测体系，组织和协调本地区应对气候变化的行动。

（二）金融危机背景下，中国加强绿色岗位开发

在金融危机背景下，"绿色经济"被看作全球经济振兴的助博器，中国在

大力加强"绿色就业"岗位的开发。中国已经将节能减排和生态工程作为"扩内需、保增长"的重点之一，4 万亿元投资计划中约有 2100 亿元投向这一领域，用于加快民生工程、基础设施、生态环境建设和灾后恢复重建。在 2100 亿元新增投资中，安排节能减排、生态建设和环境保护投资 230 亿元，主要包括四方面的内容：一是安排城镇污水、垃圾处理设施和污水管网工程 130 亿元。扩大县城污水、垃圾处理设施覆盖面，计划用 3 年时间，在全国绝大部分县城建设污水和垃圾处理设施，建设城镇污水处理能力 4200 万吨/日，垃圾处理能力 15 万吨/日，建设污水管网。二是安排淮河、松花江、丹江口库区等重点流域水污染防治 40 亿元，提高重点流域的污水、垃圾处理能力。三是安排天然林资源保护工程和重点防护林工程 35 亿元，加快建设营造林约 1800 万亩、公益林 1100 万亩。四是安排 25 亿元，支持十大重点节能工程、循环经济和重点流域工业污染治理工程建设。这将极大地刺激传统就业岗位的转化和绿色就业岗位的培育，有利于建筑节能工程师、太阳能安装师、农场主、育林人、生态保护工作者、资源回收商等绿色就业岗位的发展。

案例分析——德州市太阳能热水器产业价值链分析

一 研究背景

气候变化给人类的生存和发展带来了严峻挑战。为了应对和减缓气候变化的影响，世界各国都认识到必须减少经济发展对于化石燃料的依赖，降低碳排放。中国政府也越来越关注低碳发展，并积极展开节能减排行动，推进能源结构优化。中国在《国民经济和社会发展第十一个五年规划纲要》中提出控制温室气体排放，将单位国内生产总值（GDP）能耗降低20%的目标。然而，对产业结构和能源结构的调整不可避免地会对就业数量、就业结构和技能结构产生深远影响。如何积极利用绿色经济发展的机遇，促进绿色岗位的开发，同时促进劳动力市场的顺利转型，减少产业结构、能源结构的调整对就业的负面影响，实现经济、社会和环境的可持续发展，是我们在向绿色经济转型过程中必须解决的问题。

劳工组织（ILO）认为，"有必要对资源使用方式的转变给技术、生产和就业造成的影响进行估计，并且找到合适的发展策略，在降低温室气体排放的同时不延缓消除贫困的进程"。为此，国际劳工组织、联合国环境规划署（UNEP）、国际工会联盟（ITUC）和国际雇主组织（IOE）共同发起了"绿色工作倡议"，以促进向绿色经济的顺利转型，保障转型过程中的公平机会，并鼓励各国政府、雇主和工人合作制定和实施有效的政策措施来支持绿色经济的发展，创造体面的绿色就业机会。为了支持这一倡议，国际劳工组织亚太局在中国、印度和孟加拉三个国家启动了为期18个月的试点项目，以推进"寻找和尝试通过创造绿色工作来促进清洁发展的途径"。本研究作为该项目的一部分，旨在探讨如何通过产业价值链分析方法，探索促进太阳能热水器行业的发展，并创造绿色就业机会的途径。

二 研究方法

（一）产业价值链的初选

在接受了国际劳工组织的委托后，中国人力资源和社会保障部劳动科学研究所调研组首先根据我国的实际情况对国际劳工组织的产业价值链选择工具进行了调整，确定了七个指标，包括行业发展对改善环境的影响、行业发展基础和前景、主要消费者群体、就业潜力、国家政策的支持度、行业改变潜力、潜在干预项目的可推广性。此后，在分析文献材料和对相关机构进行访谈的基础上，调研组初步选择了绿色食品、太阳能热水器和生态林业三个产业价值链。在对这三个产业进行了综合评估之后，调研组最终确定将太阳能热水器产业价值链作为深入研究对象。

（二）对太阳能热水器产业价值链的研究方法

在确定了对太阳能热水器产业价值链进行深入研究后，调研组随即走访了国家能源局、节能协会太阳能专业委员会，以及行业内的知名企业家，并搜集了大量关于太阳能热水器行业发展的文献资料。由于国际劳工组织的产业价值链分析工具主要针对传统产业，调研组对这个工具进行了调整，编写了针对太阳能热水器产业价值链不同环节和外部服务机构的访谈提纲。如表 6-1 所示。

表 6-1 价值链初选评估

指标	绿色食品	太阳能热水器	生态林业
对改善环境的影响	发展绿色食品行业有助于减少农业对环境的污染、改善农业劳动者的工作环境	促进绿色发展的重要领域，进行能源结构调整、推动新能源的应用。与传统的燃气和电热水器相比，每平方米太阳能热水器每年减少温室气体排放大约 322 公斤；二氧化硫、二氧化氮和烟尘年排放量各 3.96 公斤、1.98 公斤、3.06 公斤。也就是说，在 10 年生命周期内，每平方米太阳能热水器可以减少温室气体排放 3220 公斤，二氧化硫、二氧化氮和烟尘年排放量各 39.6 公斤、19.8 公斤、30.6 公斤	生态造林对于减缓气候变化具有不可替代的作用。森林每生长出一立方米就能够吸收 1.83 吨二氧化碳，释放 1.62 吨氧气

续表

指标	绿色食品	太阳能热水器	生态林业
行业发展基础和前景	产业比较成熟,主要依靠市场运行。消费者认同度高,市场需求大,行业的市场发展潜力巨大。2003～2007年,无公害农产品、绿色食品和有机食品产品年均增长速度达到83%。但是,相对于普通食品,绿色食品生产规模太小,绿色食品实物年产量占普通食品年产量的比重还相当低	有了一定的技术和市场发展基础,主要依靠市场运行。消费者认同度比较高,对解决农村能源需求意义重大。市场发展潜力仍然很大。从2001～2007年,在全国销售的各类热水器中太阳能热水器的比例从15.2%上升到38.5%。2007年,全国太阳能热水器年产量2300万平方米,总保有量10800万平方米,每千人拥有面积83平方米	生态林业主要依靠政策,但是发展潜力很大。据行业专家预测,未来整个林业产业链的利润环节将逐步向林业种植转移
主要消费者	主要消费者为国内收入较高的城市家庭。此外,出口也是绿色食品的主要销售渠道	目前主要消费者为东部地区中小城市,以及农村地区消费者。由于农村缺乏能源供应,太阳能热水器能够为农民生活、养殖业和取暖提供热水,因此未来农村用户的数量将会有比较大的增长	公益性质,主要在生态比较脆弱的地区
就业潜力	属于劳动密集型行业,有利于农村劳动者充分就业,特别适合妇女和低收入人群就业和增加收入	属于劳动密集型行业。该行业的中小企业较多,促进就业效果显著,尤其是销售、安装和维修等服务企业创造的就业机会多。在中国,太阳能热水器生产工人1个人,可以带动相关服务业10人就业。据相关机构估计,2007年全行业提供就业机会250万个	造林属于劳动密集型工作,造林每亩用工71～135工日。生态林业的就业效应不仅体现在造林创造的直接工作岗位,而且包括带动产业链中的相关行业,如苗木抚育、栽培、林副业等行业的间接就业机会。 发展生态林有利于林业资源型城市中相关行业职工再就业,也有利于农民,特别是返乡农民就业。 不过,由于春季是植树造林的最佳季节,因此造林创造的就业机会中,季节性工作较多

续表

指标	绿色食品	太阳能热水器	生态林业
国家政策的支持度	国家对绿色食品发展非常支持。目前绿色食品基本制度构架已经形成,包括技术标准体系、质量认证体系、标志管理体系和质量检测体系。此外,国家层面和地方层面出台了不少针对绿色食品生产企业的优惠政策,如补贴、税收和工商行政费用减免、信贷扶持、土地使用等	国家层面制定了新能源发展战略,将太阳能利用作为能源战略的重要组成部分。在地方层面,不少城市制定了太阳能热水器强制安装、补贴的规定。此外,为应对金融危机,国家制定了扩大内需政策,其中包括家电下乡(农村用户可以享受销售价格13%的补贴),要求中标销售企业要增强网点的销售服务功能,特别是在农户分散的乡村开展巡回维修服务和集中培训服务等	国家对生态公益造林非常重视,制定了一系列优惠措施:一是建立了重点公益林补偿与补贴制度;二是建立了林木良种补贴制度及造林、抚育、保护、管理投入补贴制度;三是制定完善林业优惠政策,包括林业贴息贷款政策
行业改变潜力	改变潜力比较大,很多从业人员缺乏相应的资金、技能,产业价值链各个环节之间的合作不畅	改变潜力比较大。行业中小企业主要依靠自我力量发展,外部支持很少。制造业发展相对比较成熟,但是存在技能人才缺乏的问题;后续服务滞后,影响了行业的进一步发展	改变潜力比较大,特别是需要进一步加强从业人员的技能培训,改变传统的造林和养护手段
外部干预项目可推广性	外部项目的干预模式和手段具有全国范围的可推广性	外部项目的干预模式和手段具有全国范围的可推广性。不过,应该考虑到城市和农村地区干预项目的差异性	对于不同生态林类型,如自然保护林、环境保护林、水土保持林、防风固沙林等,外部项目的干预模式和手段有所不同。但是,对于同一生态林种的干预项目有比较强的可推广性

2009年7月,调研组在德州开展了实地调研活动。调研活动主要分为四个部分。

(1)与当地相关政府机构,包括人力资源和社会保障局、住房和城乡建设委员会、经济贸易委员会节能办公室、发展和改革委员会能源发展科、民营经济委员会、服务业发展局等部门进行了座谈。

(2)对5家生产企业进行了实地考察。调研组还与当地中小企业的代表就建立协会等问题进行了探讨。

（3）实地走访了分布在城市、县和乡镇的太阳能热水器经销商，并对他们进行了访谈。

（4）向当地的农村用户了解了他们对于太阳能热水器的需求和看法。

三　德州市太阳能热水器发展的外部环境

（一）德州市的社会经济状况

德州市位于山东省西北部，距北京大约两个小时的车程。当地人称德州市为北京的南大门，山东的北大门。目前德州市共辖 11 个县（市、区）和两个经济开发区，市区建成区面积 46.5 平方公里。过去，德州市长期以传统农业为主，曾是全国 30 个贫困地区之一；经过多年的发展，目前德州市的综合经济实力达到山东省中等发展水平。德州的民营经济比较发达，共有民营经济 9 万户，以中小企业居多。太阳能热利用、中央空调和功能糖是德州市的支柱产业。目前，德州市进入向工业化过渡的加速推进期，市政府提出了建设"低碳城市"的目标，其中的措施之一是大力发展太阳能产业。

截至 2008 年年底，德州市总人口 564.2 万人，其中农业人口 403.6 万人，非农业人口 142.6 万人。城镇从业人员 66.5 万人，在外务工人员 102 万人，城市登记失业率 3%。全市最低工资标准 500 元/月。[①] 城市居民人均可支配收入 14545 元，比上年增长 17.4%；农民人均纯收入 5659 元，比上年增长 13.5%。

（二）德州市太阳能热水器发展的政策环境

中国政府非常重视可再生能源行业的发展，将太阳能利用作为能源战略的重要组成部分。在全国层面，《节能法》规定鼓励、支持开发和利用可再生能源。《可再生能源法》进一步明确规定，国家鼓励单位和个人安装和使用太阳能热水系统、太阳能供热采暖和制冷系统等太阳能利用系统。同时要求"房地产开发企业应当根据前款规定的技术规范，在建筑物的设计和施工中，为太阳能利用提供必备条件"。在国家大力提倡保护生态环境，发展可再生能源，建设资源节约、环境友好型社会的大背景下，我国的太阳能热水器行业发展迅速。2006 年，全国太阳能热水器总保有量 0.9 亿平方米，年产量 1800 万平方

---

① 我国没有全国统一的最低工资标准。2008 年山东省最低工资标准为三类，分别为 500 元、620 元和 760 元。总体来说，500 元最低工资标准在全国来看基本偏低。

米，分别占全世界的 53.6% 和 78.2% 。

在省层面，山东省出台了《山东省节能条例》等法规和政策文件，进一步落实国家相关规定。2009 年的《关于加快新能源产业发展的指导意见》提出要进一步发展太阳能光热产业，壮大产业规模，延伸产业链条，形成具有国际竞争力的产业规模优势。在推动太阳能热水器应用的优惠政策方面，省政府建立了省节能节水专项资金，并规定三星级以上宾馆和省属高校及职业教育学校利用太阳能集热系统，日出水量在 20 吨以上、温度在 30 度以上的，用户可以获得工程总造价 30% 的补贴；有住校生的基础教育学校，使用日生产热水能力在 5 吨以上、温度在 30 度以上的，用户可以获得工程总造价 30% 的补贴；每个项目补贴资金最多不超过 150 万元。

在德州市，政府不仅扶持太阳能热水器的生产，而且非常注重太阳能热水器的推广使用。在太阳能热水器使用方面，2007 年市政府制定了《推进建筑领域应用太阳能的实施意见》，决定在"十一五"期间，在城市继续实施"百万屋顶"计划，城市居住建筑全面推广太阳能与建筑一体化，公共建筑逐步推广太阳能与建筑一体化；在农村大力实施"百村浴室工程"。当地政府的目标是：到"十一五"末期，当地城市太阳能应用面积占新建建筑面积比例达到 50% 以上，其中市区达到 80%；到 2020 年，太阳能应用面积占新建建筑面积比例为 80% 以上；全市村庄计划安装太阳能浴室 1000 个以上，使德州市成为名副其实的太阳能推广应用示范城市。

在太阳能热利用产业发展方面，市政府提出了加快"太阳城"建设的战略，通过支持太阳能骨干企业来推进产业发展、提高太阳能产业科技创新能力、城市品牌建设和推广、实施太阳能示范工程、科普和文化宣传、太阳谷建设等几个方面的措施，逐步将德州太阳能产业发展成为具有强大竞争力的产业集群。

（三）主要的相关政府机构

为了推动"太阳城"战略的实施，德州市成立了"中国太阳城"战略推进委员会，由市长担任主任，成员包括发改委、经委、民经委、城市规划、教育、科技、环保、服务业发展、税务、工商、质量监督等相关政府部门，以及银行、工会、妇联、电台、供电公司。战略推进委员会下设"太阳城"大会筹备工作领导小组、太阳城战略宣传领导小组、太阳能产业发展工作领导小组，以及太阳能推广应用工作领导小组。"太阳城"战略宣传领导小组办公室设在市委宣传部，太阳能产业发展工作领导小组办公室设在市经委，其余两个领导小组办公室均设在市建委。

目前，主要相关机构之间的分工是：市经委负责相关的产业发展规划的制订，以及企业技术改造投资管理；市建委负责太阳能热水器的推广应用、实施"百万屋顶"和"百村浴室"计划、太阳能示范工程，以及太阳城城市景观整体规划；宣传部负责加强对外宣传，提升太阳城的对外形象和知名度。发改委管理规模以上民营企业，民经委负责县级工业园和乡镇级别民营企业的发展；这两个部门要在贷款和融资等政策方面加强对民营企业的支持。

四 德州市太阳能产业价值链的情况

（一）太阳能热水器产品基本情况

按照集热器类型划分，我国生产的太阳能热水器分为真空管、平板和闷晒太阳能热水器三类。其中，真空管太阳能热水器又分为全玻璃真空管式、热管真空管式、U 管真空管式。全玻璃真空管太阳能热水器是太阳能热水器的主流产品，2007 年大约占全国太阳能热水器总产量的 90%。主要原因是我国掌握自主知识产权，并且真空管太阳能热水器的价位相对不高，有利于在我国的推广。全玻璃真空管太阳能热水器是由真空集热管、保温水筒、支架和附件组成的。我们调研的多数企业是从外部购买真空集热管，再与自行生产的保温水筒、支架组装后出售。图 6 - 1 为太阳能热水器产品示意图。

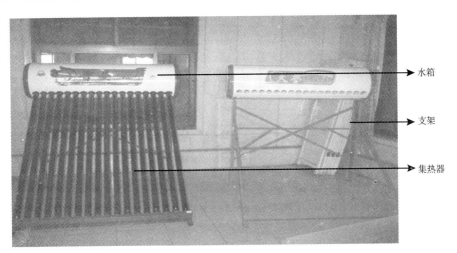

水箱

支架

集热器

图 6 - 1 太阳能热水器产品示意图

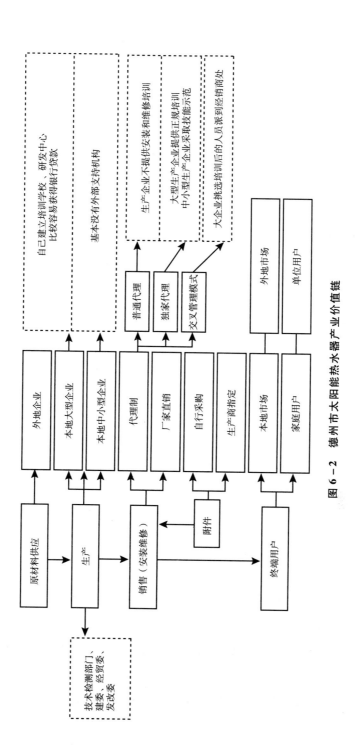

图 6 - 2　德州市太阳能热水器产业价值链

（二）太阳能热水器产业链的情况

太阳能热水器产业价值链的基本环节包括原材料供应、太阳能热水器生产、附加生产、销售（安装和维修服务）、终端用户。如图6-2所示。

1. 主要市场

太阳能热水器一直在城市市场发展较快，但是近年来这种发展势头呈现出停滞状态。主要原因是我国太阳能热水器品牌数量多，质量良莠不齐，其质量和性能难以满足消费者要求，特别是由于缺乏良好的安装和维修服务，太阳能热水器在消费者中的口碑不佳，降低了消费者的购买愿望。此外，城市楼房设计没有考虑到太阳能热水器安装问题，使很多城市居民难以使用太阳能热水器。而在农村地区，由于近年来居民收入水平的提高，以及农村养殖业发展的需要，太阳能热水器的推广速度比较快。德州市太阳能热水器生产厂家中大型企业的产品面向全国的城市和农村市场；中小型企业以满足本市及附近地区消费需求为主，一些企业在外地也享有一定知名度。

2. 终端用户

太阳能热水器终端用户包括分散的家庭用户、集体单位公用热水用户。目前，家庭用户是最主要的客户群体。城市的家庭用户主要使用太阳能热水器提供日常生活需要的热水；农村用户则主要将太阳能热水器用于养殖业。在德州，农村养殖户使用太阳能热水器的比较多，据介绍，在德州市农村养殖3～5头牛或者10头猪以上的农户，一般都会购买太阳能热水器用于搅拌饲料、给奶牛提供饮用温水，以及给牛洗澡等。对于针对家庭消费者的太阳能热水器，生产厂家一般采用专营店直销、代理经销、商场销售和建材市场销售的模式。单位客户群体主要是宾馆、饭店、学校、医院等公共场所。针对这类用户的热水器对产品质量和售后服务要求高，但是出货量大，利润空间较高。只有大型生产企业才能够生产这类产品，厂家一般会有专门的营销、安装和维护团队。

德州市太阳能热水器企业生产的产品包括高、中、低档太阳能热水器。消费者对产品档次的选择，与其所处的气候条件和收入水平密切相关。销往东北和西北寒冷地区的热水器以中高端产品为主（高端产品价格在2500元/平方米以上，中端产品价格在1600～2500元/平方米）；华北、华东以中端和低端产品为主（大约1500元/平方米以下）；南方地区四季温度都较高，因此消费者使用低端产品比较普遍。城市消费者收入水平相对较高，一般选择中高端产品；农村消费者受收入水平限制，选择低端产品比较多。

农村是太阳能热水器的主要潜在市场，所以我们对农村用户进行了访谈，发现了以下问题。

（1）市场上的太阳能热水器品牌众多，消费者难以辨别质量优劣。尽管大家都知道大型企业的产品质量过硬，但是其产品的价位比较高，难以满足农村消费者对于低价位的期望。

（2）经销商对太阳能热水器产品缺乏了解，有时候不能正确回答消费者的问题。

（3）后续服务不到位。很多厂家没有建立有效的售后服务体系。有时候用户甚至找不到售后服务。还有一些经销商使用质量不过关的附件，导致出现热水器漏水等问题。

（4）农村的消费习惯和收入水平仍然限制了太阳能热水器的推广。因此，太阳能热水器在农村地区的销售季节性比较强，夏季销售量下降。

3. 生产方面情况

目前德州市是我国的重要的太阳能生产基地。关于德州市太阳能热水器生产企业和销售企业的数量，我们从三个渠道获得了信息。从德州市工商局获得的数据显示，德州市共有注册太阳能热水器生产企业40余家，其中骨干企业20多家，其余为小型企业；经销商220家左右。生产和销售环节从业人员总计约1万人。市经委掌握的数据显示，当地太阳能利用相关企业有近百家，其中规模以上企业12家。我们访问的几家企业则认为，当地的太阳能热水器生产厂家大约有100家左右，经销商的数量应该更多。由于不同来源的数据差别较大，调研组很难进行准确研判，只能推测市经委和工商部门掌握的数字是正规经营、达到一定规模、生产比较稳定的企业的数量，而业内人士提供的是目前从事太阳能热水器生产的所有企业的数量；其中除了前面所说的那些具有一定规模、生产稳定的企业外，还包括一些生产规模小，甚至不正规经营的企业。德州市太阳能热水器生产企业的大致构成与全国整个行业的情况基本相同，比较具有代表性。2007年我国共有太阳能热水器生产企业3000多家，其中产值超过亿元的企业有25家，占市场份额的31.2%；其余的绝大多数企业为中小企业。在德州，产值超过亿元的企业有2家，占当地太阳能热水器产量的绝大部分；其余几十家甚至近百家企业为中小企业。

德州市的太阳能热水器生产企业分为三类：一类企业属于航空母舰型，其产品类型多元化，拥有自主研发能力，掌握专利技术，拥有全国性的知名度。这类企业包括同属于皇明太阳能集团下的皇明公司和亿家能公司。第二类属于正规的中小太阳能热水器生产企业。这类企业运作比较正规，有自己的品牌，至少在当地拥有一定的知名度。第三类企业属于非正规经营的企业。这些企业规模小，生产工艺落后，质量管理混乱。有的企业甚至存在偷工减料、假冒名牌、虚假宣传的问题。我们这次调研的企业是前两类。

（1）企业的基本情况。

①大型企业。第一类企业的代表皇明公司是世界上最大的太阳能生产企业，太阳能热水器年推广量200多万平方米，不仅生产适合不同气候、水质、建筑条件的家庭、单位用户使用的太阳能热水器，还雄心勃勃地在太阳能建筑一体化和太阳能高温发电方面开拓市场。在当地政府的支持下，皇明集团正在建设总规划为5000亩的太阳谷，作为太阳能生产制造、技术研发、人才培养及观光旅游等配套产业为一体的太阳能产业集聚地。除了针对品牌的直接宣传推广外，普及太阳能知识、推广科普教育也是皇明公司进行市场营销的战略之一。皇明集团的"全国太阳能科普车队万里行活动"，在推广太阳能知识和皇明品牌方面发挥了重要作用。这家大型企业不仅得到了当地金融机构的青睐，还获得了外部风险资金投入。2008年12月，美国高盛投资银行和鼎晖国际投资公司向皇明集团注资近1亿美元。

皇明公司直接雇用员工7000多人，其中管理人员占1/3，一线操作岗位和普通文员占2/3。员工平均年龄29岁，普通员工的工资在当地属于中等水平。一线员工的学历以中专、高职、高中为主；管理人员一般拥有大专以上学历。从劳动合同类型来看，与操作工人的第一份劳动合同一般为一年，一般管理人员签二年，技术人员签三年，高层管理人员则签五年。从事皇明产品经销和服务的外部人员大约有六万多人。这些人不属于皇明集团的雇员，而是皇明代理商的雇员。

由于目前职业技校和大学里设置的相关专业与太阳能热利用专业仍然有较大的差别，所以皇明集团开创性地尝试了多种培训教育手段。第一种做法是与一些大学合作开办"皇明班"，除了教材、课程设置更加专业化以外，学生在校期间就会了解皇明的生产工序、所需技能以及企业文化。第一批"皇明班"学生毕业后已经来到皇明集团工作，据说工作热情非常高，融入企业很快，解决了以前困扰企业大学毕业生理论脱离实践、难以融入企业文化、流动率比较高的问题。第二种做法是创办了皇明职业中等学校、工程技术学院和商学院。目前这三家学校的主要服务对象是皇明集团：商学院用于内训，为内部优秀员工提供提升管理能力的机会；工程学院面向社会招生，主要为皇明集团培养管理人员、销售店长和工程、销售和设计人员；职业中专培养生产、安装和营销人员。第三种做法是企业内部的培训部门定期开展针对企业员工和经销商的培训。此外，鉴于目前很多职业标准不能完全符合太阳能行业的特点，皇明集团正在开发有针对性的职业资格标准和培训教材。

②正规中小企业。这类企业有两种类型。一类企业拥有自己品牌，在当地及附近地区具有一定的知名度，销售量稳定增长。其生产方式是自己制造水箱、支架，再从外地专门生产真空集热管的厂家购买集热管，组装成成品，用自己的品牌销售。另外一类企业是国内大型生产商的生产外包商，按照发包企业提供的技术标准和工艺为其生产水箱、支架。总体来看，这些中小企业生产自动化程度较低，多采用半自动和手工生产，雇用人数不多，一般有 30～50 人从事太阳能热水器的生产。由于太阳能热水器生产的季节性比较强，企业工人的流动性比较强。有的企业还兼营其他业务，在非生产旺季时安排员工从事其他工作，人员流动率就相对较低。

小企业案例 1：

在当地属于中型企业，拥有自己的品牌，每年销售两千台左右太阳能热水器。真空管从外部购买，自己生产水箱和支架。产品属于中低价位，在城市和农村都有销售，主要市场在德州。销售人员的工资是基本工资加销售额提成 10%，大部分员工工作年限比较长。安装人员都有保险（本地的政策是企业必须加入养老保险和医疗保险，其他社会保险不是强制的）。未来市场开发重点是农村，原因是养殖业发展快；城市市场可能发展缓慢，因为现在城市建的都是高层建筑，无法安装太阳能热水器。

小企业案例 2：

企业发展比较快，开始生产太阳能热水器的第一年只销售了几百台，第二年销售量就增长到三千多台，第三年预计能卖一万台。生产的是中端产品，主要市场在德州周边的农村。有 300 多个经销商，多为独家代理。目前有员工

100 多人，除了做太阳能热水器外还生产电子仪表，从事太阳能热水器生产的员工有 30 多人。生产有淡旺季之分，天气热的时候是淡季。淡季的时候也不给职工放假，否则员工会流失。对员工的技能要求并不太高，新招用的员工一般需要一个月左右就能熟练操作。不同生产企业用的设备和生产流程不同，员工从一个企业去另外的企业必须要重新培训，并经过一定的熟练期。员工的平均工资是 1000 多元，最好的生产工人工资可以达到 3000 多元，刚来的新手工资大约 700~800 元。员工的流动率不太高。

小企业案例 3：

这家企业是纯粹的代工企业，根据大企业提供的原材料、设备、工艺和图纸，自己组织生产。企业共有 130 多人，太阳能热水器生产 36 人，年销售额 1200 万元。2000 年以前做自己的品牌，但是小企业打品牌比较难，开发推广渠道的成本高；后来与大企业合作以后，就不再生产自己的品牌了。生产工人属于熟练工种，技术含量不高，收入在 1200 元左右。开春是旺季，企业经常缺工；淡季时又不需要那么多人。员工的流动性比较大，只有 50%~60% 的员工能干满 1~2 年。

尽管德州市太阳能热水器生产企业数量众多，在某种程度上可以说形成了产业集群，但是本地的生产企业之间缺乏分工合作。大企业和小企业之间缺乏信任，大企业认为小企业对行业缺乏足够了解，质量管理落后，影响行业形象；中小企业则抱怨大企业占据太多的资源。当地一些小企业希望通过建立协会联合起来，增加对政府进行游说的能力，共同参加政府的招标；互相提供联保，推动当地银行为中小企业融资；并将协会作为太阳能生产企业之间交流的平台。但是，政府希望协会能有大企业的参与，否则协会无法代表本地的太阳能热水器行业。另外，政府希望通过协会推动大企业与中小企业之间的分工合作。对于此事，大企业认为与小企业不在一个层次，且其业务处于快速发展期，没有时间参与。尽管政府希望能够尽快推进协会建设，但是也找不到好办法。

（2）太阳能热水器生产环节的优势和机会。

①发展太阳能热水器符合我国可持续发展战略，政府非常重视行业发展，并制定了优惠政策。

②太阳能热水器的市场潜力较大。随着农村居民收入水平提高，对洗浴热水的需求增长迅速。此外，养殖业发展带动了对太阳能热水器的需求。

③德州作为"太阳城"，在全国范围内享有很高的知名度，特别是当地将举办2010年第四届世界太阳城大会，有助于进一步提升该城市太阳能企业和产品的声誉。

④已经形成了产业集群，大中小型企业能够满足消费者对不同价位产品的需求。

⑤当地的大型企业拥有专业检测中心，愿意与其他企业共享（但是，企业检测结果不具有产品上市许可的作用，仅起到技术指导的作用）。

⑥大型企业建立了面向社会的培训学校，能够培养太阳能热利用专业人才。

（3）太阳能热水器生产环节的问题和风险。

第一，在外环境方面面临的问题如下。

●关于太阳能热水器的国家标准体系不完善，特别是对长期使用的可靠性缺乏详细要求，导致很多产品无法达到宣传的寿命周期，影响整个产业的口碑。

●政府的监管力度不足，不少企业属于非正规运营，质量管理混乱，甚至假冒伪劣，影响行业整体声誉。

第二，行业内部存在的问题如下。

●专业人才缺乏，特别是技术人员和懂行的管理人员缺乏。企业之间相互挖人，大的企业人才流失问题比较突出。

●新招大学生融入职业和企业难。太阳能热利用是新兴产业，大学没有开设这个专业，因此新招大学毕业生所学专业与企业需求不对口，且理论与实际脱节，需要较长的时间才能掌握专业技能。此外，不少年轻人难以融入企业文化，对职业和企业缺乏忠诚度，离职率较高。

●普通工招工比较困难。普通工的工资不高，加之蓝领职业社会评价度不高，因此尽管职业中等学校为贫困家庭的学生提供奖学金并承诺毕业后有工作，但是仍然感觉招生难。

●中小企业的产品设计能力弱，技术含量相对较低，产品层次不高。

●中小企业宣传推广能力有限，品牌不论在当地还是外地的知名度都不高。市场上太阳能热水器品牌多，生产企业想要突破重围就必须加大宣传。一家企业的经理认为"产品成功的关键是质量、宣传推广、合理价位"。目前中小企业主要有三种宣传方式:一是在本地媒体做广告。电视广告对提升品牌知名度的效果不错,但是成本比较高,"中小企业只能偶尔为之,不能长期使用"。二是生产企业为经销商提供的产品简介。各个厂家提供的产品简介比较简单,缺乏差异性。三是在互联网的一些销售平台上打广告,介绍企业和产品种类,但是企业反映效果并不是很理想。

● 政府主要向大企业倾斜,对中小企业的关注度和支持度不足。一位企业家认为"本地只有一棵大树,没有树枝和树叶",希望政府增加对中小企业的支持。例如,在厂房用地等方面对中小企业给予支持,政府采购项目能够公开透明,让中小企业也能够参与竞争。当地技术监督部门检测每个型号的太阳能热水器要收费6000元,小企业难以承受,希望能够减少费用。

● 当地缺少针对太阳能热水器行业中小企业的培训、融资、技术和产品推广咨询服务机构,中小企业融资难。当地没有政府资金建立的担保机构,只有一家完全采取商业运作的担保机构,不能提供抵押的中小型企业仍然很难获得资金。

第三,生产环节与价值链其他环节合作方面存在的问题如下。

● 缺乏良好的售后安装和维修服务,导致用户对太阳能热水器信任度降低,影响行业信誉。

● 当地生产企业多,但是原材料和附件都由各家企业分别从外地购买,增加了成本。

4. 销售、安装和维修服务环节的基本情况

服务环节吸纳就业效果十分显著,据我们访问的行业专家估计,销售、安装和维修、仓储等人员占整个链条人员的80%。工程用太阳能热水器多由厂家直接销售和安装。针对个人用户的太阳能热水器一般有几个经销渠道:代理商、厂家直销店、市场专卖、工程市场销售,其中使用代理商是比较普遍的做法。销售、安装和维修服务一般都由经销商来完成,大型的生产厂家也设有专门的技术部门和服务热线,对经销商提供技术支持。城市地区经销商的企业规模从5~6人(小型),到100多人(大型)不等,平均规模是10~20人。农村地区的代理商则规模比较小,有时候就是夫妻店。

(1) 生产商与经销商的合作模式。

第一种是独家代理。大型企业对于独家代理的要求是,初次回款的数量在

省会城市为 40 万~50 万元，地级城市 30 万元，县级 20 万元。此外，还要建有不低于 100 平方米的形象店，要配备店长、售后经理、服务人员，要有电话、传真和计算机等设备。中小企业对于独家代理的要求要低一些，只要经销商一次性购买一定数量的太阳能热水器就可以了，以后购买数量随意。独家代理的经销商只能出售一个厂家的太阳能热水器，但是可以同时经销水暖器材、五金器材等其他产品。生产厂家对于经销商的店面位置、面积一般没有太多要求。例如，我们访问的某品牌厂商对县级别代理的要求是一次性购买 10 台太阳能热水器，并支付 1000 元保证金，以防止压低价格等违反生产厂家规定的行为，避免对其他经销商产生影响。也就是说，做一个在本地享有一定知名度的产品的县级代理，需要先购买 10 台热水器，再加上店面租金，其开办费用大约在 5 万元以下。

经销商案例：

2009 年 2 月开始经销太阳能热水器，到 7 月份一共卖了 50 多台，每台可以赚 300 元。销售主要依靠店面招徕消费者，有时也到农村去推销。目前推销成功的主要原因，一个是厂家上半年搞促销，降价不少；另外，靠亲戚朋友介绍了不少客户。此后，进入夏季就是热水器销售淡季，大家都凑合着用冷水洗澡了。农村市场虽然大，养殖业需求大，但是不好干，主要是农户没钱。当时挑选这个牌子，也不太了解，就是听说这个牌子口碑不错。等到做代理了才发现，这家企业的推广力度不够，很多农户都不知道，不好卖。厂家曾经在本地电台做过广告，效果好。平时发厂家提供的彩页广告，各个厂家的广告都差不多，农户也不知道怎么选择。

第二种是普通代理，生产商和代理商之间的关系比较松散。生产厂家对代理商是否代理其他厂家的太阳能热水器没有限制，代理商也没有事先购买其产品的义务。厂家仅仅在代理商处陈列一些产品，并为代理商提供代理标识。采用这种代理形式的一般是规模较小的生产企业，经销商一般以销售水暖器材、五金器材等为主业。这些商店代售的品牌比较多，我们看到很多商店同时挂着几个品牌的太阳能热水器的牌匾和宣传资料。

第三种是交叉管理模式，这是目前皇明公司在尝试的经销模式。由于不少经销商的企业规模不大，所以对员工的管理不到位，员工的待遇常常较低。为了降低其核心员工的流动率，增加技能积累，皇明公司开始尝试为经销商的核心员工发放基本工资和缴纳社会保险，员工只从经销商处领取提成的做法。

（2）生产企业与经销商之间的利益分配模式。

从利润分配模式来看，一般都是生产厂家定市场价位，然后以一定的折扣卖给经销商，其间的差价就是经销商的利润。在德州市，经销商出售每台太阳能热水器的利润大概在 200~300 元。销售商的另外一个收入来源是向用户提供附件的利润。生产厂家一般只提供热水器和支架，用户要想使用还必须配备室内管道、接头、花洒和水龙头等附件。附件一般由经销商购买，提供给用户使用。有的经销商为了增加利润，会使用一些质量有瑕疵的产品，导致出现漏水或者渗水等问题。同时，农村消费者经常赊账购买，在其后使用过程中发现质量瑕疵后会减少支付货款，因此经销商的利润空间可能进一步缩小。

（3）生产企业提供的附加服务。

大的生产厂家有专门针对经销商的培训，内容涉及安装、维修技术、营销和管理技能。中小型生产企业对于经销商的培训则比较简单。很多低级别的经销商本身是经销水暖器材的，所以一般是生产厂家派技术人员给用户安装一两次，经销商的人员跟着去学，之后就独立安装和维修。如果经销商在以后的服务中遇到技术问题，生产厂家会提供支持。

（4）优势和机会。

• 做中小型生产企业的经销商需要的资金量不大。

• 对安装和维修的技能要求不太高，有水暖安装维修经验的人很快就能学会。

• 农村居民收入提高，对生活质量的要求有所提高，养殖户对太阳能热水器需求大，所以本地太阳能热水器的市场潜力很大。

（5）问题和风险。

• 很多经销商自己也不了解太阳能热水器，难以选择质量好、价格适合当地消费者承受能力的太阳能热水器。我们采访的一家生产企业经理认为，"经销商懂产品和材质的不足 1%，各个厂家都会说自己的好，经销商也无法辨别"；一家受访经销商表示，自己之所以选择代理这个品牌的原因是"看到了电视广告"。

• 经销商的安装维修人员缺乏专业技能和安全防护知识。大生产企业认为，与普通热水器、空调之类的家电相比，太阳能热水器的安装和维修要复杂得多，前者是标准作业，而太阳能热水器没有作业标准，对于不同气候、建筑条件采用不同的安装方法，涉及多种知识和技能，因此安装和维修人员的技能十分重要。但是，我们访问的中小生产企业和经销商还没有认识到这一点。

●不少代理商文化程度不高，管理意识和管理水平不足，其服务流程不规范，管理制度不完善。

●经销商与生产厂家之间缺乏信任。做大品牌的代理需要投入较多，条件比较苛刻，小的经销商讨价还价的能力比较弱，导致利润空间比较小。一些经销商使用价格低廉的附件，影响热水器的使用效果。有的经销商抱怨，生产企业过于强势，代理条件苛刻，销售人员承诺多但是常常不兑现；有的厂家指责经销商不能诚信经营，重销售、轻后续服务，甚至使用质量不合格的附件，影响了生产厂家的信誉。

●中小型生产厂家对其产品的宣传力度不够大，农村消费者对这些品牌不了解，经销商的推销压力大，不大好卖。

●农村消费者一般只有到秋季才有现金，因此经常赊账购买太阳能热水器，经销商需要多次催款才能要回货款，负担很重。在使用过程中，消费者在发现产品质量的瑕疵后，常常会少支付一些钱，进一步缩小了经销商的利润空间。

5. 原材料供应

对于德州市的太阳能热水器生产企业来说，原材料包括化工、机械、电子、玻璃等很多材料，其中，对企业影响比较大的是真空玻璃管毛坯管和附件。德州市的中小生产企业采购的真空玻璃管毛坯管，主要来自全国的 3~4 家企业，例如，北京力诺、北京锁阳、滕州光谱、兖州金盾都是知名的品牌。支架也有专门厂家生产和供货。太阳能热水器的零件、附件一般从山东临沂购买，那里有专门的批发市场。尽管德州太阳能热水器企业数量众多，但是德州还没有相应的附件集散地。不少企业认为，临沂距离德州 400 多公里，从临沂采购附件增加了运输成本，因此建议在本地也开设这样的附件集散市场。

五　改善太阳能热水器产业链的建议

综上所述，德州市太阳能热水器行业的优势明显，但制约因素也很突出。具有一定规模的产业集群、城市在太阳能行业的知名度、市政府对太阳能热水器生产和使用的大力支持，都是该产业在德州市发展的优势。但是，行业发展不规范、售后服务滞后、行业人力资源缺乏、政府对中小企业支持力度不足等问题也制约着行业的进一步发展。有必要从政府和企业层面共同采取措施，改善行业发展环境，规范行业市场秩序、改善行业发展环境，推动技术创新，提升企业的竞争力，并建立产业价值链各个环节之间的共赢合作模式。

（一）改善产业发展的政策建议

首先，有必要进一步规范行业市场秩序，改善行业发展环境。在完善太阳能热水器的国家标准体系、为行业健康发展提供保障的同时，还要加强市场监管，打击生产、销售假冒伪劣产品的违法行为。

其次，制定具有可操作性的有利于产业发展的优惠扶持政策。《可再生能源法》和《循环经济促进法》为太阳能热水器行业的发展创造了大环境，但是单凭这两部法律仍不足以推动整个行业的健康稳定发展，有必要加大政策支持力度，在金融、财政、税收、科技、建筑，以及消费政策等方面对太阳能热水器行业提供支持。例如，采用减免所得税等的方式鼓励企业将等额资金用于研发和技改项目；将太阳能热利用作为建筑节能技术，享受建筑节能的优惠；简化安装太阳能热水器系统的建筑许可制度，积极引导企业在新建住宅项目中主动推广太阳能热水器与建筑的结合进行设计和施工；将太阳能热水器列入政府绿色采购名单，设立政府指定采购品牌；对消费环节的补贴等。

最后，针对绿色技能人才缺乏已经成为制约绿色行业发展的瓶颈这个问题，制定有利于包括太阳能热水器在内的新兴绿色行业的人力资源开发政策。一是进一步完善绿色职业标准的制定和推广工作。随着绿色经济的发展，很多新兴的绿色职业应运而生，很多绿色职业，都没有相应的国家职业标准，不利于这些职业的推广和相关培训的开展。对于有的职业，包括太阳能热利用，尽管已经制定了国家标准，但是标准在行业企业中的推广力度不足。例如，国家早在 2000 年就制定了太阳能热利用工的职业标准，并规定相关从业人员必须持证上岗；但是，我们调研的太阳能企业都没有听说过这个标准和相关的培训。因此，有必要在设计职业标准时吸引相关行业企业参与，以便使职业标准的设计更加贴近企业实际。二是推动企业和培训教育机构之间的合作。太阳能热利用是在企业的推动下产生和发展起来的，学校在相关专业的设置、教材开发、师资和技术方面相对滞后。因此，应该鼓励培训机构和企业、行业协会开展多种形式的合作，共同培养产业发展需要的人才。三是加大对开展太阳能热利用技能培训机构的支持。太阳能热利用对很多培训机构来说是新领域，既缺乏师资，又缺乏相关技术、设施，需要进行更多投入。中央财政从 2004 年开始，对符合条件的职业院校实训基地进行扶持，但到 2009 年才将能源环保专业作为八个重点领域之外的兼顾领域。可以说，对包括太阳能热利用在内的新兴绿色产业培训的支持远远不足。四是鼓励支持企业自行开展相关技能培训。很多培训教育机构没有开展相关的课程设置，因此企业需要花费较大的成本来开发培训教材和培训课程，因此其员工培训的费用可能要超过工资总额的1.5% ~ 2.5%（可以免除缴纳流转税）。对此，建议国家出台相应政策，对企业自行开展培训的，给予相关的税收优惠政策。

（二）改善产业发展的具体措施

1. 加强对中小型生产企业的支持

我国有太阳能热水器产品生产的企业中，绝大多数是中小企业，中小企业是产业链中比较薄弱的环节。具体包括以下内容。

（1）开展对中小型生产企业经营者的管理能力培训，提升经营者的管理能力。

（2）鼓励中小企业与大学、研究机构、设计院建立合作，改进产品设计，提高产品质量和产品的差异度，增强产品竞争力。

（3）推动中小企业与咨询服务企业合作，探索适合行业特点和中小企业特点的营销模式和营销手段。

（4）解决中小企业融资难的问题。

（5）推广适合中小企业的简易劳动合同，指导中小企业规范用工管理。

（6）支持中小企业建立太阳能热水器行业协会，促进中小企业之间的合作。例如，集中采购原材料，增强议价能力，降低采购成本；集中参加政府和开发商的招标；提供贷款联保等。

2. 改善太阳能热水器的销售、安装和维修服务

太阳能热水器的使用，必须要与水、电工配合并连接各种管道，可以说后续的安装服务对太阳能热水器的使用效果至关重要，因此行业内有"三分产品，七分安装"的说法。此外，针对农村市场的特殊营销模式是拓展农村市场的关键。目前，很多生产企业发现农村市场潜力巨大，但是不得其门而入。对于缺乏营销渠道和后续服务不足这两个制约太阳能热水器行业发展的瓶颈问题，建议外部干预重点集中在这个领域。具体建议包括以下内容。

（1）开展针对农村和中小城市经销商的培训，主要内容包括太阳能热水

器的基本知识、向当地消费者宣传推广太阳能热水器的技巧和策略、经营企业的管理技能，以及财务知识。

（2）开发专门针对太阳能热水器安装和维修人员的培训教材，组织开展技能培训。

（3）协助经销商建立服务流程，完善管理制度。

（4）推动生产厂家参与对经销商、安装维修人员培训的设计和提供，改善生产企业和经销商之间的关系，建立信任，实现共赢。

（5）为打算从事太阳能热水器销售服务的人员，提供有针对性的创业培训和小额贷款。

参考文献

［1］国家统计局、环境保护部编《中国环境统计年鉴（2008）》，中国统计出版社，2008。

［2］《中国环境年鉴》编辑委员会编《中国环境年鉴（2006）》，中国环境年鉴社，2006。

［3］国家环境保护总局：《2008年中国环境状况公报》。

［4］国家统计局能源统计司、国家能源局综合司编《中国能源统计年鉴（2008）》，中国统计出版社，2008。

［5］国家林业局编《中国林业年鉴（2008）》，中国林业出版社，2008。

［6］中华人民共和国国家统计局编《中国统计年鉴（2008）》，中国统计出版社，2008。

［7］国家统计局人口和就业统计司、人力资源和社会保障部规划财务司编《中国劳动统计年鉴（2008）》，中国统计出版社，2008。

［8］《第一次全国经济普查主要数据公报》，2005。

［9］中国电力企业联合会统计信息部：《2007年电力工业统计资料汇编》，2007。

［10］国家环境保护总局科技标准司、中国环境保护产业协会编《中国环境保护产业市场供求指南（2006）》，中国环境科学出版社，2007。

［11］《国务院关于印发节能减排综合性工作方案的通知》。

［12］普雷斯科特：《低碳经济遏制全球变暖——英国在行动》，《环境保护》2007年第6期。

[13] 徐嵩龄:《世界环保产业发展透视》,《中国环保产业》1997 年第 6 期。

[14] 周宏春:《环保产业政策的国际比较》,《节能与环保》2002 年第 12 期。

[15] 王圳:《全球可再生能源的发展》,《国际经济合作》2007 年第 6 期。

[16] 《经济日报》2009 年 3 月 25 日第 11 版。

[17] Roger Bezdek (Management Information Services, Inc.), "Renewable Energy and Energy Efficiency: Economic Drivers for the 21ˢᵗ Century", Report for the American Solar Energy Society (Boulder, CO: ASES, 2007).

[18] HowardGeller, "The Experience with Energy Efficiency Policies and Programs in IEA Countries, Learning from the Critics", Paris: International Energy Agency, 2005, http: //www. iea. org/Textbase/publications/free _ new _ Desc. asp? PUBS_ ID = 1567.

[19] Ryan Keefe, Jay Griffin and John D. Graham, "The Benefits and Costs of New Fuels and Engines for Cars and Light Trucks", Pardee Rand Graduate School Working Paper, WR – 537 – PRGS (Santa Monica, CA: November 2007).

[20] Global Electricity – generation Sector Investments from European Wind Energy Association (EWEA), "Forum for Energy and Development, and Greenpeace, Wind Force 10: A Blueprint to Achieve 10% of the World's Electricity from Wind Power by 2020 ", London, 1999.

[21] McKinsey Global Institute, "Curbing Global Energy Demand Growth: The Energy Productivity Opportunity", May 2007, http: //www. mckinsey. com/ mgi/reports/pdfs/Curbing_ Global_ Energy/MGI_ Curbing_ Global_ Energy_ full_ report. pdf.

[22] Michael Renner, "Working for the Environment: A Growing Source of Jobs", World Watch Paper 152, Washington, DC, September 2000.

[23] Paul Hawken, Amory Lovins, and L. Hunter Lovins, *Natural Capitalism: Creating the Next Industrial Revolution* (Boston: Little, Brown and Company, 1999).

[24] WorldBusiness Council for Sustainable Development, "Doing Business with the World, The New Role of Corporate Leadership in Global Development", Geneva and Washington DC, September 2007. [25] Jeremy Lovell,

"European Businesses Go Green Fast", Reuters, 14 March 2007, http: //
www. planetark. com/dailynewsstory. cfm/newsid/40831/story. htm.

[26] U. K. Department for Environment, "Food and Rural Affairs and Trade
Unions Sustainable Development Advisory Committee, A Fair and Just
Transition – Research report for Greening the Workplace", London, July
2005, http: //www. unep. org/labour _ environment/TUAssembly/ref _
docs/TUSDAC_ Greening_ the_ Workplace_ EN. pdf.

[27] United Nations Framework Convention on Climate Change, Investment and
Financial Flows to Address Climate Change, Background Paper, October
2007, Executive Summary, http: //unfccc. int/files/cooperation _ and _
support/financial_ mechanism/application/pdf/background_ paper. pdf.

[28] James Stack et al. , "Cleantech Venture Capital: How Public Policy Has
Stimulated Private Investment", CleanTech Venture Network and Environmental
Entrepreneurs, May 2007; Cleantech Group, LLC, China Cleantech Venture
Capital Investment Report , Cleantech Venture Network, 2007.

[29] Burtis, P. , Epstein, B. , & Hwang, R. , "Creating the California
Cleantech Cluster", Environmental Entrepreneurs and Natural Resources
Defense Council, September 2004 , http: //www. e2. org/ext/doc/
9. 8. 2004CreatingCaliforniaCleantechCluster. pdf.

[30] James Stack et al. , "Cleantech Venture Capital: How Public Policy Has
Stimulated Private Investment", CleanTech Venture Network and
Environmental Entrepreneurs, May 2007.

[31] UNDP, Human Development Report 2007/2008 (New York: Palgrave
Macmillan, 2007).

[32] Lisa Mastny, "Purchasing Power: Harnessing Institutional Procurement for
People and the Planet", World Watch Paper 166 , Washington, DC, World
Watch Institute, July 2003; Anne Berlin Blackman, Jack Luskin, and Robert
Guillemin, Programs for Promoting Sustainable Consumption in the United
States , Lowell, MA: Toxics Use Reduction Institute, University of
Massachusetts, December 1999.

[33] Emma Graham – Harrison, "China Plans MYM265 Billion Renewables

Spending", Reuters, 4 September 2007.

[34] UNEP, "Indian Solar Loan Programme", http: //www. uneptie. org/ energy/act/fin/india/, viewed December 10, 2007.

[35] Organisation for Economic Co – operation and Development (OECD), "Towards Sustainable Consumption: An Economic Conceptual Framework", Paris: Environment Directorate, June 2002.

[36] Norman Myers and Jennifer Kent, *Perverse Subsidies. How Tax Dollars Can Undercut the Environment and the Economy* (Washington, DC: Island Press, 2001).

[37] Janet L. Sawin, "Mainstreaming Renewable Energy in the 21st Century", World Watch Paper 169, Washington, DC: World Watch Institute, May 2004.

[38] Richard Ottinger and Nadia Czachor, 'Bringing Down the Barriers," World Conservation, July 2007.

[39] UNEP, ILO, and ITUC, "Green Jobs: Towards Sustainable Work in a Low – Carbon World", December 21, 2007.

后　记

　　本书课题研究得到了国际劳工组织北京局的资金资助和技术支持。在项目研究过程中，北京局的项目主管 Marja Paavilainen 女士、张绪彪先生、朱常有先生、佐佐木聪先生、周洁女士、潘伟女士为课题组提供了大量研究参考资料、交流研讨机会、具体工作建议和帮助，国际劳工组织曼谷局的 Ivanka Mamic 女士、Vincent Jugault 先生以及日内瓦总部的 Peter Poschen 先生、刘旭先生对课题的研究方案及研究报告提出了有价值的意见和建议。课题组还得到了中国人力资源和社会保障部国际司戴晓初副司长和钱晓燕处长的具体指导。在我们对调研行业进行选择的过程中，中国社会科学院的郑艳女士、华北电力大学的于恩海教授给予了热情的咨询帮助。在我们对课题研究进行前期设计和后期研讨的过程中，也得到了国家能源局、国家发展和改革委员会环资司和气候司、国家环境保护部技术标准司、国家住房和城乡建设部科技司、国家林业局、国家发展和改革委员会能源所、环保部环境与经济政策研究中心、中国环境保护产业协会、中国治沙学会、中国城镇供水排水协会、太阳能热利用协会、中国社会科学院宏观经济研究院等单位有关同志的大力支持。此外，天津市和内蒙古自治区有关部门对我们开展调研给予了大力支持。对于他们的帮助，课题组表示衷心的感谢。

　　"中国绿色就业研究"课题由中国人力资源和社会保障部劳动科学研究所课题组承担完成。课题由劳动科学研究所所长游钧主持，劳动科学研究所就业与人力资源市场研究室主任张丽宾具体协调，课题组成员包括：张丽宾、阴漫雪、廖骏、李宏、孙瑜香、袁晓辉。本书具体分工为：张丽宾，第一章，绿色就业研究概论和第二章，中国绿色就业研究；阴漫雪，第四章，中国绿色就业的相关法律政策和第六章，案例分析——德州市太阳能热水器产业价值链分析；廖骏，第三章，绿色就业的国际研究；李宏，第五章，中国发展绿色就业的社会环境评估。另外，孙瑜香参与了调查问卷数据的分析；袁晓辉参加了德州市太阳能热水器产业价值链分析的研究工作。书稿由游钧审定。

最后，要感谢中国劳动保障科学研究院的经费支持和社会科学文献出版社编辑的辛勤劳动，使得本书得以与读者见面。

"中国绿色就业研究"课题组

2013 年 9 月 23 日

Research on Green Employment in China

1 Introduction to Development of Green Employment

Currently, China is in the middle industrialization stage of heavy chemical industry, during which the contradictions and pressures from resource shortage, environmental deterioration and climate change are very prominent. The outbreak of the global financial crisis brought a severe challenge to the existing economic development model of our country, thus the transition to a sustainable economic and social development model became more urgent. After the outbreak of the crisis, various countries in the world, especially the developed countries, all took actions to implement Green New Deal, specifically, to promote economic recovery and create decent jobs by investing in green economy, and to reduce the environmental pressure and the threat of climate crisis to survival and development by promoting the development of green employment. As for China, among a package of economic incentive measures, there are also quite a part of funds used for investment in green economy. The transition to green and low-carbon economy is not only a trend of the global economic and social development, but also an objective requirement for future development of China.

As a matter of fact, our government has attached importance to environmental protection all the time by formulating and implementing a series of policies and measures, closing 13 key industries for eliminating backward productivity; promoting the technical transformation of traditional industries, improving energy utilization efficiency and fulfilling energy saving and emission reduction; improving comprehensive utilization level of resources and vigorously developing circular economy; strengthening environmental pollution control and developing environmental industries rapidly; strengthening eco-agricultural construction, implementing Six Key Forestry Programs and strengthening the ability of carbon sink, etc. During the process, some employment opportunities have been destroyed and some new created. Besides, the skill requirements for some jobs have changed and some employment opportunities have been substituted, all of which finally lead to the change of total employment, employment structure, employment increase and employment pattern. Therefore, the transition to green and low-carbon economy will have a great influence over employment. And as a developing country with a large population requiring employment, we must be responsible and deal with the employment problem properly in the transition to green economy.

1.1   Concept of Green Employment

Green employment is a brand new research field, and so far, no accurate definition of it has been generally accepted worldwide, thus the understanding of the issue is still in the continuously deepening process with each passing day.

1.1.1   Scope of Green Employment

1.1.1.1   Green Economy

Economy greening refers to the process of re-constructing enterprises and infrastructure in order to increase the investment return of natural, human and economic capital, reduce the emission of greenhouse gases, take and use fewer natural resources, create less waste and reduce social differentiation. So green economy is considered being capable of not only creating green employment and ensuring real sustainable economic growth, but also preventing environmental pollution, global warming, resource depletion and environmental degradation.

The Green Economy Initiative led by the UNEP (United Nations Environment Programme) aims at assisting governments of various countries in focusing on and re-formulating the policies, investment and expenditure for departments such as clean technology, renewable energy, water supply service, green traffic, waste management, sustainable agriculture and forestry for economy greening.

In practice, "greening" mainly contains six aspects: firstly, vigorously developing environment-friendly industries, primarily including eco-agriculture, ecotourism, organic food, renewable energy, service industry, high & new technology and afforestation, etc.; secondly, restricting the excessive development of the industries affecting environment greatly, mainly including heavy chemical industries like energy, metallurgy and building materials as well as light industries like papermaking industry; thirdly, greening/purifying the production process by developing new production processes, reducing or substituting the use of toxic and harmful substances, making efficient and circular utilization of raw materials, decreasing the generation of pollutants and conducting purification treatment for pollutants, etc.; fourthly, constructing and maintaining the public environmental facilities in cities and villages, protecting and governing public environment; fifthly, protecting and restoring ecological environment; sixthly, developing green service industry centering on economy greening, including green credit, green technology, green equipment, green insurance and green certification, etc.

1.1.1.2   Green Employment

Generated and developing in the process of economy greening, green employment refers to the employment engaging in greened economic activities and green economic activities. Green economy means "greening" industrial structure, technologies and processes of production, organization modes of production and life style, while green employment signifies employment adopting green technology, process and raw materials for production, employment engaging in green production and service, and also, employment directly undertaking environmental and ecological protection work.

The International Labor Organization defines green employment as a decent job created in economic departments and economic activities capable of alleviating environmental impact and finally fulfilling sustainable development of environment, economy and society.

Consistent with the development strategies for constructing a resource-saving and environment-friendly society, the green employment in China can be defined as jobs of low-investment, high-output, low-consumption, low-emission, circular and sustainable industries, professions, departments, enterprises and posts in national economy compared with the social average level. "Low Investment and High Output" generally refers to the employment related to improving organization management level and thus enhancing production efficiency. Improving production efficiency means the conservation of various production factors, with a resource-saving and environment-friendly trend, which is the main aspect of the transition of China's economic growth mode from extensive pattern to intensive pattern, which plays a fundamentally decisive role in the whole economy and thus shall be considered as a key factor of China's green employment. "Low Consumption and Low Emission" mainly refers to the employment related to fulfilling the generally-considered energy & resource saving and pollutant-discharge reduction by improving technical level, which is a basic element of green employment. "Circular and Sustainable" signifies not only the idea of ecological system's self-restoration and sustainable economic & social development, but also the employment related to circular economy, pollution control and ecological environment protection.

1.1.1.3 Relationship between Green Employment and Green Economy

Employment, in nature, is an economic relation and an economic behavior, subject to the adjustment of the supply and demand mechanism of labor market and the influence of product market. The total amount and structure of product supply, the technologies and processes of product production, and the organization modes of product production, etc. determine the employment quantity, employment structure and employment pattern. Green employment is actually a product of green economy development generated and developed in the process of economy greening, and also, a key force promoting green economy development.

1.1.2 Characteristics of Green Employment

To understand the concept of green employment, it is required to master the following characteristics of green employment:

1.1.2.1 Green Employment Has Environmental Characteristics, Namely, Green Employment Shall not only Feature Decent Work, but also Lay Emphasis on the Environmental Function of Employment.

"Green employment" specifically refers to that the economic activities undertaken by laborers are conducive to the protection or restoration of environmental quality. In terms of environmental function, green employment has four characteristics: namely, the characteristic of "dematerialization economy" aiming at reducing energy and raw material consumption, such as employment created in developing circular economy; the characteristic of "decarburation economy" aiming at avoiding greenhouse gases emission, like employment in the fields of solar thermal utilization and wind energy utilization; the characteristic of "environmental economy" aiming at minimizing waste and pollution, such as employment in electric power enterprises after their installation of dedusting and desulfurization facilities; the characteristic of "ecological economy" aiming at protecting and restoring ecological system and providing environmental services, like employment in eco-agricultural field.

Green employment refers to the employment which has far less negative influence over environment than the average level and thus can improve the environmental quality on the whole. In green employment, the degree of different employment's influence over environment varies, thus there are various types of green employment, such as "light green" employment, "deep green" employment and "dark green" employment, for example, automobile capable of energy saving and environmental protection belongs to light green employment, public transport system with large capacity belongs to deep green employment, while solar thermal utilization belongs to dark green employment. Since the working environment and working conditions are still not environment-friendly, in reality, some green employment shows no decentness.

1.1.2.2 Green Employment Has Dynamic Characteristic of Keeping Pace with the Times, not only Including the Transformation of the Existing Employment, but also Covering the Jobs Newly Added Due to Innovation.

Not all green employment belongs to a new type of employment. Certainly, some green employment provides new types of work never existing before, but most green employment is based on traditional specialties and professions only with some changes of working contents and ability requirements. Even for the brand new green employment created by completely new industries and new technologies, its supply chain mainly consists of work in traditional industries such as steel and machine parts manufacturing only with certain change of the working contents and with new skills and requirements.

Green employment includes the employment opportunities created directly, the indirect employment opportunities brought by the direct creation of employment and also the employment opportunities derived from induction. Direct green employment involves employment in enterprises engaging in waste treatment and sewage treatment, etc.; more is indirect employment, such as the employment in enterprises producing sewage treatment equipment; inductive employment covers the employment driven by aspects such as recycling and reusing of electronic waste.

Green employment features keeping pace with the times. Thus the standards of evaluating green employment are associated with the environmental standards under specific background. For instance, the non-green employment in developed countries may be green one in developing countries, and the green employment in the present stage may turn into non-green one with the development of economy.

1.2 Present Development Situation of Green Employment in China

In China, green employment has developed for a long period. Specifically, the environmental protection work in our country has been undertaken since the 1980s and the environmental protection industry has formed; afforestation has existed since the foundation of the state, and trees have been planted annually; since the 1990s, solar industry has developed and currently achieved a sizable scale; wind power generation has developed rapidly and biomass energy power generation to some extent; the three-waste treatment in industries and enterprises has been conducted with more and more strength, and for eliminating backward productivity, those with high pollution and high energy consumption have been closed successively; circular economy and waste recycling are developing under regulation. After the above process, a certain scale of green employment has been formed.

1.2.1 Industries and Employment Groups in Traditional Employment Closely Related to Green Employment

Green employment can be found in various industries. According to indexes such as the emission volume of green gases, the degree of taking natural resources as raw materials, the contribution rate to economy, and the contribute rate to employment and income, green employment is mainly centralized in six economic departments, namely, renewable energy, building, traffic, basic industry, basic agriculture and basic forestry departments. From the perspective of the employment situation in key industries closely related to green employment development [1] , the employment not covering agricultural field relates to 84.23 million people, while those covering agricultural field involves 398.67 million people, in which, 12.533 million population engage in energy and resource [2] industry, 4.643 million in metallurgic [3] industry, 8.725 million in non-metallic mineral product manufacturing industry, 5.976 million in light industry [4] , 11.36 million in chemical industry [5] , 32.53 million in building industry, 6.533 million in traffic industry, 1.93 million in hydraulic and environmental industries as well as public facility field, taking up respectively 6%, 2%, 4%, 3%, 5%, 15%, 3% and 1% of the secondary and tertiary industries in unit employment and totally occupying up to 39%. Considering the employment of the self-employed and the flexible employees neglected in the statistics, the population shall be larger and the proportions greater. Though a great number of people engage in the key industries which closely related to green employment development, so far, only a small part of posts in these industries belong to green employment indeed, and most of them can be turned into green employment only after being transformed.

1.2.2   An Analysis of Present Development Situation and Development Prospect Green Employment in Key Industries

On the whole, the direct employment effect from the transition to green and low-carbon economy seems not promising, thus emphasis must be laid on the expansion

---

[1]   Here, it only refers to the employment situation of legal entities.

[2]   Including mining industry, production and supply industry of electric power, fuel gases and water.

[3]   Including ferrous-metal smelting and calendering processing industry and nonferrous smelting and calendering furniture manufacturing industry, processing industry.

[4]   Mainly including leather, fur and feather (down) industries and their manufacturing industries, wood processing industry and woodworking, bamboo product, rattan product, palm coir product and straw-made article industries, papermaking and paper product industry.

[5]   Including petroleum processing, coking and nuclear fuel processing industry, chemical raw material and chemical product manufacturing industry, pharmaceutical industry, chemical fiber manufacturing industry, rubber product industry and plastic product industry.

of indirect employment effect. For the transition to green and low-carbon economy, in energy industry, the main way is to adjust energy structure and develop renewable energy and new energy for improving energy efficiency. Specifically, traditional energy industries will see a decline in employment, and except for solar energy, the direct employment driven by new energy is limited; for raw material industry and processing & manufacturing industry, mainly transform technologies, save resources and strengthen comprehensive utilization of resources, in which technical transformation and technical progress usually leads to the reduction of direct employment; in building industry, mainly develop energy-saving buildings and conduct energy efficiency improvement for buildings, however, the development of energy-saving buildings is subject to the market demand and the prospect of direct employment seems not promising; in traffic industry, mainly develop public transport system, but the direct employment effect is small as well; in agriculture, mainly develop eco-agriculture, and as to forestry, mainly conduct afforestation and develop ecological forestry, etc. Due to limited land resources, the potential of forestry and agriculture in creating new green employment is restricted, mainly exhibited in employment substitution. The indirect employment effect mainly comes from the contribution of environmental industry development to employment. The transition to green employment will finally lead to the change of total employment, employment structure, employment increase and employment pattern.

1.2.2.1 Employment in Relevant Industries of Environmental Protection [1]

Over recent years, the state has made more investment in constructing

---

[1] In April 2006, the State Environmental Protection Administration, the National Development and Reform Commission, and the National Bureau of Statistics jointly issued the "Communique of the Situation of Environmental Protection-Related Industries in China" executed specifically by China Association of Environmental Protection Industry in 2004. The investigation was a one-time comprehensive investigation, for which, the reference time was 2004 and the implementation time covered February to August of 2005. Apart from the special administrative regions of Taiwan, Hong Kong and Macao, the investigation covered the state-owned enterprises or institutions specially or in some aspects engaging in the environmental protection-product production, comprehensive utilization of resources, environmental protection service and clean product production as well as the non-state-owned enterprises or institutions belonging to environmental protection-related industries with over-2 million annual sales (operation) income in 31 provinces, autonomous regions and municipalities.

infrastructure for environmental protection, which effectively stimulates the market demand for relevant industries of environmental protection. Nowadays, relevant industries of environmental protection have become an important part of the national economy structure. According to the "Communique of the Situation of Environmental Protection-Related Industries in China", in 2004, people working in state-owned units and non state-owned units with an annual sales (operation) income being over 2 million Yuan belonging to relevant industries of environmental protection amount to 1.595 million, in which, 168,000 people engage in the environmental protection industries mainly producing water-pollution treatment equipment and air-pollution treatment equipment, 960,000 people in resource-comprehensively utilized industries mainly conducting recycling of renewable resources and comprehensive utilization of solid waste, 170,000 in environmental protection service industries mainly aiming at design and construction service for environmental engineering and operation service for pollution treatment facilities, and 233,000 people in the clean product industry centering on energy-saving products, low-toxic and low-harm products, low-emission products and organic food.

In short, the environmental protection industry has developed fast. According to the latest statistics made by China Association of Environmental Protection Industry, in 2008, the number of units belonging to environmental protection industry in our country arrived at 35,000 and the employees over 3 million people, occupying 0.66% of those engaged in non-agricultural employment in that year. Thus it can be foreseen that, with the establishment, issuing and implementation of the national "Development Plan of Energy Saving and Environmental Protection Industries", there will be a more significant increase of employees working in environmental protection industry, which is predicted to be millions of people.

1.2.2.2. Employment in New Energy Industry [1]

Vigorously developing renewable energy is a basic strategy of our country.

---

[1] Relevant research of Energy Institute of the National Development and Reform Commission.

Renewable energy industry is a completely new industry and its development will definitely contribute to employment increase. According to relevant research, by the end of 2007, the total employment population in the new energy industries nationwide amounted to approximately 1.1 million, mainly engaged in solar energy industry, wind energy industry and biomass energy industry, taking up 0.24% of those in non-agricultural employment.

Table 1-2-1   Employment Population (Thousand People) in New Energy Industry

Solar Water Heater	Solar Photovoltaic	Solar Thermal Power Generation	Wind Energy	Biomass Energy	Other Industries	Total
800	100	0. 150	20	200	1	1121

According to relevant research[①] , in every creation of a direct post, it is required to be invested 1.15 million Yuan for wind energy, 910,000 Yuan for solar photovoltaic cells, 700,000 Yuan for solar thermal utilization and 140,000 Yuan for biomass energy. Overall, the employment in renewable energy units demands far more investment than that in traditional industries. Since China is a developing country, the investment in such kind of posts is really costly. The primary energy in China mainly consists of coal. In 2005, among the consumption of the primary energy in our country, coal took up 68.9%, petroleum 21.0%, natural gases, hydropower, nuclear power, wind energy and solar energy, etc. only 10.1%, while in the same year, among the global primary energy consumption structure, coal took up only 27.8%, petroleum 36.4%, natural gases, hydropower and nuclear power, etc. up to 35.8%. However, in the future, China's coal-centered energy structure will hardly be changed fundamentally in a quite long period. Though by 2020, it will be realized that renewable energy occupies up to 20% of the energy supply, and more

---

① Peter Poschen. Symposium of Green Employment in China. March 30th, 2009.

employment opportunities, predicted to be up to 2.2 million, can be created, but the renewable energy industry and the traditional original energy industries will not see a reverse in employment opportunity like that of America. In a long period, the employment in traditional energy industries will still be dominant. Certainly, the development of new energy industry will drive the development of industries such as wind power equipment manufacturing and industrial raw materials, which will bring along a lot of indirect employment opportunities.

1.2.2.3 Employment in Energy-saving Reconstruction of Buildings [1]

In the continuous high-speed growth of economy and the fast promotion of urbanization in our country, building industry has developed rapidly. The building industry consumes most energy, thus promoting building energy saving is an important field in China's energy saving and emission reduction. As required in relevant laws, regulations and policies, the design and construction of newly-built buildings shall be provided with energy-saving building structure, materials, instruments and products to improve the performance of thermal insulation and reduce the energy consumption of heating, cooling and lighting; the existing civil buildings and public institution buildings shall be provided with energy-saving reconstruction.

The new construction of energy-saving buildings and the energy-saving reconstruction of the existing buildings will create a large number of employment opportunities. Since 2005, the state has developed the project of building energy saving in pilot cities, and relevant posts have been greatly increased in the pilot cities. Just for the existing energy-saving reconstruction of buildings, nowadays, our country has a building area of high up to over 42 billion Square meters. However, most buildings built before 2006 are incapable of energy saving, and the lock-in effect of no energy saving will last at least 30 years. Among 42 billion existing buildings, if reconstructing 1/3 only

---

[1] Mo Zhengchun. "Energy Efficiency and Green Employment of the Existing Buildings". "Symposium of Experience Sharing and Policies of Green Employment in China". March 30th, 2010.

calculated by 200 Yuan/square meter, the market value will reach 2.8 trillion Yuan. Moreover, in relevant report, it states that energy-saving reconstruction of buildings can newly increase around 12.6 million employment posts[①] .

However, the development of green employment will face some bottlenecks due to the energy-saving reconstruction of buildings. Specifically, the energy-saving reconstruction of buildings generally requires relatively higher initial investment, which can hardly attract the developers' interest; the existing building reconstruction has high technical content, for example, just in the energy saving of residential buildings, it includes the energy saving of building envelope, the update of heating and cooling equipment, and the heat metering alteration, etc., which requires a large number of work types with various professional technologies, while the building industry is short of skilled workers and among the construction workers, only 1/5 have been provided with training; in addition, relevant laws and regulations have not been implemented effectively so that there is still no valid provision for the acceptance check and supervision. All of the above restrict the green employment development of building industry.

1.2.2.4 Employment in Power Industry

While developing renewable energy, our country has tried to enhance energy efficiency, energy saving and emission reduction via elimination of backward productivity and other measures. Among the industries requiring energy saving and emission reduction, power industry comes first. However, while protecting environment, these environmental protection measures have influenced the employment. According to relevant research[②] , before 2020, closing down the small thermal power units as per the policy of "encouraging large projects and discouraging small energy-inefficient power plants" will make nearly 600,000 people lose their jobs. Besides, based on the investigation of thermal power

---

① "Report on Measures for Climate Change" in 2009.
② "General Report of the Subject of Empirical Study on Low-Carbon Development and Employment in China" of Chinese Academy of Social Sciences. December 2009.

enterprises conducted by the task group, among the employees losing jobs due to the closing of the power units, only 1/10 can have a new job on the assistant posts of the large power units newly built, while the other over 500,000 people have difficulties in finding another job, which requires employment assistance.

Meanwhile, because of the installation of desulfurization facilities in thermal power industry, the thermal power desulfurization industries of the corresponding period are predicted to create 1.08 million direct, indirect and inductive posts, including approximately 31,800 posts increased due to equipment running and maintenance as well as 300,000 posts created by desulfurization equipment manufacturing industry.

1.2.2.5　Green Employment of Forestry

Forest is the biggest "carbon storage" and the most economical "carbon absorber", so that employment related to this aspect is greatly promising, mainly exhibited in three aspects: firstly, employment created via continuous afforestation, restoration of degraded ecological system, construction of agroforestry system and strengthening of sustainable forest management; secondly, employment created by wood production and processing industry; thirdly, employment created in chemical industry of forest products, forest machinery manufacturing, forest tourism, forest food, forest medicinal materials, economic forest, flower and bamboo industries, etc.

According to relevant research, every increase of 1-hectare forest area can achieve a new post. From 2002, our country has started to implement the Six Key Forestry Programs and has achieved 76 million hm2, based on which it is predicted that 22.8 million people can obtain employment, with over 2 million people each year on average. As per the "China Forestry Yearbook (2008)", the state has constructed over 1200 forest parks of different kinds, and in 2001, the forest parks nationwide had received tourists of up to 83 million, creating a comprehensive income of more than 50 billion Yuan and creating directly or indirectly various posts of 3.5 million. Reputed as the "Bamboo Kingdom", the bamboo forest area and stock volume as well as the annual output of bamboos in China all come first all over the world, showing great potential of the bamboo industry; additionally, the flower industry is also recognized as one of the most dynamic industries in the world, for China has a long history of flower cultivation with rich varieties, exhibiting huge potential of development and providing employment. For employment in forestry, if 30 million people are provided with a job, the employment population in forestry will only take up 9.5% of that in agriculture.

On the other hand, the protection of forestry resources leads to serious employment problem in 135 large forestry enterprises (state-owned forestry bureaus) centering on the development and utilization of natural forest resources. Almost 412,800 workers under collective ownership have not obtained a job and the re-employment funds for 484,000 redundant workers are insufficient. Due to single forestry industrial structure and limited posts, a large number of workers have to face unemployment or seasonal unemployment. The forestry's transition to green and low-carbon economy is faced with a huge quantity of employment cost.

Therefore, the present development situation and the future development prospect of the green employment in our country require deeper research. Currently, in China, the employment population in solar water heater industry accounts for 96% of that in the whole world; it is estimated that nearly 10 million people engage in various recycling industries, among which only the recycling of electrical apparatus involves 700,000 people; at present, over 50% of the global newly-added buildings are in Asia, especially in China, thus improving the energy efficiency of buildings will provide a lot of employment opportunities as well. Thus, it can be seen that the green employment in our country has a great development potential. However, on the other hand, corresponding cost has to be undertaken while developing green employment. Eliminating the backward productivity not only makes some employees face the threat of losing their jobs, but increases huge economic and social cost for employee resettlement; green development seriously challenges the laborers' employment abilities, thus skill transformation and enhancement demands great cost; some new green employment have been created but with huge investment, costly technology cost and substitution of the original posts as the main method. In short, the development of green employment still has a long way to go.

1.3 Ideas of Promoting the Green Employment in China

1.3.1 Accurate Mastering of the Contents of Developing Green Employment

Developing green employment is conducive to employment. Raising green employment can facilitate the government to establish the development strategy for green human resources as early as possible, thus accommodating the development of green and low-carbon economy. In the long run, with great space, potential for sustainable development and ability of facilitating decent work, green employment is the development direction. Specifically, green employment can directly bring along the improvement of labor productivity and enterprise benefit, thus contributing to a faster increase of labor reward and an enhancement of labor share in income distribution; in promoting the integration of various environmental protection measures into a continuously-extended green industry chain, a large quantity of employment opportunities will be provided, which will definitely counteract the reduction of posts in traditional industries in the long run, and the employment opportunities newly created are of more safety, economic benefit and stability; using energy-saving and environmental protection facilities in production process can obviously improve the workers' working environment, thus being helpful to worker's safety and health; promoting technical progress & industrial upgrading and boosting the improvement of technical content in labor by implementing energy saving and environmental protection measures can be conducive to improve the laborers' skill quality. Our specific case study on the green employment in power industry does indicate that green employment have more occupational safety than non-green employment, and green employment is more decent than non-green employment, for the enterprises providing green employment take environmental protection measures, which can facilitate decent employment. According to the basic national policy of constructing ecological civilization, China shall unswervingly implement the strategy of green employment, that is, incorporate the promotion of green employment development into the existing strategy of expanding employment, formulate relevant policies and measures, and promote the development of green employment in the course of continuously expanding employment.

For the concept of "Green Employment" raised and the proposal of "Green Employment" initiated by the international society, the fundamental purposes are: firstly, to express that the green employment opportunities created by the transition to green and low-carbon economy are more than the non-green employment opportunities destroyed, so as to accommodate the idea of "transitioning to green and low-carbon economy" initiated by the international society in terms of employment; secondly, to incorporate green employment into decent work and enhance the international labor standards. However, when affirming its positive significance of facilitating employment, it must be pointed out that the proposal of "Green Employment" raised by the international society pays insufficient attention to the constraints on the green employment development in developing countries. Just as the transition to green and low-carbon economy requires consideration of transition cost and conditions, the transition to green employment also demands cost. Actually, our governments, enterprises, laborers and society all have undertaken tremendous cost of transition to green economy gradually. For example, the governments provided the subsidies for the electricity price of desulfurization, the subsidies for the electricity price of wind power sent into grid, the one-time resettlement cost for employees in forestry enterprises and the policy of constructing re-employment service centers for laid-off workers, etc.; many enterprises have to suffer cost increase by conducting technical transformation for they cannot release their responsibility when some workers find no place to go, for instance, the power generation enterprises undertake the responsibility for resettling the workers in the closed small thermal power units by providing training and jobs, etc. for them; the workers in the closed small enterprises lost their jobs and had difficulty in finding another job, etc. Besides, the social cost of transition to green employment is huge as well, for example, some workers in the closed enterprises appeal to the higher authorities for help to safeguard their various rights and interests, and though being resettled, some workers feel accumulated resentment due to the gap between their psychology and reality.

Analyzing from the recent 20 years of the international political and economic situation, the issue of global climate change has become more and more serious, which has already turned into an important basis for the politics and economy in the international society as well as a main tool for the western developed countries to re-divide the international political and economic pattern. Thus the raising and the incorporation into the labor standards of green employment naturally becomes an important dimension of developed countries in the game of negotiation on global climate change. We must soberly realize the dual effects possibly brought by the development of green employment, that is, we must soberly realize that for China, such a developing country, where the employment population takes up 1/4 of that in the whole world, 40% of labor force are still engaged in agricultural production, the employment's urbanization rate is less than 40%, almost 8 million rural surplus labor force go to cities for employment each year, 1/3 of the urban employment population are in flexible employment, and each year, the non-agricultural employment population requires 30 million posts while the posts created by economic growth only reach over 10 million, promoting employment at low cost is still the only feasible way to guarantee the basic employment right of our citizens. Therefore, we shall draw on advantages and avoid disadvantages, that is, in the formulation and implementation of the strategy of transitioning to green economy, we shall consider that we are now in the middle stage of industrialization with imperfect market economy system, always tremendous employment pressure and relatively backward employment structure, also, we shall consider the finance we have and the bearing capacity of the society, and we shall take into full account the economic and social cost on the transition to green employment.

1.3.2   Ideas of Promoting Green Employment

The general objective of the development strategy of green employment is to actively expand employment oriented by green employment, to be specific, vigorously develop new green employment opportunities, stabilize the existing green employment opportunities and maximize the positive influences of green economy development over employment; in the process of adjusting industrial structure and transitioning to green economy, lay emphasis on the guarantee of the laborers' legitimate rights and interests and minimize the negative influences of environment upon employment; promote the development of green economy by developing human resources. While protecting environment to the utmost extent, take measures to control the unemployment rate within a scope acceptable to the society, and the increase of unemployment rate, the reduction of the income level of laborers are unallowable to be caused due to the development of green employment, so as to avoid aggravating the unemployment problem and even making the problem exceed the acceptability of the economic society. Through active promotion of green employment development, the sustainable economic growth of environment and society will be finally fulfilled.

For developing green employment, the principles as below shall be followed:

1.3.2.1 Attach Full Importance to the Influence of Green Economy Development upon Employment in Promoting the Development of Green Economy.

Currently, our country is in the middle stage of industrialization, during which a great deal of energy is required, thus appropriate energy consumption is necessary for economic development, while low-carbon development actually means restricting the level and scale of energy utilization, which will finally restrict development and employment. In view of this, in the Intergovernmental Panel on Climate Change (IPCC), the attitude shall be made clear that, so far, the carbon dioxide emitted into the atmosphere by developing countries has only accumulated to less than 10%, so that we have a full right to keep the emission for development. To fully consider the factor of employment, it is required to find a suitable point to avoid undertaking inappropriate obligations which may cause great employment pressure and thus have a negative influence over the economic and social development in our country. At the same time, we shall strive for international funds and technologies, and while promoting economic development, mitigate the discharge of green gases.

1.3.2.2 Take the Principle of Promotion per Classification.

The development of green employment involves two aspects: one is the employment created by the market spontaneously, such as the employment in waste recycling industry; the other is the employment created by the promotion by the government, such as the employment in thermal power industry. For various green employment, it is required to take different measures and strategies on the big premise of promoting employment, rather than treat different matters as the same or find a single solution for diverse problems. As to the green employment created by the market spontaneously, the government's principle of employment promotion is to insist on the principle of marketization, and the government plays the role of eliminating the interference factors that obstruct the market mechanism from coming into play, so as to provide more and better employment service. For the green employment created by the government's promotion, it is necessary to adhere to the employment promotion principle of policy intervention and formulate specific policies for employment promotion.

1.3.2.3 Pay Equal Attention to Industrial Policies, Environmental Policies and Employment Policies.

Developing economy, protecting environment and promoting employment are all for people's livelihood, thus equal importance shall be attached to the three aspects without bias or neglect. That is, it is not allowed to ignore environmental protection and employment promotion due to economic development, nor to restrict economic development and employment increase on account of environmental protection, nor to adopt the development model without employment increase, instead, it is required to adhere to do what are possible and advance gradually in due order oriented by economy greening, and take comprehensively supporting policy levers to promote the optimization and upgrading of industrial structure, the continuous improvement of environment, the enlargement of employment quantity and the enhancement of employment quality in a coordinated way. It means that we shall encourage green industry development, promote traditional industry greening in an orderly way and perfect environmental standards gradually on the premise of adequately considering the objective of full employment.

Furthermore, to fulfill the coordinated promotion of the above three aspects, it is critical to achieve the synchronization of policies, specifically, while formulating industrial policies and plans, the synchronous employment policies and plans must be provided; while establishing environmental policies and plans, the synchronous employment policies and plans must be offered; and while setting down employment policies and plans, the effects over economic development and environmental protection must be considered.

1.3.2.4 The Policies of Green Employment Promotion Are Required to Attach Importance to the Adjustment of the Green Employment Itself.

Green employment is a continuously-developing matter with the following problems: some green employment is not decent employment in itself; some green employment is in favor of environmental protection but is not low-carbon employment; even for low-carbon employment, some is adverse to environmental protection, for example, the planting of biomass energy requires chemical fertilizer, which may cause pollution; some employment is green employment, but inconsistent with the industrial development requirements, such as the employment in capacity-redundant photovoltaic power generation industry and power generation equipment manufacturing industry; some employment is green employment, but unmatched with the resource endowment characteristic in our country, for instance, since China has limited land resources, it is not appropriate to develop biomass energy. Therefore, for green employment, it is not to encourage its development invariably, but also demands policy control. While formulating the policies for promoting green employment, it is required to proceed from the actual conditions of China to determine the field of green employment where an intervention will be made and the intervention degree.

1.3.3 Policy Suggestions on Promoting the Development of Green Employment

Formulating policies for promoting green employment development is to green more active employment policy system. On the one hand, implant the concept of "Green" into the existing policy system; on the other hand, incorporate the previous relevant policies into the policy system, such as the employment policies for resource-depleted cities, the policies for reservoir resettlement, and the policies for closing bankrupt enterprises based on policy, etc. On this base, enrich and perfect the existing active employment policy system in our country, and China's green employment policy system will be finally formed.

Firstly, guarantee the development of green employment with legal means. Make employment assessment of industrial policies and environmental policies, formulate the employment-centered social evaluation index system of environmental protection, and in various industry plans and environmental protection plans, include the employment evaluation indexes, and take the evaluation on the influence of industrial policies and environmental protection policies as the procedural prerequisite of project approval; amend and perfect relevant laws and legalize the employment evaluation of industrial policies and environmental protection policies.

Secondly, strengthen the policy support and promote the development of green employment. Green the market mechanism of human resources, establish the authentication system of enterprises providing green employment and the qualification authentication system of green employment, and green the public employment service system; green the existing active employment policies and give play to the role of the existing policies for those whose employment is affected in the transition to green economy; develop a number of green employment with potential via policy support; in the new rural construction and the western development, vigorously support the development of eco-agriculture, characteristic agriculture, characteristic agricultural product processing industry and characteristic rural ecotourism, etc., develop rural green employment, and drive the rural public service demand to create green employment for public service; support the development of small green employment-type enterprises to provide jobs.

Thirdly, formulate the development plan of green skills and promote the development of green employment. Accelerate the development and establishment of standards on green employment, develop the professional standards of green training and the training standards of green technology, so as to gradually perfect the green employment system and the standard system of green employment training; formulate and implement the technical skill enhancement planning of green industries in our country to comprehensively improve the green skill level of laborers, thus providing the human resources required by green development; green the existing entrepreneurship training; strengthen the training for job transfer in the transition to green employment; gradually develop the vocational qualification authentication of green employment and the identification & appraisal of green skills; establish the skill development system of green employment involving various laborers.

Fourthly, strengthen the rights and interests guarantee of laborers engaging in green employment. In the development of green employment, promote the improvement of the employees' labor payment and their obtaining social insurance, improve the safety and health conditions, perfect the organization and functions of trade unions, facilitate the laborers engaging in green employment to enjoy the working conditions and labor payment in conformity with the principle of decent work, and enhance the safety and guarantee of employment.

Fifthly, jointly promote green employment by social partners. To develop green employment, a consensus must be reached among the government, the employers and the employees. To be specific, the trade union organizations can take an active part in the work of promoting the development of green employment; while considering the economic benefit, the employers must undertake the social responsibility to green development and unify green employment with the economic benefit as far as possible. Besides, in the tripartite consultation mechanism of labor relations, it is required to bring the development strategy of green employment to the fore and promote the development of green employment.

Sixthly, perfect the environment promoting the green development of enterprises. Expedite the perfection of environmental standards; gradually improve the incentive and induced mechanism of policies to make the adopters of green technology and practice stand in a favorable position in market competition; keep perfecting the financing mechanism of green development and strive for the support of international technologies and funds, so as to raise funds for developing green economy and creating green employment.

Seventhly, establish the employment compensation mechanism in the international climate negotiation. So far, the emphasis of the international climate negotiation has been only laid on the emission reduction targets of various countries, without considering the social cost of emission reduction. For this, it is required to establish the employment compensation mechanism in the negotiation, and for the negative influences over employment in developing countries due to emission reduction, give compensation for the funds, technologies or emission reduction targets.

2 Research on Green Employment in China

2.1 Background of Research of Green Employment in China

2.1.1 International Background

For long, the UN (Unitied Nations) attaches great importance to the sustainability of global environment and ecology. Recently, climate change also became another hot issue. Since the financial crisis in 2008, the UN has considered green policy as an important impetus for economic resurgence. During the process, technology, mechanism and economy are the key points to be discussed with less attention on the social and employment dimension. In 2007, International Labor Orgnization (ILO) in cooperation with United Nations Environment Programme (UNEP), International Orgnization of Employers (IOE) and International Trade Union Confederation (ITUC) jointly initiated the green employment projects, first in history incorporating employment, labor market, social justice and other social aspects of sustainability into discussion of environment and ecology sustainable development. The initiative was to help countries protect and create decent, environment-friendly and productive jobs, make sure all industries abide by environmental and labor standards, and promote the just transition to green economy. In short, green employment is a brand new area, the understanding of which is yet to be deepened in the global stage. As a country with rich labor, China's effort in promoting green employment has drawn the world attention.

2.1.2 National Background

Chinese government has attached great importance to environment and ecology issues while promoting employment during the process. In 1984, Chinese government issued the *Decisions on Environmental Protection Work*, stating that promoting and improving living and ecological environment, preventing pollution and natural environment damage is the basic national policy in the construction of socialist modernity. In 2006, the State Council issued the *Decision* on implementing the scientific outlook on development and strengthening environmental protection, stating that economic and social development should be coordinated with environmental protection, committed to strengthen the environmental protection, promote recycling economy, develop environment and relevant industries, nurture new economic growth point and increase employment. Protecting environment and ecology has promoted the development of green economy, which in return results in employment increase.

Promoting green employment is in accordance with development strategy of the Chinese government. In 2003, Chinese government already initiated the concepts of comprehensive, coordinated and sustainable scientific outlook of development, coordinating harmonious development between man and the nature, and building the harmonious socialist society. Harmonious coexistence between man and the nature was one of the six characteristics of harmonious society, in which productivity will be developed, people's life will be rich and people will enjoy their lives and work. In 2006, the government put enhancing the resources efficiency and improving ecological environment as one of the nine objectives of building harmonious society, requesting the change of economic growth pattern, improvement of development quality, promotion of the development based on energy saving, clean energy and safety, in order to achieve comprehensive and sustainable development of economy and society. Therefore, with the thought of building ecological civilization, the change in production and consumption pattern will promote the green employment. In the meantime, government also noticed directly the green employment and took many measures to promote green employment development and protect rights of the workers. This is in line with the international trend.

In fact, Chinese green employment has made tremendous contribution to the global green employment in terms of volume and growth. For example, the employee in the solar water heater business has reached 600,000, 96% of the employees in such business globally. In China, it is estimated that there are 10million people engaging in recycling business of varied forms. In the home appliances recycling business alone, there are about 700,000. Six major forestry projects will create 20 million job opportunities. Globally 50% of the newly increased construction is in Asia. Improving the energy efficiency in construction will further create many job opportunities. On the other hand, many other employment opportunities will be gone. For example, if we shut down one thermal power plant, 500,000 people will lose their jobs. Pulp and paper industry will also cut thousands of jobs if using non-wood materials.

China also has many other intervention practices in promoting green employment. In the early 1990s, China issued specific policies on employment of workers from five industries like coal and forestry, on cities with energy and resources crisis, on enterprises dislocated in the three gorges areas, and on workers lost jobs due to bankrupted enterprises. In addition, there were also policies on promoting self-employment and enterprise development. The most comprehensive policy was the more positive employment policy system aiming to solve the unemployment problem of the SOEs, including human resources policy, reemployment policy for laid-off workers, policy on adjusting labor relations, policy on improving employment insurance, etc.

In short, China's strategy on developing green employment is in line with international trend. The speed of development is fast and the policies are rich. In the key period of China making the twelfth five year plan, it is necessary to clarify the green employment in China in order to further promote the idea, summarize the practices to mobilize all social sectors to promote its development, evaluate current policies to enrich and improve the employment policies. In the meantime, under the background of global climate change, China as a big developing country needs to take responsible approach to address the employment during the transition to green economy.

2.1.3   Current Research

Research on China's green employment is still new in China. There are no referable research outcomes. Current relevant researches are as the following:

2.1.3.1   Researches on Green Economy [1]

Although green employment is a brand new topic, there are still many discussions on green economy. Green economy means human activities that will generate environmental and economic results. It has two parts. Firstly, it includes activities that will reform the old economic system with greening and ecological measures, including developing new production technologies, reduce or substitute the use of toxic or harmful substance, improve efficiency and recycle of raw materials, reduce output of pollutants, purify pollutants, etc. The second part includes developing industries that has less effect or positive effects on environment, meaning green industries like ecological agriculture, ecological tourism, organic food, renewable energy, service industry, high and new technologies, forestation, etc. green economy includes recycling economy, low carbon economy, and ecological economy. Recycling economy is to solve environmental pollution issues. Low carbon is to address energy structure and GHA emission. Ecological economy means to restore, utilize and develop ecological systems (grassland, forest, ocean, wetland, desert, etc.).

Environment policies on promoting green economy mainly include: raise up the environmental entrance level, optimize industrial construction, strengthen

---

[1]   Environment policies on actively promoting green economy, by Xia Guang, International Forum on China's green economy, November 2009.

administration and law enforcement of environmental protection, incorporate environmental protection into the process of production, transportation, redistribution, and consumption, plan and implement environmental economy policies to set up incentive mechanism helpful to environment protection.

2.1.3.2 Relevant Research Abroad

ILO, in cooperation with UNEP, IEO and ITUC, issued a report in 2008, which described green employment as Towards Decent Work in a Sustainable, Low-Carbon World The report was the first ever comprehensive paper on green employment, summarizing green employment as the following:

A. scarcity of resources, deterioration of environment and climate change has posed serious threat to sustainable development of the human society. To pursue coordinated sustainable development of the environment, economy and society has become the only choice of the human society, which means the transition to the green low carbon economy. This will bring tremendous job opportunities.

B. Green employment mean jobs in all industries that will help protect and restore environment qualities. The concept is not absolute. It evolves with time. Meanwhile, the term green itself represents a color range. Different green employment have different impact on protection and restoration of environment quality.

C. transition to green low carbon economy will make some jobs substituted or lost while creating new job opportunities.

D. Green employment can be created in all industries and sectors. Based on the amount of GHG emission, using natural resources as raw materials, contribution to economy, contribution to employment and income and other indicators, green employment are mainly concentrated in the area of renewable energy, construction, transportation, basic industries, agriculture and forestry.

E. Green employment are in every corner of life. They can be created in the background of all occupation, technologies and education level.

F. Green employment can be originated from internal shifts of one sector or industry. Most of the green employment are based on conventional profession and occupations with certain change in the contents and capability of the job. Even green employment created utterly through technological and industrial innovation, their supply chains are still made of conventional industries like steel and mechanic parts where job contents have certain adjustment with new technical and performance requirement.

G. Technological gap and shortage jointly hold up the development of green economy. Reduce the technological gap and predict future needs are the fundamentals for transition towards green low carbon economy.

2.1.3.3 Relevant Research at Home

At present, there is no study on green employment. Relevant research has Impact on employment in the process of transition to low carbon economy. It conducted quantitative research and estimation on employment impact of suppression between thermal power plants and forestation.

Researches about green economy also provided theoretical calculations on green employment. So did researches about low carbon employment. Researches on green employment also provided comprehensive and inspirational references for this study.

2.1.4 Objectives and Structure

The objective of conducting the China green employment study is to put forward policy measures on promoting green employment and eventually incorporate the green employment into a more active employment system, in order to promote the coordinated development between environment and employment. While protecting the environment, we ought to develop new green employment opportunities, stabilize the current green employment opportunities. During the process of industrial structure shift and transition towards green economy, we ought to safeguard legal rights of workers. While multiplying positive impact and reducing negative impact of the environment on employment, we ought to take measures to put unemployment rate in a controllable range and pursue the economic growth with sustainable environment and society. Based on the current situation and research in China, the study is to answer the following questions:

1. What is green employment? Green employment is a completely new concept. To clarify the concept is the basis for promotion and research of green employment.

2. What is the whole picture of green employment? Green employment is rather comprehensive, involving all sectors and areas of the economy. This is the precondition of conducting study on green employment. For example, in China there are still many industries like agriculture, fishery and tourism, heavily relying on environment and climate. Lives of workers in such industries are largely affected by environment.

3. What is the impact of green employment on workers? In the area of adjusting to climate change, investment in certain areas will create more and better jobs for people who can easily lose their jobs. In the case of adjusting to sustainable production pattern, it will require big adjustment in employment scale in short term. Some workers will face problems of losing jobs or having to improve technologies. New energy and industrial policies will create opportunities for green employment.

4. How to promote green employment development and safeguard employment rights of workers? It is necessary to appropriate employment transition, provide education and trainings for workers to be qualified for other environment friendly jobs or get financial compensations. Some cities helped older laid-off workers to be reemployment through measures like water resources protection, green cities, retirement of cultivated land and return to forest and grassland, stopping wind and stabilizing sand, developing industrialization of agriculture and dragon shaped economy. And there are also cooperation between trade union and companies.

2.2　Definition of Green Employment in China

2.2.1　Current Definitions

Green employment is a completely new area for research. The understanding on such topic is rapidly deepened. At present, there are certain definitions on the international level:

One is that green employment are jobs that are economically applicable and able to reduce environmental impact and reach sustainable development [1]. Another explanation is that green employment are any of those new jobs that will improve the overall environment quality and whose environmental impact is lower than average. [2]

ILO's definition on green employment is that green employment are decent jobs created in economic sectors and activities, which will reduce environmental impact and ultimately achieve sustainable development in environment, economy and society.

In the report, Green Employment: Towards Decent Work in a Sustainable, Low-Carbon World, green employment were defined as works in agriculture, industry, service and management that are helpful to protect or restore

---

[1]　Speech by Ivanka Mamic, "Environment & CSR Specialist." ILO Regional Office for Asia and the Pacific, Jan. 21 2009, Beijing.

[2]　Speech by Ivanka Mamic, "Environment & CSR Specialist." ILO Regional Office for Asia and the Pacific, Jan. 21 2009, Beijing.

environment quality. Green employment have four characteristics. First is to reduce consumption of energy and raw materials (dematerialize economy). Second is to avoid GHG emission (decarbonizes economy). Third is to protect and restore ecosystem. Forth is to minimize waste and pollution.

Minnesota Green Employment Task Force defined green employment as employment and entrepreneurial opportunities that are part of the green economy, including the four industry sectors of green products, renewable energy, green service and environmental conservation. Green products mean products produced with reduced environmental impact and improved resources efficiency. They are mainly produced in construction, transportation, consumption and industry sectors. Renewable energy includes solar power, wind mill, water power, geothermal energy and bio-fuel. Green services mean industries or sectors that provide all kind of services to help enterprise and consumers use green products or technology, including sectors like energy infrastructure and energy efficiency, agriculture, recycling and waste management. Environmental reservation means business related to reservation of energy, air, water and land resources.

The first definition is a vague definition that stress on the economic and environmental aspects. Second definition focuses on new emerging employment that has impact on environment. Definition by ILO emphasizes on decent work. UNEP report emphasizes on industrial and technological features of green employment. The definition by Task Force refers to employment in the green sectors. All these definitions provide some explanation on green employment from different aspects, yet do not fully explain the category and characteristics of green employment.

2.2.2 Definition in China

2.2.2.1 Theoretical Definition

Green means that ecological environment is in a sound condition. In order to achieve sustainable development, it is necessary to green the economic activities and living environment of the human race, which means to green the industrial structure, technology and techniques of production, organization pattern of production, and life styles. From the practical point of view, the greening process includes six aspects. First is to develop more industries that have less environmental impact, such as ecological agriculture, ecological tourism, organic food, renewable energy, services, hi-new technology, forestation, etc. Second is to restrict the development of industries with huge environmental impact, mainly heavy industry like energy, metallurgy, building materials and light industry like paper making. Third is green production, through developing new production techniques, reducing or substituting use of toxic and harmful materials, effectively using and recycling raw materials, reducing production of pollutant, purifying the pollutant. Fourth is construction and maintenance of public environment facilities in city and countryside and protection and administration of public environment. Fifth is protection and preservation of ecological environment. Sixth is to develop green services around green economy, including green credit, green technology, green facilities, green insurance, green certification, etc.

All jobs that are able to make economic activities and living environment greener and more environment-friendly are green employment. Green employment have the following characteristics.

- Green employment emphasize on the environmental function of the employment, meaning such employment is helpful to protect or restore environment quality. Labor attribution is not the main focus. Green employment does not necessary mean decent job.

- From environmental aspect, green employment have four characteristics. One is to reduce consumption of energy and raw materials (dematerialize economy). Two is to avoid GHG emission (decarbonizes economy). Three is to protect and restore ecosystem (environment economy). Four is to minimize waste and pollution (ecological economy).

- Ways to embody the above mentioned four characteristics are as the following. In macro level, adjust production structure, use new renewable energy and raw materials, develop low-carbon economy and recycling economy and environmental protection industries, etc. In micro level, improve production technology, provide relevant service, etc.

- Green employment are not jobs that have no environmental impact but those jobs that have less impact than average\and can improve environment quality. That is to say, green employment have different degrees like dark green and light green. In the non-green employment they also have black and brown jobs.

- The proportion of green employment in the total employment is relevant with development level and pattern. The more developed the economy is, the higher the degree of the green transition. The higher percentage of industry and construction and other secondary industries and the more extensive the economic growth pattern, the lower of the green degree of employment. In short, the development of green employment is restrained by objective circumstances and historical stage. We can promote the development of green employment, but can not surpass development phases.

- The criteria for green employment are rather relative and are related to environmental standards of specific background. Non-green employment in developed countries might be green employment in developing countries. At present, green employment might become non-green employment with the development of the economy. In short, green employment have a rather dynamic development pattern.

- Green employment can be found in any industrial genres, dispersed in all segments of resources mining, transformation, transportation, production consumption, waste generation, consumption. Green employment have big potential and prospect in sectors like construction, production, technology, facilities, techniques, services. Based on amount of GHG emission, degree of relying on natural resources as raw material, contribution to economy, employment and income, the low carbon report thought green employment are mainly concentrated in six economic sectors: renewable energy sector including wind power, solar power and bio-energy, construction sector, transportation sector, basic industries, agriculture and forestry.

- Green employment also show the imbalance of industries, profession and sectors. Normally, in comparison with secondary industry, the tertiary industry is greener. In the 19 national economic sectors, agriculture, water resources, electricity, manufacture, construction, and transportation are less green. In manufacture sector, electricity, steel, building materials, electrolytic aluminum, ferroalloy, Calcium Carbide, hard coke, coal, flat glass, light industry (paper making, chemical, dyeing) are less green.

- In green employment, there are workers with all kinds of occupation, skills and educational levels. From simple physical labor to skilled workers, from manual workers and business starters to highly educated technicians, engineers and managers, they can all be green employment holders. Green employment provide opportunities for mangers, scientists, technicians and all other simple labors. Those disadvantaged groups like young people, women, farmers, villagers and poor people can also get opportunities in green employment.

- Green employment does not necessary means new job. Some green employment are brand new job types. Most of the green employment are based on conventional profession and occupations with certain change in the contents and capability of the job. Even green employment created utterly through technological and industrial innovation, their supply chains are still made of conventional industries like steel and mechanic parts where job contents have certain adjustment with new technical and performance requirement. In short, green employment are newly reformed or created on the basis of current jobs.

- Green employment include direct, indirect and derived job opportunities. Direct green employment are job opportunities in enterprises of environment devices and environment protection, like waste handling, sewage disposal. More green employment are indirect opportunities which can be found indifferent industries and enterprises. Raising environmental protection standards will affect all sectors including production and consumption. Policy, research, finance (credit, insurance, and securities), supervision and trade also generate indirect employment. Therefore, studying on green employment need coordinated consideration of direct, indirect and derived employments.

- Green employment need technological innovation. Technology gap and skills incompetence hinter the development of green economy. The weakest point of production chain will decide the level of performance. Without qualified entrepreneurs and skilled workers, the available technology and investment can not be used to achieve proposed environment and economic performance. The need to reduce the technological gap and predict the future is the basis for transition to green low-carbon economy. Simply stressing on hi-end technology and education will only result in imbalance of labor market. Therefore, to train green collar workers is important. Evaluate the potential of green employment and monitor the process will benefit the mid and long term vocational training and education system, building connections between technological innovation and policy and investment.

- Similar to the fact that solving employment needs SMEs, small enterprises and local communities can create many green employment.

- The development of green employment includes four situations: some new jobs appear, some current jobs disappear, some jobs are substituted, and some jobs have more technological needs. These will have impact on the volume, structure, increment, and pattern of employment.

- Green employment is actually an easy name without any significant meaning. The purpose or the fundamental meaning of promoting green employment lies in two aspects: one is to draw attention to the importance of greening process's impact on increasing employment and creating decent jobs. The other is to promote green economy through green employment.

- Based on China's basic policy of building ecological civilization and the fact that China is still in the middle level of industrialization and urban-rural dichotomy labor movement, we should firmly implement the green employment strategy, integrate green employment into the current strategy of expanding employment, issue relevant policy measures and promote green employment during the process of expanding employment.

● From the perspective of human resources, green employment strategy have three objectives. One is to expand employment with green employment, not to deteriorate unemployment to a level that might threat economic and social development. Second is to promote the protection of workers' rights in the green employment development. Third is to promote green economy through human resources development.

2.2.2.2 Political Definition

According to the economic and social development plan and annual government, industrial and institutional plans and policy measures, the definition of green employment in China is employment in industries, professions, sectors and enterprises in an average social level that have low input, high output, low consumption, low discharge, recycling ability and sustainability, which is in line with the development strategy of building resource saving and environment friendly society.

Low input and high output refer to employment that results from improving management level and enhancing production efficiency. Enhancing production efficiency means to save all production factors and to be able to save resources and be environment friendly. Production efficiency is the main aspect of shifting economic growth pattern from extensive to intensive level. This will play a fundamental and decisive role in the overall economy and should become the factor of green employment. Low consumption and discharge refer to employment that is created through energy and resources saving and waste reducing by improving technological level. This is the basis factor of green employment. Recycling ability and sustainability are not only the ideas of ecological self-restoration and economic and social sustainability, but also refer to employment is related to recycling economy, pollution management and ecological environment protection.

This definition is based on the current stage and major problems of economic and social development, strategy and policy measures in addressing challenges and is in line with the global trend. China is a developing country with mid-low income and in the middle of industrialization and urbanization. The major problems China is facing are to meet the basic needs of human survival, huge environmental pressure, overwhelming extensive economic growth pattern and low rate of production factors. China's eleventh five year plan states that in order to achieve coordinated sustainable development of population, resources and environment we need to build resources-saving and environment-friendly society. Shifting economic growth pattern and enhancing input-output ratio are in line with recourses saving, environment protection, pollution reduction and emission reduction. It is the combination of adjustment and reduction. Low input, high output, low consumption, low discharge, recycling ability and sustainability are the summary of strategic plan of national economic development and define the category of China's green employment. In comparison with definition by UNEP, this definition is more comprehensive. Apart from resources saving, low discharge, low pollution, protection and restoration of ecological environment, it also stresses low input and recycling and sustainable ability, which embodies the characteristics of current Chinese economic development and overall idea of promoting sustainable development of the environment.

2.2.2.3   Category of Green Employment

Green employment include low carbon and environment protection employment. Environment protection employment is the employment pattern with low pollution. Low carbon employment is the employment pattern with low consumption, low pollution, and low emission. The idea of low carbon development is 20 years behind the idea of environment protection development. The idea and approach of low carbon and environment protection development are different. So are the low carbon and environment protection employment.

Conventional pollutant discharge is regional and partial. Reducing pollutant discharge is beneficial to low carbon development, but not 100%. In return, climate change has less impact on environmental pollution. Therefore, low carbon development has less impact on environmental protection. In general, jobs in the environmental protection sector are not necessarily low carbon and low carbon jobs are not necessarily environment protection employment. There are overlaps of low carbon and environmental protection employment. Yet they are not the same.

Pollution is internal affair. Developed countries solved the problem 30 years ago. The demands of environmental protection industry abroad are relatively stable and the job opportunities are rather limited. Hence, they do not care too much about the low pollution employment and focus more one global carbon emission issues, which is the reason why green employment are more about low carbon employment. It is totally different in developing countries. They are still in the developing phase of industrialization. Protecting environment and promoting clean development are still big issues. Therefore, green employment in developing countries include both low carbon employment and environment protection employment. Neither is dispensable.

2.3 Legal, Institutional and Policy Environment for the Development of China's Green Employment

From pollution control, ecological restoration to building ecological civilization and correcting shortcomings of industrial civilization, Chinese government is mentally adopting three transitions: one is transition from stressing on economic growth and neglecting environment protection to stressing both economic growth and environment protection. Second is transition from environment protection left behind by economic development to parallel development of environment protection and economic growth. Third is transition from protecting environment through administrative measures to solving environment problems through legal, economic, technological and necessary administrative measures [1] . The transition provided the background of green employment development.

2.3.1 Legislations on Environment Protection

On September 13 1979, the Eleventh plenary session of the fifth national people's congress passed the People's Republic of China Environmental Protection Law (Trial), which was the first law on environment protection in

---

[1] Building ecological civilization: the foundation and essence of environmental protection, by Zhou Shengxian. Documents of the Fifth international forum on environment and development in China.

China. Since then, the legal system on environment and resources protection is gradually formulated. Major legislations are as the following:

One is law about ecological and natural resources protection, including Land Management Law, Water Law, Forest Law, Grassland Law, Soil and Water Conservation Law, Wildlife Protection Law, etc. Second is law on environment pollution management and public pollution control, mostly about air, water, solid waste, noise, radiate objects and standards on environment quality and pollutant discharge, including Solid Waste Pollution Prevention and Control Law, water pollution prevention and control law, Air Pollution Prevention Law, Water Pollution Control Regulations, etc. Third is law about resources saving and comprehensive use, like Energy Conservation Law. Forth is law about promoting recycling economy and clean production, like Clean Production Promotion Law, Renewable energy law, Recycling economy promotion law. Fifth is about law on specific administrative system and regulations issued by State Council and Administrative ministries, like Environmental Impact Assessment Law, Environmental Protection Supervision Rules for Construction Projects, Rules on classification and approval of assessment documents of construction projects' environmental impacts.

2.3.2 Relevant Industrial Policies

Green development will eventually be implemented on industrial policy. Relevant industrial policies include the following.

2.3.2.1 Develop Renewable Energy, Optimize Energy Structure

Energy conservation law, National Eleventh five-year economic and social development plan, Plan of Energy Efficiency and Pollutant Discharge Reduction, Environmental Protection Eleventh Five-Year Plan, National Climate Change Program, Climate change policies and actions, and New Energy Development

Plan proposed the need to optimize and develop energy industry, optimize energy production and consumption structure.

Accelerate technological innovation in thermoelectricity generation, optimize thermal power structure, eliminate old Small Thermal Power Units, develop high efficiency and clean power generation technology. Accelerate the development of renewable energies like hydro power, solar power (solar water heating, solar stove), biogas which are mature in technology and strong in market competition, promote the industrial development of renewable energy technologies like wind power, biomass energy, solar power, bio liquid fuels (ethanol fuel with non-food raw materials, bio diesel, Household Biogas pool, biogas project with large scale animal farming, solid fuel with biomass from agriculture and forestry). Promote nuclear power. Further promote clean usage of coal, strengthen the use of coal-bed and coal-well gas, and study on technologies in CO_2 capture and storage.

In the future, the energy structure strategy is that renewable energy accounts for 10% of the energy consumption around 2010 as supplementary energy, 15% around 2020 as substitute energy, 25% around 2030 as mainstream energy, 40% around 2050 as leading energy.

Renewable energy is hi-tech and emerging industry and new economic growth field, which will boost development of equipment manufacturing industries, benefit industrial structural adjustment, promote shift of economic growth pattern, expand employment and save energy and reduce emission.

2.3.2.2   Eliminate Backward Productive Power

In 2006, the State Council issued Notice of accelerating structural adjustment of overcapacity industries. The notice committed to set more strict standard on environment, security, energy consumption, water consumption, resources use and quality, technology and scale to raise the entrance level, to eliminate backward productive power by closing down a set of small enterprises (small thermal power, steel, cement and coal plants), and to promote technological innovation to reform and improve conventional industries through enhancing technological level, improving products, protecting environment, ensuring safety, reducing energy consumption and promoting comprehensive use of energy.

13 sectors including electricity, steel, building materials, electrolytic aluminum, ferroalloy, Calcium Carbide, hard coke, coal and flat glass are the key areas to reduce energy consumption and pollution and emission. In January 2007, the State Council circulated the Opinions on Accelerating Close-down of Small Thermal Power Generating Units by SDRC and State Energy Bureau, proposing the encouraging big and suppressing small policy, which means that the new power generating projects will be conducted while closing down small thermal power units. While building power units with big capacity, high indicators, low consumption, less emission, some small thermal power units will be close down. In 2007, SDRC signed liability contracts with 28 provinces on closing down and eliminating backward steel productive power. Cement sectors need to shut down their production. The nonferrous metal sector should eliminate backward productions in copper, lead, zinc smeltery and small pre-roasted vat electrolytic aluminum factories. The light industry sector should eliminate paper making, ethanol, gourmet powder, citric acid, low efficient fridge (and refrigerating cabinet), tannery, Button alkaline manganese batteries containing mercury, filament lamp. The textile sector should accelerate the close-down of dyeing enterprises with serious pollution, eliminate backward dyeing and chemical fiber factories, further eliminate backward cotton and wool spinning enterprises. The petrochemical sector should eliminate outdated refinery equipment with low efficiency and quality less than 1 million tons. The agricultural chemicals sector needs to eliminate those high toxic and risk products, eliminating products like calcium carbide and carbinol.

In November 2007, the eleventh five-year plan on national environmental protection proposed that new projects need to fit in the entrance conditions and emission levels while setting industrial entrance conditions in sectors like steel, non-ferrous metal, building materials, power plants, light industry (paper making, chemical, dyeing) with consideration of environmental protection. For areas that have no further environment capacity, it should be forbidden to start new project that will increase pollutant discharge. The outdated industries and products with high energy consumption, heavy pollution and outdated technologies need to be forced to close down.

During the eleventh five-year, 50 million kW small thermal power units were shut down. 89.17 million ton refinery capacity and 77.76 million ton steel capacity were cut, involving 917 enterprises. 250 million ton cement capacity, 300,000 ton copper refinery capacity, 400,000 ton zinc refinery capacity, 800,000 ton small pre-roasted vat electrolytic aluminum capacity, 2 million ton paper making capacity, 30 million low efficiency fridges, 30 million pieces tans, 9 billion Button alkaline manganese batteries containing mercury, 600 million filament lamps, 1 million ton alcohol, 120,000 ton gourmet powder, 50,000 ton citric acid, and 2.3 million chemical fiber capacity were eliminated. In Shanxi province alone, closing down the outdated enterprises in steel, coal carbonization, thermal power, small coal mines involved 130,000 workers. In 2007, 33 steel companies were shut down in Hebei province, involving over 20,000 workers. [1]

2.3.2.3　Promote Technological Innovation of Conventional Industries and Reduce Pollutant Discharge

In June 2007, the State council issued the Comprehensive plan to save energy and reducing emission, listing 45 policy measures to save energy and reduce emission. The policies concerning technological innovation of traditional industries are as the following:

Accelerate desulphurization of current facilities for thermal power units, enhancing the desulphurized unit's capacity to 213 million kW. Newly built or expanded coal power plants must build desulphurized facilities and reserve

---

[1]　Report on relocation of workers affected by eliminating outdated production capacity, saving energy and reducing emission. Internal report of Ministry of Labor and social security 2007.

places for denitration. Further promote Coal Washing Project and Clean-burning coal technologies. Strengthen the pollution management and technological reform of industrial waste water by paper making, brewage, chemical industries, textile and dyeing.

2.3.2.4 Save the Energy, Improve Efficiency of Using Energy, Reduce Pollutant Discharge

State Council's decision on strengthening energy conservation in 2006, and Comprehensive work program of energy-saving and emission reduction in June 2007 proposed specific measures for energy conservation in industry, transportation and construction. Industrial energy conservation needs to focus on enterprises like steel, non-ferrous metal, coal mining, power generation, petrochemical, chemical production, building materials and enterprises with over 10,000 ton coal consumption. we need to promote energy conservation in construction, develop buildings with energy saving and economic use of land, adopt the standard of 50% energy saving for new residential and public buildings, 65% for cities under the direct control of the central government and regions that meet the condition. We need to actively promote the construction of comprehensive energy-saving transportation system, accelerate the development of railway and canal transportation, prioritize public transportation and rail transportation, accelerate the elimination of outdated rail engine, car and ship, encourage the development of energy-saving and environment-friendly transportation, develop and promote cars with alternative and clean fuel. Fourthly, we need to guide commercial and civil energy conservation. The above mentioned documents listed 10 key energy conversation projects.

2.3.2.5 Promote Pilot of Recycling Economy, Pursue Clean Production, Reduce Pollutant Discharge

The government designed and issued Clean production promotion law, Law on preventing Solid waste from polluting environment, Recycling economy promotion law, Rules on managing daily waste and Regulations on recycling and handling Disposed electric and electronic products, as well as Interim Provisions on Promoting Industrial Structure Adjustment, Opinions on Accelerating the development of recycling economy, Guiding opinions on comprehensive use of resources during eleventh five-year plan, Comprehensive notice of energy conservation and emission reduction, Eleventh five-year plan of National environmental protection, Policies and actions in addressing climate change, etc. All these documents proposed the general idea, short-term objectives, basic approach and policy measures for developing recycling economy and designed the index system of evaluating recycling economy.

Chapter 6 of the Eleventh five-year plan on national economic and social development in 2006 described the plan about developing recycling economy. The plan proposed to develop recycling economy, insisted the parallel approach of exploration and conservation prioritizing conservation. The plan was to gradually set up a system mobilizing the whole society to recycle resources. Comprehensive notice of energy conservation and emission reduction proposed to strengthen recycling waste water in sectors like steel, power generation, chemical industry and coal mining.

Currently the government has set up pilot region for recycling economy and expanded 36 pilot products.

2.3.2.6　Enhance the Level of Comprehensively Using Resources

The objectives of comprehensively using resources are to achieve speed development of industries comprehensively using resources in 2010, to improve largely the efficiency of using resources and the rate of using industrial solid waste reaches 60%, to gradually raise the proportion of products with comprehensive use of resources in the overall products and establish a series of enterprises with a certain scale, high technological equipment, high efficiency of resources using and low waste discharge.

The key area of comprehensive resources using includes comprehensively using mining resources, wastes, renewable resources and agricultural and forestry wastes. The key projects of comprehensive use of resources during the eleventh five-year plan include the following. Projects of comprehensively using associated mineral resources, large solid waste resources, renewable metal processing resources, industrialization of renewable resources like abandoned home appliances and old tires, and projects of recycling renewable resources and using agricultural wastes like straw and animal wastes and wood. Lastly, the comprehensive use of construction wastes needs to be promoted.

2.3.2.7 Strengthen Management of Environmental Pollution

We need to conduct projects of handling dangerous and medical wastes and harmless disposal of daily wastes, in order to promote comprehensive use of solid waste. At the end of the Eleventh five-year plan, we will build 31 upgraded disposal center of dangerous wastes, 300 disposal centers of medical wastes and provide technical support and other supporting projects, which will need 15 billion RMB,

In waste water handling, one is to accelerate the construction of city waste water processing and recycling projects. By 2010, the processing rate of city waste water will account for 70% and all the cities need to build their own waste water processing facilities. In order to achieve this goal, we will increase the scale of processing capacity to 50million t/d, reform and improve the current water processing factories and associated pipelines, investing 210 billion RMB. The other method is to strengthen processing of industrial waste water. The key is to control the waste water discharge and reduce overall volume of the state owned key industries, which account for 65% of the Industrial emissions of chemical oxygen demand.

2.3.2.8 Actively Develop Environmental Protection Industry

The eleventh five-year plan proposed to develop large scale high efficiency clean power generation equipment and facilities for environmental protection and comprehensive use of recourses. These are the key areas to revitalize the facilities manufacture business. The plan proposed to develop equipment manufacturing for environmental protection based on the needs of environment protection key projects, and to actively develop service industry prioritizing environmental impact assessment, environmental project service, environmental technology research and development and consoling, and environmental venture investment. For example, in the area of comprehensive use of resources, the key is to promote non-regular water resources like wastes recycling, renewable water, slightly salty water, sea water desalinization, and saving water through high efficient cooling. Also we need to recycle out cars, old tires, old home appliances, electronic wastes and reuse of mine tailings. In the area of construction and operation of pollution control facilities and counseling service, the key is to promote the market drive of environmental facilities construction and operation like city waste water, wastes, dangerous wastes, etc., to process industrial wastes water at a large scale, desulfurization of power plants, and professionalization of dedusting facilities, and to develop technological counseling and management service for environment protection. Currently, the SDRC is now making a plan for industries of energy conservation and environmental protection.

2.3.2.9 Reduce GHG Emission in Agriculture and Countryside

Continue to promote high yield rice products and semi draught planting technology with low emission, adopt scientific irrigation technology, strengthen ecological agriculture in highly intensified regions, increase the management of animal waste, waste water and solid waste, promote the use of biogas and control the growth speed of methane discharge.

2.3.2.10 Promote Tree Planting, Enhance Carbon Sink Capacity

Reform and improve current industrial policy, focus on key forestry ecological construction projects. Continue to implement tree planting, promote natural forestry resources protection, return to grassland and forest, manage the sand storm origin of Beijing and Tianjin, build defending forestry system, and promote the development of wildlife protection and natural protection zone. Focus on construction of biomass forestry base. The goal is to reach 20% forest coverage by 2010 and the carbon sink capacity increase 50 million ton CO_2 on the basis of 2005.

The Eleventh Five-year Plan proposed that by 2010 energy consumption of GDP per capita decrease by 20% in comparison with 2005, which will be a very important binding indicator. The quantitive indicators related resources, environment and ecology during the eleventh five-year plan include noticeable improvement of resources using efficiency, energy consumption per unit of GDP decrease 20%, water consumption per unit of industrial increment drop 30%, water use efficiency index in agricultural irrigation reach to 0.5, rate of comprehensive use industrial solid waste increase 60%, amount of cultivated land maintain 120 million hectare, level of guaranteeing water, energy and key mineral resources improves, basically control the deterioration of ecological environment, emission of sulfur dioxide and COD drop 10% on the basis of 2005, strengthen pollution management of key rivers and accelerate processing of city waste water and waste, the rate of harmless disposal of city daily wastes no less than 60% by 2010, the proportion of renewable energy in the overall energy supply structure reaches to 10%, the emission of nitrous oxide keeps the same as the year 2005, control the growth speed of methane emission, forest coverage reaches 20%, carbon sink capacity increases 50 million tons of CO_2 on the basis of 2005, and achieve remarkable outcome in controlling GHG.

2.3.3 Relevant Economic Policy

Economic policy is an important leverage in promoting environment protection. Chinese government is actively improving relevant policy measures to promote environment protection.

2.3.3.1 Fiscal Policy

Fiscal expenditure includes direct investment, financial subsidies, governmental green purchase, and financial transfer payment to environmental protection by government.

The direct investment is investment in managing the environmental pollution. The government set up special fund for environmental management and protection, kept expanding financial input to environmental protection special fund, took the best use of central funds' role in attracting money and exemplifying model. The government also supported a few key projects in ecological construction and pollution management through national bonds, using the money in controlling sand storm sources in Beijing and Tianjin, environmental protection facilities in west region, pollution control of three rivers and lakes, recycling waste water, industrialization of wastes recycling and treated water, environmental pollution management in Beijing, and subsidizing forest ecological performance. Since 1998, the central government kept increasing financial assistance to underdeveloped central and western regions, combining ecological construction and rural infrastructure and industrial expanding, and implementing returning land to forests and grasslands policy, adjusting agricultural structure and increasing farmers' income.

At present, the most widely used subsidies include subsidies to pollution management (electricity price subsidies for Desulfurization), to ecological construction projects, to clean production projects, to environmental researches, and to production of environmental-friendly products.

The Government issued Government Procurement Law in January 2003, and in January 2005, Finance ministry and SDRC issued Opinions on implementation of government procurement of energy-saving products in 2004, which was the first specific policy regulation on government procurement to promote energy conservation and environmental protection.

2.3.3.2 Tax Policy

In terms of value added tax, the government encourages comprehensive use of resources: waiving, halving or returning VAT for products of enterprises that comprehensively use resources like waste residue, waiving VAT for waste and old materials sold by entities who recycle waste and old materials, deducting paid VAT for enterprises that buy in waste and old materials. The government also encourages tax policy for clean energy and environmental protection products, waiving or halving VAT for power generated with wind and 23 products of 14 categories in new wall materials listed in the catalog of new wall materials enjoying preferential taxation policies like Non-clay brick, building block, building boards. The government also encourages preferential measures for waste water processing. Since July 1st, 2001, waiving VAT for waste water fees collected by water plants entrusted by governments and administrative agencies at all levels.

In terms of consumption tax, reform on finished oil tax was implemented since January 1 2009, which will be beneficial to development of low emission car and to industrialization of renewable energy consumption cars.

In terms of income tax, the government will waive or deduct income tax within 5 years for enterprises using waste materials as raw material for production, waive tax for enterprises that are producing environmental protection facilities and products encouraged by the government, and introduce Tax Credit for Investment and accelerated depreciation policy for environmental protection facilities encouraged by the government.

The government introduced resources tax in April 1988 and expanded the range in 1994. currently, government is studying on carbon tax policy, cancel tax refund for exporting resource-based products like refined mineral products and crude oil, reduced the tax refund rate to 5% on copper, nickel, ferroalloy, coking coal, hard coke, etc., largely reduce or cancel tax refund for products with high energy consumption and high pollution and resources based. There are also measures to protect ecological environment in property tax, city land use tax, vehicle and vessel use tax, and contract tax, etc.

2.3.3.3 Financial Policy

July 30, 2007, former SEPA, in cooperation with People's bank, and CBRC, issued Opinions regarding the implementation of environmental policies and regulations to prevent the credit risk, asking People's bank and CBRC to cooperate with environment agencies to mobilize financial institutions of all levels to introduce different credit policies for enterprises that are forbidden, eliminated, restricted and encourage by the government according to the environmental economy policy, especially not providing new loans to project that have failed the environmental approval to avoid new non-performing loans.

December 2007, Ministry of environmental protection and CIRC together issued the opinions regarding to environmental pollution liability insurance, formally launched the green insurance system. The Opinion proposed to form the environmental pollution liability insurance mechanism based on China's situation during the eleventh five-year plan, starting pilot program in key sectors like production, operation, storage, transportation, dangerous chemical products and enterprises like petrochemical and dangerous waster processing companies that might easily occur pollution accidents. After 2012, the mechanism will be promoted nationwide.

February 2009, Ministry of Environmental protection proposed to strengthen the environment entrance level, gradually cancel relevant subsidies and tax preferential policies that might be harmful to environmental protection. In addition, the ministry will further expand the green trade policy, regularly announcing public notice of enterprises pollutant emission. For these enterprises that do not meet the standards, they will be forbidden to export. This policy will expand to other heavy pollution industries from the current citric acid and electrolytic aluminum industries.

2.4　Current Situation of China's Green Employment

Green employment have had a long development in China. The Chinese environmental protection undertaking started in 1980s. Tree planting started since the establishment of new China and lasted every year. Solar power industries started in the 1990s and now in a rather big scale. Wind power and biomass power developed in the past few years. Management and control of industrial wastes were strengthened and high pollution and energy consumption sectors were eliminated. The recycling economy and reusing waste materials business are developing recently. In such process, there have been a certain scale green employment and formed certain experiences:

2.4.1　Employment in Environment Protection Industries [①]

In the past few years, China has increased the investment in infrastructure and facilities of environmental protection, which pulled the market demands for environmental protection industries. Environmental protection industries

---

① SEPA, SDRC, and SSB jointly issued Status of the National Environmental Protection Industry Bulletin in April 2006, implemented by environmental protection association. The survey was one-off all-round one, starting from 2004, carried out between February to August 2005, coving SOEs engaging in environmental products production, comprehensive use of resources, environmental protection service, and clean products production and non-state-owned enterprises and entities with annual income over 2 million RMB in all 31 provinces apart from Taiwan, Hong Kong and Macau.

have become an important part of the national economic structure. According to Status of the National Environmental Protection Industry Bulletin, environmental protection industries include narrow contents like industries providing products and technological services in pollution control, emission reduction, pollution management and waste processing, but also include wider contents like environment-friendly technologies and products, energy saving technologies, ecological design and environmental service in the products production circle. According to the bulletin, in 2004, there were 1.595 million employees in the environmental protection industries.

Table 2-4-1   Industrial Structure of Environmental Protection in 2004

contents	total	Environmental protection products	Comprehensive use of resources	Environmental protection service	Clean products
Number of companies	11623	1867	6105	3387	947
Number of employees	1595000	168000	959000	170000	233000
Annual income(billion RMB)	457.21	34.19	278.74	26.41	117.87
Average number of employees	137	90	157	50	246
Average income per capital	290000	200000	290000	160000	510000

There are totally 5501 products of 594 categories, mostly about water and air pollution processing facilities. Average number of employees of one environmental protection product company is 90, with 200,000RMB per capita income.

Comprehensive use of resources [1] industries mainly focus on recycling renewable resources and solid waste materials. The average number of

---

[1]   Comprehensive use of resources refers to the processing of waste resources and waster materials to produce all kinds of products. It includes comprehensive development and use of associated mines during mining, recycling and use of waster residue, water, gas, surplus heat and pressure during production, recycling and renewable use of all waste materials during production and consumption.

employees is 157 for each entity with 290,000 RMB per capita income.

Among employees in environmental protection service industries[1] , 16,000 are engaged in research and development of environmental technologies and products, 53,000 are engaged in designing and constructing environmental projects, 52,000 are engaged in facilities operation of pollution management (daily waste water, industrial waste water, dedusting and desulfuration, industrial exhaust gas, daily wastes, dangerous waste processing, automatic continuous monitoring and other facilities), 27,000 are working in environmental monitoring, and 15,000 are working in environmental counseling service. The environmental service mainly focuses on services for environmental project design and construction and facilities operation for pollution management. The average number of employees for each entity is 50, with 160,000 RMB per capita income.

The survey included 9 clean products[2] , organic food and other products, low toxic or harmful products, low emission products, low noise products, Bio-degradable products, energy-saving products, water-saving product and other products. 1492 products of 52 categories were included, mostly energy-saving products, low toxic or harmful products, low emission products and organic food. The average number of employees in each entity is 246 with 510,000 per capita.

- *Wuhan opened the first ever supermarket for electronic wastes, prevent electronic waste pollution and pursue recycling use of resources*

---

[1] Environmental protection service refers to service trade related to environmental protection. The survey mainly covered research and development of environmental technologies and products, design and construction of environmental projects, environmental monitoring, environmental counseling, facilities operation for pollution control, environmental trade and financial service.

[2] Clean products refer to environmental-friendly products in the production circle (production, consumption, recycling and reusing of a new product). Such products have features of ordinary products and also meet environmental protection standards during production, use and handling. In comparison with ordinary products, they have the environmental function of low toxic and harm and resources saving.

As early as 2006, a report by Hubei Development and Reform Commission stated that Hubei was in the phase of rapidly eliminating old electronic appliances. The whole province had 300,000 TV sets, 200,000 fridges, 300,000 washing machines to be eliminated. Electronic wastes had large amount of lead, tin, mercury and other toxic and harmful substance. If not appropriately handled, the soil and water would be contaminated. It was considered another environmental killer after chemical engineering, metal melting, paper making, and dyeing industries. At present, 90% cities abandoned old home appliances, taken by mobile venders who would dismantle, burn or bury them, causing serious pollution.

Electronic wastes contain much higher level of metal than metal mines. In professional processing factory, 350 kg zinc oxide, 300 kg maganese-iron alloy, 5 kg nickel alloy can be extracted from one ton dry battery through professional method of harmless disposal, which is worthy 2000 RMB and has no waste water or waste residues. The metal powders extracted can be sold as raw materials. Plastics extracted can be reprocessed to be finished products. Electronic waste can be recycled infinitely. Old and discharged electronic appliances are like refined mines need to be exploited, which contain 30% metal.

Because of the big business opportunity, Hubei province opened the first electronic wastes supermarket, recycling old home appliances at a price of 2 rib per kg. It was to explore a new model for recycling wastes with government guidance, market operation, and social participation. In 2 years' time, Wuhan will set up 300 places. If the electronic object is over 10 kg, people can call 400889311 and staff will be sent to collect it.

Although the recycling price is not competitive in comparison with mobile venders, with the pilot program deepening, the government might offer subsidies. Moreover, according to the Recycling economy promotion law and Waste Electrical and Electronic Product Recycling Regulations, the government will force to centralize the recycling process of waste electric and electronic

products and enterprises and consumers will have to pay for processing them.
By then, the economic profits for enterprises will be more remarkable.
  Sources from People's Daily Overseas, March 19, 2009

Environmental protection industry has huge market potential. With the development of the national environmental protection undertaking, environmental protection industry will create more job opportunities. According to the Association of Environmental Protection industries, currently there are over 3 million employees in the industry. UNEP predicts that wastes processing and recycling will be very effective in lowering impact of heavy industries, creating 12 million jobs, among which 10 million are in China. China has the world biggest cement and steel company, hence having huge employment prospect.

2.4.2 Employment in Renewable energy [①]

Actively develop renewable energy is the basic national strategy. Renewable energy is a brand new industry, whose development would inevitably lead to employment increase. According to The related researches by the Energy Institute of the State Development and Reform Committee, by the end of 2007, the number of people working in the new energy industry was 1.1 million, mainly spreading across solar power, wind power and biomass energy industries, only very few worked in other industries.

Table 2-4-2 Renewable Energy Industry Workers

Solar power boiler	Photovoltaic power	Solar Power	Wind power	Biomass energy	Others	Total
800000	100000	150	20000	200000	1000	1121000

----

① Related energy researches by the State Development and Reform Committee

According to relative studies [1] , the creation of a direct work post requires investment of RMB 1.15 million in wind power, and RMB 910,000 in photovoltaic power, RMB700,000 in solar thermal utilization, RMB 140,000 in biomass energy. In generally, the input required for renewable energy employment is much higher than that for conventional industries. For a developing country such as China, such job positions are too expensive. The primary energy source in China is coal. In 2005, among China's primary energy consumption, coal accounted for 68.9%, oil accounted for 21.0%, natural gas, hydraulic power, nuclear power, wind power and solar power together accounted for 10.1%. While in the same year, in the worldwide primary energy consumption, coal only accounted for 27.8%, oil 36.4%, natural gas, hydraulic power, nuclear power and so on accounted for 35.8%. China being a developing country is still far from reaching industrialization, urbanization, and modernization. In the development towards its goals, the rationalized growth of China's future energy demand is the fundamental condition for all developing countries to achieve development. At the same time, the key role coal plays in China's energy structure will be very difficult to have fundamental changes in the foreseeable future. Although by 2020, renewable energy's percentage could reach 20% and the number of new jobs to be created is estimated to reach 2.2 million. However, unlike the US, the proportions of employment from renewable energy and conventional energy would not be switched. In a rather long period of time, conventional energy industries would still take the dominant position.

2.4.3 The Employment Impacts of Thermal Powerindustry's "Upgrading the Large and Suspending the Small" Policy

While developing renewable energies, China also improves energy efficiency, save energy and reduces emission by policies such as eliminating outdated capacities. In particular, the power industry is a big contributor for energy saving and emission

---

① Peter Poschen. China Green Employment Forum, 30 March 2009

reduction. Such environmental measures have negative impacts on employment while protecting the environment. The taskforce on "Low Carbon Development and Employment" from the Chinese Academy of Social Science, conducted studies on the data and statistics from the Development and Reform Committee, a certain power group and 12 power plants in Jiangxi and Shanxi, and estimated the affected number of employees by shutting down small thermal power plants:

553 small thermal power units were shut down in 2007, involving 14,380,000KW and 122,500 workers, of which 91,000 were incumbent workers, and 31,500 were retired. Therefore, for shutting down every 1,000KW of small thermal power capacity, the average number of workers needing replacement is 6.2. The number of workers affected by the shutdown of small thermal power unit across the nation:

(1) The number of people whose employment got affected in 2003-2008: 38,090,000KW x 6.2 workers/KW = 236,158 workers

(2) The number of people whose employ would potentially be affected in 2009-2020: 59,800,000KW×6.2 workers/KW = 370,760 workers

According to the present taskforce's investigation, among those who lost their jobs due to shutdowns, only 10% of them could be reemployed in supporting posts in the newly constructed large units. The remaining workers faced difficulties in getting back to work. According the above estimate, by 2020, among the 600,000 people whose jobs would be affected due to shutdown of small thermal units, 500,000 will need assistance in reemployment.

2.4.4　Forestry Green Employment

Forests are the largest carbon bank and the most economical carbon absorber. There are huge employment potentials in this area, which include 3 main aspects: the first are the employments created by forestation and reforestation, restorage of degraded ecosystems, building the combination system of agriculture and forestry, and improving forests sustainable development; the second are the employments by developing timber production and processing;

the third are the employments from developing forest chemicals, forest machine manufacturing, forest tourism, forest food, forest herbs, economic forest, flower growing, bamboo industry, and so on.

Since 1980, the country has invested heavily on strengthening forest ecosystem building, undertaking key forest projects, expanding the total amount of forest resources, and enhancing forest carbon trade function. According to the estimates of forest coverage targets, by 2010 when forest coverage reaches 20%, the newly created jobs would reach 17,795,000.

According to The Research on China Forestry Development Strategy, the 6 key forestry projects started in 2002 undertook forestation task of up to 760 million hm2 in 10 years, expected to create 22,800,000 jobs. In 2007, total forestation area was 2,680,000 hectares. Among this, key shelterbelt systems construction projects in the "Three North's" and the Yangtze River basin accounted for 574,000 hectares. Local people's pay for work totaled RMB 368, 570,000, using the 2007 average salary for collective enterprises of RMB 6,007, that equaled to 1 year's worth of work for 61,356 people, or 3 months' worth of full time work for 245,427 people. Registered workers for all natural forest conservation project amount to 980,000 [1] .

Table 2-4-3   Employment Potential Estimates for China's Carbon Trade Forest [2] (2010-2050)

Year	Forest coverage %	Forest area (10k ha)	Forest carbon storage (1billion MT C)	Value of CER (1b USD)	Newly increased forest (10k Ha)	Newly created no. of jobs (10k people) Note
2003	18.21	17490.92	14.43	158.73	-	-
2010	20	19210.20	15.85	174.35	1719.28	1779.5
2020	23	22091.73	18.23	200.53	4600.81	4761.8
2050	26	24973.26	20.60	226.6	7482.34	7744.2

Note: Number of jobs are calculated based on 103.5 working days per ha, 100 working days per worker. CER price is set at USD11/mt of carbon.

---

[1] China Forestry Statistical Yearbook 2008

[2] Taskforce for "Low Carbon Development and Employment" of the Chinese Academy of Social Science

According to the China Forestry Statistical Yearbook 2008, China had over 1200 forest parks, whose tourists reached 83 million in 2001, generating total income over RMB50 billion, directly or indirectly created 3.5 million jobs.

Forest related side industries: China ranks no. 1 for area of bamboo forest, storage of bamboo volume and annual bamboo output, receiving the name of bamboo kingdom. Also, the floral industry is one of the most dynamic around the world, with long horticulture history, encompassing many kinds, have vast development potentials.

By the end of 2007, total registered forestry workers amounted to 1,849,200 people, of which 1,396,000 were incumbent workers. In the state-owned forestry economic enterprises, 1,116,000 people worked in the fields of agricultural forestry and fishery, accounting to 84% of the total. Another 88,000 worked in the fields of public management and social organizations, accounting for 6.6%; 37,500 people worked in water environment and public facility management, accounting for 2.8%, 27,300 people worked in scientific research services and geological survey, accounting for 2%, 26,000 people worked in manufacturing, accounting for 2%.

The UN Food and Agriculture Organization estimates that forest restoration can create 10 million green employment. Agriculture is still the industry that offers the largest number of jobs. There are 1.3 billion farmers in the world. Green employment is mainly embodies in organic farming and bio fuel.

China linked forestation, employment expansion and national consumption together to achieve a win-win situation. Chengde City in Hebei started to explore green employment patterns since 2004, and has so far reemployed over 2400 redundant workers. Annual government investment is over RMB1.2 million, and has so far planted 2.62 million trees, increasing the urban greening rate from 24.3% to 34.6%. Recently, the topics such as hiring migrant workers to plant trees have drawn heated discussions, showing how much attention people pay to the "forestation + employment" pattern. Under the impending

Table 2-4-4 Distribution of forestry incumbent workers in 2007

Sum				139.6	
			Total	133.3	100.00%
			Enterprise	55.9	41.90%
			Institution	69.3	52.00%
			Organizations	8.2	6.20%
State-owned	Agriculture/Forestry/Animal husbandry/ Fishery		Sum	111.6	83.70%
			Forest and bamboo Logging companies	46.5	34.90%
			State-owned forest farm	34.7	26.00%
			State-owned plant nursery	3.4	2.60%
			forestry work station	12.4	9.30%
			timber check points	2.1	1.60%
			Seedling station	0.7	0.50%
			Pest control station	1.1	0.80%
			Sand control station	0.1	0.10%
			Others	10.5	7.90%
	Mining			0.1	0.10%
	manufacturing		Sum	2.6	2.00%
			Non-wood forestry product processing	0.2	0.20%
		wood processing and bamboo/ rattan/brawn straw products	Sum	1.96	1.50%
			Sawn wood processing	0.17	0.10%
			wood based panel manufacturing	1.4	1.10%
			wood product manufacturing	0.37	0.30%
			bamboo/ rattan/ brown straw product manufacturing	0.01	0.00%
		forest chemical product manufacturing		0.1	0.10%
		Special equipment and instrument manufacturing		0.04	0.00%
		craft production		0.027	0.00%
		Others		0.3	0.20%
	Power, gas and water production and supply			0.4	0.30%
	Construction			0.3	0.20%
	Distribution and retail			0.66	0.50%
	Scientific research technology services and geological survey		Sum	2.73	2.00%
		of which	Technology exchange and promotion services	0.4	0.30%
			planning, design and management	0.69	0.50%
	Water environment and public facility management		Sum	3.75	2.80%
		of which	Management of natural preserves	1.28	1.00%
			Protection of wildlife	0.1	0.10%
	Education			0.86	0.60%
	Health, Social security and welfare			0.6	0.50%
	Public management and social organizations			8.8	6.60%
	Others			0.87	0.70%
	Total of collective economic institutions			2.58	1.90%
	Total of other economic institutions			3.7	2.80%

international financial crisis, more and more migrant workers return to their hometown and take up jobs in forestry, so that "one family member as contractor leads to all family members becoming employed", and "unemployed in the city but self-employed in the forest".

Source: Chengde City "green employment" patterns opening new opportunities for reemployment. Xinhua Net, 24 November 2007

China's current state of green employment is yet to be studied. But the above analysis already shows that although China has made large contribution for worldwide green employment, but China's green employment is still on the initial stage, accounting for a very minor percentage in the face of 760 million working people. In particular, China's employment structure is still quite under-developed, overall quality of workers is quite low. The elimination of outdated capacity would lead to losses of some jobs and some workers are under the thread of unemployment. The undertaking of environmental measures would cause some jobs to change and workers would face the challenges of skill conversion. Although some new green positions would be created, which would create employment opportunities for some workers, the number is extremely limited comparing with the large number of people needing employment. On the other hand, economic development would also face the challenge from employment. Some industries might not developed as fast as they could due to labor shortages, while some industries could not make fast exit because of heavy burdens from too many redundant workers. Structural unemployment may get worse. The transformation process towards green employment must be studied in depth.

2.5 The Power Generation Industry's Transformation towards Green Employment

In order to understand the problems faced by the transition towards green employment so as to identify policy suggestions for promoting transition towards green employment, the project team conducted questionnaire surveys and in-depth interview for the power generation industry.

First of all, the project team selected 8 power plants in Tianjin, Hohhot and Wulanchabu respectively. Of those 8 plants, 3 represent the new power plants with modern technology; 1 represents renewable energy power plant; 2 represents conventional coal-fired power plants; 1 comprehensive power plant with both traditional old and small power units as well as new and large ones; 1 being representative of regional power plants, and 5 belongs to state-owned power generation groups.

In each of the 8 power plants, we hosted discussion meetings with the management as well as the employees including the plant's director, people from general departments, financial department, production and technology department, human resource department, work union, and environmental protection department. The focus of those meetings was to understand the actual situations, difficulties and problems those different types of companies face in facilitating green employment and during the transition towards a green economy. 600 employee questionnaire survey were handed out, of which 587 effective replies were received. The survey's target was strictly defined as front line operative workers that represented different types of generation equipment units, age groups, genders, and education backgrounds. The samples included both green employment as we as non green employment. Also, employees surveyed were controlled to be within a certain percentage of that respective company. In general, the sampling is quite representative.

Table 2-5-1   Basic Information on the 8 Selected Power Plants

	Hohhot No. 1 Power Plant	Hohhot No. 2 Power Plant	Hohhot No. 3 Power Plant	Hohhot No. 4 Power Plant
No. of Employees	362	1061	238	330
No. of samples	100	70	45	35
	Wulanchabu City Power Plant	Tianjin Dagang District Power Plant	Tianjin Dongli Power Generation Company Limited	Tianjin Hexi District Power Generation Company Limited
No. of Employees	193	1923	2302	801
No. of Samples	50	100	100	100

According to the Study's purposes, the employees were divided by the position's respective type of energy source, and the size of the equipment. The formers are Wind power and coal-fired power. And among the coal-fired power group, referencing the general standards used in the National policy of "promoting the large units and reducing the small units", those over 200,000 KW are called large thermal power units and those under 200,000 KW are called small thermal power units. Data for each group are listed below:

Table 2-5-2   Basic Information on Samples

		Frequency	%	Valid %	Cumulative %
Valid	Wind power	52	8.9	9.1	9.1
	Large thermal power unit	361	61.5	63.1	72.2
	Small thermal power unit	159	27.1	27.8	100.0
	Sum	572	97.4	100.0	
Invalid	System	15	2.6		
	Total	587	100.0		

The resulted data are analyzed as below:

2.5.1   The Workforce General Composition is Similar Across the Different Power Generation Industries

2.5.1.1   Age and Related Information

2.5.1.1.1   Average Age among Small Thermal Power Units is the Oldest

Workers' average age for small thermal power units was 39.1 years, older than wind power's average of 38 years, and large thermal power units' 36.3 years. Older workers accounts for higher percentage in small thermal power units, less

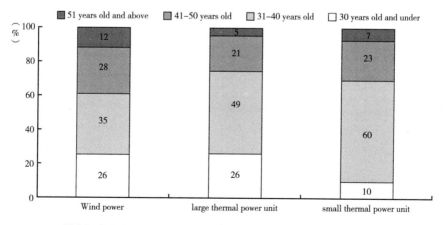

Table 2-5-1   Age Structure of Power Enterprises Employees

than 10% was 30 years old and under, those at 31-40 years old accounts for the highest percentage, at nearly 60%.

2.5.1.1.2 The Small Thermal Power Units' Workers Have the Longest Work Years

The least work years in each group are similarly 1-2 years, the most being 37-38 years. But considering the average work years for each group, the small thermal power unit group is the most, at 17.84 years, about 5 years longer than those in the large thermal power unit group (12.97 years), and nearly twice as many as those in the wind power group (9.10 years).

Grouping the samples by their worked years, it is noted that, 46% among the wind power group have work years between 1-5 years, having the highest proportion of new recruits, and distribution in the remaining 3 work-year ranges are quite in proportion; among the large thermal power unit group, distribution among all 4 work-year ranges are quite in proportion, with 37% for both 1-5 work years and 11-20 work years; over half of the small thermal power group have work years between 11-20 years, and 30.0% for 20 years and above, less than 10% is with 1-5 work-years.

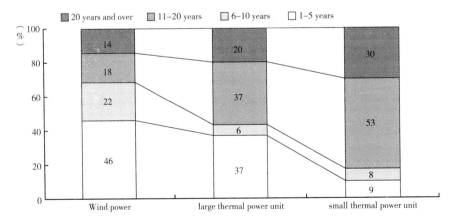

Table 2-5-2   Working Lengthen of Workers in Power Enterprises

2.5.1.2 Worker's Education and Skills

2.5.1.2.1 Workers in Small Thermal Power Units Have the Lowest Education

We gave scores to each employee based on their education (1 for junior middle school and below, 2 for senior high school and vocational high school; 3 for technical school and secondary technical school; 4 for senior vocational school, 5 for junior college, 6 for university, and 7 for Masters and above). The wind power group's average education score is the highest, at 5.3, small thermal power unit group being lowest, at 4.25, 1.05 lower than the wind power group.

Table 2-5-3 Educational Level of Workers in Power Enterprises

	Junior middle school and below	Senior high school	Vocational high school	Technical School	Vocational high school	Junior college	University	Masters and above
Wind power	0.0%	4.0%	0.0%	2.0%	4.0%	38.0%	50.0%	2.0%
Large Thermal power unit	2.5%	3.3%	3.0%	10.5%	9.8%	26.1%	43.1%	1.8%
Small Thermal power unit	4.8%	3.6%	9.6%	10.8%	14.5%	25.3%	27.7%	3.6%

Wind power is an emerging industry; its workforce has the highest education, with 0% at Junior high school and below level, and 90% for junior college and above. The large thermal power unit group uses mostly freshly built units, workforce education level is also quite high, and 71% are with junior college degree and above. Also, over 20% are with technical school and vocational high school education. Workers at the small thermal power group have relatively lower education than the other 2 groups in the survey, only 56.6% possessed junior college and above degrees. The proportion with technical school and vocational high school education is relatively high, at 25.3%.

2.5.1.2.2 Technicians Account for the Highest Percentage in the Small Thermal Power Group

Regarding the surveyed workers' vocational skill level, power generation workforce's qualification is quite high in general, most of them possessing professional qualifications. The small thermal power group has the highest percentage of workers with professional qualifications, at 90.2%; the wind power group and the large thermal power group are similar, at 84.8% and 83.8% respectively.

Table 2-5-4   Professional Qualification of Workers in Power Enterprises

	Do you possess any professional qualification?	
	Yes	No
Wind power	84.8%	15.2%
Large Thermal Power	83.8%	16.2%
Small Thermal Power	90.2%	9.8%

Regarding skill/ technical level composition, those in the wind power group are mainly with middle and senior technical personnel titles or engineers; those in the large thermal power unit group are mainly senior and intermediate technicians, or with intermediate technical qualifications; those in the small thermal power unit group are quite similar to the Large group, also with many being senior and intermediate technicians, or with intermediate technical qualifications. That is to say, wind power industry workforce is mainly made up with professional technical personnel and technicians, whereas coal-fired power plants are made up with mostly intermediate and senior technicians.

Table 2-5-5   Vocational Level of Workers in the Power Enterprises

	N/A	Junior Technician	Intermediate Technician	Senior Technician	Engineer	Senior Engineer	Junior professional technical title	Intermediate professional technical title	Senior professional technical title
Wind power	6.5%	13.0%	6.5%	2.2%	15.2%	2.2%	10.9%	28.3%	15.2%
Large thermal power	4.2%	7.7%	24.7%	25.3%	6.8%	1.2%	6.5%	18.2%	5.4%
Small thermal power	2.7%	4.1%	27.0%	24.3%	8.1%	1.4%	8.1%	17.6%	6.8%

2.5.1.3   Employee Status

2.5.1.3.1   Employees in the Small Thermal Power Unit Group Are 100% Local Non-agricultural Registered Permanent Residents

We could derive many insights from the status of the employee's residential registration. Due to wind power industry's unique working conditions, workers need to work long shifts and stay at work continuously for 10 days or even half a month without going home. Therefore many employees are non-local non-agricultural registered residents. As the large thermal power units' production efficiency has been greatly improved, they do not require many formal employees. As a result they tend to recruit local agricultural registered residents, and non-local agricultural or non-agricultural registered residents. The workers for the small thermal power units tended to be recruited long time ago when the plant was first built. They all tend to be local non-agricultural registered residents.

Table 2-5-6　Residential Status of Workers in the Power Enterprises

	Local Non-agricultural Hukou	Local Agricultural Hukou	Non-local Non-agricultural Hukou	Non-local Agricultural Hukou	Others
Wind Power	90.4%	1.9%	7.7%	0.0%	0.0%
Large Thermal	93.7%	3.3%	0.8%	0.8%	1.5%
Small Thermal	100.0%	0.0%	0.0%	0.0%	0.0%

2.5.1.3.2　Workers at Small Thermal Power Units Are 100% Formal Employees

Nearly all workers at the power plants are formal workers. Except that wind Power Company has some labor dispatch jobs, and the large thermal power units employed some temporary workers. Small thermal units exist redundant positions, but all of their workers are formal employees. Such practices are the result of each company's own production needs.

Table 2-5-7　Employment Status of Workers in Power Enterprises

	Formal workers	Labor dispatch	Hourly workers	Contractual migrant rural workers
Wind power	96.2%	3.8%	0.0%	0.0%
Large thermal power unit	98.5%	1.0%	0.3%	0.3%
Small thermal power unit	100.0%	0.0%	0.0%	0.0%

2.5.1.3.3　The Percentage of Technical Positions Is the Highest at Small Thermal Power Units

The surveyed workers' job types show that among the wind power, large and small thermal power units, the percentage of technical positions increase in turn, while the percentages for ordinary positions and skilled positions decrease in turn. This may mean that workers at coal-fired power plants requires relatively long term training, that small thermal power units have been in operation for quite some time, hence the percentage of technical positions become higher, while wind power and large thermal power units had been running for relatively short time, therefore the percentage for technical positions are relatively low. On the other hand, this may also be due to the fact that the degree of worker specialization at wind power and large thermal power units are higher, with more detailed and specific division of labor, such that production efficiency for those technical positions are higher, requiring relatively more non-technical positions for supporting. Wind power companies have a higher percentage of other positions, this may be because wind power companies in general have lean workforce, and some management positions were also included in the survey.

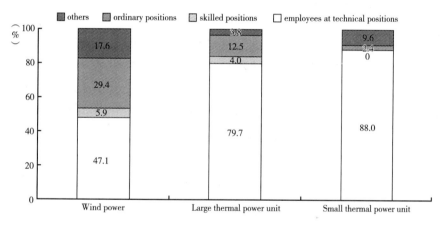

Figure 2-5-3   Skill Level of Workers in Power Enterprises

2.5.1.3.4   Employees Generally Signed Employment Contracts

Regardless the type of positions, basically all workers signed employment contracts with their companies. In particular, workers at wind power have the highest percentage of signing contracts with no fixed term, at 80%. For those wind power workers who signed fixed term contracts, the term is quite short, averaging at 4.62 years.

The percentage of workers signing contacts with no fixed term at both large and small thermal power units are also quite high, at close to 60%. Although 40% of the surveyed workers signed fixed term contracts, but the terms are relatively long, averaging 6.27 years and 5.8 years respectively, maximum fixed terms are up to 20 years and 10 years. These are much higher than that at wind power, which is only 5 years.

Table 2-5-8　Contract Status of Workers in Power Enterprises

	No fixed term	Fixed term	Project-based contract	Unclear
Wind power	80.4%	15.7%	0.0%	3.9%
Large thermal power	55.0%	40.6%	0.3%	4.1%
Small thermal power	59.3%	38.3%	0.0%	2.5%

Among the surveyed workers who signed fixed term contracts, nearly all of them were willing to renew contract with the company, and most of them felt that this expectation would materialize. Among those fixed term contract workers at coal-fired power plants, a small proportion felt that there was uncertainty regarding their contract renewal.

Table 2-5-9　Worker's View on Renewing Contracts With Power Enterprises

	Will renew	Won't renew	Hard to say now
Wind power	100.0%	0.0%	0.0%
Large Thermal	90.3%	0.6%	9.1%
Small Thermal	94.3%	0.0%	5.7%

2.5.1.4　Job Seeking and Job Changing

2.5.1.4.1　Workers at Small Thermal Power Units Got Their Position Mostly by State Allocation, while Those at Wind Power Got Their Job Through Reassignment

Historically, power generation industries were all state owned, and all employees were allocated by the state. All employees over 40 years old mainly got their job through state allocation. Since the introduction of market oriented employment in 1993, employment needs have been met through recruitments with employer and graduate's mutual selection. State allocation was abandoned. New recruits in those companies have mostly been university graduates. Since the recruitment channels are quite mature, and remuneration package is quite attractive, the companies did not need to rely on other market oriented approaches such as agency, recommendation by relatives and friends, etc. to meet their recruitment needs.

Wind power is an emerging industry in China, however, specialized university graduates for this industry are not yet available. Therefore, the recruitment needs were mostly met by internal position relocation, training, and reassignment from other companies. The survey shows that 41.2% of wind power workers joined the company through job reassignment.

Table 2-5-10   Ways to Find Jobs in Power Enterprises

	State allocation	Reassignment	Self-application	Merger & reorganization	Agency	Recommendation by friends & family	Labor dispatch	Others
Wind power	43.1%	41.2%	7.8%	0.0%	0.0%	2.0%	3.9%	2.0%
Large thermal	60.1%	19.0%	16.5%	0.5%	0.2%	1.5%	0.2%	2.0%
Small thermal	80.5%	4.9%	11.0%	0.0%	0.0%	0.0%	0.0%	3.7%

2.5.1.4.2   Job Post Changes in Power Generation Industry Are Mostly Internal Relocation

Workers' job post changes are related to equipment unit's years of operation. Since small thermal power units have been in operation for a long time, the proportion of workers who experienced job post changes became higher. Among those experienced job post changes, about 1/4 of the workers across all 3 groups experienced it once; over 1/4 of the small thermal group workers experienced job post change twice, which is the highest proportion, while in large thermal group and wind power group, more workers experienced job changes three times than those experienced it twice.

2.5.2 Different Frontline Worker's Working Conditions in Power Generation Industry

2.5.2.1 Working Conditions

2.5.2.1.1 Work Instruments Are Mainly Automated Tools

Judging from the work instruments in use at the moment, the wind power group has the highest rate of automated tool usage, at 74.5%; large thermal power units are the lowest, at 52.5%. This is to do with the distribution of each group's positions. Wind power uses fully modernized management system, with high level of mechanization and automation. Even for workers at ordinary positions, they mainly involve automated operation, and hence the highest rate of automated tool usage. Technical positions at large thermal power units accounts for a lower percentage compared with small thermal power units, the respective automated tool usage for their workers become lower.

It is worth noting that the level of automation varies across the different automation tools. For example, the production technology and flow are more or less the same for the large and small thermal power units, however, the main control equipment is different. Also, some semi-automatic tools may be categorized differently.

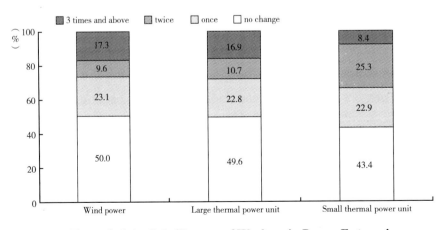

Figure 2-5-4   Job Changes of Workers in Power Enterprises

Table 2-5-11　Equipment Used by Workers in Power Enterprises

	Manual instrument	Automated instrument
Wind power	25.5%	74.5%
Large thermal	47.5%	52.5%
Small thermal	37.7%	62.3%

2.5.2.1.2　Among Small Thermal Power Unit Workers, More Work Shifts

Shifts in small thermal power units are very common. Half of the surveyed workers work shifts; while this among wind power and large thermal power units are around 1/3. It could be interpreted that after implementing eco-friendly measures, more workers can enjoy normal work hours.

Table 2-5-12　Working Shifts of Workers in Power Enterprises

	Yes	No
Wind	33.3%	66.7%
Large Thermal	31.6%	68.4%
Small Thermal	49.4%	50.6%

2.5.2.1.3　Working Overtime Is Common among Power Generation Industry, while Their Rights and Interests Are Mostly Protected

Overtime work in all 3 categories are very common, percentage of those worked overtime in the past year are all over 85%, increasing in turn from small thermal, to large thermal and wind power.

Table 2-5-13　OT of Workers in Power Enterprises

	Have you worked overtime in the past year?	
	Yes	No
Wind power	93.5%	6.5%
Large thermal	89.3%	10.7%
Small thermal	87.7%	12.3%

The majority of workers that worked overtime got overtime pay or supplementary leave according to the country's regulations. As working long shifts are very common in the wind power group, those workers mainly received compensation in the form or supplementary leave, accounting for 60%. The other 40% got overtime pay.

In the two coal-fired power groups, workers' overtime compensation are mostly by overtime payment, accounting for 60-70% who got basic rate compensation for their overtime, less than 10% got supplementary leave. In the small thermal group, more workers got no compensation for their overtime work compared with the large thermal group.

Table 2-5-14   OT Payment for Workers in Power Enterprises

	Got full overtime pay	Got partial overtime pay	No overtime pay	Supplementary leave	No clear
Wind	20.0%	20.0%	0.0%	57.5%	2.5%
Large thermal	18.4%	50.6%	15.8%	9.0%	6.2%
Small thermal	44.4%	19.4%	26.4%	9.7%	0.0%

2.5.2.1.4   Workers at Wind Power Enjoyed the Highest Average Annual Income, while Biggest Income Differentiation Existed in the Small Thermal Power Units

Wind power workers' average annual income is the highest, at RMB 51,687.50, nearly RMB 10,000 higher than that of the small thermal power units which ranked the lowest. From wind power to large thermal power units, then to the small thermal power units, the differences between the respective workers' average annual income became higher.

Table 2-5-15   Annual Income of Workers in Power Enterprises

	Last year's income			
	Lowest	Highest	Average	Standard Deviation
Wind power	27000	100000	51687.50	14715.446
Large thermal power	7500	120000	46792.74	17750.316
Small thermal power	15000	95000	42219.34	20373.406

Grouping the samples by their ranges of annual income, wind power's income shows a normal distribution pattern, where middle income range of RMB40,001-50,000 accounts for 41%, while the percentages of higher and lower income are both lower. This appears to be scientific and reasonable. Coal-fired power workforce represents a descending pattern, where lower income groups accounts for higher proportion, and percentage becomes less as income gets higher. Over half of the surveyed workers at large thermal power units have annual incomes below RMB 40,000, while this percentage is over 70% of those surveyed at small thermal power units.

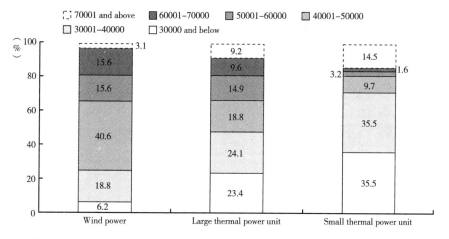

Figure 2-5-5   Annual Income Structure of Workers in Power Enterprises

The principle rule for income distribution at power generation industry is leaning towards frontline workers, income levels are differentiated. The higher percentage of lower income workers means higher percentage of non-frontline workers at the generator unit.

2.5.2.1.5   Workforce's Social Security Participation Rate is Higher than the Country's General Situation.

Judging from the participation rate for the 5 social insurances required by laws and regulations, nearly all surveyed workers at wind power group participated in urban worker's basic retirement insurance and medical insurance schemes, while a small portion of surveyed employees from coal-fired power plants did not participated in those 2 insurances. Among these, workers at small thermal power units have a higher rate of non-participation or uncertainty than those at large thermal power units. All 3 groups' participation rate of child birth insurance is relatively low, with small thermal power units being lowest: 31.8% clearly stated they did not participate in child birth insurance, and an additional 15.9% said they were not sure. The percentages at wind power and large thermal power units are slightly better.

Other than the basic social insurances, power generation companies all offered annuity. The differences across each group are very little, wind power group appears to be a little better.

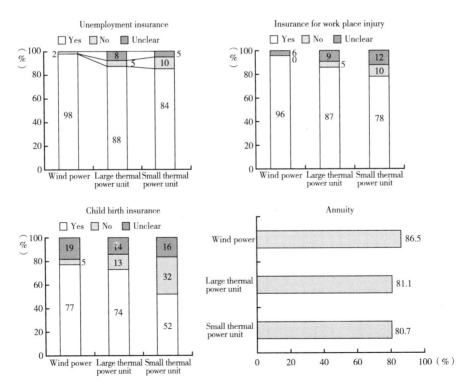

Figure 2-5-6　Social Insurance for Workers in Power Enterprises

2.5.2.1.6 Workers' Benefits at Power Generation Companies are Generally Quite Good

Almost all surveyed employees had housing subsidies or (and) housing fund (wind power at 94.2% and the other 2 groups both at 97%)

Major differences exist at each group's meal/skipped meal subsidies, and transportation subsidies. Only 1/3 of those at wind power group could get meal/ skipped meal subsidies, while that in large thermal power units are over 3/4.

At wind power group, only 26.9% got transportation subsidy, only half of that at small thermal power units, while large thermal power units are the best at 73%.

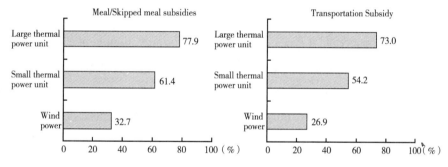

Figure 2-5-7-1   Subsidies for Workers' Meal and Transportation of Workers in Power Enterprises

Additionally, power companies also organized health checks for their employees periodically, and provide living allowance to those in need. But differences do exist in such benefits. Regarding health checks, wind power group is better as almost all enjoyed this benefit, while just short of 20% at the coal-fire power groups did not have this benefit.

Regarding living allowance for needy employees, 40% of those from wind power group said their companied offered such benefit, while 60% and 50% from large and small thermal power units respectively said they had such benefit.

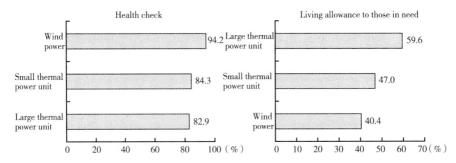

Figure 2-5-7-2   Health Check and Living Allowance for Workers in Power

Enterprises

2.5.2.2   Working Environment

2.5.2.2.1   Major Differences Exist at the Groups Regarding Occupational Hazards

This survey concerned 4 types of occupational hazards: high temperature, noise, dust, and radiation. Wind power company clearly displays green employment characteristics: none of the surveyed workers considered they experience any hazard concerning high temperature, only 2% considered they experienced dust, less than 1/5 experienced noise, and less than 1/3 felt they were exposed to radiation at work.

On the contrary, coal-fired power groups displayed clear non-green employment characteristics: in large thermal power units, 2/3 felt they were exposed to noise hazard at work, the percentage at small thermal power units are over 75%; in both thermal power units around 2/3 felt they were exposed to dust hazard, over half in those 2 groups felt they experienced high temperature, an 42.4% and 44.6% respectively felt they were exposed to radiation.

2.5.2.2.2   Workers Were Generally Happy about Their Work Environment, while There Were Clear Difference Between Wind Power and Thermal Power Groups

Most workers in the wind power group considered their work environment "very good", as much as 76.9% picked this option. In the 2 thermal power groups, 18.2% and 13.3% respectively considered their work environment "very good", the majority felt it was "general".

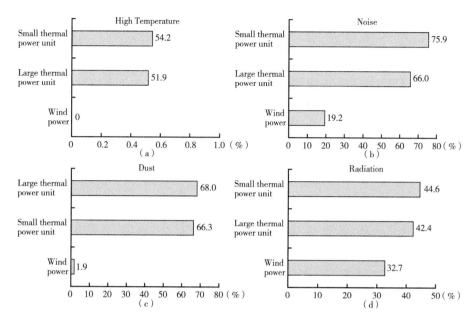

Figure 2-5-8 Occupational Hazards for Workers in Power Enterprises

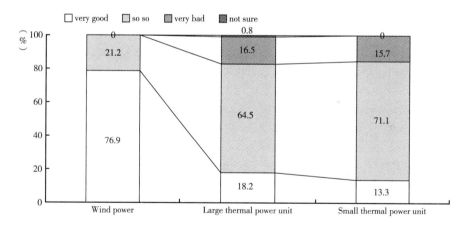

Figure 2-5-9 Worker's View on Working Conditions of Power Enterprises

2.5.2.2.3 Workplace Protection Measures

Among all the protection measures adopted in each group, wind power companies have the least occupational hazards and enforce the highest level of workplace protection measures. However, small thermal power units which have the most serious occupational hazards, provides the lowest level of protection measures.

Nearly 90% of those surveyed at the wind power said their company held safety education, while this percentage at small thermal power plants are less than 75%; nearly 85% of the surveyed wind power plant workers said there

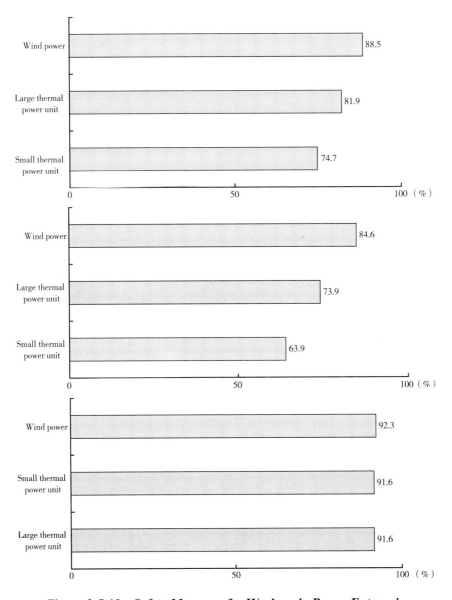

Figure 2-5-10   Safety Measures for Workers in Power Enterprises

were safety measures and facilities at their workplace, while this percentage at small thermal power units are less than 65%. About 92% in each of the surveyed groups said their companies provided safety protection supplies.

2.5.2.2.4   Health conditions among wind power workers are the best

98% of those surveyed at wind power said they were "healthy", while less than 80% of those surveyed at coal power said so, nearly 20% of them said their health condition was average. The general health conditions of those from small power units are not as good as those from large power units. Nearly 5% were quite frail. Large thermal power units also employed about 0.3% disabled people and placed them at suitable positions, displaying corporate sense of social responsibility.

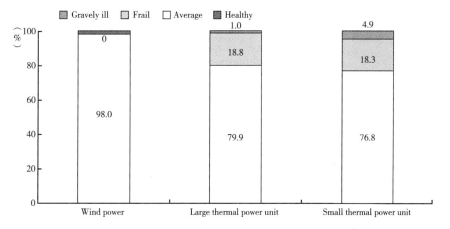

Figure 2-5-11   Health of Workers in Power Enterprises

2.5.2.2.5   Occupational diseases

Regarding occupational diseases, the wind power group's condition is the best. Except the 10.9% were not sure if they had any occupational diseases, the other 89.1% said they had no occupational disease from the current job. In the 2 thermal power groups, over 1/4 were not sure if they had any occupational diseases in the current job, and 45.6% in large thermal power units had occupational diseases from their current jobs, and this percentage for the small

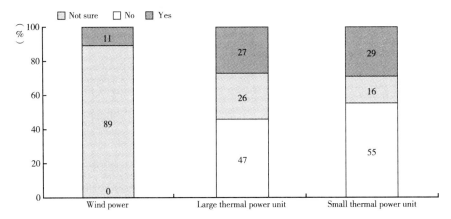

Figure 2-5-12   Occupational Diseases of Workers in Power Enterprises

power units was even higher, at 55.4%.

By briefly analyzing the answers to this particular question, it showed that Silicosis was the most common among these types of companies. Also, Neurasthenia and Tinnitus are quite common.

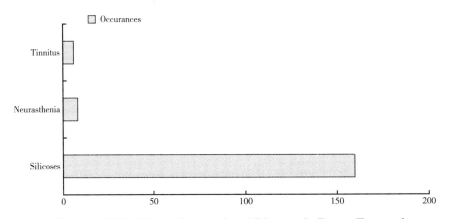

Figure 2-5-13   Major Occupational Diseases in Power Enterprises

There existed clear differences among the different groups of surveyed workers on their risk assessment for occupational diseases. Nobody at wind power felt there was "significant risk", and the majority felt that it "would not happen" or likelihood is "average". In the 2 thermal power groups, nearly 1/3 in each of them felt that there was "significant risk", nearly half felt the risk is "average"; among the small thermal power group, only 1.2% felt there would be no risk of occupational diseases.

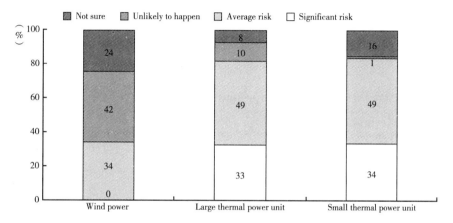

Figure 2-5-14   Workers' Awareness of Occupational Diseases in Power Enterprises

2.5.3   Labor Relations

2.5.3.1   Labor union's participation in the company's decision-making

All surveyed employees said their companies had labor unions. And over 90% of them belong to their respective companies' labor unions. There is little difference across the 3 groups on this regard. Also, the unions or the labor representatives were able to participate in the companies' democratic management, having their say in consultations regarding the companies' reform and structural adjustment. In particular, participation in democratic management at wind power is slightly better than the other 2 groups, nearly 90% of those surveyed expressed their unions or representatives could take part in the consultations regarding the company's reform and structural adjustment, while this percentage at the 2 thermal power groups are respectively 81.6% and 80.5%.

Table 2-5-16   Workers' Participation of Management of Power Enterprises

	Are labor representatives allowed to take part in consultations regarding the company's reform/structural adjustment?	
	Yes	No
Wind	89.8%	10.2%
Large Thermal	81.6%	18.4%
Large Thermal	80.5%	19.5%

2.5.3.2   Worker's Participation in Company's Democratic Management Mostly Concerned Technical Training

Almost all of those surveyed felt that their companies should listen to take more into account the workers' opinions. The workers were most concerned about skill training. Over half in each of the 3 groups felt strong needs for skill training. In wind power group this proportion is as high as 3/4. While in the 2 thermal power groups, this proportion is over half respectively.

Thermal power workers were also very concerned about their wage. 57% of those survey at large thermal power units expressed their concerned about wage. Wind power workers had the lowest level of concern regarding salary. This may be because they were already quire happy about their current pay level. ---- Average income level being the highest and income differences among them are the lowest. Also, the company did not need to cut wage to compensate for implementing environmental protection measures.

Workplace safety is another most concerned issue. The small thermal power workers were particularly so. This may be because their actual workplace safety condition was the worst.

Large thermal power workers were also quite concerned about the "introduction of new technology" and the "worker's transfer to new position". This may be because some workers needed to learn new skills after transferring from small thermal power units to large ones.

There was also some minor concern about "redundancy and compensation". This again shows that employment in power industry is relatively stable.

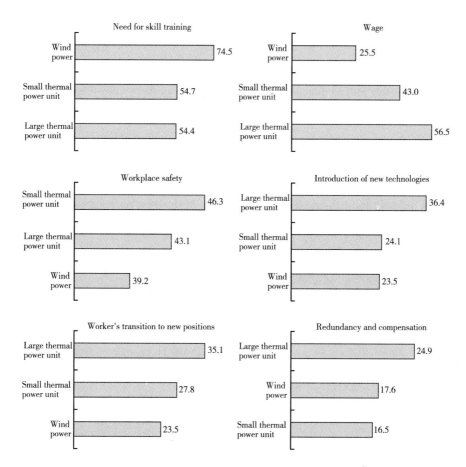

Figure 2-5-15　Questions Most Concerned by Workers in Power Enterprises

2.5.4　Training for the Different Power Generator Units' Workers

2.5.4.1　General Conditions

Regarding employee training, overall speaking, the situation at coal-fired power plants are quite good, over 97.5% received training; it is relatively not as well at wind power, around 88.5% of their employees received training.

Table 2-5-17　Training for Workers in Power Enterprises

	Received training	No trained
Wind power	88.5%	11.5%
Large thermal power	97.5%	2.5%
Small thermal power	97.6%	2.4%

2.5.4.2　Training Classification

Regarding classified training, wind power employees received better classified training than those at thermal power plants. The percentages of Wind power employees receiving training in qualification, continuous education, and adaptive training are all higher than those of thermal power plants workers, only lower on the percentage of technical level training.

Table 2-5-18　Trainings Participated by Workers in Power Enterprises

	Qualification training		Adaptive training		Technical level training		Continuous education	
	No	Yes	No	Yes	No	Yes	No	Yes
Wind Power	48.1%	51.9%	69.2%	30.8%	57.7%	42.3%	57.7%	42.3%
Large thermal	64.8%	35.2%	84.6%	15.4%	38.2%	61.8%	66.0%	34.0%
Small thermal	72.3%	27.7%	83.1%	16.9%	34.9%	65.1%	75.9%	24.1%

2.5.4.3　Employees Gave High Ratings for the Trainings, and Their Desire for More Training Was Very Strong.

All the surveyed employees in each group who received training expressed gave high rating for their trainings. The surveyed workers at wind power all said the training was "very useful" or "somewhat useful", without any negative or average comments. However, small percentage of thermal power workers said their training did not think much of their training.

All employees felt a strong need for training. 85% of the surveyed employees thought that they needed more training in order to fit into the current company or department better; relatively, small thermal power workers' need for training was lower than the other 2 groups.

Table 2-5-19 Needs and Evaluation of Trainings for Workers in Power Enterprises

	Do you feel the need for further training in order to fit into the company/ department's technology development?		How would you rate the training you have received so far?				
	Yes	No	Very useful	Somewhat useful	Average	Not very useful	No
Wind power	88.4%	11.6%	61.9%	38.1%	0.0%	0.0%	0.0%
Large thermal	86.5%	13.5%	51.0%	35.0%	12.2%	1.3%	0.5%
Small thermal	76.8%	23.2%	54.9%	29.3%	8.5%	7.3%	0.0%

2.5.5 Effects on Employment by Adapting Environmental Protection Measures

2.5.5.1 Environmental Protection Measures Adapted

All surveyed companies adapted some level of environmental protection measures: wind Power Company protects the environmental by generating power from wind; large thermal power plants preserve the environment by deploying large thermal power generators; small thermal power plants preserve the environment by adopting technical enhancement measures such as using desulphurization equipment.

2.5.5.2 Effects of the Environmental Protection Measures

2.5.5.2.1 Have Significant Effect on Workers' Skill and Work Instruments

Over 70% in the wind power group said there were significant changes on the skills and equipment /instruments at work. In large thermal power plants, less than half of employees felt significant changes towards the skills and equipment/

instrument at work. Also, over 1/4 felt there were a little change, and the balance 1/4 felt no change at all. At small thermal power plants, only 1/4 felt the change was significant, over 70% felt there was a little or no change.

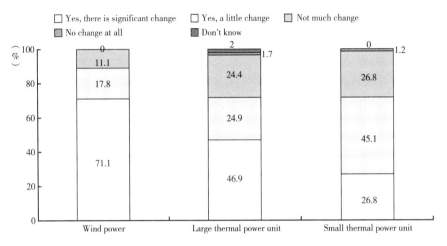

Figure 2-5-16   Impact of Environmental Protection Measures on Workers' Tools and Skills

2.5.5.2.2   Clear Effects on Income Level

After adaptation of environmental protection measures, 40-50% in each group said their income had no changes. In wind power, none of the surveyed workers said their income became less after the company adapted environmental protection measures; on the other hand, nearly 60% said their income increased "considerably" or "a little". In the large thermal power plants, the number of workers with increased income was more than those with reduced income, 3.5% said their income increased "considerably", and 23.6% said their income increased "a little", while those with reduced income accounted for over 1/5. In small thermal power plants, the number of workers with reduced income was more than those with increased income, 23.2% with increased income, no one had their income increased considerably, and 1/3 had their income reduced.

2.5.5.2.3   Effects on Working Hours

The effect of adapting environmental protection measures on working hours

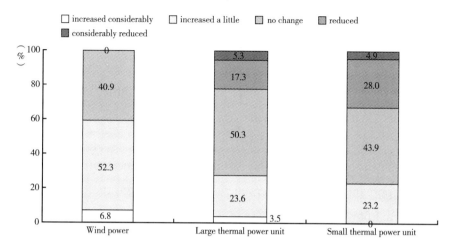

Figure 2-5-17   Impact of environmental Protection Measures on

Worker's Income

was similar to that on workers' income. In general, the surveyed workers enjoyed stable working hours. 3/4 of those in large thermal power plant had no change to their working hours, in small thermal power and wind power this percentage is also very high, at 68.3% and 57.1% respectively.

In wind power plants, 43% said their working hours had become longer, and none had shortened working hours. The situation at thermal power plants varies.

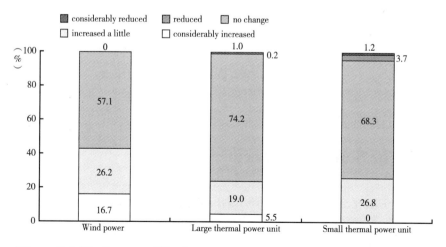

Figure 2-5-18   Impact of Environmental Protection Measures on Worker's

Working Time

Compared with small thermal plants, a smaller percentage of those at large thermal power plants had their working hours reduced. In the large thermal power group, 5.5% said their working hours had increase considerably, and another 19% said their working hours had increased a little. In small thermal power plants, 26.8% employees had extended working hours

2.5.5.2.4 Effects on Work Intensity

Work intensity generally got increased across all three sample groups. The following percentages of workers at wind power, large thermal power and small thermal power, 50%, 53.8% and 45.1%, respectively felt work intensity increased.

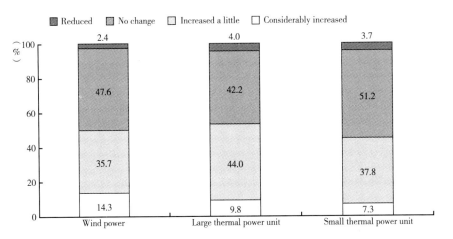

Figure 2-5-19   Impact of Environmental Protection Measures on Worker's Working Intensity

2.5.6   The State of Job Security

2.5.6.1   Effect of Financial Crisis on the Companies: Mildest on Wind Power Plants

The 2008 worldwide financial crisis had reduced the demand for electricity, which eased coal power plants' operation load. This caused some negative effect on employees' income. A certain proportion of employees had wage cuts. The financial crisis did not have clear effect on wind power company's employees. 98% of them said they did not experience shortened working hours, temporary no pay leave, wage cut, training leave, and so on.

Table 2-5-20 Impact of Financial Crisis on Employment of Power Enterprises

	Did any of the below happen since the 2008 financial crisis?					
	Shortened working hours	Temporary no pay leave	Wage cut	Training leave	Others	None of the above
Wind	.0%	.0%	2.0%	.0%	.0%	98.0%
Large thermal	1.5%	.3%	18.1%	.5%	1.5%	78.1%
Small thermal	.0%	.0%	38.6%	1.2%	.0%	60.2%

2.5.6.2 Job Security

2.5.6.2.1 Self-appraisal on Job Security

In general, the surveyed employees felt their own jobs were relatively secure. In wind power group, 76.9% felt that the job is "very secure", 19.2% felt "quite secure". Most coal power workers felt "quite secure", and an additional 20% felt "very secure". A small percentage in small thermal power plants felt there

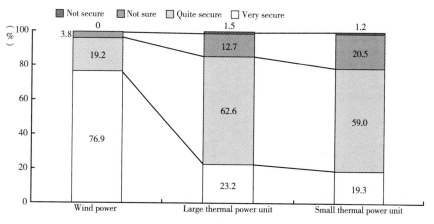

Figure 5-20 Sense of Job Security of Workers in Power Enterprises

existed uncertainty to their jobs.

2.5.6.2.2 Factors Affecting Job Securities

The main reason for job insecurity/ uncertainty for the 3.8% wind power workers were skill limitation. The reasons among large thermal power workers are, in descending order, insufficient government support, fierce industry competition, limited skill, industry evolution. The reasons for small thermal power workers are, in descending order, insufficient government support, limited skill, industry evolution, and short contract terms.

Table 2-5-21   Reasons for Worker's Job Uncertainty in Power Enterprises

	Short contract terms	Current skill set becoming increasing insufficient to meet work demand	Competition becoming more fierce	Insufficient government support on employment	Headcounts required decreases as the industry develops	Others
Wind	.0%	100.0%	.0%	.0%	.0%	.0%
Large thermal	13.2%	15.1%	18.9%	34.0%	15.1%	3.8%
Small thermal	18.8%	18.8%	6.2%	31.2%	18.8%	6.2%

2.5.6.2.3 Levels of Job Satisfaction

Although coal fire power workers had some worries about their job security, the overall rating of job security is satisfactory. Wind power workers' job satisfaction rate for their present jobs is very high, over half of them were "very satisfied", and another 42.6% "quite satisfied"; none were unhappy. In the 2 thermal power groups, although those that were "very satisfied" with their jobs did not account for high percentage, most surveyed workers were "quite satisfied"; those that were unhappy about their jobs were only of a small percentage.

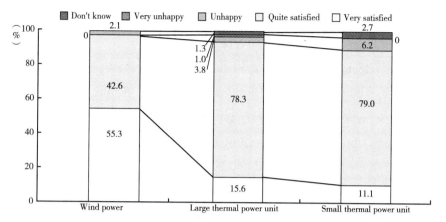

Figure 2-5-21   Job Satisfaction of Workers in Power Enterprises

2.5.7   The Approaches Power Companies Took for Green Employment Development and the Problems and Difficulties They Faced

Power companies' approaches adapted for green employment development mainly fall into the following four categories:

2.5.7.1   Take Corporate Social Responsibility and Try Their Best to Find Ways to Relocate Surplus Employees

When carrying out the programs of upgrading large units and suspending small units, and energy saving emission reduction, the companies tried their best to relocate the surplus workers, giving full considerations to the industry and the company's own features as well as their own human resource characteristics, so as to avoid adding pressures to the community's unemployment. For those workers from the suspended units, the company would place them in new supporting positions after giving them training based on new units' requirements. The company also had various ways to relocate those who could not fit into the new production lines:

First is to relocate them to the maintenance and repair team so that their experience and skills could be utilized, and encourage them to go beyond the company for other maintenance and repair works.

Secondly, relocate them to the company's tertiary industry-type subsidiaries. For instance, a conventional coal fired power place in Tianjin had nearly 2000 employees. It had 12 tertiary industry-type subsidiaries, involving restaurant and catering, hotel, food, logistics, construction materials, construction, etc., which were already very well developed and became main tax payers in Tianjin. The desalination operation alone already helped to absorbed 60 surplus workers. In another example, Inner Mongolia's economy is not as good as Tianjin, and power company's tertiary industry-type subsidiaries were not as competitive.

Thirdly, to implement job sharing for some positions, work intensity was reduced and the respective employees' incomes would be affected.

2.5.7.2　Strengthen Training

Employee training is a very important routine activity in power companies. The more dated the company, the more standardized the training programs.

The first is induction training. After an employee starts in a position, generally he would receive half month induction training, involving company rules and regulations, safety requirements, fire safety requirements, first aid for electric shock and cardiopulmonary resuscitation, production process, explanations on the employment contract and social insurances. After the induction training followed on-site training, which would be followed by job-training or operation training. Its training stages included on-site attendant internship, work under supervision, and work independently. It would normally take 1 year for the new recruit to get through all the above trainings, and then take a qualification test before becoming a formal employee. It would generally take no less than 5 years for a new recruit to become a master attendant. After a new recruit enters the company, he would normally sign apprenticeship agreement with an experienced technician to receive one-to-one training.

The second is equipment specific training. When the company purchased a new piece of equipment, the equipment supplier would be responsible for providing training. The most common way is the supplier would come to the company's site to host a training section, and then arrange another section during trial run period. Also, some would host lecture series given by industry experts; other forms would include arranging for study visits to similar power plants, appointing specialist training organization to host on-site learning, and simulation training, etc. Sometimes the company would also corporate with universities to organize classes for subject-specific theoretical study. For example, when a Tianjin power plan installed desulphurization equipment, they allotted the elitists among that year's university graduates to the dust removing workshop and let them take part in the preparation for desulphurization, and also send them off to visit the installation and operation of desulphurization equipment in other power plants, and study on-site as trainees and interns. Meanwhile, the company sent a repair and maintenance team to intern for the desulphurization equipment. After the desulphurization equipment came on line, the company set up full course training as follow up, and comprehensive assessment, making use of company-level professional examination on dust removal and desulphurization.

The third is daily training. Daily training includes routine and special trainings. For example, a company would specify that there must be a shift specifically for training for each operation team's shift circle. And the maintenance and repair team would host a 2-hour training section in an afternoon on a weekly basis. On-site trainings were taken as special trainings, explanation and random testing would be given as and when problems arose.

The forms of training generally involve every member in each shift to attend technical presentation, on-site examination, technical Q&A, technical tests, and anti-accident drills. The company's training center would have monthly random checking. The evaluation of training is done through company- and workshop-level tests. The annual company level test involved all production positions and the main management positions. The test results were linked to the company's talent project evaluation, where employees with outstanding results would be well rewarded.

The fourth is to apply joint management, joint training, joint exams, joint certification and joint reexamination for employees working on the special positions. The company would send them to attend industry-wide training and certification programs, fully implementing the national professional qualification entrance system, strengthening the management on special equipment operators' training and qualification, standardizing the above by setting respective rules.

The fifth is to encourage employees to attend relevant academic education in their spare time, and reimbursement of partial tuition fees upon graduation according to the terms of the company's academic education award program. This is to improve workforce capability portfolio, enhance employee's professionalism and learning capability.

Strengthening training is an important counter-measure on employment effects caused by a power company's environmental protection measures. After the adaptation of environmental protection measures, over 2/3 in wind power joined their company's relevant training. This proportion for large coal power units also reached 59%, while at small coal power units it was 42.5%. The employees gave high evaluation to the trainings they received, and expressed high demand for further training. When employees exercise their right for the company's democratic management, training is the issue they most cared about.

Table 2-5-22   Trainings After the Introduction of Environmental Protection Measures by Power Enterprises

	Did the company arrange any respective training after adapting environmental protection measures?	
	Yes	No
Wind	67.7%	32.3%
Large thermal	59.0%	41.0%
Small thermal	42.5%	57.5%

2.5.7.3 Emphasize Employee Participation

Employees in these power plants are mostly union members. Union chairmen played an important role in each company. In the worker representatives' annual meeting, all important company decisions must be passed by the union. Workers participated in the company's democratic management through this channel, having their says in the consultations for the company's reform and restructuring, expressing their views and suggestions so as to ensure their rights and interests were protected. The unions also carry out help and support program for employees in difficulties. All these helped maintain stability of the company's operating conditions and its workforce. As a result, the employees expressed relatively high level of satisfaction towards their jobs.

2.5.7.4 Find Ways to Enhance the Employee's Environmental Awareness

The companies emphasized the needs for energy saving and environmental protection to enhance employee's environmental awareness by science education campaigns, questionnaire surveys, and quiz. As a result, the employee's environmental awareness at work as well as in their daily lives got increased, and they became very sympathetic and supportive of, and actively participate in the company's environmental measures.

Power Company's green employment development has been met with the following 2 problems and difficulties:

1. Small Companies Faced Considerable Difficulties in Production and Operation when Adapting Environmental Measures

Taking the example of desulphurization transformation, coal fired power companies generally upgraded the older units' desulphurization and dust removing functions, and added efficient desulphurization and dust removal components to the new units. Installing desulphurization equipment generally involved significant investment, and after the installation, maintenance and operation would increase power consumption, which in turn increase coal input on supplying the required power. More new equipment means more expenses on maintenance, material and water. All these increased the company's operation costs by 10%. The government subsidizes the companies by adding RMB0.015 per kilowatt when they supply power generated by those units with desulphurization equipment to the grid, but the actual increased cost is RMB0.02 per kilowatt, therefore the subsidy is not enough to make up the increased costs. Large companies can afford to invest in environmental measures, while small ones could not afford to. They are faced with 2-folded difficulty: the company could not survive and lose their competitive edge without adapting the required pollution reduction measures; however investing in environmental equipment would increase operation costs, and put the company in deep difficulty to keep their workforce.

2. Hard to Find Re-employment for Older Workers

Thermal power plants' management underwent an increasingly scientific rationalization process. For the oldest Phase One units (those small thermal power units already suspended or to be suspended soon), jobs are managed in 3 specialized groups: turbine, boilers, and electrical operation. The special feature of this arrangement is that specialized skills could be utilized for relative long period of time, the worker's skills tended to be high in specialization and low in diversity. This made it difficult for the worker to learn interdisciplinary skills. Phase Two were mainly those units constructed since the 1990s, mainly at 200,000KW. The positions were on the stage of transition, everyone was trying hard to learn new skills, and the capable ones became more diversified in their skill portfolio. Phase Three was mainly the newly constructed units at 300,000KW. The companies intend to run them by all-round employees. Workers from older units would have difficulty fitting into the new positions. Due to aging and outdated skills, these workers face considerable difficulties for learning new skills. Together with major psychological gap in position transition, they have considerable difficulty in reemployment.

2.5.8 Summary

2.5.8.1 Industry Characteristics

2.5.8.1.1 Power Generation Industry Deeply Affected by Government Policy

Power generation is an industry under major state supervision and regulatory reform. Firstly, since power generation and power grids' separation and reform took place in 1984, power plants started to face market competition. The price of coal, being the main raw material, has become market oriented. The volume and price of power supplied to the grid are controlled by the state and the grid companies. Since 1997, the state started to implement policies of "upgrading the large and suspending the small", and elimination of outdated production capabilities, some small thermal power plants gradually got shut down and replaced by large ones. Since the 1990s, the state started to promote renewable energy, in which fields power companies had since invested heavily in order to seize the markets. In particular, wind power and hydropower grew rapidly.

2.5.8.1.2 Power Plants are Mainly State-owned Companies

The power industry is monopolized by the big 5 state-owned power companies. All of them being "red companies", have been always committed to take corporate social responsibilities and highly responsible to the employees. They did their best to absorb and relocate their surplus workers during restructuring, without letting them loose into the community.

2.5.8.1.3 Safety Is the Top Priority

Power concerns the country's development and people's livelihood. Production safety comes first on the list. The plants are managed in semi-military style to ensure production safety is failure-proof. Each company implements comprehensive and strict production safety measures, is quite demanding on staff capability, who in turn enjoy relatively good remuneration packages. Therefore the workforce has been very stable.

2.5.8.1.4　A Knowledge-based instead of Labor-intensive Industry

This characteristic determines the power industry workforce to be among the highest in all industries in terms of education level and skill capability. The companies only recruit graduates from colleges and vocational schools.

This characteristic also determines the need for their workforce's ongoing training. The operation of large thermal units requires workers with diversified skills that encompass a broad spectrum, requiring long term training. Awareness training is only for the short term. In-post continuous training is most important. University graduates must start from the lowest level on the team, going through different on-job training for 1 to 2 years before becoming qualified as normal workers. It takes much longer to be a team leader or engineer.

This industry and training characteristic also determines that its employees could only be relocated within the industry. This is the result of each worker's skill being too specific after long period of training, hence difficult to fit into other industries. Beside, job relocation also depends on the state of local economy. Even if relocation is within the same industry, and each generator's control system is similar, each unit's installation varied. Re-education would still be required for each relocated worker. In the backdrop of overall technology upgrade and adequate power supply, coal-fired power workers' reemployment is facing a very difficult situation.

2.5.8.2　Conclusions and Analysis

2.5.8.2.1　Restructuring Brought Significant Negative Effects to Power Industry's Direct Employment

First of all, renewable energy industries have limited potential in absorbing surplus workers. Based on the 3 categories of generator units of wind power of over 300,000 KW, large thermal power and small thermal power, their employment potentials are respectively 30-50, 300-500 and over 1000 workers. Technology advance and the restructuring of energy supply would reduce demand for employment in the power industry significantly.

Secondly, large thermal power units could only limited workers. On one hand, the demand for workers by large thermal power units are smaller, on the other hand, only 1.4 of those who lost their jobs from the suspended small units could get back to supporting positions after training. The company had to try other ways to absorb the other 3/4.

Thirdly, direct employment opportunities created by installing desulphurization units and other environmental measures are limited. Generally speaking, a unit's desulphurization transformation could only create 1 to 2 additional positions, and there are generally 5 units in a power plant, amounting to 10 additional jobs at most.

In all, it is a necessary advancement process for the power industry to "upgrade the large and suspend the small, and to develop renewable energy. Under a given power supply, the need for labor would become less and less. While high quality jobs are being created in the process, a much bigger number of jobs would be eliminated.

2.5.8.2.2 Employment Problem Would Become More and More Serious as Restructuring in the Power Industry Deepens

There is less and less room for the small thermal power units that are not yet suspended. They have lower production efficiency than large units, and under the same market conditions, their operation costs are much higher than large ones. In order to meet environmental requirements, small thermal power units have to go through much technical transformation, leading to increase in its own power consumption, which means increased operation costs. The effect of increase of raw material prices such as limestone on small thermal power units are also much larger than on large thermal power units.

Under such circumstances, job creation at small thermal power plants is extremely limited. As the units were constructed some time ago, the employee age structure tend to be aging, the number of years they have worked tend to be quite long, their level of education tend to be quite low, and their skill level is quite outdated. It is an inevitable trend that all small thermal power units would be suspended eventually, so close attention must be paid to address the redundant workers in the future.

2.5.8.2.3 Suspension of Small Thermal Power Units Were Met with Significant Internal Resistance

The income distribution rule in power plants leans towards the front line workers. Their income is 10 times more that of the supportive positions or the tertiary positions. Once the small thermal plant is closed, those frontline workers would be relocated to supportive positions, where incomes drop drastically. Although the companies could try to relocate the redundant workers, they would still feel discontent.

As the industry itself has higher and higher requirements on its workers, those small thermal unit team members who could not return to frontline would be unlikely to feel very good about their own career prospect, increasing their job insecurity.

Separately, the company's narrowing survival space and pressure from increasing operation costs also cast a shadow on its workers, increasing their job insecurity and discontent. Among the reasons affecting thermal power workers' job security, insufficient support from the government ranks the top spot.

2.5.8.2.4 Policies for the Energy Sector Led to Changes in Employment across Different Industries and Regions

The power industry's restructuring leads to reduction of direction employment, as well as the increase of indirect employment and induced employment. For example, the use of desulphurization equipment led to the development of an entire product chain that contributed positively to local society: limestone is used as the raw material for desulphurization, this increased job opportunities at limestone production factories; after desulphurization, the resulted gypsum could be used for construction, also creating job opportunities for motor transportation; also the needs for desulphurization equipment's production and maintenance are created. Another example is that wind power development could lead to new jobs for wind turbine production and installation. In another word, while suspension of small units would lead to lost jobs, it would also lead to new jobs in the upper and lower production streams as well as the relevant sector's industries and regions. The energy policies cause changes of employment situations across different industries and regions.

2.5.8.2.5 Green Employment Offer Higher Job Security Than Non-green Employment

Industry prospect determines a job's safety and security. Wind power is an emerging industry with high growth potential, and its demand for labor is very strong. Workers do not need to worry about lack of positions. What they worry about is whether they have sufficient skills to meet the job's requirements. For those who signed fixed term contract with wind power plants, basically everybody was willing to renew contract with their company, and almost all of them felt this could be achieved. This generally shows that wind power workers have very high job security.

On the other hand, small thermal power workers worried whether they could keep their current positions. As thermal power plants are increasingly affected by market factors, competitions became increasingly fierce, and demand for labor gradually reduced as technology advanced, more and more workers felt their jobs were under fundamental threads. The personal skill issue comes next. Among those workers who signed fixed term contracts with their company, a small portion of them felt the uncertainty for renewal. This shows there is relatively more room for personnel adjustment among coal-fired power plants.

2.5.8.2.6 Green Employment Shows a Higher Level of Flexibility and a Lower Level of Loyalty Than Non-green Employment

Regarding the type of labor used, wind power companies employed a small amount of labor dispatchers, large thermal power units uses a small amount of temporary workers, while the entire workforce at small thermal power units were formal employees. Regarding the employee status, wind power plants hire relatively more non-locally registered workers, large thermal power units hired some locally registered agriculture workers and some non-locally registered workers, while small thermal power units' workers were hired since their startup, and were all locally registered non-agriculture workers. Regarding the length of contract terms, wind power workers had shorter contract terms than those at thermal power units. Regarding the ways of recruitment in each type of units, wind power is the most flexible. Regarding the mobility of workers, wind power and large thermal power workers had higher frequencies of job changing. All these above show that green employment in generally have higher flexibility than non-green employment.

The back side of increased employment flexibility is reduced employee loyalty toward the company. The key staff would change jobs as soon as they found better opportunities. For some regular posts that could be replaced easily, the company would hire some temps with relatively low education level, to make sure they could fire them when they are no longer needed. This group generally account for 10% of a company's total workforce. Also temp workers had similar wage compared with formal workers, they do not have any benefits such as annuity and house fund. They would not feel strong loyalty towards the company either.

After the implementation of Labor Law, the companies changed all temp workers to be labor dispatchers, who enjoyed the same level of wages for same type of job. This would increase the company's dismissal cost and labor costs, and employment flexibility would be lower. This is another new question the companies have to deal with.

2.5.8.2.7 Green Employment Are More Decent than Non-green Employment

First of all, wind power plants offer the best workplace environment, having the least health effect on the workers. The specific operation conditions of thermal power plants means high temperature and noise are inevitable, which would have some considerable effects on worker's health. There are also considerable differences between the old and new generator units. Older units were designed with production as its first priority, and had very little regard for worker's health. New units' designs took more and more human factors into consideration, and their workplace environment is continuously improved.

However, wind power also faces some new problems. As wind power plants are far away from the city, workers would generally work long shifts: working nonstop for 10-15 days before taking long break for 10-15 days at home. There would be only a few people in each shift, therefore, in the long run worker's communication skills would be affected. Also, open air operation is largely affected by naturally weather factors, equipment repair and maintenance and operation management are very demanding on the worker's physical requirements. Therefore, worker's age and gender are quite specific, and thus generally young males in their 20s would be quite suitable.

Secondly, regarding income, wind power offers abundant employment opportunities as new wind power plants are being started up in record speed under the state's heavy promotion through the policy on encouraging the development of renewable energy industries. However, the pool for reserve staff is very limited, therefore, the income for this sector becomes higher than coal-fired power plants. Wind power companies offer relatively good wages as well as benefit packages in order to avoid losing talent too fast. Conventional coal-fired power industry is in generally good shape, workers' income is quite stable. However, in the adaptation of environmental measures, some non-green positions, while still existed, faced reduced incomes.

Thirdly, regarding overtime work, wind power workers' overtime work is more common, and workers could generally get overtime pay or compensation leave, but there existed some differences among the different groups. Wind power workers would all get over time for their overtime work, while more people in the small thermal power group did not get overtime pay.

Fourthly, regarding the impact of financial crisis, it had little impact on wind power companies and had some impact on coal-fired power plants.

Additionally, green employment is more superior than non-green employments in terms of work instruments, working hours, enrollment of social insurances, the company's benefit package, worker's health, occupational hazard, workplace safety measures, worker's satisfaction rate towards work environment, and worker's participation in the company's democratic decision making.

2.5.8.2.8   The Adaptation of Environmental Measures Helps to Promote Decent Employment

After the company adapted environmental measures, wind power companies had the most changes in terms of production skills and equipment/tools. The small thermal power units had some changes on these regards too. Worker's overall working hours remain unchanged, but wind power worker's night time work hours became much longer. Over 1/4 of small thermal power workers also had some increase to their work hours. Intensity in each group all got increased. Nearly 60% of wind power workers had increased income, and nearly 1/4 of small thermal power workers had higher income. Overall speaking, after the adaptation of environmental measures, there have been positive changes and improvements across all groups on production skills and equipment/tools, income, working hours and intensity. The adaptation of environmental measures helps promote decent employment.

2.6 The Principles and Policy Suggestions for Green Employment Development

As the initial study on China's green employment, this report conducted some initial explorations on the theoretical concepts of green employment, the macro-development conditions for green employment, and the micro-practices of the transformation towards green employment. The initial results show that the development of green employment has broad potential, and could promote decent employment.

The transformation towards and the promotion of green economy are the direction and inevitable trend for China's future economic and social development. These have continuously generated more and more emerging industries, which are becoming the new points of economic growth that lead the way for economic development and job creation. Green employment across all walks of life that could benefit all kinds of workers are yet to be exploited.

Also, environmental protection is a continuous process, and hence green employment has vast potential for sustainable growth. Take the example of desulphurization: the old desulphurization furnaces were based on immature technology, wear and tear was very serious, which meant frequent maintenance and high costs. The desulphurization operator's workplace environment was quite good but that of the repair workers is worse, as they would need to get into the furnace for repair work and had to bear with the stinking odor. At this moment the equipment still in their healthy phase where frequent maintenance and repair are not required. However, in the next 5 to 6 years, workload for maintenance and repair is likely to increase. Therefore environmental protection requires continuous input with progressive technology advancement, and green employment is a sustainable development process.

Green employment directly leads to increase of productivity and efficiency, helps to promote faster income growth for workers and the growth of labor share in income distribution. The promotion of various environmental protection measures leads to an ever expanding green industry chain with numerous hidden employment opportunities that would be enough to offset the number of jobs lost in the conventional industries. The newly created jobs would be safer, more economical and stable. The adaptation of energy saving measures in production processes could largely improve workplace condition and hence worker's health and safety. It could also promote technology advance, industry update, as well as the increase of technical content in labor, and help to improve worker's quality of skills. In sum, green employment helps to promote decent employment.

The only option faced by human resource policy is to follow the trend of green development and effectively promote green employment.

2.6.1　The Guiding Ideology and Basic Principles of Green Employment Promotion

2.6.1.1　The Principle of Promotion by Classification

There are 2 kinds of green employment, one is self-generated in the market, such as waste recycling jobs, and the other is directed by the government, such as the employment in the thermal power industry. Different kinds of promotional ideas and principles must be used for different types of green employment. They cannot be generalized nor standardized. For the market self-generated green employment, the government should follow the market-oriented principle, eliminating interfering factors obstructing the proper functioning of market mechanism, and try to provide more and better employment services. For the government directed type of green employment, policy interference principle must be followed, to design specific employment promotion policies.

2.6.1.2   Industrial, Environmental and Employment Policies are Equally Important and Should be Considered Simultaneously

Economic development, environmental protection and employment promotion are all for improving people's lives, so all three are equally important and none should be neglected. Neither could the economy be developed by ignoring the environment or employment, nor could the environment be well protected by limiting economic growth and job creation, nor could a development model without employment growth be adopted. The development direction should be firmly towards a green economy, while the pace should be within economic development's means, one step at a time. Policy should provide leverage for integrated support, coordinating the promotion of industrial structure optimization, the environment's continuous improvement, job quantity increase and job quality improvement. All these mean that, under the premises that employment goals are given gull considerations, we should encourage green industries, promote the green transformation of traditional industries and gradually improve environmental standards.

The key to realize the coordinated development of the 3 aspects is to achieve synchronized policy making, i.e. when deciding on industrial policy and planning, there should simultaneous be employment policies and planning; when making employment policies and planning, their effects on economic development and the environment must be considered.

2.6.1.3   Attentions Must Be Paid to Its Effects on Employment While Promoting Low-carbon Development

China is in the middle of industrialized development with high energy consumption, appropriate level of energy consumption is the inevitable trend for economic development. Low carbon development is in fact restricting the level and scale of energy consumption, ultimately would become constraints on development and employment. Therefore, China must take full consideration of the employment factor so as to find a balance point to use international funding and technology to promote economic development while mitigate greenhouse gas emission.

2.6.1.4 Green Employment Promotion Policies Requires Adjustments on Green Employment Itself

Some green employment themselves are not decent employment; some green employment are good for the environment but are not low carbon employment, for example, desulphurization emits carbon into the air; some low carbon jobs are bad for environmental protection, for example, growing of biomass energy crops involves the use of fertilizer which causes pollution; some green employment do not meet the need for industrial development, such as photovoltaic power plants and PV power generation equipment manufacturing industry where over capacity is pervasive; some green employment do not meet the characteristics of resource endowments, for example, China has limited land resources and is not suitable to develop biomass energy. Therefore, green employment development should not be solely promotion without policy constraint and control. When the government is making up green employment promotion policies, it must be based on China's actual situation, identify the areas and levels of interference for green employment.

2.6.1.5 Industry-specific Green Employment Promotion Policies

Green employment exist in all kinds of industries and sectors, and all levels of workers, varying widely in different industries. Therefore, under the general guiding ideology and principles, industry-specific survey and research must be conducted, and industry specific green employment promotion policies must be devised.

2.6.2 Policy Suggestions for Green Employment Promotion

China formally established market economic system in 1992, followed by large scale state-own enterprise reform in the mid-1990s. 1998 saw the start of re-employment project, which involved employee reduction and productivity enhancement, layoffs and reposition of redundant personnel, leading to the change of 30 million state workers in state owned enterprises to become social persons. This project ended in 2002. On the basis of summarizing the lessons learned from the reemployment project, an active employment policy system with Chinese characteristics was set up in 2002. After 3 years exploration, the system was further expanded, enriched, extended and enhanced in 2005. Experiencing the 2008 financial crisis, the policy system has been further improved to become more aggressive.

The International Labor Organization fully affirms China's active employment policy, considering the system to have included all elements of the existing employment policies in other countries: emphasizing the role of active promotion of employment, while also including measures to prevent job losses beforehand; simultaneous emphasis on job creation and skill development, and emphasis on entrepreneurship. These not only display fundamental characteristics of decent employment, but are also enforceable.

The making of green employment promotion policies is the greening of a more active employment policy system. The "green" concept must be implanted into the current policy system on one hand, and include past policies into this policy system on the other, for instance, employment policies for resource depleting cities, water reservoir immigrant employment policy, treatments for policy-induced closure and bankruptcy, etc. On these bases, the more aggressive employment policy system would be further enriched and improved, ultimately becoming China's green employment policy system.

At present, the annual non-agricultural employment demand is around

30million in China, and the current economic growth only creates about 10 million new jobs. To accelerate economic growth and expand employment are still the government's most urgent task with the highest priority. In such employment situation, the making of green employment promotion must give proper consideration to the following issues: firstly, green employment promotion should not cause great employment fluctuation, and the respective employment plans must be well designed. Secondly, when it is difficult to fully transfer agricultural labor surplus to meet shortage, the government should support the greening of labor intensive employment in the agricultural domain. Thirdly, like other policies, green employment promotion should be focused on non-public sectors, including individual, private-owned, and village and township enterprises etc. On one hand, such enterprises generate the majority of jobs, and on the other hand, the greening potential is quite considerable. Fourthly, flexible employment is still the key channel for job creation at present, green employment promotion must not strangle this employment channel.

According to this research, the following policy suggestions are raised:

2.6.2.1 Ensure Green Employment Development by Legal Means

2.6.2.1.1 To Conduct Employment Evaluation on Industrial and Environmental Policies

First of all, a social evaluation index system centered on employment should be set up for environmental protection. In the making of various industrial and environmental planning, employment evaluation indexes must be outlined scientifically, including the number of new jobs the project could possibly create, the number of lost jobs caused by the project, the impact on local human resource supply-demand situation, the impact on local population's income level, the matching of local human resources for the project, etc.

Secondly, it is important to make employment planning. Setting up employment evaluation indexes should be followed by employment planning. This means the policies and measures to address the project impacts on employment. If job losses are likely, plans must be made to encounter unemployment; if there are needs for the supply of human resources, a supply plan must be devised. Such planning mainly concerns the issue of ensuring sufficient funding.

Thirdly, organize employment budget. The setup of employment evaluation indexes and plans should be followed by employment budgeting, i.e. the cost-benefit calculation for the project employment, which includes employment budgeting and funding budgeting.

Lastly, project evaluation should be conducted. The evaluation of the industrial and environmental policies' impacts on employment should be taken as a pre-approval procedure for project approval.

2.6.2.1.2 Modify and Improve Respective Laws and Legalize the Employment Evaluation for Industrial and Environmental Policies

Firstly, clear goals for green employment must be raised in the Twelfth Five planning in the aspects of environmental protection, main industries, and human resources and social securities. Ultimately, employment targets during industrial development and environmental protection must be stated clearly in the Twelfth Five-Year planning for economic and social development, so as to ensure our country's green employment development during the Twelfth Five period.

Secondly, as the Twelfth Five-Year plan is being carried out, respective laws and regulations shall be modified. These include Environmental Protection Law, Cyclical Economic Promotion Law, Energy Conservation Act, Employment Promotion Law, Labor Contract Law, and so on. Also, elements of green employment should be included in the formulation of new laws and regulations such as Vocational Ability Development Ordinance and Social Insurance Law.

2.6.2.2 Policies and Measures for Green Employment Promotion

2.6.2.2.1 The Greening of Human Resource Market Mechanism to Promote Green Employment

Firstly, a green employment certification system should be set up to promote green employment. The green employment certification system could award companies in green industries and the green companies in non-green industries the title of Green Employment Enterprise, which could become a reference for receiving related policy supports. For example, they could be qualified to join the list of suppliers for government green procurement.

Secondly, a professional green employment certification system could be set up, promote worker's transformation towards "green collar". While improving our professional certification system, green employment standards should be developed, and workers should be encouraged to participate in the professional green employment certification, so as to encourage more and more people to join the rank of green employment.

The third point concerns the public employment service system. A green employment service zone should be set up in public employment service agencies, in order to collect and advertise green employment information, promoting matching between green employment demand and supply. The labor and social security community platform should be used so that green employment information could reach every single worker.

2.6.2.2.2　The Greening of Existing Active Employment Policy to Promote Green Employment

At present, China's active employment policy mainly targets the redundant workers and the unemployed. To green the active employment policy is to broaden the current program to include those affected during the transformation towards green economy. These could include workers affected in the state-owned forest farms' reform, and workers from the 13 industries that are required to shut down or suspend outdated production capacities. They are power, steel, construction material, electrolytic aluminum, ferroalloy, calcium carbide, coke, coal, plate glass and paper making. Their jobs were affected because of the state's industrial policies and institutional factors, and should be provided with employment policy support, including policies to promote job stabilization, and to promote employment.

The first is to encourage companies to expand employment. Policy leverages such as tax benefits, social insurance subsidies, guaranteed loans and interest subsidies should be used to encourage employment of those affected in the transformation towards green economy. Policy supports such as tax benefits should be provided to those companies that use multiple channels to relocate their own affected workers by the use of their existing facilities, sites and technology for diversification.

The second is to help companies overcome difficulties to create as many jobs as possible. Preferential treatments such as delaying payment of social insurances, reducing social insurance rates, and providing social insurance subsidies, job subsidies, and worker training subsidies, should be given to those companies who are in the transformation towards green production and have the potential to absorb surplus workers, so that they could maintain stable employment, and eliminate or minimize redundancy.

The third is to encourage self-employed entrepreneurs. Entrepreneurship should be encouraged by providing free training, fixed amount tax relief and guaranteed micro loans. For those started their own businesses, cottage craft businesses and privately owned businesses, their administrative fees and taxes could be reduced or waived. For those lacking operation funding, certain amount of guaranteed micro loans and the respective interest subsidies could be provided. A good environment suitable for workers to find their living should be created through taxes and fees waivers, venue arrangement, guaranteed micro loans, and interest subsidies.

The fourth is to promote reemployment through public employment services and reemployment training. The government's public employment agencies should provide free employment services to these people. Employees from the sun-set industries should be retrained, focusing on resource substitution industries and skill training so that their reemployment could be realized smoothly.

The fifth is to provide employment support for those in difficulties. The government could create charitable positions with social insurance subsidies and job subsidies, which those having difficulty in finding reemployment could enjoy priority. The government could provide social insurance subsidies to those with reemployment flexibility, and coordinate placement for the key groups such as those having reemployment difficulties.

The sixth is to carry out early retirement for some old workers. Some older workers with difficult to retrain and relocate should be allowed to take early retirement, so that they could exit the employment market in a decent way.

The seventh is to provide good support for the difficult regions. The regions that are hurt in the transformation towards green economy, especially the middle and western regions where economy is relatively backwards, need special funding from the central government to help them overcome employment problems.

2.6.2.2.3　Develop Green Employment Posts through Policy Support

Some green employment are themselves very competitive hence become very well developed without the need for any policy supports. Environmental equipment, cleansing products and organic food manufacture are examples of such industries. However, in general, green employment is an emerging phenomenon, most of which still need to rely on policy support to be developed rather quickly. This does not necessarily translate to heavy investment but offers enormous employment potentials.

For example, some cities piloted waste collection and recycling stations, which could not compete with the private recycling operators. To nurture their growth, waste recycling posts in the communities could be created so that a network is built up, and in its initial stage job subsidies or social insurance subsidies could be given. As the green employment gets developed to a formal industry, it could be left alone to operate in the market.

In another example, each year large amounts of Chinese universities graduates majored in environmental subjects have difficulty finding employment, while the companies could not recruit enough suitable employees, feeling the shortages. If each company is required to hire an environmental assessed, a large quantity of new jobs could be created. From The 2008 China Statistical

Yearbook on Environment, among China's professional environmental workers, 188,000 spread across the 70,612 companies in the collection of industrial solid wastes, 6,463 in 2,681 companies working on environmental protection archives. According to the first national economic census, if each of the 5,169,000 legal person status units and 6,824,000 industrially activity units hire one environmental worker, and this could create 12 million positions alone.

2.6.2.2.4 Develop Green Employment in the Socialist New Countryside Construction and West Development

There is broad potentials in countryside's green employment. Agriculture is the foundation of national economy. Ecological environment construction is the basic national policy, and countryside economy is a miniature national economy. The development of agricultural knowledge-intensive industry is the countryside's future and the source of green employment. Such industries in agriculture, forestry, glass, sand and ocean use the sun as direct energy source, rely on photosynthesis for production and make full use of biological resources and modern production technology, to conduct flow type productions. Long sunshine duration and rich land and other resources in the west give it the biggest potential for developing agricultural knowledge-intensive industries. Countryside green employment could take place mainly in the following six areas:

The first is to develop eco-agriculture employment. Eco-agriculture is a knowledge and labor intensive hybrid, can increase rural labor's localized transformation by 20% and increase an ordinary farmer's income by over 50% by efficiently producing energy saving green food.

The second is developing employment in special agriculture. Special agriculture based on market and regional advantages is the development direction for modern agriculture. This would lead to the creation of groups of specialized households and specialized villages, which help to increase farmer's income.

The third is to develop employment in special agricultural product's processing industry. Special agricultural product's processing industry is the combination of agriculture, industry and commerce, with the company or farmers, cooperation as the leading flagship, connecting the farmers and processing industry to become an operation chain.

The fourth is to develop special eco countryside travel industry, which could achieve 15% growths in production, revenue and employment.

The fifth is developing new energy industries. Country energy consumption is undergoing fast increase. The development of biomass energy, straw manure biogas and so on, not only helps to meet countryside energy demand, but also important areas for green employment.

The sixth is to drive up demand for rural public services and create green public service positions on the basis of developing the rural economy.

The promotion of countryside green employment should firstly develop an energy and ecology compensation mechanism, to charge an eco-resource tax, and realize the end stream industry compensate the source industry, finished products compensate resources, the second and tertiary industries compensate the first industry. The received eco resource tax funding should be used to develop rural green public services, such as improve rural conditions, water supply systems and hygiene facilities.

Secondly, in order to optimize the present policies on promoting university graduates to take up grass root jobs, and guiding technical people to start up green businesses in the countryside. What the countryside lacks is professional talents and entrepreneurs but not village officials. The policy for promoting university graduates to work at grass roots must be expanded to include those graduates working in the fields of green public services. The policy for promoting entrepreneurship to boost employment must be expanded to include rural green entrepreneurship.

Thirdly, there should be increased publicity in order to let more people become aware of the broad potential of rural green employment. Comparing with industries that have great effect on GDP such as energy, agriculture does not have apparent economic benefits, so rural green economy tends not to receive much attention. But in fact, it contains not only technology element, but is also labor intensive, is an emerging industry with enormous prospect for development. In coordinating township and rural employment development, promotion of rural green employment should be taken as a key aspect for further exploitation.

Fourthly, rural worker's education must be strengthened. At the moment, there exist great conflicts between rural worker quality and the needs of rural economic development. The present rural workforce, mainly made up of elderly and female, have difficulties in taking up the responsibility of rural green economic development. Developing countryside green economy would attract those with knowledge and skill to join the rural workforce. Meanwhile, expanding specific training for rural workers could help to optimize rural human resource profile, promoting the rural area's sustainable development.

2.6.2.2.5 To Drive Employment Growth by Supporting the Development of Green Employment Type Small Enterprises

Small businesses have always played a key role in creating and absorbing employment, it is the same for green employment. For those classified as green employment type small enterprises, Green Employment Organization Certificates should be given, which could be used as the basis for enjoying respective supportive policy. For example, green employment type small enterprises could be given support in loans, enjoy reduction and waiver of income taxed for 3 years, followed by 2 years of 50% off income tax, or enjoy suitable subsidies. For those who started up green employment type small enterprises, the business tax, personal income tax, urban maintenance and construction tax and education surcharge should all be waived for 3 years; they should also be provided with micro loans; their industrial and commerce registration should be simplified, where once the Green Employment Organization Certificate is given, business license is no longer needed. Technology promotion policy should be made to drive the implementation and popularization of green scientific research results, and to promote green collar entrepreneurship.

2.6.2.3 Draw up Green Skill Development Plan to Promote Green Employment Development

Skill development is the key in the transformation towards green employment. On one hand, we should try to green all existing trainings, such as rural practical skill training, sunshine training, dew program, skill training for rural labor employment transformation. Green skill development should be included in all these training programs. On the other hand, new skill development plan should also be drawn up.

2.6.2.3.1 To Survey Green Employment Status and Draw up Functional Spectrum for Green Employment

There are many kinds of green employment in China already, and some green employment are included in the professional qualification system, such as environmental assessment engineers, recycling of renewable resources, sewage treatment operator, and solar power worker, biogas production operator, etc. On one hand, we should continue to discover green employment in each industry, and on the other, the development of green employment standards must be speeded up, so as to develop green training professional standards and green skill training standards and gradually improve our functional spectrum for green employment and the system of green employment training standards.

2.6.2.3.2 Draw up Plans for Technical and Technological Enhancement for Green Industries

To draw up and implement the plan for China green industry technical and technological enhancement, improve worker's overall green skill level, supply the necessary human resources for green development.

To achieve this, industry-specific outlines on green technology and skill and human resource plans must be drawn up. For new technologies and skills, industries and universities could be lined up to explore the most suitable training methods together. An example is Vocational skill training school under Himin Group continuously develops various technologies and professional training for solar thermal utilization. The existing education system and training system must institutionally accept and promote such new technology and skills. For relatively mature technologies and skills, there should be respective incentive policies, for example, to provide unemployment insurance fund to motivate companies to give green skill training for the entire workforce, to encourage various educational and training institutions to conduct training by providing training subsidies, and to give out training coupons to encourage workers take up training.

2.6.2.3.3   To Green the Existing Entrepreneur Training

This includes green entrepreneurial philosophy and projects, green industrial skills etc.

2.6.2.3.4   To Strengthen Reorientation and Relocation Training during the Transformation towards Green Employment

The exist for non-green employment includes reorientation, relocation and complete exist from the labor market, in other words, job post substitution, job post conversion and job post being lost. Retraining for skill improvement and conversion must be given to workers on those positions, to realize fair transformation towards green employment.

Reorientations trainings for job post substitution mainly involve skill conversion training, which could be provided by the enterprise itself with given support from the community. Training for job post conversion is relocation training, which is quite difficult as the skills needed are not what the worker is usually good at, so they would require government and community to provide support on training. The government should draw up specific job conversion training plans for the industries and regions facing lost job opportunities, and assign specific funding in order to carry out meaningful skill re-training.

2.6.2.3.5　To Gradually Develop Green Employment Practitioner Qualification and Green Skill Appraisal

Green collar assessment and evaluation standards should be developed according to green employment standards, in order to gradually develop green employment practitioner qualification and green skill appraisal.

2.6.2.3.6　To Set up a Green Skill Development System Encompassing All Workers

Green employment exist in every industry and involve all kinds of workers. Therefore,　green skill development should cover all workers too. All kinds of channels such as vocational schools, community training centers, public employment service institutes and companies, must be used to spread the concept and skills of green employment, so that upcoming workforce possess green employment awareness; to provide green reemployment trainings for the unemployed; to provide skill enhancement and conversion trainings for workers in difficulties; to provide green vocational skill training for migrant workers; to provide free green vocational training for demobilized soldiers; to provide green entrepreneurial training for university graduates and those wanting to start their own businesses; to provide green vocational enhancement training for incumbent workers. Training subsidies policies could be used to expand training scale, extend training duration and improve training's target accuracy and effectiveness.

2.6.2.4　To Strengthen Protection for Green Workers' Rights and Interests.

Green employment helps to protect the environment, but the rights and interests of some green employment workers are not well protected. The first case is that, the workplace conditions are not good. For example, wind power workers' jobs are largely affected by the natural environment, and have to work long shift circles. This calls for special subsidy mechanism to address problems caused by long shift circles. Other than providing subsidies, improving the company's welfare facilities, the most important is to address the problem concerning worker's offspring's education.

The second case is that the worker's way is very low, and they lack social protection, especially for some flexible employment groups. This could include those trash recycling workers spreading across the streets and roads in cities. Their employment should be formalized as much as possible, so as to improve their employment stability and safety, improve income level.

The third case is that some green employment security is relatively low, with short employment contract terms, and the likelihood that they get fired any time, and worker's rights and interests often get abused. These are most common in small and medium enterprises as well as private enterprises. Improving the supervision over law enforcement, as well as collective negotiation mechanism would help to increase workers' employment security.

The fourth case is where the labor relations are not in harmony. For example, many fresh graduate recruits have conflicts with the company in Himin Group. The company feels that the new recruits cannot fit into their jobs in terms of work attitude and capability, while the new recruits feel that the company is asking for too much. Confrontations often take place. Wage level is too low, causing high staff turnover rate. Therefore, assisting the company to improve management quality and system, develop harmonious labor relations would ultimately help green employment development.

2.6.2.5 To Align Social Partners for Green Employment Improvement

Mutual understandings must be reached between the government, the employers and the workers. When the employers are considering economic benefits, they must shoulder the social responsibility for green development at the same time, and try to align green employment with economic benefits. The development strategy should emphasize green employment in the coordination of the 3 parties in labor relation, in order to promote green employment.

Worker's unions can take part in promoting green employment development actively. Firstly, they would carry out skill improvement activities, to improve worker's capability for green employment. For example, the union can help workers learn new skills and new approaches for green production by providing topical training and consultation with green development as the main theme, publish related books, and hosting respective talks. The union can continuously discover and summarize green operation skills and tips created by the workers, helping workers to improve resource saving capability. The union can also conduct respective position drill and skill contest, to motivate workers' enthusiasm for improving their own skills.

Secondly, company management must be improved, and community supervision must be strengthened on the company's green development. The workers' participation into company management could be penetrated into the company's entire production and operation process. The workers could be encouraged to carefully identify weak links from their own positions and from the smallest places, plugging the loopholes, reduce resource wastes, improve resource utility rate so as to improve environmental protection. The workers can also learn about the company's environmental situations, check on the company's environmental measures, actively assist the company to design planning, identify responsibilities, and ensure various environmental protection measures are implemented effectively. The workers can also organize worker supervision team to strengthen community supervision.

2.6.2.6 To Improve Publicity, Create an Atmosphere for the Entire Society to Promote Green Employment Development

Different types of activities can be undertaken, such as publicity on typical examples of green employment, important projects and important events, to gradually promote the formation of a social atmosphere where green employment is well understood, respected and developed. Publicity events can also be road shows, the programs to collection and awards for worker's rationalization recommendations, organize release of worker's innovation on energy saving and emission reduction, host energy saving environmental knowledge contest, give awards to selected groups and individuals in recognition of their contribution to green employment then widely publicize their deeds and promote their innovations.

2.6.2.7 Improve the Environmental for Promoting Company's Greening Development

2.6.2.7.1 Improve Environmental Standards

At present, China's environmental protection standard system is undergoing development, environmental standards for many industries are still lacking or incomplete. Therefore, the development for environmental standard system must be speeded up. Meanwhile, the standards should be within the reach of the majority of companies, excluding only a small number of companies. When the state is setting up the standards, the country's actual situations must be given thorough considerations, allowing companies to reach the standards in stages on one hand, and on the other hand, make it feasible for the companies to implement the standards by funding inputs and policy inputs. The actual effects on the society, especially the impact on employment must be given full consideration when implementing environmental standards.

2.6.2.7.2 Promote Companies' Sustainable Development by Rewards and Penalties

Refusing to fulfill environmental responsibilities equals to externalizing the environmental and social costs for the responsibilities. The promotion of a company's transformation towards green development firstly requires a gradually improved incentive and motivation mechanism in place, where green technology and their users are put on an advantageous position in market competition. For instance, increase government subsidies for those environmental products and services that have no or at present not yet have any economic returns. The second is to improve law enforcement. Right now state own enterprises would normally perform national environmental policies, while some small private enterprises would not. Rectifications and environmental law enforcement should be strengthened for those small enterprises.

2.6.2.7.3 Continuously Improve the Financing Facilities for Green Development

The development, utilization and popularization of environmental technologies are critical in promoting the transformation towards green economy, and the key for environmental technology's adaptation is funding. Financing facilities must be continuously improved, including imposing resource tax, environment tax, carbon tax, and so on, to generate funding for green economic development and green employment creation. Meanwhile, we should also try to get international technological and funding supports.

3 International Research on
Green Employment

Developing green energy-saving and environmental protection industry, implementing the low-carbon economic development mode, utilizing renewable energies are the only ways for sustainable development of future economy and society. The development of environmental protection industry, low-carbon economy and renewable energy and creation of jobs are the recipes for coping with the domestic employment pressure under the shock of existing financial crisis. The aim of this research is to provide reference for China's green employment through the summarization of the relevant legislations, policies and measures of the world in such fields as environmental protection industry, low-carbon economy and renewable energy.

3.1 Definition of Green Employment

Currently, there is no strictly uniform definition for green employment (green employment).

One definition is that, green employment refers to the employment that is economically feasible, can reduce environmental impact and realize the sustainable development.

Another definition is that, green employment refers to any emerging job which exerts an impact lower than the average level on the environment, and can improve the overall environmental quality.

The definition of green employment by the International Labor Organization is that, green employment refer to the decent work created in economic sectors and economic activities, which can reduce the environmental impact, and ultimately realize a sustainable development in terms of environment, economy and the society.

In the report named "Green Employment: Realizing Decent Work in a World of Low-carbon and Sustainable Development" UNEP,ILO,ITUC , the green employment is defined as the work contributing to the protection and restoration of environmental quality in such fields as agriculture, industry, services and management. Green employment has four basic features: first, it can reduce the consumption of energy and raw materials ("dematerialized economy"); second, it can reduce greenhouse gas emissions ("carbon-free economy"); third is the protection and restoration of ecological system; forth is the reduction of waste and pollution.

The Task Force in US Minnesota is of the view that, the job opportunities in green economy includes the employment in such four industrial sectors as green products, renewable energy, green service and environmental protection. Here, the green products refer to the products produced in order to reduce the environmental impact and improve the resources utilization efficiency; it is mainly used in such four fields as building, transportation, consumer products and industrial products. Renewable energy refers to such energies as solar energy, wind energy, water energy, geothermal energy and bio-mass fuel, etc. Green service refers to the industries and professions providing various services for enterprises and consumers to use green products or technologies, including energy infrastructure construction and the professions related to the energy efficiency, agriculture, recycling and waste management. Environmental protection refers to the industries related to the protection of energy, air, water and land resources.

3.2 International Industrial Policies on Environmental Protection

3.2.1 American Policies

America's environmental protection industry (including state-owned enterprises and private ones) has two forms : one is the public infrastructure existed in history, such as the provision of drinking water, sewage treatment and waste management; the other is the enterprises rapidly rising with the formulation and implementation of domestic environmental protection laws and regulations, most of which are private-owned enterprises, mainly engaging in the businesses like pollution control and pollution remediation. Environmental protection industry includes all value-creating enterprises in connection with the following activities: 1) complying with environmental regulations; 2) environmental assessment, analysis and protection; 3) pollution control, waste management and pollution remediation; 4) supply and transportation of water, recyclable materials and clean energy; 5) technical activities that could improve the energy and resources utilization efficiency, increase productivity and promote the sustainable economic development.

America's environmental protection policies include the following aspects after conclusion:

3.2.1.1 Implementation of Rigid Environmental Standards and Regulations is the Foundation of Environmental Protection Industry Development

America formulated the first Clean Air Act in 1963, limiting the emissions from burning fossil fuels. With the strengthening of pollution control, during 1970-1990, America amended the Clean Air Act for three times in succession, and every time the regulations are stricter than before. During this period, the America's air pollution control equipment market was developed rapidly, new technologies and new processes were developed continuously and the market was on the rise. In addition, the Clean Water Act also directly promoted the rapid development of environmental protection industry in terms of water pollution control.

3.2.1.2 Adopting the Economic Stimulus Means is the Impetus of Development of America's Environmental Protection Industry

Compared to other industries the environmental protection is still an emerging industry. In the process of developing environmental protection industry, America adopted many economic means as supplementation of laws and regulations, so as to stimulate the enterprises to meet the environmental standards and comply with the environmental laws and regulations. The economic stimulus means adopted mainly include:

1) Financial subsidies. It means that, the government gives some capital subsidies for the environmental industries and related projects by legislations. For example, the America's Federation Water Pollution Control Act stipulates that, if the urban sewage treatment plants adopt the "best practical treatment technology" recognized by the Federal Environmental Protection Agency, they may apply to the Federal Environmental Protection Agency for subsidies, and they may get a large portion of construction subsidy upon approval, provided that the sewage treatment management plan is implemented properly. Since the beginning of 1970s, the U.S. federal government encouraged the states to

establish "water pollution control circulation fund", and each state may get a certain proportion of subsidy from the federal government into the fund, so as to alleviate the financial pressure of the federal government.

2) Tax incentives. Generally governments impose fixed asset tax on commercial enterprises, but in order to encourage enterprises to install environmental protection facilities, special tax relief measures were taken in terms of local taxation.

3) Collection of sewage clean-up charges. In May 2000, U.S Federal Environmental Protection Agency imposed a fine of $ 37,250,000 on 51 enterprises polluting the drinking water source at the San Fernando Valley in California, which was used for paying the charges required for cleaning the drinking water reservoir at San Fernando Valley.

4) Pollution-discharge right trade. In 1979, U.S government firstly proposed the overall policy for pollution-discharge right trade, stipulating the total pollution discharge amount within certain regional area and the minimum standard for environmental quality, and that sewage discharge amount for some pollution sources difficult to control and costing too much for governance shall be increased and discharge amount for other pollution sources shall be reduced. To 1986, America had initially established a whole set of relatively complete pollution-discharge right trade system. In 1990, America firstly realized the successful pollution-discharge right trade in controlling the discharge of carbon dioxide and sulfur dioxide, and the charges spent was only a half of the charges needed by the "plant-by-plant control" method.

The pollution-discharge right trade refers to that, in a regional area, based on the environmental pollutant carrying capacity and with premise of implementing total amount control, the government distributes the pollution-discharge right to enterprises through the market, which is relatively fair and efficient, and helpful to the coordination between regional economic development and environmental protection, therefore such policy has great prospect of development.

3.2.1.3 Increase Investment in Environmental Protection Funds, Providing Driving Source for Development of Environmental Protection Industry [①]

The investment in environment protection funds is a guarantee for the development of environmental protection industry. The money invested by America in reducing pollution and protecting the environment is considerable in amount, and still showing a trend of increase. For example, in 1991, the total amount of environment governance costs in America reached 129 billion dollars, and in 1995, the costs for reducing and controlling pollution in America amounted to 170 billion dollars.

The environmental protection funds of America are not undertaken solely by the government, the participation of enterprises is also an important source of environmental protection funds. It's just the large quantity of investment by the government and enterprises in environmental protection funds that promoted the continuous development and utilization of various new technologies and new products used for preventing pollution, resulting in a more prosperous and active environmental protection industry.

3.2.1.4 Accelerate the Technical Innovation of Environmental Protection Industry and Improve the International Competitiveness of Environmental Protection Industry

America is an all-around super superpower in each field of economy and technology. In order to keep its superpower position, it needs to put more investment in high-tech industry and emerging industries, and more importantly, it should take the advantage of America's leading edge in science and technology to promote the development of the environmental protection industry, thus ensure that the environmental industry is matched with other

---

① Yi Dong, "Simple Analysis on America's Government Act in Becoming an Environmental Protection Industry Power", Environmental Protection, October, 2003

industries (especially the high-tech industry), dominating a leading position in international environmental protection industry market.

3.2.2 Britain's Policies

Development of Britain's environmental protection industry has many difficulties, such as laws and regulations, capital, market and technology, etc. The capital shortage is very prominent, especially when starting a business and expanding new businesses, the capital is even more in shortage. While investors are always unwilling to make investment in environmental protection industry, they think that the environmental projects are highly risky and the policies are not stable.

Britain promulgated the Environmental Protection Industry Control Act in 1994. In recent years, in order to solve the bottleneck problems hindering the development of environmental protection industry, Britain has been taking some measures, which mainly include: reform of environmental protection laws and regulations and technological innovations; research and development policies; application of high-tech technologies in industry; promoting and assisting the development of export business; international trade and international environmental protection policies; establishing a database for environmental protection industry.

Currently Britain's environmental protection industry has the following features and trends [1] :

(1) Among the basic policies for environmental protection industry, the support for environmental protection measures with high technological content is increased;

(2) Support the environmental protection research and development;

(3) Promote the development of environmental protection industry in Britain as a national strategy;

(4) Reform of environmental protection laws and regulations

---

[1] Zhang Jianting"Current Situation of Britain's Environmental Protection Industry and Development Trend", Global Technology Economy Lookout, April, 1999.

(a) Gradually standardize various major environmental protection enterprises in Britain and promote the Britain's environmental protection industry standards to the world's highest level;

(b) Strengthen the implementation and management of environmental protection laws and regulations, ensure that they are totally implemented in accordance with the standards of Britain and European Union;

(c) Research and formulate the preferential policies for compliance with environmental protection laws and regulations to encourage companies to actively select the innovative environmental protection technologies, actively create the supporting conditions for research and development and provide tax preference policies to environmental protection investors;

(d) Use the government procurement plans to motivate the development of domestic environmental protection technologies and the related service market, put more investment in environmental protection infrastructure construction.

(e) Internationalization of environmental protection technologies and services;

(f) Develop new ways for research of environmental protection technologies and service innovation technologies in order to get new breakthroughs in encouraging the innovative activities, and reduce the barrier of innovative activities.

3.2.3　Belgium's Policies

Belgium is a small country, but it is one of the founding members of European Union. Same as other western European countries, in the economic and social development of last several decades, Belgium has been going a long way for "pollution first and treatment later", drawing a painful lesson from it. In order to pay attention to the environment governance work, Belgian government formulated the Environmental Technology Research and Development Plan as early as in 1991. In 1995, the government again comprehensively researched and analyzed the national environmental status, and carried out various researches and technological development activities based on such four fields as atmosphere, water, waste and soil. The policy essentials may be concluded as the following: [1]

(1) For such four environment fields as atmosphere, water, waste and soil, the federal government and governments of each administrative region should strengthen organization and coordination and give strong financial support;

(2) Actively guide and support industrial enterprises (including small and medium-sized enterprises) to participate in the development of new technologies, new processes and new products of environmental protection;

(3) In the development of each technology, the high-tech feature and long-term safety should be assured, which should be suitable for a variety of environmental protection fields, and may not be limited to a certain area;

(4) Organize elite units (especially research institutions and enterprises) to jointly overcome technical difficulties for large-sized environmental protection equipment, research and develop a new generation of high-level equipment and apparatuses;

(5) Formulate uniform international standards for various types of new environmental protection products;

(6) Strengthen the trainings for various professional persons and technical leaders in the environmental protection field, cultivate and reserve excellent professional talents for future environmental protection;

(7) Intensify the international cooperation, especially the cooperation between it and European Union as well as the other members of European Union, and actively participate in the European Union's overall plan for research and technological development.

---

① Zhou Hongchun, "An International Comparison of Environmental Protection Policies", Energy Saving and Environmental Protection, October, 2002;

3.3 Low-carbon Economic Policies and Measures in Selected Countries

3.3.1 European Union: Transformation to High Energy Efficiency and Low Emission [1]

The "a package of energy plans" proposed by the European Union Committee is to drive the transformation of European Union's economy to a high energy efficiency and low emission, and lead the world to enter an era of "post-industrial revolution".

European Union has always been an advocator for coping with climate change, actively promoting the greenhouse gas reduction activity around the world. Since the Britain proposed the concept of "low-carbon economy", EU members gave positive evaluations at varying degrees, and adopted similar strategies.

Why the EU vigorously advocates the low-carbon economy is also the consideration of guaranteeing the energy and climate safety within the whole EU system. As the world's largest economic system and the second largest energy consumption system, the EU energy shortage problem has always been one of the biggest obstacles for economic and social development.

At present, the entire EU is the largest importer of oil and natural gas in the world, 82% oil and 57% natural gas are from other countries and regions, and it

---

① "Ecological Economy" , Economic Daily, 11th edition, March 25, 2009

is expected that in the future 25 years the oil and natural gas import ratio will be higher than 93% and 84% respectively. Among which, the western European developed countries (such as France and Germany) will be particularly dependent on imported energy. The "oil crisis" occurred many times in the last century promoted the development and utilization by EU countries of oil-alternative energy and cleaner and safer renewable energy, the new round of world energy price soar started from 2006 and the oil and natural gas disputes between Russia and Ukraine as well as Belarus respectively in recent two years greatly impacted EU countries, highlighting EU's potential energy crisis and the weakness of energy policies.

In order to further push forward the diversity of energy supply and realize the greenhouse gas reduction goals specified in the Kyoto Protocol, leaders of EU countries passed in March 2007 the "a package of energy plans" proposed by the EU Committee, thus drive the transformation of EU economy to the direction of high energy efficiency and low emission, and lead the globe to an era of "post-industrial revolution".

Based on this plan, EU promised that up to 2020, the proportion of renewable energy in the total energy consumption would be increased to 20%, the consumption of such one-off energies as coal, oil and natural gas would be decreased by 20%, and the proportion of bio-mass fuel in the transportation energy consumption would be increased to 10%. Furthermore, EU made a unilateral commitment that, up to 2020, the greenhouse gas emission will be reduced by 20% compared to 1990, if other major countries take similar actions, the proportion may be 30% and it is expected to reduce emissions by 60%~80% up to 2050. At the end of 2007, the EU Committee passed the European Strategic Energy Technology Plan, which clearly proposed that the "low-carbon energy" technology would be encouraged and popularized, and the establishment and development of sustainable energy utilization mechanism for EU in the future would be promoted.

The governments of major EU countries led by France and Germany have been putting more investment in the energy conservation and environmental protection field in a long term, boosting the technological upgrading of environment, energy and related industries. At the same time, EU countries, by their advantages in technologies of renewable energy and greenhouse gas emission reduction etc., actively promote the international cooperation for coping with the climate change and greenhouse gas emission reduction, making efforts to create conditions for EU enterprises to enter the energy environmental protection markets of developing countries by means of technological transfer.

3.3.2 Practice of Britain in Implementation of Low-carbon Economy

Britain is the first country raising and actively advocating the concept of "low carbon". In 2003, the British government proposed four goals in the Energy White Paper: first is to reduce the British CO_2 emission by about 60% before 2050, and achieve real progress in 2020; second is to guarantee reliable energy supply; third is to promote a more competitive market in Britain and even broader market; forth is to guarantee that each British family could obtain the most adequate heating within the affordable economic capacity.

In order to realize the above goals, the major measures taken by Britain include [1] :

3.3.2.1 Establish a Free Market with Competitive Edge

Free and competitive market is the foundation of energy policies. A well-designed market mechanism has the capacity of healthy competition, which can produce reasonable prices and provide safer energies and more choices and under the market mechanism the currency value can truly be reflected.

---

[1] Jin Zhiyong, "Britain Implements Low-carbon Economy Energy Policy", Global Technology Economy Lookout, October, 2003.

3.3.2.2   Implement Relevant Standards and Regulations

Britain implemented the Energy Efficiency Standards and amended the new Regulations Governing Buildings to improve the energy utilization efficiency and reduce the CO_2 emission. In implementing the Energy Efficiency Standards, the Department for Environment, Food and Rural Affairs established an overall target and relevant laws and regulations; The Office of Gas and Electricity Markets is responsible for management and supervision; while the suppliers not only expect the further effective utilization of energy, but also want to save the family energy consumption with priority.

3.3.2.3   Utilize Renewable Energy

The renewable energy will play an important role in reducing carbon emission. At the same time, through development of cleaner technologies, products and processes the energy reliability will be enhanced and the industry competitiveness will be improved. By 2003, 3% of British power supply had come from renewable energy. Currently the British government has formulated the following goals: as long as the cost can be accepted by consumers, up to 2010, the power generation capacity of Britain's renewable energy will account for 10% of the total generating capacity. That is to say, in each year 1250MW newly added renewable energy power generation will be required in Britain. Moreover, in order to reach the goal of reducing 60% CO_2 emission in 2050, Britain needs to increase 30%~40% renewable energy power generation.

Britain's practice shows that, the economic growth and low-carbon emission could be realized at the same time. Advancing to low-carbon is not only the method coping with climate change but also the opportunity for economic prosperity. Over the past decade, British realized the longest economic growth period in 200 years, and the economy has increased by 28%, and the greenhouse emission has been reduced by 8%. Britain's practice shows that, the economic growth and low-carbon emission could be realized at the same time. Advancing to low-carbon is not only the method coping with climate change but also the opportunity for economic prosperity. Britain's successful experience may be summarized as two aspects: [1]

On one hand, cope with the climate change by legislation. In recent years, Britain has always been taking the climate change solution and development of low carbon technology and economy as an important strategy for economic and social development of Britain. In June 2007, Britain published the draft of Climate Change Bill, clearly promised that to 2020, 26%—32% greenhouse gas emission would be reduced, to 2050, the greenhouse gas emission would be reduced by 60%, which is a long-term goal. The bill proposed that a Climate Change Committee should be established, which is responsible for making suggestions to the government in terms of investment and policy mechanism for carbon emission reduction. The bill also formulated a plan for future 15 years, providing a clear framework for facilitating the realization of carbon reduction and ensuring the investment by enterprises and individuals in low carbon field.

On the other hand, actively utilizing the policy tool is another initiative used by Britain for developing a low-carbon economy.

In family field, British government proposes that up to 2016, the zero carbon emission will be realized for all newly built residences. The Department of Environment, Food and Rural Affairs of the government sets up carbon trust fund, providing energy conservation services and loans; adopts the EU standards for home electrical appliances; uses the financial tools like value-added tax reduction, formulates fuel poverty subsidy measures; provides information and suggestions for residents; establishes energy conservation trust fund, which is responsible for providing green housing service, establishing energy logo and building energy conservation performance certificate system.

For enterprises, British government specifies that, all units above 20 MW

---

[1] "Ecological Economy", Economic Daily, 11th edition, March 25, 2009

should participate in the carbon discharge trade system; set up "carbon trust fund" to be responsible for carbon management, energy audit and loans (providing low-interest or no-interest loans to small and medium-sized enterprises), install smart meters, establish the building energy efficiency certificate system; introduce financial incentives, develop "climate change tax", the government and users of heavy-industry energy sign a voluntary agreement that if the enterprises could realize relatively low emission through new investments, they do not need to pay all tax, and the highest tax exemption will be 80%.

Britain also actively advocates the carbon capture and sequestration technology. Among the innovation of various technologies related to low-carbon economy, British government particularly concerns about the vital role carbon capture and sequestration technology plays in realizing the greenhouse gas control target around the world.

3.3.3 Italy's Low-carbon Economy Development Policy

At present, Italy is making great efforts to develop a low-carbon economy, or even zero-carbon economy, using the energy conservation and emission reduction policies and measures as well as technological development to influence Italy's economic policies and economic development. 80% of Italy's energy is dependent on import, so Italy attaches great importance to the development and utilization of renewable energies and new energies, pays more attention to the low-carbon economy development with the implementation of Kyoto Protocol, overall European energy policy and the change of world energy market.

The government of Italy pays attention to the implementation of Kyoto Protocol, adopting policies and measures to improve the energy efficiency, develop renewable energy and encourage the development of low-carbon technologies, so as to reduce the carbon dioxide emission level in the production and consumption of major energies, including the "green certificate" system encouraging the development of renewable energy, the "a package of energy plans" in the 2015 Bill promulgated recently and the energy efficiency action plan proposed to the EU, etc. [1]

3.3.3.1 "Green Certificate" System

In order to support the development of renewable energies, Italy started to implement the so-called CIP6 mechanism since 1992 to support the construction of renewable energy power plants by means of guaranteeing the purchase price. Different prices are specified according to the construction costs, running and maintenance costs and fuel costs of renewable energy projects, the development facilitating costs and the varieties of renewable energy equipment, the costs are fully used or partially used for renewable energy and the energy products are totally sold or only the remaining products are sold, thus the development of renewable energy is promoted in terms of policy orientation. After 1999, Italy started to implement the "green certificate" system by legislation.

3.3.3.2 Energy Efficiency Action Plan

According to EU's energy conservation target that the energy consumption will be saved by 9% in 2016, Italy proposed an energy efficiency action plan to the EU and the measures implemented and to be implemented. The action includes the following three facets:

(1) Continue to implement the measures already adopted for several years, such as, make energy certification for buildings, reduce taxes for oil and liquefied gas, establish eco-car parks and formulate pollution reduction measures; provide preference measures for agriculture energy system, reduce and relieve taxes for high-efficiency industrial motors; reduce and relieve taxes for high-efficiency household appliances; and promote the high-yielding

---

[1] "The World is Moving Towards a Low-carbon Economy", Environmental Protection, February, 2007.

cogeneration plants.

(2) Some measures to be implemented and being discussed. Such as the EU ordinance relating to ecological design stipulates that all products and services must have energy labels as specified by EU.

(3) From 2009, the average carbon dioxide emission from cars will be limited at 140g/km, and the corresponding energy conserved will be 2326 billion KWh/ year, which accounts for 18% of the overall energy conservation target.

3.3.4   Germany's Policies and Measures in Developing Low-carbon Economy

Germany as a technologically advanced industrialized country, its energy development and environmental protection technologies are all at the first place in the world. The German government implements a climate protection high-technology strategy, incorporates the climate protection and greenhouse gas reduction into its strategy of sustainable development, and formulates specific goals and timetables for climate protection, energy conservation and emission reduction through legislations and implementation mechanism with strong binding effect. [1]

3.3.4.1   Implement the Climate Protection High-technology Strategy

In order to realize the climate protection goals, from 1977 to now, the German Federal Government promulgated five Energy Research Plans in succession, the latest plan was implemented starting from 2005, in which the energy efficiency and renewable energy is the focus, for which the Germany's "high-technology strategy" provides capital support. In 2007, the Federal Ministry of Education and Research formulated the "climate protection high-technology strategy" under the framework of "high-technology strategy".

---

① "The World is Moving Towards a Low-carbon Economy", Environmental Protection, February, 2007.

3.3.4.2 Improve the Energy Utilization Efficiency and Promote the Conservation

1) Impose ecological tax. The ecological tax is a quantity tax taking the energy consumption as the subject, which is an important policy of Germany to improve ecological environment and implement the sustainable development plan.

2) Encourage enterprises to carry out modernized energy management. Exerting the huge energy saving potential of industrial economy is the important goal of Germany's climate protection. Germany's industry also contains great potential of energy efficiency improvement, such as the power plants, illumination systems, heat using and boiler equipment, all of which have a space for energy conservation transformation. German government plans to sign an agreement with the industry community before 2013, specifying that enterprises' enjoying the tax preference depends on whether the enterprises implement a modernized energy management or not. For small and medium-sized enterprises, the German Federal Ministry of Economic Affairs has established a special fund for energy conservation to promote small and medium-sized enterprises to improve the energy efficiency, the fund will mainly provide capital support for enterprises in their acceptance of specialized energy conservation guidance and adoption of energy saving measures.

3) Popularize the technology of "combined heat and power generation". In order to support the development and utilization of the technology of combined heat and power generation, the German federal government formulated the Heat and Power Cogeneration Act (effective from April 2002).The act mainly stipulates the subsidy amount for the electric energy generated by the technology of heat and power cogeneration, such as, for the electric energy generated by heat and power cogeneration equipment upgraded before the end of 2005, 1.65 euro cents subsidy may be obtained for each kilowatt. German government plans that up to 2020, the ratio of power supply by the power and heat cogeneration technology will be doubled compared to present level.

4) Implement the building energy conservation transformation. German

government plans that 700 million euros will be allocated to conduct energy conservation transformation for existing civil buildings, in addition, another 200 million euros will be used for transformation of local facilities, the purpose of which is to fully excavate the potential of energy conservation in buildings and public facilities.

3.3.4.3   Vigorously Develop the Renewable Energy

Through the Renewable Energy Law, the government guaranteed the position of the renewable energy, providing subsidy for renewable energy power generation, thus the disadvantage of high production cost for renewable energy is balanced, so the renewable energy is developing very fast. Germany fixed the following key areas at the same time of extensively developing various renewable energies:

(1) Promote the replacement of existing wind power installations and develop offshore wind power parks.

(2) Promote the use of renewable energies. In 1991, Germany promulgated the Law on Renewable Energy Power Generation Combination, stipulating the combination method for renewable energy power generation and the acquisition price that is sufficient to bring profits to the power generating enterprises.

(3) Germany also stipulated the Law on Heating by Renewable Energy, promoting the renewable energy to be used for heating, it is planned that up to 2020, the proportion of heating by renewable energy will be increased to 14% (6% for 2006).

3.3.4.4   Reduce the Carbon Dioxide Emission

(1) Develop plants which adopt low-carbon power generation technology. German government believes that, though the renewable energy is developing fast, lignite and stone coal power plants will continue to play a role in medium and long term, therefore, the power plants with higher efficiency and using clean coal technologies must be developed.

(2) Lower the carbon dioxide emission of various vehicles. For motor vehicles, currently the average carbon dioxide emission of newly sold cars in Germany is approximately 164g/km, but according to the EU's provisions, up to 2012, the emission of new cars should be reduced to 130g/km.

For heavy-duty vehicles, since 2005, Germany started to impose truck fee for trucks with a loading of more than 12 tons driving on the federal superhighways and several key federal highways, and this measure played an active role in improving the transportation efficiency and increasing the proportion of low-emission vehicles.

As for air freight, German government actively advocates to incorporate it into Europe's carbon dioxide emission trading system to promote competition. Meanwhile, German government also supports the suggestion of "European Aviation Integration", and wishes to reduce the carbon dioxide generated from aviation by 10% through the integration.

(3) Pollution-discharge right trade. Germany started to prepare the discharge right trade since 2002, at that time, the Federal Environmental Protection Agency established special discharge trade office, and drafted relevant laws, and currently a relatively integrated law system and management system have been formed.

3.3.5 Japan: the Draft Low-carbon Action Plan Materializes the Emission Reduction Goals [①]

In 2007, Japan proposed the new solution for preventing the global warming ——"Fukuda blueprint", the long-term emission reduction goal is that to 2050, the greenhouse gas emission will be reduced by 60% to 80% compared to current level. Moreover, Japan has always been paying attention to the energy diversity, and making great efforts in improving the energy utilization efficiency.

Japan is the country initiating and advocating the Kyoto Protocol. Japan

----

① "Ecological Economy", Economic Daily, 11th edition, March 25, 2009

always attaches importance to the energy diversity because Japan's domestic energy resources are scarce, and it has made great efforts in improving the energy utilization efficiency. Japan invests a lot of money to develop and utilize the solar energy, wind energy, light energy, hydrogen energy, fuel cells and other alternative energies and renewable energies, and actively carries out research on tidal energy, hydro energy and geothermal energy.

Japan also adopts various laws and incentive measures to encourage and promote the energy conservation and consumption reduction. Aside from emphasizing the industrial structure adjustment, stopping or limiting the development of energy-intensive industries and encouraging the transfer of energy-intensive industries to foreign countries, Japan has also formulated energy conservation planning, making specific regulations for the energy conservation indicators, and developed rather strict energy consumption standards for some energy-intensive products.

Japan takes the Photovoltaic Power Generation as a key field to implement, and proposes that before 2030 the solar energy power generation will be increased by 20 folds. The photovoltaic power generation equipment of Sharp Corporation alone accounts for one third of the world's total, and those of the enterprises at the second to the forth place in Japan also account for 24%. Nowadays, Japan has already been the world's largest exporter of photovoltaic power generation equipment, dominating a leading position in the market. In May 2007, the Japan's Ministry of Economy Trade and Industry proposed a new plan, in which it is planned that in the future five years 209 billion Japanese yen will be invested to develop the clean vehicle technology, the purpose of which is not only to reduce the fuel consumption significantly but also to lower the emission of greenhouse gas.

In June 2007, Japan's Prime Minister Yasuo Fukuda proposed a new solution for preventing the global warming ——"Fukuda blueprint", the long-term emission reduction goal for Japan is that, to 2050, the greenhouse gas emission will be reduced by 60% to 80% compared to current level. On July 26, 2007, Japanese government published the draft action plan formulated in order to realize a low-carbon society, in which the content of significantly reducing the price of solar energy power generation equipment is included.

3.4 Renewable Energy Policies in Foreign Countries

The policies of foreign countries in encouraging the development of renewable energy are mainly reflected in such aspects as objective guiding, price incentives, financial subsidies, tax preferences, credit support, export encouragement and the facilitation of scientific research and industrialization. [1]

3.4.1 Objective Guiding

Establishing a development strategy or a development roadmap is the successful experience of a majority of countries in the world. The idea of developing renewable energies by many developed countries is that: the State formulates specific development objectives and plans for certain stage, and develops a series of preference policies under the framework of the development objectives, and encourages various fields to invest and utilize the renewable energies through market economy means.

In 1997, EU promulgated the White Paper on Renewable Energy Development, stipulated that in 2010, the renewable energy should account for 12% of the total energy consumption in EU, and in 2050, the renewable

---

① Li Junfeng, Shi Guili, "Renewable Energy Policy at Home and Abroad", Renewable Energy, No.1,2006.

energy should account for 50% in the total energy source composition in the entire EU countries. In 2001, EU Council of Ministers proposed a common directive for the use of renewable energies in power generation, which requires that, to 2010, the proportion of renewable energy of EU countries in the total energy consumption should be 12%, and among the power consumption, the proportion of renewable energy will amount to 22.1% in the total. According to this directive, EU member countries formulated their own development objectives, for example, Britain and Germany promised that, in 2010 and 2020, the proportion of renewable energy would reach 10% and 20% respectively; Spanish expressed that, in 2010, its proportion of renewable energy power generation would be more than 29%; Denmark formulated an energy action plan named "21st Century's Energy", promising that, before 2030, the proportion of renewable energy in the energy composition of the entire country will be increased by 1% each year. Some Nordic countries proposed the strategic goals that using wind power and bio-mass power for gradually replacing the nuclear power.

In 1999, Australia published the State goal of supporting the development of renewable energy. It's that to 2010, the power generating capacity by renewable energies will be increased to 25.5 billion kWh, equivalent to 12% of the country's total generating capacity; and the supply of renewable energies will be increased by 2%.

Japan started to implement the "New Sunshine Program" in 1993 to accelerate the development and utilization of photovoltaic cells, fuel cells, hydrogen energy and geothermal energy; in 1997, it published the plan for solar energy photovoltaic roofs, the purpose of which is to install 7,600,000 kW solar energy cells up to 2010.

U.S Department of Energy proposed the plan for gradual improvement of green electricity development, formulated a development roadmap for technologies for wind power generation, solar energy power generation and bio-mass power generation, wishing to increase the proportion of green energy through wind power generation, solar energy power generation and bio-mass power generation.

3.4.2   Price Incentives

Nowadays the price policies for renewable energies in the world are mainly targeted at power products. Apparently the price policy mainly includes the following aspects:

3.4.2.1   Fixed Price

Fixed price refers to that the government directly specifies the market price of renewable energy products clearly. Germany is a representative country for such price policy. Germany formulates different renewable energy power prices by laws and according to the technological form of the renewable energy technology and project resource conditions. There are more than 10 countries adopting such price mechanism in the world, mainly in Europe. The characteristic of such mechanism is that it could promote a balanced development of various renewable energies according to government's willingness and could also push the preferred development of some renewable energy technologies.

3.4.2.2   Floating Price

Some countries adopt floating prices, which is that they take normal power sales price as reference and design an appropriate ratio, and the real price will be floating with the market change of normal power price. For instance, the Spanish government specifies that, the renewable energy power price will be floated in the range of 80-90% of the normal power sales prices, but the specific price level of each year will be negotiated and fixed within the floating range by power generation enterprises and power transmission enterprises.

3.4.2.3 Market Price

Through mandatory quota (that is, requiring enterprises to produce and sell renewable energy power at specific ratio when they producing and selling normal power) and trading system (the government issues green trade certificate to enterprises for the renewable energy power generation, and the certificate may be traded among energy enterprises, the price will be determined by market), the market regulation function can be exerted, and the price of renewable energy products can be enhanced. By this method, the price of renewable energy power generation is the aggregation of average online electricity price and the price of green trade certificate. Britain, Australia and a portion of states in America implemented such policy. In such case, the governments specify the amount of punishment for the enterprises that fail to realize the mandatory quota. Such quota is always the upper limit of the cost of renewable energy power generation trade. Under such price mechanism, different renewable energy powers have the same price, but the price levels are changing with the market demand and supply situation of renewable energies, and the total price will be floating with the change of power market.

3.4.3 Financial Subsidies

Financial subsidy is the most common economic incentive, which is varied in forms.

3.4.3.1 Investment Subsidy

Investment subsidy is to give direct subsidy to the investors of renewable energy projects development. In the countries the price policy is not clearly defined, investment subsidy is very common, and covers a number of renewable energy technologies. For instance, Greece provides subsidy for all renewable energy projects with a ratio of 30-50% of the investment amount; Sweden provides 10-25%, and India provides 10-15% for wind power. In countries where the price policy has been defined, the investment subsidy is always complemented with the price policy. For example, Belgium implements preferential power price for renewable energy power, and provides 10-20% investment subsidy for other renewable energy projects beyond the power generation. Holland provides 20% subsidy for private-invested wind power based on green power price. Aside from the fixed power price, Spanish provides 40% subsidy for the photovoltaic power generation projects which are suffering from high cost. Britain also provides 40% subsidy for high-cost offshore wind power projects based on uniform market power prices. Most European countries also provide subsidies for the renewable energy projects in which individuals have investment or stocks. No matter what subsidy methods are adopted, there are detailed regulations to be referenced for governments of each country. The advantages of subsidy mechanism are that it can mobilize the activeness of investors, increase the production capacity and enlarge the industrial scale, but the shortage is that it is not related to the production and operation situation of enterprises, so it can not stimulate enterprises to upgrade technologies and reduce costs.

3.4.3.2 Product Subsidy

Product subsidy is to provide subsidy according to the output of renewable energy equipment. The advantage of such subsidy is obvious, it is conducive to increase output, reduce cost and improve the economic efficiency of enterprises. It is also an incentive measure being adopted by America, Denmark and India. For example, in America's Energy Policy Act, the wind power can receive product subsidy.

3.4.3.3 User Subsidy

User subsidy is to provide subsidy for consumers. For instance, most European countries provide 20-60% subsidy for users of solar water heaters, and Australia provides 500 Australian dollars for each user installing the solar water heater. The subsidy for consumers is not always unchanged. It is adjusted with the market development and technological advances. For example, Japan's subsidy ratio for family users installing photovoltaic power generation products is gradually reduced from the initial 40% to less than 10%, and prepares to cancel the subsidy at proper time.

3.4.4 Tax Preference

3.4.4.1 Tax Preference for Renewable Energies

The supporting methods of each country are varied and the technical fields supported are also different. For example, India's import tariff for complete wind power generators is 25%, but adopts zero tariff for spare parts import; Greece exempts tax for all renewable energy projects and products; Denmark exempts the imposition of income tax for private-invested wind power, and Portugal, Belgium and Ireland exempt income tax for private-invested renewable energy projects; moreover, Ireland exempts corporate income tax for the funds invested by some enterprises on wind power, bio-mass energy, photovoltaic and hydropower projects.

3.4.4.2 Implement Mandatory Tax Policy for Non-renewable Energies

For example, Sweden and Britain impose electricity tax for non-renewable energy power. Mandatory tax policy, especially the high-standard and high-intensity charging policy, can not only encourage the development and utilization of clean energies, but also promote enterprises to adopt advanced technologies and improve technological levels.

3.4.5 Credit Support

Financial policies such as low-interest loan and soft loans could alleviate the burden of enterprises in repaying the current interests, which is beneficial to lower the production cost, but the government needs to raise certain funds to support the discounts and interest rate cuts, the higher the loan amount is, the larger the discount will be, and the funds need to be raised will be more. Therefore, the availability of capital supply is a key factor influencing the ongoing of such policies. Currently, Germany grants low-interest loans for wind power projects and photovoltaic projects; Italy, since 2001, has been providing interest-free loans for the installation of small-sized photovoltaic system on roofs or other parts of buildings, the amount of which is equivalent to 85% of the project investment.

3.4.6 Export Incentive

Developed countries provide aid for foreign countries to help their equipment manufacturing enterprises to expand into overseas market, including providing various money donations, government loans and hybrid loans to developing countries to increase the export of their equipment manufacturing enterprises. For example, Denmark and Holland push the export of wind power generators by money donations and government loans; Spain and Japan push the export of solar energy products by using channels of assistance.

3.4.7 Joint Promotion of Scientific Research and Industrialization

Aside from using the above policies to generally push the development of renewable energy industrialization, most countries provide strong support for domestic manufacturing industry.

The first is scientific research. Developed countries are making great efforts to promote scientific research. For example, they establish national laboratories and research centers, provide technical guidance, research funds and subsidies etc. for institutions and enterprises. America, Denmark, Germany, Spain, Britain and India all have special national renewable energy institutions, which are responsible for organizing and coordinating the research and development and industrialization of renewable energy technologies of the country on a uniform basis.

The second is expanding market. For example, Denmark and Spain, in the initial period of the development of wind power generation equipment manufacturing industry, required power companies to install a certain number of wind power generators in each year, so as to support the equipment manufacturing enterprises to form a scaled production capacity rapidly. Most European countries require the purchase of their equipment before provide import and export credit so as to help their enterprises to expand overseas market.

3.5 Influence of Energy Utilization and Green Technologies Used to Adapt to Climate Change on China's Employment

3.5.1 Five Areas Influenced

The economic development and the change of population habitation structure bring a severe challenge, i.e. the carbon dioxide emission. Economic growth and gathering of population in cities and towns may bring more carbon dioxide emission, which will have profound influence on the environment. But through the development and utilization of green technologies, in future development process, it is possible to find an important opportunity for sustainable development that will bring a new scene to China's employment, which is mainly reflected in five areas, i.e. the energy industry in which the power is the subject, the transportation industry in which the use of cars is the subject, high-emission industry, building and home appliance industry, and ecological industry (including agriculture and forestry). They will be detailed as follows:

First, in the energy industry, with the development of green energy technologies, cleaner energies will definitely be used to replace the conventional oil and coal. Even in the conventional oil and coal area, the development of green technologies will cause the change of its inner structure, such as the green coal and green power generation, etc. The carbon dioxide capture and storage may become an important part in future's energy composition. China has relatively rich wind resources and solar energy resources, among the green energies, the utilization of wind energy and solar energy has the greatest potential. With the application of new green technologies, the skill structure of practitioners in these fields will definitely be impacted, and a large number of new occupations will be generated along with it.

Second, in the high-emission industry, the values of green industry can be realized, the most important technology is to effectively manage the waste from high-emission industry and city life, and convert these wastes into new energies and materials by new technologies. The constant development of China's green industry requires the conversion of life waste and industrial waste into new power. In the future development years, with the constant popularization of waste utilization technology, the skill structure of practitioners will certainly be changed and new occupations will be generated continuously.

Third, in the area of green building and home appliance, designing and building more energy-conservative public and civil constructions has become an obvious trend of current time, which means using more energy-conservative illuminating equipment and other home appliances in buildings, thus to reach the goal of carbon dioxide reduction. Facing the rapid development of urbanization, it is a non-ignorable important area in the sustainable development of future society. The utilization of some technologies will greatly reduce and effectively control the carbon dioxide emission from human activities. For instance, in the self-owned office buildings in some enterprises, a new profession appears, they are called as energy managers, who are responsible for energy utilization and management system in buildings. The energy conservation measures of many enterprises apparently have significant results. Of course the more important goal is to design and construct more energy-conservative buildings to make our energy utilization more effective. There is another rather important and new design idea and design technology, it is called "passive design", and a new profession is generated as passive designer, the role of which is to research how to make the energy utilization in buildings more effective by effectively using existing conditions, including topography and climate.

Forth, in the transportation area, the clean energies and hybrid cars may be used and finally the electric vehicles will be used widely to reduce and control emission. Such change will bring profound reform for professional activities in manufacturing, sale and maintenance of automobiles, including the supporting industries.

Fifth, in green ecology area, the main method is forestation in large quantity, better water and soil conservation and the full utilization and effective management of chemical fertilizers in agriculture area, thus to enable our ecology could be restored and China's carbon sink can be conserved. In this field, there are already some new professions appeared, such as the fertilization guider and fertilizer manager, whose responsibility is to prevent the abuse of chemical fertilizers and fully use the fertilizer effect and ultimately reduce the fertilizer use.

3.5.2 Overall Trend

Generally speaking, the trends for change of employment and professions resulted from green revolution in these fields include the following:

First is the generation of new professions. For example, the application of Integrated Gasification Combined Cycle Technology in green coal-based power generation area is generating a demand for professional and technical personnel; the users of wind energy and solar energy will be rather popular talents in future employment market; There are also other new professions such as urban waste management persons, the technical persons turning garbage into power, and technicians for carbon capture and storage etc. At present, the energy efficiency technical engineers, energy management engineers and energy conservation engineers have started to play a role in the society.

Second, the technological reform will cause more internal professional adjustments, for instance, in the above five big areas, the utilization of these technologies will definitely make all practitioners face the adjustment, updating and upgrading of knowledge and skills. At the same time, the practitioners of related industries will also be adjusted in terms of skills. For example, urban planning engineers will need to understand and apply lots of green technologies and their knowledge and capacity structure will definitely be adjusted greatly.

Again, the traditional fields and traditional posts may be shrinking or even disappear. For example, in the power field, with the utilization of green power technologies and the seizing of opportunities, the utilization of traditional energies will be downsized. The traditional posts retained in the entire energy industry system and its practitioners will definitely be shrinking and employment capacity will be reduced with the decrease of total quantity and structural adjustment.

Relevant data shows that, in many green fields, the job opportunities are increasing continuously due to the emergence of new professions. According to statistics by the United Nations, up to 2030, the employment capacity in the wind energy field alone will be increased by 7 folds compared to 2005. In China, the employment quantity created in the renewable energy field alone is a large number. According to statistics by relevant departments, in 2007, the total employment quantity in the new energy industry in the country was approximately 1,100,000. It is of great significance for China to solve the employment problem and promote the green employment.

3.6 Influence of China's Workforce Condition on the Energy Utilization and the Work of Adapting to Climate Change

The workforce condition will also exert influence on whether the working goals in environmental protection, energy utilization and responding to climate change could be realized. The workforce quality and skill is one of the major barriers influencing the application and popularization of green technologies. There is no doubt that, the green technologies in environmental protection, energy utilization and responding to climate change need the practitioners have corresponding technologies and professional skills. Generally speaking however, China's labor quality is not high and the skill structure is single, which will become a big challenge for China's human resource development strategy in the future. Green talent is becoming the bottleneck of green technology application. In addition, green thinking and green skill are not fully valued in existing education field and other social and economic policies, which will become an important factor restricting the realization of China's green policy goal. [1]

---

[1] [1] China Environmental Awareness Project hosted "2007 Survey on China's Public Environmental Awareness", the Chinese Academy of Social Sciences Sociology Institute undertook all works, and it was implemented from December 2007. This survey was conducted by going to households, and the survey object is China's urban and rural residents at the age of 15-69, the sample size is 3001 persons, covering 20 provinces/autonomous regions/municipalities.

3.7 Influence of Social Partners on Energy Utilization and Adaption to Climate Change

Some social partners, such as labor unions and enterprises, play a vital role in realizing their working goals in such fields as environmental protection, energy utilization and response to climate change. For example, without strong support from labor unions, and more importantly, the actual implementation and active assistance by enterprises, policies concerning energy conservation and emission reduction cannot be smoothly implemented, measures for energy utilization and climate change responding can not be effectively executed.

4 Laws and Policies for Green Employment

Since the reform and opening up of China, China's economy has grown rapidly, the people's income levels have been raised significantly, and a large quantity of Chinese have shaken off poverty. But China's development is not balanced. Despite great achievements in economic growth, the environmental situation is very severe, which is mainly reflected by the following facts: Pollution emissions have exceeded the environmental bearing capacity, air pollution in many cities has been serious, the area of polluted soil has expanded, ecology has been seriously damaged, water loss and soil erosion have been enlarged in quantity and wide in range, biodiversity has been decreasing and the ecological system function has been degrading. The environmental problems, appeared in phases in industrialization process of developed countries for hundreds of years, have broken out in recent 20 years in China in a concentrated manner, showing structural, compound and shortened features. In the next 15 years, China's population will increase continuously, 1 economic aggregate will continue to expand, the resources and energy consumptions will grow constantly, and the pressures on environmental protection will become greater and greater. But China is in the phase of rapidly-developing industrialization and urbanization. In the face of multiple pressures from economic development, poverty elimination and pollution reduction, in order to promote employment, eliminate poverty and improve people's living standard, China must keep a relatively high economic growth rate; but in view of serious damages to the ecological environment, China must transform the extensive growth and the mode of "pollution first and treatment later", make great efforts to develop green economies and promote the green growth.

In order to transform to a green development mode, China has promulgated a series of laws, regulations and policies, and has established a series of legal policy framework systems including environmental protection laws, industry policies and environmental economic policies. These policies take environmental protection as the new economic growth engine, and turn the environmental protection work into an opportunity and power for economic growth rather than additional cost and burden on economic development. The promulgation of these policies will be helpful to coordinate the relations between environmental protection and economic development, and push forward the development of green industries. In 2008, a global financial crisis swept the world, bringing about some shocks on China's economic development. But this financial crisis has also afforded opportunity for economic structure adjustment. China has taken the energy saving and emission reduction and ecological engineering as one of the key tasks in "expanding domestic demand and maintaining growth". It is estimated that for a considerable part of 4000 billion investments incentive plan will be invested in such field, which will greatly stimulate the transformation of conventional jobs and the creation of green employment.

4.1　Framework of Legislations and Policy Systems for Green Development

The environmental overview for green development and green employment includes:

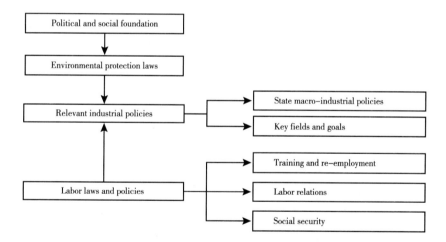

4.2　The Social and Political Foundation for China's Green Development

In May 1984, the State Council issued *Decision on Environmental Protection*, which provides that protecting and improving the living environment and ecological environment, preventing and remedying pollution and natural environment damage is a basic state policy in the socialist modernization construction of China", and resolved to set up the State Council Environmental Protection Commission, which is responsible for researching, reviewing and approving the guidelines, policies and planning requirements in terms of environmental protection, organizing and coordinating the environmental protection across the country.

Proposal on The 11th Five-year Plan for National Economy And Social Development by the Central Committee of the CCP points out that the recycling economy should be developed with great efforts, and the development of recycling economy should be adopted as the main approach to constructing a resource-saving and environmentally-friendly society and achieving sustainable development. The 11th Five-Year Plan for National Economy and Social Development (2006-2010) issued by the State Council in March 2005 specifies the resource saving as the basic national policy of our country.

In terms of the relations between environmental protection and economic construction, work focus of Chinese government has started fundamental adjustment since 2006. [1] Environmental Protection Law of the People's Republic of China enacted in 1989 stipulates that "Environmental protection work should be coordinated with economic construction and social development", the essence of which is that the economic construction should take precedence over environmental protection. However, in the 6th National Environmental Protection Meeting in 2006, Premier Wen Jiabao emphasized that the policy of emphasizing economic growth and paying little attention to environmental protection should be transformed as paying equal attention to environmental protection and economic growth, and seeking after development in environmental protection. After this meeting, in February 2006, the State Council issued Decision on Implementing Scientific Outlook on Development and Strengthening Environmental Protection, placing environmental protection at a more important strategic position and put forward that "Economic and social development must be coordinated with environmental protection", which has raised the priority of environmental protection and has emphasized environmental protection and economic development equally. In addition, the Decision also pointed out to strengthen environmental protection, develop recycling economy with great efforts, actively develop environmental protection industries and relevant industries, cultivate new economic growth engines and increase employment, thereby laying a political foundation for development of green employment.

In October 2006, *Decisions by the Central Committee of the CPC on Some Major Issues in Building a Harmonious Socialist Society* takes "significantly increase of resource utilization efficiency and remarkable improvement of ecological environment" as one of nine goals for constructing a socialist harmonious society, and demands the transformation of economic growth mode, improving the development quality, pushing forward the conservative

---

[1] Sun Youhai, *Experience and Problems in China's Environmental Legislations Since the Reform and Opening Up*, Journal of China University of Geosciences (Social Science Edition), Issue 4, Vol.8, July 2008

development, clean development and safety development, and achieving sustainable development for economy and society in an all-round way.

In May 2007, the State Council promulgated *National Program for Coping with Climate Change*, which specifies guiding ideas, principles and goals for China to cope with climate change, as well as the relevant policies and countermeasures in this regard. In August 2009, National People's Congress made *Resolution on Copping with Climate Change*. It was the first decision made by China's highest legislative body for coping with climate changes. The Resolution mainly expounds the practical measures for actively coping with climate change at five facets: 1) intensifying energy saving and emission reduction, and striving to control the greenhouse gas emissions; 2) reinforcing the capability of adapting to climate change; 3) putting the supporting and leading role of science and technology into full play; 4) developing green economy and low carbon economy based on national conditions; 5) integrating active coping with climate change as a long-term task for sustainable development strategy into *Plan for National Economy And Social Development*, with clear-cut goals, tasks and requirements.

4.3　Relevant Environmental Protection Legislations

Environmental Protection Law of the People's Republic of China (Trial Implementation), enacted by the 11th Standing Committee of the Fifth National People's Congress on September 13, 1979, is the first environmental protection law of China; since then, China's environmental protection legislation have made progress constantly, and a legal system for environment and resources protection with the Chinese characteristics has been basically formed. The general trend of China's environmental protection legislations is from end treatment to clean production and development of recycling economy; from pollution control to ecological protection; from environmental management oriented to administrative orders to environmental management with the use of technical, economic, legal, educational and other means; from emphasizing on the role of the state in the environmental management to emphasizing on the composite role of governments, enterprises and citizens in the cause of environmental protection. [1]

4.3.1　Overview of China's Laws Concerning Environment and Natural Resources Protection

At the national level, China's environment and natural resource legislations

---

[1]　Li Yongjin, etc, China Population Resources and Environment, No.5, 2008

fall into the following several categories generally:

The first category: Comprehensive environmental protection laws, which mainly include *Environmental Protection Law*. *Environmental Protection Law* is the fundamental regulation of the state for guidelines, policies, principles, systems and measures in environmental protection, which features principled and comprehensive legal norms. The basic principles set forth by this law include: including environmental protection into economic and social development planning, following the principle of coordination between economic development and environmental protection; the principle of prevention first, combined prevention and treatment and comprehensive treatment; environmental impact assessment system, sewage charging system, system of treatment within deadline and licensing system, etc.

The second category: laws and regulations committed to environmental pollution prevention and public hazard control. It mainly includes the laws on prevention for air, water, solid waste, noise, radioactive pollution and supportive environment quality standards and pollution emission standards, including *Solid Waste Pollution Prevention Law, Water Pollution Prevention Law, Air Pollution Prevention Law, Enforcement Regulation for Water Pollution Control Law*, etc.

The third category: laws on natural ecology and resource protection, including *Land Management Law, Water Law, Forest Law, Grassland Law, Water and Soil Conservation Law, Wild Life Protection Law*, etc.

The fourth category: laws and regulations on resource saving and comprehensive utilization, such as *Energy Conservation Law*.

The fifth category: laws and regulations on promoting recycling economy and clean production, such as *Cleaner Production Promotion Law* and *Renewable Energy Law and Recycling economy Promotion Law.*

The sixth category: laws on administrative systems for specific environment and supporting regulations issued by the State Council and competence administrative authorities, such as *Environmental Impact Assessment Law* and *Environmental Protection Management Regulation for Construction Projects and Rules on Classified Review and Approval for Environmental Impact Assessment Files of Construction Projects.*

4.3.1.1 Brief Introduction to Main Legislations

Renewable Energy Law (in force since January 1, 2006)

Renewable Energy Law ranks the development and utilization of renewable energies as the priority for energy development, encourages and supports the power generation by renewable energies, encourages the clean and efficient development and utilization of biomass fuel, encourages the development of energy crops, and encourages individuals and entities to install and use solar energy water heating system, solar energy heating and cooling system, solar energy photovoltaic power generation system and other solar energy utilization systems. Renewable Energy Law also encourages and supports the development and utilization of renewable resources in rural areas. For this, special fund for development of renewable energy, preference loans with financial discounts and taxation preferences will be provided.

Energy Conservation Law (the amended Energy Conservation Law has been in force since April 1, 2008)

Energy Conservation Law stipulates that "Energy conservation is the basic national policy of our country. And the state should implement the energy development strategy with equal attention to saving and development, which should give top priority to saving". *Energy Conservation Law* further intensifies the standardization of industrial energy saving, with a view to ensuring the advancement of energy conservation and emission reduction from law perspective. The amended *Energy Conservation Law* emphasizes the strengthening of supervision on "major energy consumers"; and it stipulates that "major energy consumers" should annually submit reports on status of the resource utilization of last year to the competent authorities in charge of energy saving work.

The amended *Energy Conservation Law* makes clear incentive policies to be adopted by China in terms of energy conservation, including the production and utilization of the energy conservation technologies and products required to be supported as specified in the promotion list and the implementation of tax preference according to the laws; supporting the popularization and use of energy-efficient lighting apparatuses and energy conservative products through fiscal subsidy, listing products and equipment with energy conservation certifications into the government procurement with priority; as for financial support, laws specify that the state should guide the financial institutions to increase the loan support for energy conservative projects, implement the price policies in favor of energy conservation and guide the energy consumers and individuals to save energy.

In addition, *Energy Conservation Law* also stipulates the implementation of energy saving target responsibility system and energy saving appraisal and evaluation systems, and making fulfillment status of the energy saving targets as a component of appraisal and evaluation on local people's governments and the leaders.

Recycling economy Promotion Law (in force since January 1, 2009)

Recycling economy Promotion Law stipulates that reducing, reusing and recycling should be implemented in the process of production, circulation and consumption, and under the premise of technically-feasible, economically-reasonable and favorable for resource saving and environmental protection, the principle of reducing should be implemented with priority. In addition, *Recycling economy Promotion Law* makes a series of major institutional arrangements for the development of recycling economy as follows.

- Establish a recycling economy planning system. It is required for people's governments above the county level and competent authorities to develop planning for national economy and social development and annual plans, and make plans for environmental protection, science and technology, which should include the contents on development of recycling economy.

- Establish an overall regulatory system. The local people's governments above the county level should plan and adjust the industrial structure of local administrative areas and promote the development of recycling economy according to the control index for emissions of major pollutants, construction land and total water consumption set by superior people's governments.

- Establish producer responsibility extension system. *Recycling economy Promotion Law*, under different circumstances, expressly stipulates producer's responsibilities for recycling, utilization, disposal and the like after the products are discarded.

- Implement key management for key enterprises. For the key enterprises engaged in such industries as steel, non-ferrous metals, coal, electricity, petroleum processing, chemical engineering, building material, construction, paper making, printing and dyeing with annual composite energy consumption and water consumption beyond the total volume stipulated by the state, key supervision and management system for energy consumption and water consumption should be implemented.

- Intensify the standardization and guidance for industrial policies. *Recycling economy Promotion Law* emphasizes that the formulation of industrial policies should be in line with the requirements for development of recycling economy.

- Establish reasonable incentive mechanism, which mainly includes: setting up special fund for development of recycling economy; providing fiscal support for major scientific and technological projects in the recycling economy; giving tax preference for activities promoting the development of recycling economy; investment orientation to relevant recycling economy projects; implementing price policies conducive to resource saving and reasonable resource utilization, etc.

Management Regulation for Recycling and Disposal of Waste Electrical and

Electronic Products (in force since January 1, 2011)

- The state should implement multiple channel recycling and concentrated disposal system for waste electrical and electronic products.

- The state should implement qualification licensing system for disposal of waste electrical and electronic products.

- The state should establish a fund for disposal of waste electrical and electronic products so as to subsidize recycling and disposal of waste electrical and electronic products. The manufacturers of electrical and electronic products and the receivers or their agents of imported electrical and electronic products should perform the obligation of contribution to such a fund.

- The responsibilities that should be undertaken by every producer, seller, recycling operator and disposal enterprise are defined. For example, the electrical and electronic products made and imported by producers, receivers or their agents of imported electrical and electronic products shall comply with the relevant state regulation concerning pollution control over electrical and electronic products. The design scheme in favor of comprehensive resource utilization and decontamination treatment should be used. Non-toxic and harmless materials or low-toxic and low-harm materials, which could easily be recycled, should be adopted; and seller, maintenance agency and after-sales service agency for electrical and electronic products should take responsibility for marking indicative information about recycling and disposal of waste electrical and electronic products at the eye-catching position of the business place.

4.4 China's Industrial Policies on Green Development

China's industrial policies concerning promoting the green development enjoy the following characteristics:

4.4.1 Adopting Different Policy Orientations to Promote the Industrial Structure Adjustment, Forming a Conservation-oriented Growth Mode with Low Input, Low Consumption, Low Emission and High Efficiency

The state restricts the overly fast growth of such industries characterized by high energy consumption and high pollution, and encourages the development of advanced production capacity with low energy consumption and low pollution. In November 2005, the State Council approved *Interim Provisions on Promotion of Industrial Structural Adjustment*; in December, with approval of the State Council, National Development and Reform Commission issued *Guiding Catalogue of Industry Structural Adjustment*. These documents classify three types of industries: encouraged, restricted and eliminated. And different policy orientations have been respectively followed for them. [1]

(1) Encouraged: It mainly includes the key technologies, equipment and

---

[1] http://www.chinaenvironment.com/view/ViewNews.aspx?k=20090227103959087,Reading Date, March 20,2009

products that significantly promote the economic and social development, help resource saving, environmental protection and industrial structure upgrading, for which policies and measures should be taken to encourage and support. For the investment projects in the category of Encouraged, credit support, tax preference and other preferential policies should be provided.

(2) Restricted: It mainly include the industries with out-of-date technologies, without improvement on industrial structure; going against work safety, resource saving and energy conservation; going against environmental protection and recovery of ecological system; with serious low-level repeated construction and obviously production overcapacity. The newly established projects in the category of Restricted will not be approved, verified or filed by investment management authorities. Any financial institution cannot offer loans, and such authorities in land administration, urban planning and construction, environmental protection, quality inspection, firefighting, customs, industry and commerce cannot handle the relevant formalities;

(3) Eliminated: It mainly refers to the out-of-date technologies, equipment and products in unconformity with relevant laws and regulations, characterized by serious waste of resources, significant environment pollution without safety production conditions. Eliminated projects should not be permitted for investment. Financial institutions should stop various types of credit-granting support and take measures to recover the granted loans. All regions, all authorities and all relevant enterprises should take effective measures so as to eliminate within specified period.

Guiding Catalogue of Industry Structural Adjustment includes more than 20 industries including agriculture, water conservancy, coal, electricity, transportation, information industry, iron and steel, nonferrous metals, petrochemicals, building materials, machinery, textile, service, environmental and ecological protection, resource conservation and comprehensive utilization, etc. Of which, 539 are Encouraged, 190 are Restricted and 399 are Eliminated.

4.4.2 Establishing Environmental Access System for Key Industries

In 2006, the State Council issued *Circular Concerning Expediting Promotion of Structural Adjustment in Overproduction Industries*, which specifies that economic, legal and necessary administrative means should be taken to promote the structural adjustment for overproduction industries. Firstly, it is required to formulate more rigid standards in terms of environment, safety, energy consumption, water consumption, comprehensive resource utilization, quality, technique, scale and the like to lift up the access threshold. Secondly, it is required to eliminate the out-of-date production capacity, shut down a batch of small enterprises, damaging resources, polluting environment without work safety production conditions according to laws, and eliminate enterprises with lagging production capacity. For example, small coal mines falling short of scale and safety standards specified in industrial policies should be eliminated. Thirdly, it is required to push forward the technical transformation, improve and reform convention industries with focus on enhancing the technological level, improving varieties, protecting environment, assuring safety, reducing consumption and conducting comprehensive utilization. [1]

The 11ᵗʰ Five-year Plan on Environmental Protection formulated by the State in November 2007 points out that in determining the access conditions for such key industries as iron and steel, nonferrous metals, building materials, electricity, light industry, environmental protection requirements should be fully considered, and the newly established projects must comply with the access conditions and emission standards stipulated by the State. For the regions without environment capacity, it is not permitted to set up new projects increasing the pollutant emissions. In February 2009, Ministry of Environmental

---

[1]   http://www.gghf.org.cn/xm/hd4-1.htm, National Transferring Outdated National Production Capacity to Funds, Reading Date, June 9, 2009

Protection put forward that environmental access conditions should be tightened up. The relevant subsidies and tax preferences adverse to environmental protection will be abolished gradually. For enterprises falling short of environmental protection requirements and seriously polluting the environment, the relevant tax preferences for them should be cancelled. Moreover, green trade policies will be further expanded and the emission compliance notices for enterprises should be published on a regular basis. Products from the enterprises not listed in the compliance notice should not be allowed to be exported. Based on the current notices for such industries as citric acid and aluminum, other industries with heavy pollution will be covered. [1]

4.4.3 Developing Recycling Economy, and Constructing a Resource-conserving and Environmentally Friendly Society

The State has formulated and implemented *Cleaner Production Promotion Law* , *Solid Waste Pollution Prevention Law*, *Recycling Economy Promotion Law*, *Municipal Solid Waste Management Practices*, *Management Regulation for Recycling and Disposal of Waste Electrical and Electronic Products* and other laws and regulations, has promulgated *Interim Provisions on Promoting Industrial Structure Adjustment*, *Several Opinions on Accelerating the Development of Recycling Economy*, *Guiding Opinions on Comprehensive Utilization of Resources in the 11th Five-year Plan*, *Comprehensive Circular on Energy-saving and Emission Reduction*, as well as *The 11th Five-Year Plan for National Environmental Protection*, *White Paper for Policies and Actions Responding to Climate Change* and other policies and documents, which put forward the general idea, the near-term objectives, basic approaches and policy measures for development of recycling economy. Evaluation index system for recycling economy has been publicized.

Chapter 6 of *Outline for the 11th Five-Year Plan for National Economy*

---

[1] Same as above.

and Social Development published in 2006 makes planning for development of recycling economy. The Outline proposes that the basic national policy of energy conservation and environmental protection should be put into practice. A recyclable and sustainable national economy system with low input, high output, low consumption and few emissions should be established, and a resource-conserving and environmentally-friendly society should be built. The Outline points out to develop recycling economy, pay equal attention to development and conservation, prioritize the conservation, gradually establish a resources recycling system in the whole society on the principle of reducing, reusing and recycling in terms of resource exploitation, production and consumption, waste generation and consumption, etc.

4.4.3.1 Optimizing the Energy Structure

Energy Conservation Law, The 11th Five-Year Plan for National Economy And Social Development, Comprehensive Working Program on Energy Conservation and Emission Reduction, The 11th Five-Year Plan for Environmental Protection, National Program for Coping with Climate Change, and Policies and Actions Responding to Climate Change point out to optimize and development energy industry, develop coal industry in an orderly manner, achieve diverse development, increase the proportion of renewable energy in the energy structure, and optimize the structure of production and consumption.

White Paper for Policies and Actions Responding to Climate Change emphasizes that the hydropower should be developed with great efforts so as to promote the transformation of China's energy structure towards clean and low-carbon direction; meanwhile, the technological advances for thermal electricity should be accelerated to optimize the thermal power structure, eliminate the out-of-date small thermal power units on an accelerated basis, and make great efforts on such high-efficient and clean power generation technologies. The development of bio-mass energy should be boosted, focusing on bio-mass power generation, marsh gas, bio-mass solid forming fuel and liquefied fuel. And it is necessary to vigorously promote the development and utilization of bio-mass energy.

The development and utilization of renewable energy are important choice for exploiting new economic growth fields, promoting the economic transformation and enlarging the employment. The renewable energy is also a high-tech and emerging industry. The rapidly-developing renewable energy has become a new economic growth engine, which can effectively drive the development of equipment manufacturing-related industries, adjust the industrial structure, promote the transformation of economic growth mode and enlarge the employment.

4.5 Main Objectives and Key Fields of Green Development

4.5.1 Main Objectives

Outline for The 11th Five-Year Plan for National Economy And Social Development points out that during the 11th Five-year Plan period, the energy consumption of 10000 yuan GDP will be lowered from 1.22 ton standard coal in 2005 to below 1 ton standard coal, i.e., an decrease by about 20%; and water consumption unit industrial added value will decrease by 30%. During the "11th Five-year Plan", the total emission of major pollutants will decrease by 10%. By 2010, the sulfur dioxide emissions will be decreased from 25.49 million tons in 2005 to 22.95 million tons. COD will decrease from 14.14 million tons to 12.73 million tons; urban sewage treatment ratio of each city around China will not be at least 70%, and comprehensive utilization of industrial solid waste will reach more than 60%. [1]

4.5.2 Key Fields

4.5.2.1 Eliminate the Outdated Production Capacity

Great efforts should be MADE to eliminate the outdated production capacity

---

[1] *Guide for Market Supply and Demand in China's Environmental Protection Industry,* prepared by Technology Standard Department of State Environmental Protection Administration, and China Environmental Protection Industry Association, China Environmental Science Press, 2006

of such industries as electricity, iron and steel, building materials, electrolytic aluminum, ferroalloy, calcium carbide, coke, coal and flat glass. Chinese government has issued the guiding opinions on structure adjustment of 13 industries including cement, electrolytic aluminum, electric power and iron and steel, and has closed a batch of small thermal power plants, small steel plants, small cement factories and small coal mines according to law. These shutdown measures are of very importance for energy and water conservation and pollution reduction. For example, there exists great difference between advanced steel plant and small steel plant in terms of power consumption, water consumption and pollution discharge: In terms of power consumption, in some provinces with large economic scale, the power consumption per ton of steel for steel plants with small electric range is about 700 KWH, while the power consumption per ton of steel of relatively advanced steel companies in these areas is only about 300 KWH. In terms of water consumption, the production water of many steel plants with small electric range hasn't been recycled and discharged to rivers directly, while production water recycling ratio of some modernized steel enterprises can reach 98%; in terms of pollutant discharge, the volume of dust contained in flue gas per cubic meter for small plants reaches 500 mg, while the volume of dust contained in flue gas per cubic meter for modernized steel enterprises is only 25 mg.

Power industry: the key field for energy saving and emission reduction. In January 2007, the State Council approved and forwarded *Opinions on Closing Down Small Thermal Power Generating Units* issued by National Development and Reform Commission and the Energy Office and put forward the "launching large units and inhibiting small units", i.e., the newly established power plants should be linked with the closedown of small thermal power plants. In the construction process of a series of power units with high capacity, high parameter, low consumption and few emissions, a portion of small thermal power units should be closed down. During the 11th Five-year Plan, the specific working objectives of "launching large units and inhibiting small units" are:

Firstly, small coal-fired thermal power units to be closed down across the country must be over 50 million KWH. Secondly, it is necessary to close down small thermal power units to save more than 50 million tons of standard coals and reduce more than 1.6 million tons of sulfur dioxide. Thirdly, it is necessary to construct a batch of large-scale, high-efficient and environmentally-friendly units and other power generation units using clean energy and renewable energy. In 2007, China closed down 553 small thermal power plants in total, with generating capacity of 14.38 million KW.

Iron and Steel industry: is another key industry for energy saving and emission reduction. In 2007, the National Development and Reform Commission signed the Responsibility Letter for Closing and Eliminating Outdated Steel Production Capacity with 28 provinces (autonomous region districts and cities municipalities) in succession. According to the responsibility letter responsibility letter, during the 11th Five-year Plan, China will close down and eliminate outdated iron-melting capacity of 89.17 million tons and 77.76 tons of steel-melting capacity of 77.76 million tons on an accumulated basis, involving with 917 companies. In 2007, China had eliminated 46.59 million tons of outdated iron-melting capacity of 46.59 million tons and outdated steel-melting capacity of 37.47 million tons.

Cement industry: by the end of 2008, 1066 vertical kiln cement plants would stop production, leading to unemployment of about 320,000 employees. During the 11th Five-year Plan, the outdated production capacity will be eliminated by 250 million tons.

Non-ferrous metal industry: by 2009, 300,000 tons of outdated copper smelting capacity, 600,000 tons of outdated lead smelting capacity and 400,000 tons of outdated zinc melting capacity will be eliminated. By the end of 2010, 800,000 tons of outdated small pre-baked electrolytic aluminum capacity will be eliminated.

Light industry: by the end of 2008, China had eliminated 5.47 million tons of outdated paper making capacity, 945,000 tons of outdated alcohol capacity,

165,000 tons of outdated monosodium glutamate capacity and 72,000 tons of citric acid. By 2011, China will eliminate more than 2 million tons of outdated pulp and paper making capacity, 30 million sets of low energy-efficiency refrigerators (including ice tanks), 30 million pieces of leather products, 9 billion button alkaline manganese batteries containing mercury, 600 million electric incandescent lamps, 1 million tons of alcohol, 120,000 tons of monosodium glutamate and 50,000 tons of citric acid.

Textile industry: It is necessary to accelerate the shutdown of printing and dyeing enterprises causing serious pollution. By 2011, 7.5 billion meters of printing and dyeing capacity with high energy and water consumption and low technological level will be eliminated with priority. 2.3 million tons of outdated fiber production capacity will be eliminated. It is necessary to accelerate the elimination of outdated cotton spinning and wool spinning production capacity.

Petrochemical industry: Regional equivalent alternation method for the oil refining industry will be adopted. By 2011, the low-efficiency and low-quality oil refining equipment with 1 million tons or below will be eliminated. For pesticide industry, a batch of high-poisonous and highly-risky pesticide varieties will be eliminated according to administrative rules and regulations. It is necessary to accelerate the elimination of the outdated production capacity for calcium carbide and methanol, etc.

4.5.2.2 Engineering Emission Reduction and Pollution Abatement

In terms of emission reduction of sulfur dioxide, the priority should be given to the construction of desulphurization utilities at thermal power plants, and the construction of existing desulphurization utilities at thermal power plants should be accelerated so as to make desulphurization installed capacity for existing thermal power units up to 213 million KW. For the newly established (expanded) coal-fired power plants, with the exception of the ultra-low sulfur coal pithead power plants stipulated by the State, desulphurization utilizations must subject to synchronized construction and denitration places must be reserved. In addition, with state-controlled major pollution sources accounting for over 65% of industrial sulfur dioxide emission as focus, the air pollutant emission standards and total volume control system should be implemented strictly. Pollutant emission licensing system should be promoted at an accelerated pace. It is necessary to continue to properly control the waste air sources for such industries as coal, iron and steel, non-ferrous metals, petrochemicals and building materials, etc. Great efforts should be made to accelerate the construction of coal washing projects and popularize the clean coal combustion technology.

It is necessary to control the solid waste pollution, and accelerate the recycling and decontamination. It is necessary to launch the hazardous waste and medical waste disposal project and household garbage decontamination project, and accelerate the comprehensive utilization of solid waste. By the end of 11th Five-year Plan, 31 hazardous waste centralized disposal centers will be established, 300 urban medical waste centralized disposal centers will be set up, as well as construction projects for technical support and supervision capacity, total investment amount of which will reach 15 billion yuan. The comprehensive utilization of bulk industrial solid waste will be accelerated with priority, such as coal refuses, fly ash, metallurgical and chemical residues, tailings, etc. By 2010, the comprehensive utilization ratio of industrial solid waste will reach 60%. The comprehensive utilization of construction waste, straws and livestock manure should be intensified. It is necessary to establish producer responsibility extension system, perfect the recycling system for renewable resources, and achieve the comprehensive utilization of waste electrical and electronic appliances on a scaled and decontaminated basis.

In terms of waste water treatment, firstly, it is necessary to accelerate the construction of urban sewage treatment and recycling engineering. By 2010, the urban sewage treatment ratio will be at least 70%, and every city will construct sewage treatment facilities. To achieve this goal, 50 million t/d urban sewage treatment scale will be newly established, and the existing sewage treatment plants and supporting pipe network will be transformed and perfected, with an investment amount of 210 billion yuan. Secondly, it is necessary to strengthen the industrial waste water treatment. The waste water discharge standards and the total emission volume reduction of state-controlled major enterprises (accounting for 65% of the industrial chemical oxygen demand) should be supervised properly.

4.5.2.3 Save energy and Improve the Energy Utilization Efficiency

The main fields of energy saving are industry, transportation and construction. The initiatives in *Decision of the State Council on Strengthening Energy Saving Tasks* issued in 2006 include the following measures:

Firstly, industrial energy conservation. should be carried out energy conservation work for key energy consuming industries and the enterprises annually consuming more than 10,000 tons of standard coals should be targeted with priority, and these industries include iron and steel, non-ferrous metals, coal, electricity, petroleum and petrochemicals, chemical engineering, building materials, etc.

Secondly, the building energy conservation should be promofed. It is necessary to make great efforts to develop the energy-saving and land-conservative buildings, promote the rigid implementation of the design standard of energy conservation ratio at 50% for newly built residential and public buildings, and implement the standard of energy conservation ratio at 65% for municipalities directly under the central government and the regions where the conditions permit.

Thirdly the energy conservation in transportation should be strengthened .It is necessary to actively accelerate the construction of energy-conservative comprehensive transportation system, develop the railways and inland water transportation, develop the public transport and rail transport with priority, accelerate the elimination of outdated railway motors, autos and ships, encourage the energy-conservative and environmentally-friendly transport tools, develop and popularize the automobile-used alternative fuels and automobiles using clean fuels.

Fourthly, it should be given directions for the commercial and civilian energy conservation.

4.5.2.4   Develop Renewable Energy and Optimize the Energy Structure

The strategic positioning of renewable energy in China's energy structure: Before or after 2010, the renewable energy will account for about 10% of the total energy consumption, which will be positioned as supplemented energy. Before or after 2020, the renewable energy will account for about 15% of the total energy consumption, which will be positioned as alternative energy. Before or after 2030, the renewable energy will account for about 25% of the total energy consumption, which will be positioned as mainstream energy. Before or after 2050, the renewable energy will account for about 40% of the total energy consumption, which will be positioned as dominant energy.

In order to realize this strategic goal, *The 11th Five-year Plan for Renewable Energy Development* formulated by National Development and Reform Commission in March 2008 points out to accelerate the development of renewable energy with mature technology and strong market competitiveness such as hydropower, solar energy heat utilization, marsh gas and so on, and raise the proportion of renewable energy in the energy structure; actively push forward the industrialized development of wind power, bio-mass power generation, solar energy power, bio-liquid fuel and others with basically mature technology and great development potential, and lay a solid foundation for greater development and utilization of renewable energy. The specific goals include:

- Hydropower: During the 11th Five-year Plan, the newly added installed capacity of hydropower around the country will be 73 million KW.
- Bio-mass power generation: By 2010, the installed capacity for bio-mass power will reach 5.5 million KW. For the ethanol made from non-food raw materials, the annual utilization volume will be 2 million tons, and the annual utilization volume of bio-diesel will be 200,000 tons. The number of households

using marsh gas tank will reach 40 million in rural areas, 6,300 large-scale marsh gas projects will be constructed, and the annual utilization volume of marsh gas will be 19 billion cubic meters. The annual utilization volume of bio-mass solid formed fuel will be 1 million tons. The commercialized and scaled utilization of the bio-mass energy will be achieved preliminarily.

• Wind power: By 2010, the total installed capacity of the wind power will reach 10 million KW.

• Solar energy: By 2010, the accumulated installation volume of solar energy heaters will reach 150 million cubic meters, and the installed capacity for solar energy will reach 300,000 KW.

• Renewable energy in rural areas: By 2010, by 40 million households around the country will use marsh gas tanks, and there will be 4700 marsh gas projects in large-scale plant. The total collector area of solar energy heaters in rural areas will reach 50 million square meters, and the inventory of solar cookers will total 1 million.

4.5.2.5 Promote the Comprehensive Utilization of Resources

The goal of the comprehensive resource utilization: By 2010, the industries with comprehensive resource utilization will rapidly develop, the utilization efficiency will increase significantly, the proportion of products for comprehensive utilization among similar products will be raised, and a batch of comprehensive utilization enterprises characterized by certain scale, relatively high technological equipment level, relatively high resource utilization ratio and relatively low waste emission.

The key fields of comprehensive resource utilization include: comprehensive utilization of mineral resources, comprehensive utilization of "Three Wastes", recycling of renewable resources and comprehensive utilization of wastes from agriculture and forestry.

The key projects in comprehensive utilization during the 11th Five-year Plan include as follows:

- Comprehensive development and utilization project for paragenetic and associated minerals.
- Recycling utilization project for bulk solid waste.
- Recycled metal processing industrialization project.
- Industrialization project for waste household appliances, waste tires and other renewable resources.
- Demonstration project for renewable resource recycling system.
- Comprehensive utilization project for agricultural waste and timbers.

4.5.2.6 Vigorously Develop Environmental Protection Industry

Outline for the 11th Five-Year Plan for National Economy and Social Development specifies the development of large-scale and high-efficient clean power generation equipment, environmental protection equipment and comprehensive resource utilization equipment as the key fields for promoting the equipment manufacturing industry.

The 11th Five-Year Plan for Environmental Protection points out that the environmental protection equipment manufacturing industry should be developed with great efforts to meet the needs for key projects of environmental protection; focus on the environmental impact assessment, environmental engineering service, environmental technology R&D and consulting and environmental risk investment, actively develop environmental protection service industry. For example, in terms of comprehensive resource utilization, the recycling and reclamation of waste will be developed with priority, such as the recycling of unconventional water resources such as reclaimed water, brackish water and seawater desalination, efficient cooling water for saving, the reusing of abandoned cars, waste tires, waste appliances, electrical wastes and tailings, etc. In terms of construction, operation and consultation for pollution treatment facilities, the marketization of the construction and operation of environmental protection facilities for urban sewage, garbage and hazardous waste should be advanced with priority. Specialized operation for installations used in scaled industrial waste water treatment, power plant desulphurization and dust removal should be conducted. The technical consultation and management service for environmental protection should be developed vigorously. [①]

4.5.2.7 Emission Reduction in Agriculture Industry

The greenhouse gas emission in agriculture and rural areas should be reduced. It is necessary to continue to popularize the high-yielding paddy rice varieties and semi-drought cultivation techniques with low emission, and adopt scientific irrigation technologies; intensify the ecological agriculture construction for the regions with high degree of intensification; strengthen the management over animal wastes and solid wastes, tighten up the marsh gas utilization, and strive to control the growth rate of methane emission.

4.5.2.8 Forestry

State Administration of Forestry issued *Forestry Action Plan Responding to Climate Change* to implement the roles of forestry to respond to the global climate change as specified in *National Program for Coping with Climate Change*. The Action Plan sets forth 22 major actions, including 15 actions for alleviating the climate change and 7 actions for adapting to the climate change on the part of forestry industry. The main fields in developing forestry and responding to the climate change include: Implementing the key forestry ecology projects, implementing the integration project for energy forest cultivation, processing and utilization, reasonably developing and utilizing bio-mass materials, and enhancing the high-efficient recycling of timbers, etc. Three phased targets for the national forest coverage are set as follows: 20% by 2010, 23% by 2020 and over 26% by 2050, the forest carbon sink capacity will be improved constantly and ultimately

---

① "Talents with high professional skills" refer to the personnel at the frontline positions in production, transport and service, who have accomplished professional skills, play a role in key sections and can resolve difficulties in production and operation. They mainly include the personnel obtaining the job qualification for highly skilled worker, technician and senior technician as well as corresponding position ranks.

keep relatively stable. In the afforestation, China is implementing six key forestry projects. In the next decade, the afforestation area will aim at 76 million hm2, and it is expected to provide employment for 22.8 million people. The construction of bio-mass energy forest is another positive initiative taken by the Chinese government responding to the climate change. According to National Energy Forest Construction Plan prepared by State Administration of Forestry, during the 11th Five-year Plan, China is going to construct more than 10 million mu (667,000 hectares) of energy forest demonstration bases. By 2020, the energy forest will reach 200 million mu (13.34 million hectares), which can provide more than 6 million tons of bio-diesel to meet the fuel demand of power plants with installed capacity of more than 11 million KW. [1]

---

[1]   Cited from meeting presentations by Ivanka Mamic, an expert of ILO in Asia Pacific region, Jan.21, 2009, Beijing.

4.6 Labor Protection Policy in Connection with Green Development

The impacts of transformation to green development mode on the employment is reflected at the following aspects: Firstly, the increase of green occupations and green employment such as the development of renewable energy, will create a large quantity of job opportunities for new energy sectors, relevant manufacturing sectors and consulting service sectors, involving urban waste recycling and management, carbon dioxide capture of thermal power plant, carbon emission trader and environmental impact assessor, etc. Secondly, some gray posts may be shrunk or even disappear. For example, the elimination of outdated production capacity of such traditional energy utilization industries as cement, iron and steel, chemical engineering and non-ferrous metals means that the enterprises falling short of industrial standards will be closed down, merged and reorganized. Some production lines of enterprises will be demolished, causing the disappearance of relevant working posts. Thirdly, the working contents and technical requirements of existing posts have changed. For example, the conventional planting relying on chemical fertilizers and pesticides are being transformed to organic planting, and farmers need to master green manures and control injurious insects through biological control means. Urban planning engineers need to understand and utilize more green technologies. After the thermal power generation equipment are upgraded and transformed from the original separated operation to centralized control operation, the working contents and skill requirements of relevant operational and technical persons will be changed correspondingly. In order to ensure the smooth transformation of traditional posts to green employment and the development of green employment, corresponding labor protection policies should be in place to provide support. Currently, China's policies in this respect include vocational training policies, employment promotion policies, reduction, compensation, rearrangement and job-transfer trainings for the employees from enterprises closed, merged or transferred for production. [1]

4.6.1 Vocational Training

4.6.1.1 Job Qualification and Vocational Training System

China's vocational training system includes pre-employment training, on-the-job training and re-employment training. In addition, China has also established professional standards and qualification examination system, in which the State formulates professional skill standards or job qualification conditions, and the examination and accreditation organs recognized by the governments carry out evaluation and accreditation on the skill level or professional qualification for labors. The qualified labors get corresponding national job qualification certificates. The National Job Qualification Certificate is divided into five grades, i.e., Junior (5th Grade National Job Qualification), Middle-Level (4th Grade National Job Qualification), Senior (3rd Grade National Job Qualification), Technician (2nd Grade National Job Qualification) and Senior Technician (1st Grade National Job Qualification). The occupations with formulated national standards in connection with green employment include environment impact assessors, renewable resources recyclers, sewage treatment engineers and solar utilization engineers, etc.

---

① Cited from meeting presentations by Ivanka Mamic, an expert of ILO in Asia Pacific region, Jan.21, 2009, Beijing.

For the laborers engaging in the jobs with complicated technology, broad versatility and involving with state properties, people's life safety and the consumer interests, they cannot be employed until accepting training and obtaining the job qualification certificates, such as marsh gas producers.

4.6.1.2 Encouraging the Construction of Training Bases and Improving the Skill and Practice Capacity for Graduates from Vocational Colleges

Since 2004, the central finance special fund for vocational education has provided financial support for qualified training bases in various vocational colleges so as to improve the skill level and practice capacity of students from vocational colleges. There are two modes for central finance special fund to support the vocational education training bases: regional comprehensive training base and vocational training base. At the beginning of this project, the central finance will focus on supporting the digit control technology, automobile maintenance technology, computer application and software technology, electrical and electronic technology and building technology, and then gradually expand the supported fields with priority. In 2009, Ministry of Education specified that eight key fields for vocational training bases, with equal attention to the energy and environmental protection. The central finance special fund has focused on the following several types of colleges and training institutions characterized by: 1) orientation to employment, and cultivating a large quantity of skilled personnel in shortage in the society; 2) making breakthrough and innovation in terms of deepening the vocational education reform and strengthening the cooperation between colleges and enterprises; 3) making outstanding contributions to social training, re-employment training for laid-off workers and the training for labor force transferred from in rural areas. The capital from central finance is primarily used for updating and purchase of equipment for the training bases. For the construction of training bases in secondary vocational schools backed by central finance, the local finance should provide supporting capitals. [①]

4.6.1.3   Encouraging Students to Accept Secondary Vocational Education

For the grade one and grade two students with registered residence in rural areas, the students in counties or towns without households in rural areas, as well as the students confronted with financial hardship in cities in secondary vocational schools, each student can get subsidy of 1500 yuan every year.

4.6.1.4   Vigorously Promoting the Professional Skill Training for Rural Migrant Workers

The 17th Party Congress of the CPC clearly points out to strengthen the employment training for laborers transferred from rural areas. Since then, relevant authorities have formulated the rural migrant workers training plan supported by central finance, the priority of which is professional skill training. The skill training refers to such training carried out by regional goals, industry goals and occupational goals to which the rural workers will be transferred in consideration to the skill shortage of rural laborers in terms of adapting to the employment transfer. *National Training Plan for Rural Migrant Workers* (2003-2010) jointly formulated by six ministries and commissions in 2003 (including Ministry of Agriculture and original Ministry of Labor Security) is an example. In 2005, the original Ministry of Labor Security formulated *Plan for Labor Skill of Rural Migrant Workers*, which specified that vocational training would be launched for 40 million rural migrant workers in cities in the next five years.

4.6.1.5   Encouraging Enterprises to Conduct Employee Trainings to Improve Their Vocational Skills

Outline of the 11th Five-year Plan for Training System Construction for

---

① Chen Lvjun, Wen Donghui and Chen Weimin, "Development Status of America's Environmental Protection Industry", Environmental Protection, September, 2002

Talents with High Professional Skills (2006—2010) encourages enterprises to input more funds for trainings for the skilled workers at the frontline of production and service, especially for the talents with high professional skills. [1] Enterprises should withdraw employee education expenditure in full at the ratio of 1.5%—2.5% of total employee wages according to relevant regulations so as to guarantee the cultivation of talents with high professional skills.

When enterprises carry out technical reform and project introduction, they should provision employee technical training expenditure according to the specified ratio and enter it into project cost. For the enterprises which are incapable of conducting employee trainings and fail to carry out trainings for talents with high professional skills, local governments above the county level can make overall arrangement for the employee education spending according to laws. And the labor and social security authorities should organize the training service on a uniform basis.

The employees, participating in off-job trainings or semi-off-job trainings with consent of the employer enterprises, should enjoy the same wages and benefits as the on-the-job employees. For the personnel participating in training for talents with high professional skills in occupations (types of work) in urgent demand, obtaining the corresponding job qualification and being employed by enterprises, the enterprises can give certain subsidies for training and appraisal fee.

4.6.2　Special Vocational Training Plan in the Face of Financial Crisis

In order to cope with the shocks from international financial crisis on China and keep the employment situation stable, Ministry of Human Resources and Social Security, National Development and Reform Commission and Ministry

---

[1] Gu Wenyan"Development of America's Environmental Protection Industry and the Push Factors",International Data and Information, May, 2000.

of Finance have decided to implement special vocational training plan, and focus on vocational trainings for four categories of groups on a targeted basis from 2009 to 2010.

Firstly, it is necessary to carry out on-the-job skill improvement training and job transfer training for the employee of enterprises in difficulties, which is the core content of this plan. The focus of near-term work is active launching of on-the-job trainings for employees in large and medium-sized enterprises greatly shocked by the financial crisis, which see a large number of employees and undergo production and operation difficulties. The capital required in carrying out trainings in this respect will be disbursed from employee education and training expenditure according to relevant stipulations, and the insufficient section can be properly supported by special employment fund of the governments exercise the jurisdiction over the enterprises. The enterprises in difficulties can present relevant certifications and file an application to local human resources and social security authorities and finance authorities. Examined by human resources and social security authorities and reviewed by the finance authorities, the local finance authorities should directly transfer the subsidy fund to the basic account opened by the enterprises in banks, the amount of which should not be higher than 50% of the training expenditure to the greatest extent.

Secondly, it is necessary to carry out vocational skill trainings and training in starting businesses for the unemployed rural migrant workers going back to their hometowns. The skill trainings can be carried out for the rural migrant workers according to their requirements for job transfer and their intentions for labor service export so as to create conditions for their future employment. Order trainings can also be conducted vigorously according to the demands from local industrial structure adjustment, enterprise technological transformation and the newly started construction projects. Meanwhile, for the rural migrant workers with certain enterprising spirit and enterprising conditions, who go back to their hometowns, entrepreneurship trainings can be organized for them to help improve the capability of self-employment and setting up their own business. For rural migrant workers joining in various vocational trainings, special employment fund and relevant special funds can provide subsidies according to the regulations.

Thirdly, it is necessary to conduct 3-6 month medium and short-term skill trainings for the unemployed to help them realize re-employment. The unemployed include two categories generally: 1) Persons transferred from being employed into being unemployed (including the unemployed rural workers that continue to find job in cities and towns), who have working experience and some skills. The employment fields locally expanded with priority, industries complying with industrial adjustment policies and the occupations needed to be developed should be closed combined. The service-category skill training programs for the urban employment should be developed with priority, flexible and varied training forms and means should be adopted, and practicability of trainings should be emphasized. 2) Undergraduates registered for unemployment, such kind of persons have some theoretical knowledge but lack practical working skills. So skill trainings should be organized for them based on their educational background, emphasize on trainings on operational skills and improve their employment capabilities. For the unemployed with the intentions and demands for starting a business, entrepreneurship trainings can be organized for them. For the capital required in trainings for various unemployed persons, the special employment fund and unemployment insurance fund can provide subsidies according to the regulations.

Fourthly, it is necessary to carry out 6-12 month reserved skill trainings for emerging labor force to improve their employability. In special period, the training period for emerging labor forces should be extended appropriately. Effective measures should be taken to enlarge the recruitment of mechanic colleges, and guide schools to accelerate the cultivation of a batch of high-quality reserve skilled talents according to the national industrial structure adjustment and in view of demand on the labor market. For the regions where conditions permit, demobilized soldiers can also be organized to join in the vocational trainings. For the capital required in trainings for emerging labor force, local special employment fund and relevant special funds can provide subsidies according to the regulations.

4.6.2.1 Policies for Promoting the Re-employment of Laid-off Workers

4.6.2.1.1 Promoting the Re-employment of Laid-off Workers through Public Employment Service and Re-employment Training

The public employment service agencies under the leadership of the governments will provide employment services to laid-off workers free of charge. The private employment agencies helping re-employment of laid-off workers will be provided with employment introduction subsidy. For the laid-off workers joining in trainings, training fee subsidy and occupational skill appraisal subsidy will be provided.

4.6.2.1.2 Encouraging the Self-employment of Laid-off Workers

It is necessary to encourage the self-employment of laid-off workers by such policies as entrepreneurship trainings, fixed tax relief and granting of small secured loans. The laid-off workers can join in the entrepreneurship trainings free of charge. For the eligible laid-off workers engaged in small private business, the administrative charges can be exempted within three years. Based on the tax amount ceiling of 8,000 yuan for each household on an annual basis, the tax amount exceeding this ceiling will be relieved. In the event of insufficient operation capital, small secured loans below 50,000 yuan and corresponding fiscal interest subsidies will be granted.

4.6.2.1.3 Encouraging Enterprises to Employ Laid-off Workers

It is necessary to encourage enterprises to employ laid-off workers by such policy leverages as tax preference, social security subsidy, secured loan and interest subsidy. For commerce trade enterprises and service enterprises, according to the number of recruited laid-off workers and based on the ceiling of 4,000 yuan for each person on an annual year, the tax amount of such enterprises should be reduced within three years, and social insurance subsidy will be given. The eligible labor-intensive small enterprises will be provided with secured loans and fiscal interest subsidies.

4.6.2.1.4　Implementing Employment Assistance for Vulnerable Groups

It is necessary for governments to develops public welfare jobs, arrange for the persons with employment difficulties with priority, and give social insurance subsidy and job subsidy. Social insurance subsidy will be given for the persons undertaking flexible employment.

4.6.3.1　Preference Polices for Promoting Undergraduate Employment in Connection with Green Employment

4.6.3.1.1　Graduate Internship System

Ministry of Human Resources and Social Security has established internship system for unemployed college graduates who left universities so as to enrich their working experience and increase their competitiveness on the job market. In selecting internship bases, the advantageous industries primarily developed locally should be preferred, and the internship posts must have certain technical level and business content. During the internship period, enterprises should pay certain basic allowance for the students. Such period for every college graduate interning in the same entity generally last for 3-12 months.

4.6.3.1.2　Support for Starting Businesses

For the persons who are willing to start business, such "one-stop" entrepreneurship services as project development, program design, risk evaluation, guidance for opening business, financing service and follow-up support will be provided.

4.6.4.1　Standardizing the Cancellation Procedures of Labor Relations in Enterprise Bankruptcy, Closure or Downsizing

Article 41 of *Labor Contract Law of the People's Republic of China* stipulates the procedures for reduction in personnel: Where an enterprise is restructured, changes the production lines, introduces major technological innovation or adjust business mode, upon amendment of employment contracts, in the event that such enterprise still needs reduction in personnel and employees to be laid-off total over 20 or accounts for more than 10% of the total employees although employees to be laid-off total fewer than 20, the employer enterprise should make statements to the labor union or all employees 30 days in advance and listen to the opinions from the labor union and employees, and submit the program for reduction in personnel to labor administration organs. Under this premise, reduction in personnel may be implemented.

In the event of reduction in personnel, an enterprise should primarily retain the following personnel:

(I) signing fixed-term labor contract with the employer for long period.

(II) Signing labor contract without fixed term with the employer.

(III) Whose family members are not employed, and old people or minors need to be raised.

Where the employer makes reduction in personnel according to Article 41 (1) of *Labor Contract Law* but recruits within six month, it should notify previously reduced employees. And previously reduced employees should be preferably recruited under the same conditions.

Under the following circumstances, the labor contract cannot be terminated by the employer:

(I) The laborers are engaged in operations in contact with occupational hazards subject to no occupational health check before leaving post, or the suspected occupational disease patients are in the period of diagnosis and medical observation.

(II) The laborers suffer from occupational disease or work-related injuries, and they are confirmed as those losing or partially losing the labor capability.

(III) The laborers suffer diseases or injury unrelated to work within the specified medical treatment period.

(IV) The female workers in the pregnancy, childbirth and breast-feeding period.

(V) The laborers work continuously for 15 years and there is less than 5 years to the statutory retirement age.

(VI) Other circumstances specified by laws and administrative regulations.

Article 44 of *Labor Contract Law of the People's Republic of China* stipulates that where the employer is announced as bankrupted, ordered to close down or cancelled according to the laws or the employer decides to dissolve in advance, labor contract should be terminated. For the procedures of closedown and bankruptcy of state-owned enterprises, Article 17 of *Circular of the State Council on Further Promoting Employment and Reemployment stipulates* that where state-owned enterprises implement reorganization and bankruptcy, employee placement program should be discussed and approved by workers' congress or employees' assembly. In the event that employee placement program and social security methods are not clear and funds are unallocated, state-owned enterprises should not be permitted to proceed with the procedures of reorganization and bankruptcy.

4.6.5.1 Employee Security in Enterprise Bankruptcy, Closure or Downsizing

4.6.5.1.1 Compensation for Employee in Case the Company is Bankrupted, Closed or Downsized

China's state-owned enterprise bankruptcy system has been gradually established and improved along with the process of economic system restructuring. Therefore, in terms of asset disposal and employee placement for bankrupted state-owned enterprises, there are a lot of administrative factors, the laws and policies have been implemented in parallel.

Policies: the State Council has started to issue a series of administrative regulations since 1994, including *Circular on Relevant Issues about the Pilot Implementation of Bankruptcy of State-owned Enterprises in Some Cities and Supplementary Circular on Relevant Issues about the Pilot Implementation of Merger and Bankruptcy of State-owned Enterprises in Some Cities and Workers' Reemployment*. In 1996, National Economic and Trade Commission and the

People's Bank of China also issued *Circular on Relevant Issues about the Pilot Implementation of Merger and Bankruptcy of State-Owned Enterprises*. According to these circulars, the employee placement in the enterprises entering into the bankruptcy procedure has enjoyed special preference beyond the legal norms. In terms of the bankruptcy properties used for debt solvency, the land use right should firstly be used for resolving the employee placement, even the realization of mortgaged land use right can be used for compensating for the employee placement fees. Employee housings and other social assets (such as kindergartens) should be excluded from bankruptcy properties. Breakthroughs have also been made in scope and standard for actual liquidation of debts. Moreover, in 111 pilot cities designated by the State Council, if employees of bankrupted enterprises choose to be self-employed, the placement fee can be paid in a lump sum, the amount of which should not be higher than 3 times last year's average wage of the employees in enterprises in pilot cities. The specific standard should be determined by the liquidation panel according to the working term and job rank, etc. That is to say, the application range of one-off placement fee should cover employees of planned bankrupted enterprises approved by National Merge and Bankruptcy Coordination Panel. For the employees of planned bankrupted enterprises, employee placement fee and economic compensation cannot be simultaneously drawn. After the pilot state-owned bankrupted enterprises enter into bankruptcy procedure, the employees' life allowance should be paid from the bankruptcy liquidation fees.

Laws: China promulgated the first generalized legal norms applicable to the bankruptcy of state-owned enterprises in 1986, i.e., *Law of the People's Republic of China on Enterprise Bankruptcy (Trial Implementation)*, in which it specifies that "employees' wages and labor insurance fees owed by bankrupted enterprises should be liquidated in the first order. *Regulations of Supreme People's Court on Several Issues in Court Trial of Enterprise Bankruptcy Cases 2002* also stipulates that "employee compensation for dissolving labor relations" and "raised funds by employees" will also be liquidated in the first order. New *Law of the People's Republic of China on Enterprise Bankruptcy* enforced since June 1, 2007 still provides space for policy-oriented bankruptcy, which stipulates that special matters in bankruptcy of state-owned enterprises within the period and scope specified by the State Council before the enforcement of the law should be handled according to relevant regulations of the State Council. *Enterprise Bankruptcy Law of the People's Republic of China* expressly stipulates that after the bankrupted properties are firstly used for satisfaction of bankruptcy charges and public debts, the items listed in the first order of satisfaction should also include "wages, medical treatment costs, disability benefits, pension costs due to the employees basic endowment insurance and basic medical insurance that should be transferred into employees' individual accounts,, compensation that should be paid to employee as specified in laws and administrative rules". The social insurance fees owed by the bankrupted enterprises should be in the second order of satisfaction. Although mortgaged creditor's rights can be covered when employee creditor's rights are not sufficient for distribution, such duration and scope should be strictly limited.

According to *Labor Contract Law*, at the time of bankruptcy and downsizing, enterprises must pay economic compensation to the laborers. The economic compensation should be based on working duration in the employer. For each calendar year, monthly wage should be paid to the laborer. If a laborer only works for more than six months and less than twelve months, this should also be deemed as one year. If a laborer only works for less than six months, half of monthly wage should be paid to the laborer. If the laborer's monthly wage is 3 times higher than last year's monthly average wage of workers as published by a municipal people's government of the municipalities and autonomous regions where the employer is located, the economic compensation paid to the laborer should be 3 times such monthly average wage. Term for paying the economic compensation should not be more than 12 years.

4.6.5.1.2 Early Retirement in the Event of Enterprise Bankruptcy and Closedown

The existing policies stipulate that in the event of enterprise bankruptcy, the eligible employees can retire at an early date. For example, Provisional Measures for Employee Placement in Bankrupted State-owned Enterprises in Beijing stipulates that retirement formalities can be handled for employees in the enterprises to be bankrupted upon application by themselves in the month the court announces the bankruptcy, under the premise that the male employees attain the age of 55 (physical age) and female employees attain the age of 45 (physical age). However, during the early retirement period, the pension should be appropriately reduced as the case may be.

5 Evaluation of Social Environment for Developing Green Employment in China

The period China develops green employment is just the critical period in which the industrialization, urbanization, marketization and internationalization are carried out simultaneously and the society and economy are developed comprehensively, and there are contradictions and challenges between rapid economic development and resources consumption as well as ecological protection. Domestic and overseas practices have proved that the high-input, high-consumption and high-pollution economic growth mode is non-sustainable; we should set foot on the road of new industrialization and sustainable development, and establish a resources-saving and environmental-friendly society.

China's employment problem is very prominent. In China, the newly added employment population in each year is 10 million, millions of workers are laid off from their posts, ten millions of surplus labor force exist in the rural areas, and if the economic growth rate does not reach 8%-9% or higher, the social security can not be guaranteed. China's urbanization process is developed steadily at the rate of 1% to 1.5% each year. The demand from urban infrastructure construction will drive the continued enlargement of scale of such industries as chemical, building materials, metallurgy with heavy pollution; the level of regional economic development is decreasing from east to west, the ecological environment in inland is weaker, and the contradiction between economic development and the ecological environmental protection becomes more prominent.

Since China is a responsible developing power, Chinese government attaches great importance to the promotion of green development, and has created good social environment for green development. This report is to make assessment on the social environment for China to develop green employment from such four aspects as China's economic policies for promoting green development (including fiscal policy, tax policy and monetary policy), China's public awareness in promoting green development, China's science and technology environment for promoting green development, China's social supporting system in promoting green development.

5.1 China's Economic Policies for Promoting Green Development

5.1.1 China's Fiscal Policies for Promoting Green Development

Financial input is a very important policy means for macro-economy regulation, which specifically includes: government's direct investment on environmental protection, financial subsidies, government's green purchase system, transfer payment from the exchequer due to environmental factor.

5.1.1.1 Chinese Government's Green Budget and Expenditure Policy

Government's direct investment on environmental protection is mainly used for controlling environmental pollution. From 2001 to 2005, the accumulated input on the environmental protection by central finance was more than RMB110 billion yuan.

(1) The environmental protection expenses are increased year by year to ensure that the environmental protection departments perform their duties.

During the "10th Five-year Plan" period, the central finance, through departmental budget, arranged RMB1.06 billion yuan for the environmental protection expenses on an accumulated basis, an average annual increase of 25.3%, which was mainly used to support such works as environmental monitoring, environmental protection law enforcement and the environmental standards formulation and amendment.

(2) Increase the input of environmental protection funds to exert the guiding function of central financial capital.

The total amount of special funds for environmental protection allocated by the central finance was increased from RMB30 million yuan in 2001 to RMB930 million yuan in 2005, the accumulated special expenditure allocated was RMB1450 million yuan, guaranteeing the successful implementation of special works, and driving local governments and social funds to participate in the environmental protection.

(3) Support the key ecological construction and pollution control projects with national debt funds.

During the "10th Five-year Plan" period, the central finance, through national debt fund, directly arranged expenditure of RMB 108.3 billion yuan for ecological construction and pollution control on an accumulated basis, which was mainly used for sandstorm source control for Beijing and Tianjin, construction of environmental protection facilities in western center cities, pollution prevention and control of "three rivers and three lakes", sewage and waste industrialization and reclaimed water reusing, Beijing environmental pollution control, and compensation for forest ecological efficiency.

5.1.1.2 Chinese Government's Green Purchase Policy

In 2004, the Ministry of Finance and the National Development and Reform Commission jointly issued the Opinions on Implementation of Government Procurement for Energy-saving Products, and it is the first specific policy in China to promote energy-saving and environmental protection by means of government procurement. This policy was formally implemented from January 1, 2005. Some local governments promulgated some environmental protection procurement standards, for example, the Qingdao Finance Bureau and the Qingdao Environmental Protection Agency issued the first batch of "List of Environmental Protection Products by Government Procurement in Green Purchase Project" on December 27, 2005, in which the first batch of environmental protection products by government procurement were determined.

5.1.1.3 Chinese Government's Green Fiscal Transfer Policy

Since 1998, the central government continuously increased the financial assistance for the less developed central, western areas, combined the ecological construction with rural infrastructure construction and industry development, implemented the policy of returning farmlands to forests and grasslands, and strengthened the environmental protection investment ability in local areas.

5.1.1.4 Chinese Government Established Special Funds for Promoting the Development of Green Environment

In recent years, Chinese government increased the special funds for environment management and protection, and provincial finance departments established corresponding special funds in connection with "green" environmental development and protection. For example, during 2000-2003, Zhejiang province arranged special funds totaling RMB1.7 billion yuan for the projects involving ecological construction, including the "construction of ecological agriculture and new countryside", "construction of ecological public welfare forest", "construction of thousands of clean water riverway", "ecological environment control", "construction of ecological cities and towns", "blue sea construction" and "green culture construction", which greatly improved the ecological environment.

5.1.1.5 Chinese Government's Green Financial Subsidy (Interest Subsidy) Policy

Currently the widely used subsidies mainly include the subsidy on pollution control projects, subsidy on ecological construction projects, subsidy on clean production projects, subsidy on environmental researches, and subsidy on environmental-friendly products.

5.1.2 China's Tax Policy for Promoting Green Development

The items of taxation in connection with green development mainly include two facets: firstly, the resource tax, urban land use tax and farmland occupation tax imposed on units and individuals exploiting and using natural resources (including land), which have a direct function in protecting resources and promoting green development. Secondly, consumption tax, urban maintenance and construction tax, having indirect function in promoting green development.

Various taxes conducive to green development are mainly reflected in the value-added tax and corporate income tax. In addition, they are also reflected in the consumption tax and some local taxation items.

5.1.2.1 Chinese Government's Green Value-added Tax Policy

Chinese government implements the green value-added tax policy, which can be classified as following categories in general:

(1) Incentives for products of comprehensive utilization of resources

Including: ① Conduct VAT exemption for the gold and silver produced by enterprises by using waste liquid (slag) (CSZ [1995] No.44 and CS [1996] No. 120). ② Conduct VAT exemption for building materials (including commercial concrete) containing not less than 30% coal gangue, stone coal, fly ash and bottom slag from coal-fired boilers (excluding blast furnace slag), and the blending proportion may be calculated by weight or by volume (GSH [2003] No. 1151, CSZ [1995] No. 44 and CSZ [1996] No. 20). ③ For the electricity produced by using coal gangue, coal slime, stone coal and oil shale and the quantity (weight) of which accounts for more than 60% (inclusive 60%) of the fuels for power generation, the VAT imposed will be halved (CS [2004] No. 25, CS [2001] No. 198). ④ For the comprehensive utilization products produced by enterprises by using such raw materials as "three residues" and "sub-small fuel wood" in forested area, the taxation agency will implement the "levy-refund policy" for VAT before December 31, 2005. ⑤ For the flue gas desulphurization by-products from coal-fired power plants (including plasters in which the content of calcium sulfate dehydrate is not lower than 85%; sulphuric acid with a concentration no less than 15%; and ammonium sulphate in which the total content of nitrogen is not lower than 18%), the "levy-refund policy" for VAT will be implemented (CS [2004]No.25).

(2) Preferential measures for promoting the recycling of waste and used materials

For waste and used materials recycling units, the preferential VAT policy of "levy first and then return 70%" was changed from May 1, 2001 to VAT exemption for the sale of waste and used materials purchased. For the production enterprises as VAT general taxpayer, when they purchase waste and used materials, it is allowed to calculate the VAT based on 10% of the amount written on common invoices to deduct input tax amount (CS [2001] No. 78).

(3) Preferential measures for clean energy and environmental protection products

The VAT will be halved for the electricity generated by wind energy and the new-type wall materials listed in the Catalogue of New-type Wall Materials Enjoying Preferential Tax policy, including 23 kinds of products in 14 classes, such as non-clay bricks, building blocks and building boards.

(4) Preferential Measures for Waste Water Treatment

Since July 1, 2001, VAT has been exempted for the sewage treatment fee charged by governments and authorities at various levels by entrusting water plants to collect together with the water rate (CS [2001] No. 97).

5.1.2.2 Chinese Government's Green Consumption Tax Policy

Since January 1, 2009, the refined oil tax reform contemplating for 14 years was formally implemented, six charges beyond the oil price were cancelled, and they are: road maintenance fee, waterway maintenance fee, highway transport management fee, highway passenger and freight surcharge, waterway transport management fee and the surcharge for waterway passenger and freight transport. The unit tax amount of gasoline consumption tax within the imposed price was increased by RMB 0.8 yuan per liter, that is, the price was enhanced to RMB1 yuan from the original RMB0.2 yuan for every liter; the unit tax amount for diesel consumption tax was increased by RMB0.7 yuan per liter, that is, the price was enhanced to RMB0.8 yuan from original RMB0.1 yuan for every liter; and the unit tax amount of other refined oil consumption taxes was also increased correspondingly. It was made clear that the price of domestic refined oil will be linked indirectly with the refined oil price in the international market on a controlled basis, which will be determined based on the refined oil price on the international market, plus average domestic processing cost, tax, costs at flowing links and appropriate profit. Meanwhile, it stipulates that the consumption tax at the import link of refined oil will be adjusted.

From the angles of environmental protection and resources conservation, the timely launching of such refined oil tax reform greatly pushed forward the degree of green for China's tax system, which is mainly reflected in the following two aspects.

(1) Refined oil tax reform will promote consumers to change the concept for automobile consumption.

After the refined oil tax reform, the consumption tax for refined oil such as gasoline and diesel will be imposed according to quantity at fixed amount, rather than imposed according to price. This means that the tax amount is not related to the change of oil prices, but to the oil consumption quantity. This reform will definitely urge consumers to change the concept of automobile consumption, encourage the purchase of fuel-efficient vehicles and development of public transport. At the same time, it will push the industrial structure upgrading in automobile industry and promote the utilization of new energies and new technologies.

(2)Refined oil tax reform will promote the industrialized development of new energy vehicles.

The refined oil tax reform is not only beneficial to the development of energy-saving and environment-friendly low-emission vehicles, but also conducive to the industrialized development of new energy vehicles in the long run.

5.1.2.3　Chinese Government's Green Income Tax Policy

In recent years, in order to further promote green development, China promulgated some special income tax policies for saving resources and protecting environment. Which mainly include:

(1) Tax exemption for enterprises using "three wastes"

If enterprises use waste water, waste gas and waste slag as the main raw materials to conduct production, their corporate income tax may be reduced or exempted within five years (CS [1994] No.1), which specifically include: ① for the earnings of an enterprise from products mainly produced by using the resources in the Catalogue of Comprehensive Resources Utilization that are generated from the production process of the enterprise beyond the originally designed and specified products, income tax will be exempted from the date of production and operation; ② for the earnings from producing building materials by using bulk coal gangue, slag and fly ash coming outside of the enterprise as the main raw materials, the income tax will be exempted for five years from the date of production and operation; ③ for the newly established enterprises in order to dispose of and utilize the resources abandoned by other enterprises and as listed in the Catalogue of Comprehensive Resources Utilization, the income tax may be reduced or exempted for one year upon approval by competent tax authority.

(2) Tax exemption policy for the enterprises specialized in producing environmental protection equipment (products) currently encouraged by the State.

It stipulates that, for the enterprises (factories and workshops) specialized in producing the equipment and products as listed in the "Catalogue of

Environmental Protection Equipment (Products) Currently Encouraged by the State". If they are independent in accounting and in calculation of profit and loss, and their annual net revenue is less than RMB 300,000 yuan (including RMB 300, 000 yuan), the corporate income tax will be exempted temporarily. For the portion exceeding RMB 300,000 yuan, the corporate income tax shall be paid in accordance with the law (GJMZY [2000]No. 159, GJMZY [2002] No. 23).

(3) For the environmental protection equipment encouraged by the State, investment credit and accelerated depreciation policy will be implemented.

Chinese government stipulates that, where in the technological transformation projects, the domestic manufactured equipment as listed in the "Catalogue of Environmental Protection Equipment (Products) Currently Encouraged by the State" (first batch) are used by an enterprise, the preferential policy of corporate income tax credit will be enjoyed by the enterprise in accordance with the "Notice on Printing and Issuing the Provisional Measures for Corporate Income Tax Credit for Domestic Produced Equipment in Technological Transformation" (CSZ [1999] No. 290), and the accelerated depreciation method may be used.

(4) Policy of deduction of charitable donations

Since January 1, 2004, the public welfare donations made by enterprises and institutions, social groups and individuals through China Environmental Protection Foundation shall be allowed to be deducted before paying corporate income tax and personal income tax (CS [2004] No. 172).

(5) Preferential policy for productive foreign-invested enterprises

The foreign-invested enterprises engaging in sewage and waste treatment business may be recognized as productive foreign-invested enterprises, and they can enjoy the preference of exemption of enterprise income tax for the first two years of making profit, and 50% tax reduction for the following three years (GSH [2003] No. 388).

5.1.2.4 China's Tax Policy for Promoting the Resources Saving

In order to promote the reasonable use of resources and limit the abuse of resources, the resource tax has been imposed from April 1988, and in the 1994 tax reform, the collection range was further enlarged. Although China started imposing the resource tax, generally speaking, China's resource tax system is far from perfect. The prominent feature is that the resource tax fails to cover all resources, for instance, currently China does not impose resource tax on water resources and biological resources (including forests, grasslands and marine fishery resources).

5.1.2.5 Chinese Government's Export Rebate Policy for Promoting Green Develo-pment

In terms of export rebate, in order to limit the export of high-pollution, high-energy consumption and resource-based products, the central finance successively adopted a series of measures, including the elimination of export rebate policy for various mineral concentrates and refined oil and other resource-based products. In addition, the tax rebate rate for certain products as copper, nickel, iron alloy, coking coal and coke was reduced to 5%. The export rebate rate for "high-pollution, high-energy consumption and resource-based products" was lowered significantly or totally cancelled, reflecting the regulation goals in optimizing industrial structure.

5.1.2.6 Other Tax Incentives of Chinese Government in Promoting Green Develo- pment

Among some local taxation items such as house tax, urban land use tax, operation tax of vehicle and ship and deed tax, there are also some measures conducive to ecological environment protection, which mainly including: For the houses, lands, vehicles and ships owned and used by the environmental protection units for which the State financial sector allocates business funds, the house tax, urban land use tax and operation tax of vehicle and ship will be exempted. For the transformed abandoned lands (No. 17 order by State Council in 1988), water conservancy facilities and the protection lands (GSDZ No.

014 [1989]), forested areas and protection lands in the forestry system (GSHF [1991] No. 1404), the urban land use tax will be exempted. For various sprinkler trucks, garbage trucks and ships used by environmental protection departments (GF (1986) No. 90), the road sweepers, environment monitoring vehicles used by sanitation and environmental protection departments (CSD [1987] No. 3), city buses and electric buses ((86) CSDZ No. 008), the operation tax of vehicle and ship will be exempted. Moreover, during the period from January 1, 2004 to December 31, 2010, for the houses, lands, vehicles and ships owned by the enterprises and units implementing the natural forest protection program in state-owned forests, the house tax, urban land use tax and operation tax of vehicle and ship would be exempted respectively. If the houses and lands owned by forest industry enterprises are left unused for more than one year due to the fact that the country implements the natural forest protection program, the house tax and urban land use tax will be exempted temporarily (CS [2004] No. 37).

5.1.3 China's Financial Policy for Promoting the Green Development

5.1.3.1 Chinese Government's Green Credit Policy

On July 30, 2007, the original State Environmental Protection Administration in conjunction with the People's Bank of China and the Banking Supervision Commission, promulgated the Opinions on Implementing Environmental Protection Policies and Rules and Preventing Credit Risks, more than 20 provinces issued specific implementation schemes around the country, the Industrial and Commercial Bank of China, China Construction Bank and the Industrial Bank of China implemented the "one-vote veto for environmental protection". The Opinions has become the fundamental file of green credit. It is required for the People's Bank of China and the Banking Supervision Commission to assist the environmental protection agencies and guide financial institutions at various levels to make differential treatment to the credit granting for different types of enterprises that are prohibited, eliminated, restricted and encouraged by the country according to the requirements of environmental and economic policies. Especially for the projects not approved by environmental protection agencies, new credit shall not be provided in order to avoid bad debt.

On November 6, 2008, the Ministry of Environmental Protection and the World Bank jointly issued the International Experience in Promoting Green Credit: Original Equator Performance Standard and Guideline (hereinafter referred to as Green Credit Guideline). Green Credit Guideline fully introduced the content of "equator principle", the performance standards for social and environmental sustainability, and the guidelines for environment, health and safety for 62 industries. The publication of green credit guideline is an important mark showing that China's green credit policy is deepening, and meanwhile it is a new starting point for perfecting the green credit technical system.

5.1.3.2 Chinese Government's Financing Policy for Environmental Protection Industry.

At present, the financing size of China's green economy projects is increasingly enlarged, just from the perspective of the environmental protection project financing, during the periods of "9th Five-year Plan" and "10th Five-year Plan", the funds allocated by the central finance was RMB351.6 billion yuan and RMB839.51 billion yuan respectively. According to planning by the State Environmental Protection Administration, during the "11th Five-year Plan period, the environmental protection financing in the society will reach RMB1375 billion yuan, accounting for about 1.6% of GDP over the same period. However, we should also see the fact that, the financing problem has already become a bottleneck for the industrialized development of China's environmental protection. At present, aside from government investment for China's environmental protection enterprises, the indirect financing means are mainly used to raise funds.

On one hand, for large-scale environmental protection projects, the funds are raised by the country through policy banks as special loans, there are some external problems so the capital shortage is difficult to be obtained from other commercial banks. On the other hand, the small and medium-sized enterprises with good growth potential and considerable benefits have difficulties in gaining loans and guarantees.

5.1.3.3 Chinese Government's Policy on Environmental Pollution Liability Insurance

In December 2007, the Ministry of Environmental Protection and the China Insurance Regulatory Commission jointly promulgated the Guiding Opinions on Environmental Pollution Liability Insurance Work, thus the green insurance system construction was started formally. The Opinions proposed that an environmental pollution liability insurance system in line with China's national conditions should be established initially, the pilot demonstration work should be carried out for environmental pollution liability insurance in key industries and areas, and the pilot objects include the enterprises producing, operating, storing, transporting and using hazardous chemicals, petrochemical enterprises prone to pollution accidents, and enterprises disposing of hazardous wastes. After 2012, the Environmental Pollution Liability Insurance will be implemented around the country.

For example, in 2008, Hunan province launched insurance products covering 18 key enterprises in such fields as chemical industry, nonferrous metal and steel, in which seven enterprises have bought the insurance. Jiangsu province launched the ship pollution liability insurance in 2008, for which a co-insurance body consisting of four insurance companies as PICC, Ping An, CPIC and Yongan was organized, covering the ship pollution liability insurance projects in Jiangsu province from 2008 to 2009. In 2008, Hubei province started pilot work for the Environmental Pollution Liability Insurance, which was carried out in Wuhan city circle, and Wuhan specifically arranged RMB2 million yuan as government guidance fund and provided subsidy for the enterprises buying insurance at 50% of the insurance premium. Shenyang firstly made breakthrough in local legislation, Shenyang Regulations on Prevention and Control of Hazardous Waste Pollution clearly stipulates that, "support and encourage insurance companies to set up hazardous waste pollution damage liability insurance; support and encourage the units generating, collecting, storing, transporting, utilizing and disposing of hazardous waste to buy the hazardous waste pollution damage liability insurance".

5.2 Influence of China's Economic Policy for Promoting Green Development on Employment

5.2.1 Influence of China's Fiscal Policy for Promoting Green Development on the Employment

5.2.1.1 Chinese Government's Green Budget and Expenditure Policy not only Promoted the Green employment Directly, but also Increased Green Employment through the Multiplier Effect Driving the Social Investment

The fiscal policy, by its multiplier effect, enlarged the total employment from two aspects. One is direct effect. The fiscal expenditure directly formed industry capital thus creating jobs. Chinese government, through increasing the environmental protection expenses, environmental protection funds and national debt year by year, supported a large number of key ecological constructions and pollution treatment projects, directly enlarging the total green employment. The other is indirect effect. The increasing fiscal expenditure by Chinese government will multiply the national income due to the multiplier effect, and the continuous growth of Chinese economy will definitely promote the increase of the number of green employment.

Under the financial crisis, China implemented a proactive fiscal policy, effectively stabilized and recovered the economy and also increased job opportunities. According to the estimation made by the Human Resources and Social Security Department of Labor Science Research Institute, Chinese government's investment totaled 4 trillion will create 24,160,000 jobs.

5.2.1.2   Chinese Government's Green Budget and Expenditure Policy Has Limited Effect on Small Enterprises, and the Potential for Job Creation is to be Excavated.

Chinese government's green budget and expenditure policy had big effect on promoting green employment, but there are also some defects, for example, less support and assistance were given to small enterprises. Small enterprises are an important force in pushing China's national economic development and promoting employment. While the fiscal expenditure policy has limited support for small enterprises, for instance, in the government's green procurement policy, there is no quota specified for buying products of small and medium-sized products, and the support for various business guide, information service and marketing for small and medium-sized enterprises was less.

5.2.2   Influence of China's Tax Policy for Promoting Green Development on the Employment

5.2.2.1   China's Tax Policy Has Formed Good Guide for Promoting Green Development

China's existing tax policy has formed an orientation of encouraging resource saving, environmental protection and limiting pollution, which, along with the government's other related measures such as charging system, pollution discharge licensing system and fiscal subsidies, has played an active role in alleviating or eliminating pollution, saving and reasonably using resources, strengthening the environmental protection and promoting China's sustainable development.

5.2.2.2   The Effect of Chinese Government's Green Tax policy on Promoting Employment is Remarkable

Since 1994 tax reform, China promulgated a series of tax preference policies for promoting employment. Including: The tax preference policy before 2002 for employment and reemployment of job-waiting people, four classes of disabled persons, demobilized cadres and demobilized soldiers from army; tax preference policy promulgated successively during 2003-2005 targeted at service enterprises, new businesses and laid-off workers; in 2006, the tax policy emphasized on encouraging enterprises to create jobs and encouraging self-employment, encouraging state-owned large and medium-sized enterprises to separate parent company with subsidiaries, and encouraging the subsidiaries to reform; in order to cope with the financial crisis, from September 2008 to February 2009, Chinese government promulgated seven documents promoting employment, and implemented six initiatives. By improving the entrepreneurial environment and giving strong support for the persons starting their own businesses in such aspects as tax relief and small-secured loans, the employment multiplier effect was exerted, thus driving the employment of other labor workers.

Compared with the fiscal expenditure policy, investment policy, procurement policy, transfer payment policy adopted by the government, the type of tax preference incentive policy combined with market-oriented operation has obvious effect and the function will last longer. As of June 30, 2004, there were 2,290,000 laid-off workers enjoying the tax preference policy in reemployment around the country, the tax department had allocated RMB10.729 billion yuan for reemployment tax burden relief, and the tax registration fee abated was RMB 36,350,000 yuan.

5.2.2.3 Chinese Government's Green Tax Policy Promoted Small and Medium-sized Enterprises to Make More Contributions in Creating Jobs

A 2008 investigation by a scaled private enterprise showed that, under the influence of international financial crisis, Chinese private enterprises showed relatively strong resistance, maintaining a relatively high growth level in both scale index and social contributions. Though the profit margins of these enterprises were squeezed, their contributions to tax and employment were increased. In 2008, the total tax amount paid by 500 private enterprises was RMB148.446 billion yuan, average tax per enterprise was RMB297 million yuan, an increase of 12.76% year-on-year, among which, there were 341 enterprises whose tax payment exceeded RMB100 million yuan. They were particularly prominent in creating jobs, the total employment number was 4132700, an increase of 685000 compared with 2007, an increase of 19.87% year-on-year.

Small and medium-sized enterprises are regarded as "a machine creating jobs". According to statistics, the number of employment of China's small and medium-sized enterprises account for 70% of the total employment number, and account for 80% in the new job opportunities. At present, the important growth point in developing green employment is also the small and medium-sized enterprises, it is observed that, small and medium-sized enterprises have become a reservoir for Chinese labor force, and the development speed of small and medium-sized enterprises is directly linked to China's green employment level. The country should formulate a differential tariff combining with fiscal policy to support and encourage small and medium-sized enterprises. Therefore, the tax policy promoting green development needs to favor small and medium-sized enterprises on a continued basis.

5.2.3 Influence of China's Financial Policy for Promoting Green Development on the Employment

5.2.3.1 "Moderately Easy Monetary Policy" Provides a Good Development Space for Green Development.

Since the implementation of moderately easy monetary policy, the strength of finance supporting economic development has been intensified. In the first half of 2009, the increase of various RMB loans was 7.4 trillion, an increase of 4.9 trillion year-on-year. The rapid growth of loans is conducive to promote the economy to develop faster in terms of total amount, providing good development space for promoting green employment.

5.2.3.2   There is Less Support for Small and Medium-sized Enterprises in Monetary Policies, and the Financing Difficulty of Small and Medium-sized Enterprises is Still Very Prominent.

According to the employment law of the world, the residue workforce transferred from rural areas, newly added workforce in cities, and the workforce extruded from structural adjustment and mechanism reform will concentrate more on small and medium-sized enterprises with the change of industries. Compared with large enterprises, small and medium-sized enterprises have disadvantages in capital, information, talent, technology and management, so supporting small and medium-sized enterprises should be a key content concerned in the construction of financial policies by China in promoting green development.

Currently, the financial policy adopted by China in promoting green development is conducive to the development of China's green economy, but the support for small and medium-sized enterprises, which create a majority of jobs, is obviously inadequate, small enterprises are in capital shortage and financing difficulties and the development is weak, which greatly limited the enlargement of employment capacity. The major problems faced by small enterprises are high financing cost and the supporting policies for small and medium-sized enterprises are not in place, in order to breakthrough this bottleneck, the inclination, supporting and assistance by financing policies are needed.

5.3 Chinese Public's Awareness of the Promotion of Green Development

5.3.1 China's Publication and Public Participation in Promoting Green Development

Green development not only needs the participation of governments and enterprises, but also needs public engagement, thus a long-term push force for green development can be formed fundamentally. China has always attached importance to the education, publication and public participation in promoting green development.

The "Survey on Green Employment Status of Enterprise Workers" conducted by Human Resources and Social Security Department of Labor Science Research Institute showed that, 80.1% workers' working places have environmental protection actions or relevant rules and regulations; 89.4% enterprises have actions in connection with recycling, reusing and emission reduction.

"2007 Survey on China's Public Environmental Awareness" showed that, more than 70% Chinese public have a higher awareness on the importance, necessity and urgency of the environmental protection. With the decrease in age, the assessment on the importance of environmental protection is improved gradually, the higher the level of education, the environmental awareness and environmental behavior is better. The assessment on the importance of environmental protection by city resident population is higher than that by resident population in rural areas. There are more than eighty percent Chinese public believes that environmental protection is not only the responsibility of government but also closely linked to individuals.

5.3.2 Degree of Social Recognition for China to Promote Green Development

In recent years, the State proposes some advanced ideas such as implementing scientific thought of development, constructing a harmonious society and adhering to a road of sustainable development, continuously guiding the whole society to improve the green development awareness and set up an idea of harmonious development between people and the nature. The State takes the construction of resource-saving and environmental-friendly society as an important content in education and press campaign, uses various means to popularize the knowledge related to green development and improve the recognition level of the whole society.

"2007 Survey on Chinese Public Environmental Awareness" showed that the Chinese public's recognition for environmental protection has the feature of high awareness rate and low accuracy: there are more than 80% respondents knowing of at leas one concept related to the environmental protection; but there are only 10% respondents being able to correctly point out the exact meaning of the environmental protection concept they know.

China has published a large number of publications, movies and audiovisual works in connection with the climate change, launched the China Weather TV channel, established information database, and popularized the knowledge about climate change by using mass media. The "Survey on Green Employment Status of Enterprise Workers" conducted by the Human Resources and Social Security Department of Labor Science Research Institute shows that, the TV and radio are the main channels for the public to receive environmental protection knowledge and information(See Figure 5-3-1).

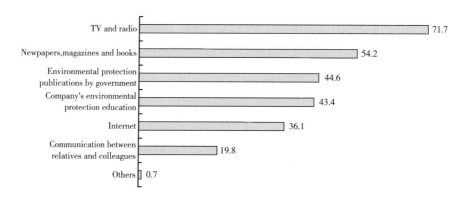

Figure 5-3-1　Survey Results of Green Employment Status of Enterprise Workers

5.3.3　Practical Actions by Chinese Public in Participating in Green Development

Since 1992, China has successively held 18 National Energy-saving Propaganda Week activities. In 2007, the State promulgated the National Action Implementation Plan for Energy-saving and Emission Reduction, implemented a national campaign of energy-saving and emission reduction, including such 9 special actions as family community action, youth action, enterprise action, school action, barrack action, government agency action, science and technology action, science popularization action and media action, forming an working mechanism for energy-saving and emission reduction which government pushes, enterprises implement and the society as a whole participate in. The energy-saving orientation function of government agencies and government staff was exerted by actions such as creating energy-saving government agencies.

"2007 Survey on Chinese Public's Environmental Awareness" showed that, the occupational groups like state public servants have relatively higher environmental awareness. For the occupational groups in which the occupations are highly organized and need higher educational level, their recognition on environmental protection issues and environmental awareness are higher. This is mainly because that the higher degree of organization guarantees that such occupational groups have more chances to accept the environmental information and environmental protection activities provided by their occupational organizations, and thus they can understand the environmental issues in an even larger scope.

China implements the propaganda and education activities for energy conservation and emission reduction by enterprises, mobilizes staff to participate in the management of energy conservation and emission reduction by enterprises. To increase the energy-saving and emission reduction awareness of the public, China is developing such activities as rebuilding the household consumption mode, setting up community platform for energy-saving and emission reduction, actively encouraging the citizens and social communities to participate in afforestation voluntarily, carrying out restrictions and compensation for the use of plastic bags, Theme educations in schools and social practice activities concerning energy conservation and emission reduction are actively carried out to help students set up energy conservation and environmental protection awareness. In recent years, some social communities and non-governmental organizations also participate in the national energy saving and emission reduction in various forms, playing an active role.

The "Survey on Green Employment Status of Enterprise Workers" conducted by Human Resources and Social Security Department of Labor Science Research Institute showed that, 96.9% enterprise workers heard of garbage classification, 98.1% enterprise workers correctly know the relevant knowledge of garbage classification. Energy saving has become a major environmental protection action for Chinese public. In terms of the environmental protection acts of enterprise workers, the environmental protection acts mainly include the acts of reducing living expenditure or being beneficial to their own health. A high proportion of enterprise workers can fulfill the following environmental protection acts: do not use plastic bags when shopping, do not use one-off tableware when dinning out, do classified treatment for home scraps, put waste batteries into specialized recycling bins, use energy-saving products, shut the tap at any time, and pull out plugs after watching TV or using computer.

5.3.4 Chinese Enterprise Workers' Satisfaction Evaluation on Environmental Protection

The "Survey on Green Employment Status of Enterprise Workers" conducted by Human Resources and Social Security Department of Labor Science Research Institute showed that 55.8% enterprise workers are satisfied with the environmental protection work done by the central government; 48.2% enterprise workers are satisfied with the environmental protection work done by local government; 64% enterprise workers are satisfied with the environmental protection work done by the company; 60.9% enterprise workers are satisfied with the consciousness of compliance with environmental protection laws of the company they work for; 62.3% enterprise workers are satisfied with the environmental protection propaganda work done by medias; 93.9% enterprise workers believe that enterprises should participate in and support the environmental protection, which is an important part of enterprises' social responsibilities, not only by providing capital, but by implementing environmental protection measures to reduce pollution.

5.4 The Science and Technology Environment for China to Promote Green Development

Scientific and technological progress is the core method for promoting green development. The improvement of efficiency of energy conversion and utilization, reduction of energy consumption or the development and utilization of renewable energies and optimization of energy structure are dependent on research, development and popularization of advanced technologies. In the long run, whether to acquire the relevant core technologies or not will embody the overall competitiveness of a country.

5.4.1 China's Achievements in Science and Technologies in Promoting Green Development

Currently China is the biggest developing country in the world, and the country attaches great importance to green development and takes a series of measures to deal with it actively. China National Plan for Coping with Climate Change clearly proposes that scientific and technological progress and innovation should be relied on in coping with the climate change, the leading and fundamental role of scientific and technological progress in alleviating and adapting to the climate change should be exerted to promote the development of various technologies and accelerate the pace of technological innovation and technology import, the "development and popularization of advanced applicable technologies" will be deemed as a key field in greenhouse gas emission reduction, they include clean and efficient coal development and utilization technology, oil and gas resources exploration, development and utilization technology, nuclear power technology, renewable energy technology, transmission and power network safety technology, etc. Chinese government also promulgated the Special Scientific and Technological Action in Coping with Climate Change as the scientific and technological support for the National Program. China also takes the low-carbon technology as the priority field and incorporates it into the National Guideline on Medium and Long-term Planning for Science and Technology Development (State Council, 2007). In terms of technical direction, the Guideline tracked the research and development direction of advanced energy technology raised by developed countries. In specific measures, it is proposed that research and development input should be increased and the ability of independent innovation should be improved, the technology introduction should be combined with domestic digestion, absorption and innovation to accelerate the pace of advanced technology industrialization. At the same time, it is proposed that the construction of system and mechanism for mitigation of climate change such as laws and regulations should be strengthened, thus the laws and regulations and policy incentive mechanism promoting the scaled industrialization of advanced energy technologies will be formed gradually.

Through the National Science and Technology Plan, National High-tech Research and Development Plan and the National Basic Research and Development Plan, China successively organized and carried out a series of scientific and technological projects promoting green development, which focused on the prediction of global climate change and its influence, the trends of China's future living environment, solution and supporting technologies for the global climate change, China's formation mechanism and prediction theory for major climate and weather hazards, clean and efficient energy utilization technology, energy saving and improvement of energy efficiency, development and utilization technology of renewable energy and new energy.

Meanwhile, China also actively participated in international science and technology cooperation for global climate change, such as the four international scientific research plans as WCRP, IGBP, IHDP and DIVERSITAS under the framework of ESSP, participated in the GEO and GCOS, conducted the fundamental research on global climate change with Chinese characteristics and global importance.

Through the supports of national scientific and technological plan and international scientific and technological cooperation, China has obtained many achievements and important progresses in such respects as the basic science research on climate change, research on impact and solution of climate change, development and utilization of technologies controlling greenhouse gas emission and mitigating climate change, analysis on social and economic impact of climate change and the research on the mitigation measures, compiled and finished the National Climate Change Assessment. At the same time, the construction of infrastructures for scientific research, personnel training and the construction of scientific research institutions have also been strengthened significantly. The above achievements provide strong support for China to cope with climate change, and at the same time lay a solid foundation for the further development of China's scientific and technological work in coping with climate change.

5.4.2   The Science and Technology Goals for China to Promote Green Development

The science and technology goals for China to promote green development in 2020 are: the ability of independent innovation is increased significantly in the field of responding to climate change; some key technologies with intellectual property rights controlling greenhouse gas emission and mitigating the climate change have breakthroughs; and they are widely utilized in economic and social development; the ability of adapting to climate change of key industries and typical weak areas is strengthened obviously; the science and technology supporting ability of participating in cooperation for climate change and formulation of major strategies and policies is improved significantly; construction of disciplines for climate change is developed greatly, the basic conditions for scientific research are improved obviously, the level of scientific and technological personnel is improved notably; and the scientific awareness of the public on climate change is increased markedly.

5.4.3   China's Key Task in Promoting Green Development

5.4.3.1   Scientific Problems of Climate Change

Including: new generation of climate system mode with independent intellectual property rights, detection and attribution of climate change, monitoring, predicting and early-warning technology for climate change, Asia monsoon system and climate change, the formation mechanism for China's extreme weathers/climate events and disasters, changing process and trend of cryosphere, energy conversion of ecological system, and the response of circulation of materials to the climate change.

5.4.3.2   Technological Development for Controlling Greenhouse Gas Emission and Mitigating Climate Change

Including: energy conservation and improvement of energy efficiency technology, renewable energy and new energy technology, clean and efficient coal development and utilization technology, oil and gas resources and coal bed gas exploration and the clean and efficient development and utilization technology, advanced nuclear technology, carbon dioxide capture and storage technology, bio-sequestration technology and other carbon sequestration engineering technology, greenhouse gas emission control technology in utilization of agriculture and lands.

5.4.3.3 Technologies and Measures Adapting to Climate Change

Including: the climate change impact assessment mode with independent intellectual property rights, impact of climate change on China's major weak fields and the adaptation technologies and measures, the impact of extreme weathers/climate events and disasters and the adaptation technologies and measures, determination of sensitive and weak areas impacted by the climate change and the establishment of risk management system, influence of climate change on major projects and the solutions, interaction between climate change with other global environmental problems and the solutions, determination of risk level of climate change impact and the adaptation ability, case study on adaptation to climate change.

5.4.3.4 Major Strategies and Policies Responding to Climate Change

Including: response to climate change and China energy safety strategy, international system for future climate change, China's future energy development and greenhouse gas emission prospect, clean development mechanism and carbon trade system, responding to climate change and low-carbon economy development, international product trade and greenhouse gas emission, science and technology strategy coping with climate change.

5.4.4 Problems

Whether China could utilize late-development advantage to realize the green economy development in the industrialization process depends on capital and technological ability to a great extent. For China, it mainly refers to the technology access and absorption, and the technological innovation ability could be improved. Technologically, China is restricted by various controls of military technology, and at the same time, China lacks of the ability of absorption, the technologies introduced cannot be fully absorbed, and the skills in maintenance and use are in shortage, thus advanced technologies produced no effect. As China is suffering weak technological innovation ability, it is a net importer of technologies. Though the United Nations Framework Convention on Climate Change stipulates that developed countries have the obligation to transfer technologies to developing countries, the real progress is far from the expectation, and the Clean Development Mechanism program provides very limited technological transfer to developing countries. Therefore, it is very necessary to properly solve the relation between intellectual property rights protection and technological transfer by institutionalized means. China should actively utilize various ways inside and outside the Framework Convention to promote the transfer of technologies from developed countries to developing countries.

5.5 Social Supporting System for Promoting Green Development in China

5.5.1 China Has Established Sound Management System for Coping with Climate Change

Chinese government established relevant agencies coping with climate change in 1990, and set up the National Coordination Committee on Climate Change in 1998. In order to further strengthen the leadership in the work coping with climate change, in 2007, the National Leading Group on Climate Change was established, the group leader is the premier of State Council, who is responsible for formulating major strategies and polices for the country to respond to climate change and to coordinate and resolve the major problems in the work responding to the climate change. In 2008 the leadership for work responding to climate change was further intensified, the member units of the National Leading Group on Climate Change were increased from the original 18 to 20, the specific work of which was undertaken by the State Development and Reform Commission, the leading group was established at the State Development and Reform Commission, and a special agency was established to be responsible for organization and coordination of the national work for coping with climate change. In order to improve the scientificalness of the decision made for coping with climate change, an Expert Committee on Climate Change was established, which had done a lot of works in supporting government decisions, promoting international cooperation and carrying out civil activities.

Currently, each region and department has established a management system, coordination mechanism and special agency on climate change, set up expert group on local climate change, and according to the geographical environment, climate conditions and economic development levels of each region, the relevant policies and measures coping with climate change were formulated, the statistics and monitoring system were established to organize and coordinate the actions coping with climate change in local area.

5.5.2 China Strengthened the Development of Green Employment under Financial Crisis

Under the financial crisis, "green economy" is regarded as the pace maker for global economy revitalization, and China is intensifying the development of green employment with great efforts. China has taken the energy saving, emission reduction and ecological engineering as one of key points of "expanding domestic demand and maintaining growth". Among the RMB4 trillion yuan investment, about 210 billion Yuan was invested to such field, which will be used to accelerate the construction of livelihood projects, infrastructures and ecological environment and post-disaster recovery and reconstruction. Among the 210 billion new investments, 23 billion Yuan will be used for energy saving and emission reduction, ecological construction and environmental protection investment, which mainly include the following four aspects: first, 13 billion Yuan for constructing urban sewage and waste treatment facilities and sewage piping engineering. Expand the coverage of sewage and waste treatment facilities in counties, and it is planed that in three years, most counties nationwide have sewage and waste treatment facilities, with a sewage treatment capacity of 42 million tons and waste treatment capacity of 150000 tons per day in urban areas, and sewage piping network will be constructed. Second, 4 billion Yuan will be arranged for water pollution control in such key watersheds as Huaihe River, Songhuajiang River and Danjiangkou reservoir, improving the sewage and waste treatment capacity of key watersheds. Third, 3.5 billion Yuan is arranged for natural forest resources protection program and key protection forest projects, so as to accelerate the afforestation of 18 million mus and public welfare forest of 11 million mus. Fourth, 2.5 billion is arranged to support 10 big energy-saving projects, recycling economy and industrial pollution control engineering for key watersheds. This will greatly stimulate the transformation of traditional jobs and the cultivation of green employment, which is conducive to the development of energy-saving engineer, solar energy installer, farmer, forest cultivator, ecological protection worker and resources recycling dealer and other green employment.

6 Case Study: Value Chain Analysis of Solar Water Heater Industry in Dezhou City

6.1　Research Background

Climate change has created a serious challenge for human survival and development. All the countries around the world have recognized the need to reduce the dependence of economic development on fossil fuels and lower carbon emissions in order to cope with and mitigate the influence of climate change. The Chinese government also increasingly concerns about low-carbon development and has been actively pursuing energy-saving and emission reduction actions to promote the optimization of energy structure. China set the target of controlling greenhouse gas emissions and reducing energy consumption per unit of gross domestic product (GDP) by 20% in the "Eleventh Five-Year Plan". However, adjustment of the industrial structure and energy structure will inevitably have a far-reaching impact on the number of jobs, employment structure and skill structure. How to actively use the opportunities of green economic development to promote the development of green employment while promoting the transition of grey jobs into green ones, reducing the negative impact of adjustment of the industrial structure and energy structure on employment to achieve sustainable economic, social and environmental development is a problem we must solve in the process of transition into a green economy.

International Labor Organization (ILO) thinks that "it is necessary to estimate the impact of change in the way resources are used on technology, production and employment and find a suitable development strategy to reduce greenhouse gas emissions without delaying the process of poverty eradication". To this end,

International Labor Organization, United Nations Environment Program and International Trade Union Confederation jointly launched the "Green Employment Initiative" to promote policy-making making for coordinated development of employment, poverty alleviation and climate mitigation. To support this initiative, the ILO Regional Office for Asia and the Pacific started an 18-month-long pilot project in China, India and Bangladesh to advance efforts to "promote clean development through the creation of green employment". As part of the pilot project, this research aims at exploring ways to promote the development of the solar water heater industry and create green employment opportunities through the method of value chain analysis.

6.2　Research Methodology

6.2.1　Preliminary Selection of Value Chains

After accepting the commission given by the International Labor Organization, the research team of the Institute for Labor Studies first adapted the International Labor Organization's value chain selection tools in accordance with China's actual situation and set up the eight indicators of "impact of industrial development on improving the environment", "foundation and prospect of industrial development", "principal market", "employment potential", "conformity with policy priorities", "feasibility of external intervention and potential for change", "innovativeness of intervention projects" and "replicability of intervention projects". After this, the research team primarily selected the three value chains of green food, solar water heater and ecological afforestation after analyzing existing literature and interviewing relevant organizations. After carrying out a comprehensive assessment of these three industries, the research group finally decided to take the value chain of the solar water heater industry as the object of in-depth study. Result of the assessment is as follows:

Table 6-2-1   Preliminary Assessment of Value Chains

	Green Food	Solar Water Heater	Ecological Afforestation
Impact on improving the environment	Developing the green food industry can help reduce environmental pollution caused by agriculture and improve agricultural laborers' working environment.	Important areas for promoting green development are adjusting the energy structure and promoting the use of new energy. Compared with traditional gas and electric water heaters, a solar water heater can reduce about 322 kilograms of greenhouse gas emissions per square meter each year and 3220 kilograms in its 10-year life cycle.	Afforestation through carbon sequestration plays an irreplaceable role in mitigating climate change. One cubic meter of forest can absorb 1.83 tons of carbon dioxide and release 1.62 tons of oxygen each year.
Foundation of and potential for industrial development	The industry is quite mature and mainly relies on market operations. With a high degree of consumer recognition and a big market demand, the industry's market development potential is huge. From 2003 to 2007, the average annual growth rate of pollution-free agricultural products, green and organic food products reached 83%. However, compared with ordinary food, the production scale of green food is too small. The proportion of the annual physical output of ordinary food accounted for by green food is still quite low.	It has a certain technical and market development foundation and mainly relies on market operations. It has a quite high degree of consumer recognition and is of great significance for solving rural energy needs. Its market development potential is still big. From 2001 to 2007, the proportion of various types of water heaters sold across the country accounted for by solar water heaters rose from 15.2% to 38.5%. In 2007, the annual output of solar water heaters nationwide was 23 million square meters, the total inventory was 108 million square meters and the area owned by every thousand people was 83 square meters.	Carbon sequestration forestry relies on policy, but it has a huge development potential. According to industry experts' prediction, the profit link of the entire forestry industry chain will be gradually transferred to forest planting.

Continued

	Green Food	Solar Water Heater	Ecological Afforestation
Principal market	All parts of the country, as well as foreign markets	Currently the markets are mainly in small and medium-sized cities in the eastern region. In the near future, the central region has a great potential for development; the western region, especially rural areas where energy is relatively scarce is yet to be developed.	Mainly in forested areas
Employment potential	It is a labor-intensive industry and is conducive to full employment of rural laborers and especially suitable for increasing the employment and income of women and low-income groups.	It is a labor-intensive industry. This industry has many small and medium-sized enterprises and plays a significant role in promoting employment. Especially enterprises engaging in sales, installation, maintenance and other services create many employment opportunities. In China, one solar water heater production worker can bring employment to ten people in related service sectors. According to the estimate of relevant organizations, the whole industry provided 2.5 million employment opportunities in 2007.	Afforestation through carbon sequestration is labor-intensive work and afforestation of each mu (land unit) takes 71-135 man-days. The development of ecological forest is conducive to not only the employment of workers in forest resource-based cities, but also the employment of farmers, especially those who returned to their hometown.

Continued

	Green Food	Solar Water Heater	Ecological Afforestation
Conformity with policy priorities	The state is very supportive of the development of green food. The framework of the basic systems of green food has been formed, including the technical standards system, quality certification system, sign management system and quality inspection system. In addition, many preferential policies for green food manufacturers have been introduced at the national and local levels, such as subsidies, remission of taxes and industrial and commercial administrative costs, credit support and land use.	At the national level, a new energy development strategy has been formulated to make the utilization of solar energy an important component of the energy strategy. At the local level, many cities have formulated regulations for mandatory installation of and subsidy for solar water heaters. In addition, to deal with the financial crisis, the state has formulated policies for expanding domestic demands, including the policy of "home appliances going to the countryside" (rural users can enjoy a subsidy equivalent to 13% of the selling price). All sales enterprises won the bidding need to enhance the sales service function of outlets and especially need to carry out itinerary maintenance services and centralized training services in villages with dispersedly located farmer households.	The state attaches great importance to public welfare-oriented ecological afforestation and has worked out a series of preferential measures: firstly, it established the compensation and subsidy system for key public welfare forests; secondly, it set up the subsidy system for improved varieties of forest trees and subsidy system for investment in afforestation, tending, protection and management; thirdly, it formulated and perfected forestry preferential policies, including the policy of providing discounted interest loans for forestry.
Feasibility of external intervention and potential for industrial change	The potential is quite big. Many jobholders lack appropriate funds and skills; cooperation between the various links of the value chain is impeded.	The potential is quite big. The manufacturing industry is relatively mature, but it is beset by a lack of skilled personnel; the lag of follow-up services affects further development of the industry.	The potential is quite big. Skills training for jobholders needs to be further strengthened.

Continued

	Green Food	Solar Water Heater	Ecological Afforestation
Replicability of intervention projects	They can be propagated around the country.	They can be propagated around the country.	They can be propagated in forested areas.
Innovativeness of intervention projects	There are relatively more external projects, such as poverty alleviation projects and environmental protection projects.	There is quite limited external intervention, mainly rely on the development of enterprises.	External projects include projects of afforestation through carbon sequestration carried out under the clean development mechanism and projects of afforestation through carbon sequestration voluntarily undertaken by nongovernmental organizations.

6.2.2   Research Methods for the Solar Water Heater Value Chain

After deciding to conduct in-depth study of the value chain of the solar water heater industry, the research group presently visited the National Energy Board, the Solar Energy Society and well-known entrepreneurs in the industry and collected a large number of literature materials concerning development of the solar water heater industry. Because the International Labor Organization's value chain analysis tool mainly aims at traditional industries, the research group adjusted this tool and compiled the outline of interview with external service organizations in view of different links of the value chain of the solar water heater industry.

In July 2009, the research group carried out field research activities in Dezhou. The research activities are mainly divided into four parts.

(1) Had workshop with relevant local government agencies, including the Labor and Social Security Bureau, Construction Commission and the energy conservation office of Economic and Trade Commission, Energy Development Division of the Development and Reform Commission, Private Economy Commission and Service Industry Development Bureau.

(2) Conducted a field visit to large and small manufacturers that have their own brands and small manufacturers that provide outsourcing services for large enterprises in other places and interviewed managerial staff of these enterprises. The research team also discussed needs and possibility of setting up an local business association with representatives of local small and medium-sized enterprises;

(3) Visited and interviewed solar water heater distributors located in cities, counties, villages and towns;

(4) Interviewed local rural users.

6.3 External Environment for the Development of Solar Water Heater Industry in Dezhou

6.3.1 Social and Economic Conditions of Dezhou

The city of Dezhou is situated in the northwest of Shandong Province. Located in about two hours' driving away from Beijing, Dezhou is known as Southern Gate of Beijing and Northern Gate of Shandong Province. Dezhou is comprised of 11 counties (urban districts) and two economic development zones. The built-up areas of the urban districts cover an area of 46.5 square kilometers. Dezhou had been primarily engaged in traditional agriculture for a long time and was once one of the country's 30 poverty-stricken areas; after years of development, the overall economic strength of Dezhou has reached the medium level of Shandong Province. The private economy of Dezhou is highly developed with a total of 90 thousand private enterprises, the majority of which are small and medium-sized enterprises. Solar heat utilization, central air conditioning and functional sugar are pillar industries of Dezhou. Dezhou has entered a period of accelerated transition towards industrialization. The municipal government set the goal of building a "low-carbon city". One of the 0measures is vigorously developing the solar energy industry.

At the end of 2008, Dezhou had a total population of 5.642 million, of which 4.036 million was agricultural population and 1.426 million was non-agricultural population. There were 665 thousand urban employed persons and 1.02 million

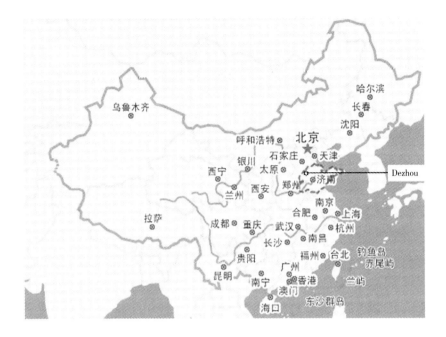

persons who worked outside the city. The registered urban unemployment rate was 3%. The city's minimum wage standard was 500 yuan / month. The per capita disposable income of urban residents was 14,545 yuan, up 17.4% over the previous year; the per capita net income of farmers was 5,659 yuan, up 13.5% over the previous year.

6.3.2 Policy Environment for the Development of Solar Water Heaters in Dezhou

The Chinese government attaches great importance to the development of the renewable energy sector and has made utilization of solar energy an important component of the energy strategy. At the national level, the Energy conservation Law stipulates that the development and use of renewable energy sources shall be encouraged and supported. The Renewable Energy Law further explicitly stipulates that the state shall encourage organizations and individuals to install and use solar water heating systems, solar heating and cooling systems and other solar energy utilization systems. Meanwhile, it also requires "real estate development enterprises to provide necessary conditions for the utilization of solar energy in design and construction of buildings in accordance with the technical specification stipulated in the previous provision". Against the backdrop of the State strongly advocating protecting the ecological environment, developing renewable energy sources and building a resource-saving and environment-friendly society, China's solar water heater industry has been developing rapidly. In 2006, total inventory of solar water heaters across the country was 90 million square meters and the annual output was 18 million square meters, accounting for 53.6% and 78.2% of the world's total respectively.

At the provincial level, Shandong Province promulgated the Energy Conservation Regulations of Shandong Province and other legislation and policy documents to further implement relevant national regulations. The Guidance on Accelerating the Development of the New Energy Industry promulgated in 2009 proposed to further develop solar thermal industry, expand the industrial scale and extend the industrial chain so as to build internationally competitive scale advantages of the industry. In terms of promoting of preferential policies for the use of solar water heaters, the provincial government established a special provincial fund for energy and water conservation and stipulated that hotels rated above three star and provincial universities and vocational schools that use solar collector systems capable of producing more than 20 tons of water above 30 degrees each day could get a subsidy equivalent to 30% of the total construction cost and basic education schools with resident students that use solar collector systems capable of producing more than 5 tons of water above 30 degrees each day could get a subsidy equivalent to 30% of the total construction cost. The amount of funds for subsidizing each project shall not surpass RMB1.5 million yuan.

In Dezhou, the Government not only supports the production of solar water heaters, but also attaches great importance to popularizing the utilization of solar water heaters. Regarding the use of solar water heaters, the municipal government drew up the Implementation Opinions on Promoting the Application of Solar Energy in the Construction Sector in 2007 and decided to continue to implement the "one million roofs" plan, comprehensively promote the integration of solar energy with urban residential buildings, gradually expand the integration of solar energy with public buildings and vigorously implement the "100 Village Bathroom Project" in rural areas during the "Eleventh Five-Year" period. The local government's goal is that the area of solar energy application accounts for more than 50% of the area of newly built buildings in the city and 80% in urban areas by the end of the "Eleventh Five-Year" period and the area of solar energy application accounts for more than 80% of the area of newly built buildings by 2020;solar water heaters will be installed for more than 1000 bathrooms in villages across the city to make Dezhou truly a model city in popularizing the application of solar energy.

Regarding the development of the solar energy heat utilization industry, the municipal government put forward the strategy of accelerating the construction of a solar city and gradually developing the solar energy industry of Dezhou into a strongly competitive industry cluster through measures such as supporting key solar energy enterprises to promote industrial development, enhancing the technical innovation capabilities of the solar energy industry, city brand building and promotion, implementing solar energy demonstration projects, popularization of science and cultural promotion as well as building of the solar valley.

6.3.3　Relevant Government Agencies

In order to promote implementation of the "Solar City" strategy, Dezhou set up a "China Solar City" Strategy Promotion Committee headed by the mayor. Its members include the Development and Reform Commission, Economic

Commission, Private Economy Commission, Urban Planning Bureau, Bureau of Education, Science and Technology Bureau, Environmental Protection Bureau, Service Industry Development Bureau, Tax Bureau, Industrial and Commercial Bureau, Quality Supervision Bureau and other relevant government departments, as well as banks, trade unions, women't federations, radio stations and power supply companies. The Strategy Promotion Committee consists of the Solar City Congress Preparatory Work Leading Group, Solar City Strategy Propaganda Leading Group, Solar Energy Industry Development Work Leading Group and Leading Group of Popularizing the Application of Solar Energy. "The office of the "Solar City" Strategy Propaganda Leading Group is located at the Propaganda Department of the Municipal Party Committee, the office of the Solar Energy Industry Development Work Leading Group is situated at the Municipal Economic Commission and offices of the other two leading groups are both set up at the Municipal Construction Commission.

At present, the division of work between the main relevant agencies is: The Economic Commission is responsible for the formulation of relevant industrial development plans and technological upgrading and investment management of enterprises; the Construction Commission is in charge of popularizing the application of solar water heaters, implementation of the "Million Roofs" and "100 Village Bathroom" plan and the solar energy demonstration project as well as overall planning of the urban landscape of the Solar City; the Propaganda Department takes charge of strengthening the propaganda to enhance the image and popularity of the Solar City. The Development and Reform Commission administrates private enterprises above the designated size and the Private Economy Commission takes responsibility for the development of county-level industrial parks and township and village-level private enterprises. Both the two departments need to strengthen their support for private enterprises in terms of loan and financing policies

6.4   Overview of the Value Chain of Dezhou's Solar Energy Industry

6.4.1   Solar Water Heater Industry Cluster in Dezhou

Dezhou currently is China's largest solar energy production base. Its annual solar energy production capacity reaches more than 3 million square meters, accounting for 70% of the province's total output and about 10% of the total national output. Because Dezhou has been committed to the solar energy industry and popularizing the application of solar energy products, it was awarded the "China Solar City" title jointly by the China Solar Energy Society, China Association of Resources Comprehensive Utilization and China Association of Rural Energy Industry in the year of 2005. In addition, Dezhou also successfully bid to host the 4th International Solar Cities Congress in 2010.

At present, solar energy enterprises of Dezhou are producing a wide range of products including high, medium and low-grade all-glass vacuum tube solar water heaters, and their customers are mainly household users in this area and other areas of the country. With regard to the number of solar water heater manufacturing and sales enterprises in Dezhou, we obtained relevant information from three sources. The data obtained from the Dezhou Municipal Industrial and Commercial Bureau show that Dezhou has a total of more than

260 registered solar water heater manufacturers and distributors, of which more than 40 are manufacturers, including more than 20 key enterprises and other small enterprises and about 220 are distributors. About 10 thousand people are employed at the production and the sales links. Data of the Municipal Economic Commission show that there are nearly one hundred enterprises using solar energy and related enterprise in this area, of which 12 enterprises are above the designated size. Several enterprises we visited thought that there were about 100 solar water heater manufacturers and more distributors in this area. As the data from different sources vary greatly, the research group feel it is very difficult to make an accurate judgment, and can only speculate that the number grasped by the Municipal Economic Commission and Department of Industrial and Commercial is the number of enterprises that have reached a certain size and whose production is relatively stable, while the number provided by insiders is the number of all the enterprises currently engaging in solar water heater production. Among them, besides enterprises that have reached a certain size and whose production is relatively stable as mentioned above, there are also some enterprises with a small production capacity or even engaged in irregular operations.

6.4.2   Solar Water Heater Value Chain in Dezhou

Basic links of the value chain of the solar water heater industry include raw material supply, solar water heater production, value-added production, sales (installation and maintenance services) and end user.

6.4.2.1   Principle Markets

Solar water heaters have been enjoying a rapid development in urban markets. However, such development momentum has been stagnant in recent years. The primary cause is that there are many solar water heater brands in China and their quality and performance can hardly meet consumers' requirements,

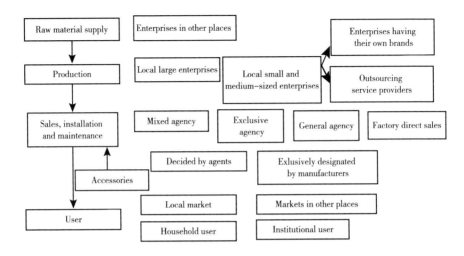

Figure 6-4-1   Diagram of the Value Chain of the Solar Water Heater Industry in Dezhou

especially the lack of good installation and maintenance services has led to a poor reputation of solar water heaters among consumers, dampening consumers' willingness to purchase. In addition, the design of urban buildings hasn't taken into account the installation of water heaters, making it difficult for many urban residents to use solar water heaters. On the contrary, as the rural residents have been enjoying an increasing income in recent years, and there is a demand to develop rural aquaculture, solar water heaters has been popularized relatively quickly. Products of Dezhou's large solar water heater manufacturers are oriented towards urban and rural markets across the country; small and medium-sized enterprises mainly meet the consumer demand of the city and surrounding areas; some enterprises also enjoy certain popularity in other places.

6.4.2.2   End Users

End users of solar water heaters are mainly dispersedly located household users, users of public hot water of collective units and users of hot water of projects integrated with buildings. Urban household users mainly use solar water heaters to provide hot water needed for daily life while rural household users mainly use solar water heaters for livestock breeding. In Dezhou, rural livestock breeders often use solar water heaters. It is reported that farmer households that breed three to five cattle or more than ten pigs will generally buy solar water heaters for providing warm water for mixing cattle feed, for cows to drink and washing cattle. For solar water heaters aimed at household consumers, manufacturers generally adopt the modes of direct selling through franchise stores, agency and distribution, sale through shopping malls and sale through building materials market.

Organization customer groups mainly refer to hotels, restaurants, schools, hospitals and other public places. Hot water projects integrated with buildings refer to large-area application projects in which solar water heaters on buildings are uniformly planned, designed, installed, checked and accepted as well as projects of central hot water supply systems capable of supplying more than 600 liters of hot water. Although the water heaters aiming at the two kinds of users need to be of high quality and excellent after-sales service is required, they sell well and are quite profitable. Only large manufactures can produce such kind of products, and manufacturers generally have dedicated marketing, installation and maintenance teams. In future, solar water heaters aimed at organization customers and projects integrated with buildings will have a relatively large potential for development. But at present, like those produced in the rest of the country, solar water heaters manufactured in Dezhou are mainly oriented towards individual users that install solar water heaters on finished buildings and are in small local systems.

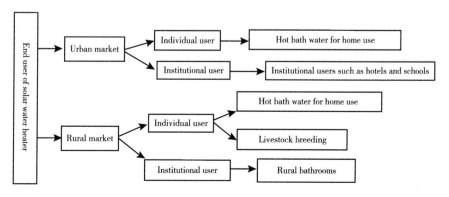

Figure 6-4-2   Diagram of End Users of Solar Water Heaters

The countryside is the major potential market for solar water heaters, so we interviewed some rural users and found the following problems.

(1) There are numerous solar water heater brands in the market, making it difficult for consumers to choose a good one. Although everybody knows that product quality of large enterprises is excellent, prices of their products are relatively high and can hardly meet rural consumers' expectation for low prices.

(2) Distributors do not understand solar water heater products, and sometimes cannot answer consumers' questions correctly;

(3) Follow-up services are inadequate; many manufacturers haven't established an effective after-sales service system. Sometimes users even cannot find after-sales service, and some distributors use substandard accessories, leading to many problems such as water heater leakage;

(4) Spending habits and income levels in rural areas still restrict the popularization of solar water heaters.

6.4.2.3 Manufacturers

Dezhou's solar water heater manufacturers are divided into three categories: enterprises in the first category are aircraft carrier-type enterprises. They have diverse product types, possess independent research and development capabilities, master patented technologies and enjoy nationwide popularity. Enterprises in this category include the Himin Company and Yijianeng Company under Himin Solar Energy Group. The Second type is consisted of regular small fleet-type enterprises and are small and medium-sized solar water heater manufacturers. Enterprises in this category are relatively regular, having their own brands and at least enjoying certain popularity in their areas. Enterprises in the third category are "irregular troop" enterprises. Their sizes are small, production technologies are backward and quality management is chaotic. Some enterprises do not follow prescribed rules in operation and engage in shortchanging on work and materials, counterfeiting of famous brands and false propaganda. Enterprises involved in our research are enterprise in the first two categories.

(1) Large Enterprises

Himin Company, the representative of enterprises in the first category, is the world's largest solar water heater manufacturer and popularizes more than 2 million square meters of solar water heaters each year. It not only produces solar water heaters suitable for household and institutional users under different climate, water quality and building conditions, but also ambitiously develops markets in areas of integration of solar energy with buildings and solar thermal power generation. Under the local government's support, Himin Group has been building a solar valley with a total planned area of 5000 mus, which will be used as a solar energy industry gathering place that integrates supporting industries such as solar energy manufacturing, technical research and development, personnel training and tourism. In addition to direct publicity and promotion aimed at brands, spreading solar energy knowledge and popularizing popular science education are also marketing strategies of Himin Company. The "nationwide popularization of solar energy science motorcade long march activity" of Himin Group played an important role in promoting solar energy knowledge and the Himin brand. This large enterprise not only won the favor of local financial institutions, but also obtained venture capital investments of outside sources. In December 2008, the U.S. investment bank Goldman Sachs and CDH International Investment Company injected nearly 100 million U.S. dollars into Himin Group.

Himin Company directly hired more than 7,000 employees, of which managerial staff account for 1/3 and front-line operators and general clerks account for 2/3. The average age of employees is 29 years old and wages of ordinary employees are at the local medium level. Front-line employees mostly have received secondary education, vocational education and senior middle school education; managerial staff generally hold college degree or above. In terms of the type of labor contracts, the first labor contract signed usually has a term of one year for operators, two years for general managerial staff, three years for technicians and five years for senior managerial staff. There are about 60 thousand external personnel engaging in distribution and services of Himin products Himin Company now is trying to convert some of them into its own employees. The reason is that distributors generally operate on a small scale, so their employees are poorly remunerated and many of them are not covered by social insurance, leading to a high employee turnover and a lack of skill accumulation, which is disadvantageous for the development of the Himin brand.

In the present relevant majors of vocational technical schools and universities are still considerably different from the specialty of solar heat utilization, so Himin Group innovatively tried a variety of methods of training and education. One method was setting up the "Himin Class" in cooperation with some universities. Special teaching materials are used and the curriculum is more specialized, so that students will understand the production process of Himin, skills required and corporate culture in the school. The first batch of "Himin Class" graduates have already come to work at Himin. It is said they are very enthusiastic about their work and integrated into the enterprise very quickly, solving the problems of gap between the theory learned by university graduates and practice, their difficulty of adapting to the corporate culture and high turnover that previously troubled the enterprise. The second method was establishing the Himin Vocational Secondary School, College of Engineering & Technology and Business School. At present, these three schools mainly serve Himin Group: Business School is used for in-house training to provide opportunities for outstanding in-house employees to enhance management capabilities; the College of Engineering & Technology recruits students from society and mainly trains managerial personnel, sales directors and engineering, sales and design personnel for Himin Group; the Vocational Secondary School trains production, installation and marketing personnel. The third method was that the in-house training department trained the enterprise's employees and distributors on a regular basis. In addition, in view of the fact that many existing professional standards can not fully conform to the characteristics of the solar energy industry, Himin Group has been developing targeted professional qualification standards and training materials.

Major Problems Currently Besetting Large Solar Water Heater Manufacturers:

(a) There are few national standards for standard solar water heaters, especially there is a lack of detailed requirements for reliability during long-term use, consequently many products are unable to reach the advertised life cycle, affecting the reputation of the entire industry;

(b) Some small manufacturers do not pay attention to product quality, produce fake and shoddy products or resort to abnormal methods of competition, not only affecting the development of the industry, but also posing considerable risks to users' personal and property safety;

(c) Government regulation is inadequate, the cost of cracking down on fake products is too high for enterprises;

(b) There is a lack of professionals within the industry, enterprises poach each other's talents and the brain drain problem of big enterprises is quite prominent;

(e) Newly recruited university graduates have difficulty adapting to their professions and enterprises. Newly recruited university graduates' majors do not fit enterprises' needs and the theory they learned are divorced from reality, so it takes them a long time to master professional skills. In addition, many young people have difficulty integrating themselves with the corporate culture, lack loyalty to their professions and enterprises, so the turnover is high.

(f) Recruitment of workers and students is quite difficult. The entire society doesn't think much of blue-collar occupations. So, despite vocational secondary schools offer scholarships to students from poor families and guarantee jobs after graduation, they still feel it is quite hard to recruit students;

(g) Employees' expectation for continuously growing enterprises to pay higher wages is in conflict with enterprises' need for reinvestment. Employees believe that enterprises develop quickly and expect wage increases, but enterprises want to develop further and activities such as research and development, training and promotion of their own brands require a lot of money, so they want to keep the wage level at the local medium level;

(h) At present, all product parts are produced by Himin Company itself. Although the enterprise wants to outsource part of its operations, it is worried about the difficulty of quality control after outsourcing due to inadequate development of the industry.

(2) Situation of Regular Small and Medium-sized Enterprises

Enterprises in the second category are small and medium-sized enterprises engaging in quite regular production. Such enterprises are divided into two types. Enterprises of the first type have their own brands and enjoy certain popularity in their areas and surrounding areas and their sales volume grows steadily. Their mode of production is to manufacture their own water tanks and stands, and then purchase evacuated tube collectors from other places to assemble them into finished products and sell the products under their own brands. Enterprises of the second type are production outsourcing service providers of large domestic manufacturers and produce water tanks and stands for enterprises awarding the contract in accordance with the technical standard and process provided by them. All in all, these enterprises have low degrees of automation, mostly use semi-automatic and manual production and employ few people. Many of them also concurrently run other businesses, but generally they will have 30 to 50 people engaging in solar water heater production.

Small Enterprise Case 1:

It is a medium-sized enterprise in its area and has its own brand, and it sells around 2000 solar water heaters each year. It buys vacuum tubes and produces water cylinders and stands itself. Its products are priced at a low to medium level and sold in both urban and rural areas. The principle market is Dezhou. Wages of sales personnel are composed of basic wage plus 10% sales commission; most employees have been working for quite a long time. Installation personnel are all covered by commercial insurance (the local policy is that enterprises must participate in old-age insurance and medical insurance, other social insurance is not mandatory). The focus of future market development is rural areas due to the rapid development of livestock breeding; urban market may develop slowly because nowadays buildings in cities are all high-rise on which solar water heaters cannot be installed.

Small Enterprise Case 2:

The enterprise has been developing quite fast. It sold only a few hundred solar water heaters in the first year of production. That figure grew to more than three thousand in the second year and is expected to reach ten thousand this year. It produces middle-end products and the principle market is Dezhou's surrounding rural areas. It has more than 300 distributors, mostly exclusive agents. It currently has more than 100 employees, of which over 30 engaging in solar water heater production. Besides solar water heaters, it also produces electronic instruments. Production is divided into low and high seasons. It is the low season when the weather is hot. It does not give employees time off even during the low season, or it will suffer loss of employees. Skill requirements for employees are not too high, and newly recruited employees generally will be able to operate skillfully in about one month. Different manufacturers use different equipment and production processes. Employees switching to a new enterprise must be retrained and go through a certain practice period. The average wage of employees is more than RMB1000 yuan; wages of the best production workers can reach as much as more than RMB3, 000 yuan; wages of new comers are about 700 to 800 Yuan. The employee turnover is not very high.

Small Enterprise Case 3:

The enterprise is purely an outsourcing service provider and organizes production according to the raw materials, equipment, processes and drawings provided by large enterprises. The enterprise has a total of more than 130 employees, 36 of which engage in solar water heater production. Its annual sales reach RMB 12 million yuan. It produced products of its own brand prior to 2000, but due to small enterprises' difficulty of creating their own brands and the high cost of development and promotion channels, it no longer produced products of its own brand after cooperating with large enterprises. Production workers engage in skilled work with low technical content and earn about RMB1200 yuan each month. Early spring is the high season when the enterprise often lacks workers; it does not need so many people during the low season. The employee turnover is quite high and only 50-60% of them can stay there for 1 to 2 years.

Problems Currently Besetting Small and Medium-sized Solar Water Heater Manufacturers.

(a) There are few national standards for solar water heaters, leading to numerous manufacturers and a great number of solar water heater brands. "It is even difficult for distributors to distinguish between the true and the false, let alone consumers". This has a negative impact on the entire industry's development.

(b) Small and medium-sized enterprises do not have the ability to promote their own brands. There are many solar water heater brands on the market. To break the siege, manufacturers must step up promotion. The manager of an enterprise thought that "the key to product success is quality, publicity and promotion and reasonable price." The enterprise once advertised itself on a local TV station, which worked well for enhancing the popularity of its brand and products. However, "the cost of advertising on TV stations is high for small and medium-sized enterprises, so this method can only be used occasionally rather than in the long term".

(c) Governments mainly favor large enterprises and pay little attention to and provide little support for small and medium-sized enterprises. An entrepreneur thought that "there is only one big tree with no branches and leaves in this area" and expected the government to increase support for small and medium-sized enterprises. For example, the governments' procurement projects shall be open and transparent to allow small and medium-sized enterprises to participate in competition and support shall be given to small and medium-sized enterprises in areas such as land used for factory buildings.

(d) It is difficult for small and medium-sized enterprises to get financing. There is no government-funded guarantor institution and only a fully commercial guarantor institution in this area, so small and medium-sized enterprises that can not provide collateral still have difficulty in obtaining funds;

(e) The test fee is high. The local technical supervision department charges RMB6000 yuan for testing each type of solar water heaters, which is hardly acceptable for small enterprises;

(f) Small and medium-sized enterprises are limited in both production and financial capacity and can hardly participate in government or real estate developers' tenders alone. In addition, developers often pay by installments, which is unbearable for small and medium-sized enterprises.

(3) Problem of Industry Cluster

Although Dezhou has a large number of solar water heater manufacturers, which to some extent has formed an industry cluster, there is little communication between manufacturers, let alone division of work and cooperation. There is a lack of trust between large and small enterprises. Large enterprises think that small businesses do not know much about the industry, fall behind in quality management and affect the image of the industry while small and medium-sized enterprises complain that large enterprises take too many resources. Local small and medium-sized enterprises hope that large enterprises can focus on the development and production of high-end solar energy products and leave low and medium-end markets to small and medium-sized enterprises; the local government hopes that leading enterprises can prompt large enterprises to outsource the production of low and medium-end products and promote the development of supporting service enterprises, such as enterprises engaging in sales and processing of parts and accessories. However, given the current situation, it is very difficult to form such a cooperation arrangement in the short term.

Some local small enterprises hope to set up an association so as to increase the ability to lobby the government and jointly participate in government tenders; prompt local banks to provide financing for small and medium-sized enterprises by providing joint guarantee for each other and make the association a platform for communication between solar energy manufacturers. However, the government wants large enterprises to participate in the association, and thinks the association cannot represent the local solar water heater industry otherwise. In addition, the government also hopes to further cooperation

Table 6-4-1　SWOT Analysis of Manufacturing Stage

Advantages	Disadvantages
• Local large enterprises have strong research and development capabilities and have successfully applied to become national laboratories;	• There are many small and medium-sized enterprises with little science and technology input, weak independent innovation ability and low product level;
• Local large enterprises have professional testing centers and are willing to share them with other enterprises (but the test results do not play a role in approving marketing of products and only play a role of technical guidance);	• Market development is not standardized, many enterprises engage in irregular operations, implement management in a disorderly manner and even produce fake and shoddy products, affecting the industry's overall reputation;
• There are local training schools that can train professionals specializing in solar heat utilization;	• There is a lack of appropriate human resources, especially professional and technical personnel;
• An industry cluster has already been formed and enjoys some popularity throughout the country;	• Small and medium-sized enterprises haven't spent enough effort on publicity and promotion and the popularity of their brands is low both locally and in other places;
• Local large, medium and small-sized enterprises can meet consumers' demand for products at different prices.	• There are many manufacturers in this area, but raw materials and accessories are purchased respectively by various enterprises from other places, thus increasing the cost.

Continued

Opportunities	Obstacles
• The market potential of solar water heaters is big. As income of rural residents increases, their demand for hot bath water has been growing rapidly. In addition, the development of livestock breeding drives the demand for solar water heaters; • As development of solar energy water heaters is in line with China's sustainable development strategy, the government attaches great importance to development of the industry and has formulated preferential policies; • As a solar city, Dezhou enjoys high reputation across the country, which helps enhance the brand popularity of local enterprises; • Dezhou will host the 4th International Solar Cities Congress in 2010, which helps further enhance the reputation of the city's solar energy enterprises and products.	• Incomes and spending habits of rural residents may limit the further expansion of rural markets; • The country's standard system for solar water heaters is imperfect and the industry regulation is ineffective, resulting in poor quality products that interfere with the market and affect the development of the industry; • At present, many urban buildings are not suitable for the installation of solar water heaters. In addition, in order to maintain the appearance of buildings, some local real estate developers prohibit owners from installing solar water heaters in property management; • There is a lack of good installation and maintenance services, dampening users' confidence in solar water heaters and affecting the industry's reputation; • There is a lack of relevant external services, small and medium-sized enterprises have difficulties getting loans and the product test fee is high; • The government's preferential policies lack operational rules and cannot benefit enterprises; • The government's attention to and support for small and medium-sized enterprises are inadequate.

between enterprises through the association to promote division of labor and cooperation between large enterprises and small and medium-sized enterprises and cause large enterprises to share their research and development, testing and training capabilities with small and medium-sized enterprises. Regarding this matter, large enterprises think they are not at the same level with small enterprises and have no time to participate as their business is undergoing rapid development. Although the government hopes to carry forward the building of the association as soon as possible, it is in an awkward situation for the above-mentioned reasons.

6.4.2.4　Sales, Installation and Maintenance Services

Solar water heaters used for projects are mostly directly sold and installed by manufacturers. Solar water heaters aimed at individual users are generally sold through several distribution channels, including agents, factory outlets, market monopoly and project market sale, of which the use of agents is a quite common practice. Sales, installation and maintenance services are generally done by distributors, large manufacturers also have specialized technical department and service hotline to provide technical support for distributors. The service link has a very remarkable effect on providing employment opportunities with personnel engaging in sales, installation & maintenance and warehousing accounting for 80% of the personnel on the entire chain. The size of distributors' businesses in urban areas ranges from 5 - 6 people (small) to more than 100 people (large), the average size is 10 - 20 people. Agents in rural areas are quite small, and some are simply family-run shops.

There Are Several Modes of Cooperation Between Manufacturers and Distributors.

The first is exclusive agency. Large enterprises' requirement for exclusive agency is: the initial amount of accounts payable collected is RMB400-500 thousand yuan in provincial capitals, RMB300 thousand yuan in prefecture-level cities and RMB200 thousand yuan in county-level cities. In addition, an image store covering an area of no less than 100 square meters shall be built and equipped with store manager, after-sales service managers, service personnel and equipment such as telephone, fax machine and computer. Small and medium-sized enterprises' requirement for exclusive agency is a little lower. As long as distributors buy a certain number of solar water heaters at the first time, they can buy any number of solar water heaters thereafter. Exclusive distributors can only sell solar water heaters of a single manufacturer, but they can sell plumbing and heating equipment, hardware equipment and other products at the same time. Manufacturers do not have too many requirements for the location and area of distributors' stores. For example, a manufacturer we visited requires county-level agents to buy 10 solar water heaters at a time and pay a deposit of RMB 1,000 yuan to prevent violations of the manufacturer's rules such as driving down the price, thus avoiding affecting other distributors. In other words, to become a county-level agent of a kind of product which enjoys a certain reputation in its area, one has to buy 10 water heaters at first and the start-up cost including the store rent is about less than RMB 50 thousand yuan.

A Case of Distributor

The distributor just started selling solar water heaters in February 2009 and has sold a total of more than 50 units by July. It can earn RMB300 yuan each unit. It mainly solicits consumers through its store and sometimes promotes sales in the countryside. The success of its marketing so far is mainly attributed to the sales promotion carried out by the manufacturer in the first half of the year that cut the price a lot. In addition, relatives and friends have recommended many customers. Summer is the low season for water heaters when people make do with cold water bath. Although the rural market is large and demand of livestock breeding is big, it is not an easy job mainly because farmers do not have much money. We did not know much about the brand when we chose it and just heard that the brand was well spoken of by the public. Only after we became an agent did we find that the enterprise hadn't done much in promotion, many farmers did not know the product and the product did not sell well. The manufacturer once advertised itself on a local radio station and the effect was quite good. Usually we distribute color ads provided by the manufacturer. As Ads of various manufacturers are similar, farmers do not know how to make their choice.

The second is general agency in which the relationship between manufacturers and agents is relatively loose. Manufacturers do not restrict agents from selling other manufacturers' solar water heaters and agents are also not obligated to buy manufacturers' products in advance. Manufacturers only display some products at agents' places, and provide agent identification code for agents. This form of agency is generally used by small manufacturers and distributors generally have selling plumbing and heating equipment and hardware equipment as their main business. These stores sell solar water heaters of many brands. We saw that many stores were hanging the boards and promotional materials of solar water heaters of several brands.

The third is cross-management, which is a distribution mode currently tried by Himin. Many distributors are small in size, so they cannot manage employees well and their employees are often poorly remunerated. In order to reduce the turnover of their core employees and increase skill accumulation, Himin has begun to try the practice of paying basic wages and social insurance premiums for distributors' core employees and employees only receiving commission from distributors.

Large manufacturers have specialized training for distributors that covers skills of installation, maintenance, marketing and management. Training provided for distributors by small and medium-sized manufacturers is relatively simple.

Many distributors themselves sell plumbing and heating equipment, so usually after learning with technicians sent to install heaters for users by manufacturers once or twice, distributors' personnel will be able to carry out installation and maintenance independently. If distributors encounter technical problems in future services, manufacturers will provide support. In addition, large manufacturers can provide start-up loans for distributors.

In terms of the profit distribution mode, usually manufacturers set the market price and then sell products to distributors at a discount. The price difference is distributors' profit. In Dezhou, distributors earn a profit of 200 to 300 Yuan from each solar water heater sold. Another source of distributors' income is the profits from providing accessories to users. Manufacturers usually only provide water heaters and stands, to use water heaters, users must also have accessories such as indoor pipes, fittings, showers and faucets. Accessories are generally purchased and provided to users by distributors. In order to increase profits, some distributors will use some defective products, resulting in problems such as water leakage or seepage. Meanwhile, rural consumers often buy on credit and will reduce payment after finding quality defects in subsequent use, so the profit margin of distributors may shrink further.

Major Problems Currently Faced by Distributors:

(1) Many distributors themselves do not understand solar water heater and have difficulties selecting brands. The manager of a manufacturer we interviewed thought that " less than 1% of distributors understand the products and materials, all manufacturers will say that their own products are good and distributors cannot differentiate"; a distributor interviewed indicated that the reason why he chose the brand was that "he saw the TV ad";

(2) Distributors' installation and maintenance personnel lack professional skills and safety protection knowledge. Large enterprises think that compared with home appliances such as ordinary water heaters and air-conditioners, installation and maintenance of solar water heaters are much more complex. The former involves standard operations, while solar water heater has no operation standards, different installation methods are used for different climate and building conditions and a variety of knowledge and skills are involved, so the skill of installation and maintenance personnel is very important. But the small and medium-sized manufacturers and distributors we interviewed haven't realized this yet;

(3) There is a lack of trust between distributors and manufacturers. Some distributors complain that manufacturers are too domineering and set rigorous conditions for agency, sales personnel make many promises but often fail to fulfill them; some manufacturers accuse distributors of failing to conduct business honestly, "emphasizing sale and ignoring follow-up services" and even

using substandard accessories which will consequently affect manufacturers' credibility;

(4) Manufacturers' support for distributors is inadequate; sales personnel do not understand the basics of solar water heaters and the characteristics of products sold, so it is difficult for them to sell products to consumers;

(5) As small and medium-sized manufacturers haven't put much effort into publicity, rural consumers do not know these brands, therefore, distributors are under great sales pressure and the products do not sell well;

(6) Rural consumers usually do not have cash until autumn, so they often buy solar water heaters on credit. Distributors need to repeatedly press for payment, which is a heavy burden. After finding defects of the product quality in use, consumers will often pay less, further reducing distributors' profit margin.

Table 6-4-2   SWOT Analysis of the Distribution Stage

Advantages	Disadvantages
• It does not require a large amount of funds to become distributors of small and medium-sized manufacturers; • The requirement for installation and maintenance skills is not very high, people with experience in installation and maintenance of plumbing and heating equipment can learn very quickly.	• The solar water heater industry as a whole lacks a sound follow-up service system, consumer satisfaction with services of the solar water heater industry is low; • Agents themselves do not know much about solar water heaters, so it is difficult for them to select solar water heaters with good quality and prices suitable for the affordability of local consumers; • Many agents are not well-educated and their awareness and level of management are insufficient, service processes are not standardized and management systems are imperfect; • Sellers' employees do not have enough service skills, lack strong service awareness and are replaced frequently; • An agent for big brand products needs a lot of investment and has to accept rigorous conditions. As small distributors' bargaining power is relatively weak, they can only enjoy a relatively small profit margin. Some distributors use cheap accessories, affecting the use of water heaters. • There is a lack of external service providers for the solar water heater industry in this area.

Continued

Opportunities	Obstacles
• As the income of rural residents has increased, they require higher quality of life, and livestock breeders' demand for solar water heaters is big, so the market potential for solar water heaters is huge in this area; • The government has been vigorously promoting the use of solar water heaters.	• There are many solar water heater brands on the market, and strenuous small and medium-sized manufacturers haven' t launched strong promotion of their products, leading to low popularity of their brands, therefore, it is difficult for distributors to make sales; • Many farmers buy the products on credit, and it is very difficult to press for payment

6.4.2.5   Raw Material Supply

For solar water heater manufacturers in Dezhou, raw materials include chemicals, machinery, electronics, glass and many other materials, of which semi-finished evacuated glass envelopes and accessories have a bigger effect on enterprises. Semi-finished evacuated glass envelopes purchased by small and medium sized manufacturers in Dezhou mainly come from 3 to 4 enterprises across the country, such as Beijing Linuo, Beijing Suoyang, Tengzhou Guangpu and Yanzhou Jindun, all of which are famous brands. Stands are also produced and supplied by specialized manufacturers. Parts and accessories of solar water heaters are usually purchased from Linyi of Shandong, because there is a special wholesale market there. Although Dezhou has many solar water heater enterprises, it lacks a distributing center for relevant accessories. Many enterprises think that purchasing accessories from Linyi that is more than 400 kilometers away from Dezhou increases the transportation cost, so they suggest opening such an accessories terminal market in this area.

6.5　Suggestions for Improving the Solar Water Heater Value Chain

In conclusion, Dezhou's solar water heater industry has obvious advantages, but the constraints are also very prominent. An industry cluster of a certain size, the city's popularity in the solar energy industry and the municipal government's vigorous support for the production and use of solar water heaters are all advantages for developing the industry in Dezhou. However, problems such as irregularity in the development of the industry, lag of after-sales services, lack of human resources and inadequate government support for small and medium-sized enterprises also restrict further development of the industry. It is necessary that the government and enterprises jointly take measures to improve the industry's development environment, standardize the industry's market order, purify the industry's development environment, promote technical innovation, enhance enterprises' competitiveness and build a mode of win-win cooperation between various links of the value chain.

6.5.1　Creating a Conducive Macro-policy Environment

Firstly, it is necessary to further standardize the industry's market order and purify the industry's development environment. While improving the solar water heater technical standards system to provide safeguard for the industry's healthy development, we also have to strengthen market supervision and crack down on illegal acts of producing and selling fake and shoddy products.

Secondly, we should formulate preferential support policies that are operable and in favor of the industry's development. "The Renewable Energy Law" and "the Circular Economy Promotion Law" created a broad environment for the development of the solar water heater industry, but the two laws alone cannot promote healthy and stable development of the entire industry. It is necessary to strengthen policy support and provide support for the solar water heater industry in terms of financial, fiscal, tax, technology, construction, and consumer policies. For example, we can encourage enterprises to use matching funds for development and technical transformation projects through income tax relief and other means; classify solar energy heat utilization a building energy-saving technology that enjoys preferential treatment for building energy conservation; simplify the construction permit system for the installation of solar water heating systems and actively guide enterprises to voluntarily prompt the design and construction combining solar water heater and building in new residential projects; include solar water heaters into the government's green procurement list and establish brands designated for procurement by the government; subsidize the consumption.

Thirdly, we should formulate policies conducive to the reservation of human resources and development of emerging green industries, including the solar water heater industry. We should also further improve the formulation and promotion of green employment standards. We found out that people engaging in jobs relating to solar power utilization were closely related to the production of solar water heaters. The state has a professional standard in this regard and there are also organizations providing relevant training, but none of the enterprises we surveyed has heard of this professional standard, let alone participated in training. The solar water heater industry is an emerging industry and suffers a serious shortage of both human resources and training resources. It is recommended that the state take into account emerging industries' demand for human resources when formulating national plans for the development of job skills. It is recommended that mature technologies of green industries be introduced into training programs and support be given to organizations that promote green technologies and workers who participate in green skills training courses. In addition, many training and education institutions do not have relevant curriculum, so enterprises need to spend a lot on developing training materials and courses. The cost of employee training may exceed 2.5% of the gross payroll (turnover tax may be exempted). In this regard, we suggest that the state introduce relevant policies to provide relevant preferential tax policies for enterprises in emerging green industries that conduct training on their own.

6.5.2 Strengthening Support for Small and Medium-sized Enterprises

Like the home appliance and motorcycle markets, the solar water heater market is likely to undergo reshuffle in future. Only large enterprises can survive and develop. However, rural residents are limited by their income levels and spending habits and differences in their requirements for solar water heater products have widened, so small and medium-sized enterprises' low and medium-end products will still have a big market space for quite some time in future. Therefore, the policy support should be guided by the market demand and differentiation according to enterprises' sizes should be avoided. Seen from the perspective of future development, products' technical content and variability, distribution channel and quality of after-sales services will be important conditions for the survival and development of solar water heater enterprises, yet these three factors are precisely the weaknesses of many small and medium-sized enterprises. Therefore, it is necessary to strengthen the support for small and medium-sized enterprises by starting from the following several aspects:

- Encouraging small and medium-sized enterprises to carry out technical innovation and transferring technologies to small and medium-sized enterprises to enable them to improve product design, product quality and variability so as to enhance the competitiveness of their products;

• Strengthening training for managers of small and medium-sized manufacturing enterprises and sales enterprises to enhance their management capabilities;

• Establishing an association of small and medium-sized solar water heater enterprises to promote self-discipline of enterprises and encourage cooperation among small and medium-sized enterprises, such as purchasing raw materials together to enhance their bargaining power and reduce the purchase cost, participating in bidding together and providing joint loan guarantee for each other.

• Providing financial support for small and medium-sized enterprises to solve their difficulties in financing, and provide conditions for them growing stronger and bigger;

• Stepping up promotion of local brands through a variety of means such as participating in exhibitions under the government's centralized organization.

6.5.3 Improving Follow-up Services

Solar water heaters must be used in coordination with water, electrical works and connected with various channels. We can say the follow-up installation service is of crucial importance for the use of solar water heaters, hence the saying "thirty percent product, seventy percent installation" in the industry.

In addition, a special marketing mode aimed at the rural market is the key to expanding the rural market. Many manufacturers have found the great potential of the rural market has, but they cannot find their way in regarding the two bottlenecks of lack of marketing channels and inadequacy of follow-up services that restrict the development of the solar water heater industry, we suggest taking measures to improve the follow-up service system. Specific suggestions include:

• Developing professional qualification standards and training materials specifically for solar water heater installation and maintenance personnel, formulating unified assessment standards and organizing efforts to carry out skill training for installation and maintenance personnel to improve the quality of after-sales services of solar water heaters;

• Helping distributors establish service processes and improve the management system;

• Carrying out training for distributors in rural areas and small and medium-sized cities, which mainly covers the basics of solar water heaters, skills and strategies of prompting solar water heaters to local consumers, management skills for operating enterprises as well as financial knowledge;

• Urging manufacturers to participate in designing and providing training for distributors and installation and maintenance personnel and improving the relationship between manufacturers and distributors to build trust and achieve win-win.

• Providing targeted training for starting businesses and small loans for people who intend to engage in solar water heater sales services.

References

Anne Berlin Blackman, Jack Luskin, and Robert Guillemin. 1999. Programs for Promoting Sustainable Consumption in the United State. University of Massachusetts Press.

Burtis, P., Epstein, B., and Hwang, R. 2004. "Creating the California Cleantech Cluster." Working Paper of the Environmental Entrepreneurs and Natural Resources Defense Council.

http://www.e2.org/ext/doc/9.8.2004CreatingCaliforniaCleantechCluster.pdf.

Emma Graham-Harrison. 2007. "China Plans $265 Billion Renewables Spending." Reuters, 4 September.

Howard Geller. 2005. The Experience with Energy Efficiency Policies and Programs in IEA Countries, Learning from the Critics. International Energy Agency.

Janet L. Sawin. 2004. "Mainstreaming Renewable Energy in the 21st Century." Worldwatch Paper 169.

Jeremy Lovell. 2007. "European Businesses Go Green Fast." Reuters.

http://www.planetark.com/dailynewsstory.cfm/newsid/40831/story.htm.

Lisa Mastny. 2003. "Purchasing Power: Harnessing Institutional Procurement for People and the Planet." Worldwatch Paper 166.

Michael Renner. 2000. "Working for the Environment: A Growing Source of Jobs." Worldwatch Paper 152.

McKinsey Global Institute. 2007. "Curbing Global Energy Demand Growth:

The Energy Productivity Opportunity".

http://www.mckinsey.com/mgi/reports/pdfs/Curbing_Global_Energy/MGI_C urbing_Global_Energy_full_report.pdf

Norman Myers and Jennifer Kent. 2001. Perverse Subsidies: How Tax Dollars Can Undercut the Environment and the Economy. Island Press.

Organization for Economic Co-operation and Development. 2002. Towards Sustainable Consumption: An Economic Conceptual Framework. Environment Directorate Press.

Paul Hawken, Amory Lovins, and L. Hunter Lovins. 1999. Natural Capitalism: Creating the Next Industrial Revolution. Little Brown Company.

Prescott. 2007. "Low-carbon Economy to Curb Global Warming—Britain in Action." Environmental Protection.

Resources and Social Security Ministry. 2008. China Labor Statistics 2008. China Statistics Press.

Richard Ottinger and Nadia Czachor. 2007. "Bringing Down the Barriers." World Conservation.

Roger Bezdek. 2007. Renewable Energy and Energy Efficiency: Economic Drivers for the 21st Century. Report for the American Solar Energy Society, Boulder press.

Ryan Keefe, Jay Griffin, and John D. Graham. 2007. "The Benefits and Costs of New Fuels and Engines for Cars and Light Trucks". Pardee Rand Graduate School Working Paper, WR-537-PRGS.

Scientific Standard Department of CEPA and CAEPI. 2007. Guide Book on Market Supply and Demand in China Environmental Protection Industry 2006. China Environmental Science Press.

SSB. 2008. China Statistics Yearbook 2008. China Statistics Press.

SSB and MEP. 2008. China Environment Statistical Yearbook 2008. China Statistics Press.

SSB and MEP. 2006. China Environment Statistical Yearbook 2006. China Statistics Press.

State Forestry Bureau. 2008. China Forestry Yearbook 2008. China Forestry Press.

Statistics Department of SSB and General department of NEB. 2008. China Energy Statistical Yearbook 2008. China Statistics Press.

UNEP. 2007. "Indian Solar Loan Programme."

http://www.uneptie.org/energy/act/fin/india/.

United Nations Framework Convention on Climate Change. 2007. "Investment and Financial Flows to Address Climate Change." Background Paper.

http://unfccc.int/files/cooperation_and_support/financial_mechanism/application/pdf/background_paper.pdf.

United Nations Framework Convention on Climate Change. 2007. Investment and Financial Flows to Address Climate Change. Background Paper.

http://unfccc.int/files/cooperation_and_support/financial_mechanism/application/pdf/background_paper.pdf.

UK Department for Environment, Food and Rural Affairs and Trade Unions Sustainable Development Advisory Committee. 2005. "A Fair and Just Transition - Research report for Greening the Workplace."

UNDP. 2007. Human Development Report 2007/2008. Palgrave Macmillan Press.

http://www.unep.org/labour_environment/TUAssembly/ref_docs/TUSDAC_Greening_the_Workplace_EN.pdf.

UNEP, ILO, and ITUC. 2007. Green Employment: Towards Sustainable Work in a Low-Carbon World.

http://www.unep.org/publications/search/pub_details_s.asp?ID=4002

Wang Zhen. 2007. "Global Renewable Energy Development." International Economic Cooperation.

World Business Council for Sustainable Development. 2007. Doing Business with the World: The New Role of Corporate Leadership in Global Development.

Xu Songling. 1997. "World Environment Industry Development Perspective." China Environmental Protection Industry.

Zhou Hongchun. 2002. "An International Comparison of Environmental Protection Policies." Energy Saving and Environmental Protection.

Postscript

The subject research was provided with funds and technical support from ILO Beijing Office. In the course of the project research, Ms. Marja Paavilainen (the project supervisor), Mr. Zhang Xubiao, Mr. Zhu Changyou, Mr. Zuozuomucong, Ms. Zhou Jie and Ms. Pan Wei from ILO Beijing Office, had provided a lot of reference data for the research, opportunities for communication and discussion as well as specific suggestions and assistance for our work. Also, Ms. Ivanka Mamic and Mr. Vincent Jugault in ILO Bankok Office as well as Mr. Peter Poschen and Mr. Liu Xu in the headquarters of ILO in Geneva had provided valuable opinions and suggestions for our research scheme and research reports. Besides, our task group obtained specific guidance from Dai Xiaochu and Qian Xiaoyan, both of whom are respectively the Deputy Director and the Division Director in the Department of International Cooperation, Ministry of Human Resources and Social Security of the People's Republic of China. In the process of our selecting industries for investigation, Ms. Zheng Yan from Chinese Academy of Social Sciences and Professor Yu Enhai from North China Electric Power University had offered enthusiastic consultation help. During the early-stage design and the later-stage discussion of the subject, strong support had also been provided by relevant comrades from units such as National Energy Administration, Department of Environment and Resources and Department of Climate Change of the National Development and Reform Commission, Department of Science, Technology and Standards of the Ministry of Environmental Protection, Department of Science and Technology of the Ministry of Housing and Urban-Rural Development, State Forestry Administration, Energy Institute of the National Development and Reform Commission, Policy Research Center for Environment and Economy of the Ministry of Environmental Protection, China Association of Environmental Protection Industry, China National Sand Control and Desert Industry Society, China Urban Water Association, China Solar Thermal Industry Federation, Academy of Macroeconomic Research of China Academy of Social Sciences. In addition, relevant departments of Tianjin City and Inner Mongolia Autonomous Region offered great support for our conduction of the investigation. To their guidance and help, our task group expresses sincere gratitude.

The subject of "Research on Green Employment in China" was undertaken and completed by the task group of the Institute for Labor Studies of the Ministry of Human Resources and Social Security of the People's Republic of China. The subject was led by You Jun, the former director of the Institute for Labor Studies of the Ministry of Human Resources and Social Security (the present director of the Department of Rural Social Insurance of the Ministry of Human Resources and Social Security), and coordinated specifically by Researcher Zhang Libin, the director of the Employment and Labor Market Research Office of the Institute for Labor Studies, including the following members: Yin Manxue, Liao Jun, Li Hong, Sun Yuxiang and Yuan Xiaohui. Specific division of labor to the book is as below: Director You Jun provided the general idea and the framework arrangement; Researcher Zhang Libin took the responsibility for the first chapter "Introduction to Development of Green Employment" and the second chapter "Research on Green Emplayment in China" ; Research Associate Yin Manxue undertook the forth chapter "Laws and Policies for Green Employment" and the sixth chapter "Case Study: Value Chain Analysis of Solar Water Heater Industry in Dezhou City"; Doctor Liao Jun wrote the third chapter "International Research on Green Employment"; Research Associate Li Hong completed the fifth chapter "Evaluation of Social Environment for Developing Green Employment in China". Meanwhile, Sun

Yuxiang participated in the data analysis of the questionnaires; Yuan Xiaohui took part in the research on the value chain analysis of the solar water heater industry in Dezhou City. The manuscript was approved by Director You Jun and Researcher Zhang Libin.

In the end, we would like to thank China Academy of Labor and Social Security Sciences for the funds support and the editors in Social Sciences Academic Press for their hard work, without which the book will not be published.

Task Group of "Research on Green Employment in China"

September 23, 2013

图书在版编目（CIP）数据

中国绿色就业研究/游钧等著. —北京：社会科学文献
出版社，2014.1
（科思论丛）
ISBN 978 - 7 - 5097 - 5345 - 3

Ⅰ.①中…　Ⅱ.①游…　Ⅲ.①劳动就业 - 研究 - 中国
Ⅳ.①D669.2

中国版本图书馆 CIP 数据核字（2013）第 278662 号

·科思论丛·
中国绿色就业研究
——————————

著　　者／游　钧　张丽宾 等

出 版 人／谢寿光
出 版 者／社会科学文献出版社
地　　址／北京市西城区北三环中路甲 29 号院 3 号楼华龙大厦
邮政编码／100029

责任部门／经济与管理出版中心　（010）59367226　　　责任编辑／陈凤玲　于　飞
电子信箱／caijingbu@ ssap. cn　　　　　　　　　　　责任校对／王洪强
项目统筹／恽　薇　　　　　　　　　　　　　　　　　责任印制／岳　阳
经　　销／社会科学文献出版社市场营销中心　（010）59367081　59367089
读者服务／读者服务中心（010）59367028

印　　装／三河市尚艺印装有限公司
开　　本／787mm×1092mm　1/16　　　　　　　　　印　　张／30.75
版　　次／2014 年 1 月第 1 版　　　　　　　　　　　字　　数／512 千字
印　　次／2014 年 1 月第 1 次印刷
书　　号／ISBN 978 - 7 - 5097 - 5345 - 3
定　　价／98.00 元